SOCIAL JUSTICE AND S(
POLICY IN SCOTLAND

Edited by Gerry Mooney and Gill Scott

First published in Great Britain in 2012 by

The Policy Press
University of Bristol
Fourth Floor
Beacon House
Queen's Road
Bristol BS8 1QU
UK

Tel +44 (0)117 331 4054
Fax +44 (0)117 331 4093
e-mail tpp-info@bristol.ac.uk
www.policypress.co.uk

North American office:

The Policy Press
c/o The University of Chicago Press
1427 East 60th Street
Chicago, IL 60637, USA
t: +1 773 702 7700
f: +1 773-702-9756
e:sales@press.uchicago.edu
www.press.uchicago.edu

British Library Cataloguing in Publication Data
A catalogue record for this book is available from the British Library.

Library of Congress Cataloging-in-Publication Data
A catalog record for this book has been requested.

ISBN 978 1 84742 702 1 paperback
ISBN 978 1 84742 703 8 hardcover

The right of Gerry Mooney and Gill Scott to be identified as editors of this work has been
asserted by them in accordance with the 1988 Copyright, Designs and Patents Act.

Cover design by Qube Design Associates
Front cover image: 'Glasgow Study' by Michael Scott, © Michael
Scott estate
Printed and bound in Great Britain by TJ International, Padstow
The Policy Press uses environmentally responsible print partners.

Contents

List of figures and tables

Figures

Tables

List of contributors

Eddy Adams is an independent consultant, writer and facilitator. He has a particular interest in youth employability and has chaired two independent workstreams for the Scottish government. The first led to the development of the national NEET (not in education, employment or training) strategy, More Choices, More Chances (MCMC), and the second investigated learning and skills provision for young offenders. He has also reviewed work experience in Scotland for the government. In addition, he is a European Union (EU) Expert Adviser on youth engagement and employability, contracted by Rotterdam to support a network of 10 European cities under the URBACT Programme. Contact: eddy@eaconsultants.com

Margaret Arnott is Reader of Political Science, Department of Social Sciences, Glasgow Caledonian University. Her main research areas are post-devolution territorial politics and governance in the UK, with a focus on education policy. Research topics include nationalism and policy development and post-devolution social policy.

Christine Bertram is Research Officer at the Policy Studies Institute where she currently works on qualitative evaluations of major labour market programmes. Her research focuses on front-line service delivery, governance of welfare services and welfare-to-work policies. She has completed her PhD at the University of Stirling, where she was also involved in a European research project comparing employment advice services for out-of-work adults in five countries.

Hazel Croall is Professor Emerita (Criminology) at Glasgow Caledonian University where she set up the BA programme in Criminology. She has taught on a wide range of criminology courses and has published extensively in the areas of white-collar and corporate crime, crime and inequality and Scottish criminal justice. She is the co-author of *Criminal justice in England and Wales* (Pearson, 2010), now in its fourth edition, has recently completed the second, enlarged edition of *Crime and society in Britain* (Pearson, 2011), and co-edited the recent collection on *Criminal justice in Scotland* (Willan, 2010) with Gerry Mooney and Mary Munro.

Sue Dumbleton is Senior Lecturer and Staff Tutor in the Faculty of Health and Social Care at The Open University in Scotland. Sue has a long-standing interest in the lives of people who have a learning disability through work, research and personal experience as a family carer.

Alex Law is Professor of Sociology at the University of Abertay Dundee. His recent publications include *Key concepts in classical social theory* (Sage Publications, 2011).

Philomena de Lima is Director of the Centre for Remote and Rural Studies, University of the Highlands and Islands, Scotland. Her research interests include equalities and social justice with a particular focus on migration, ethnicity and belonging. Recent publications include 'Welcoming migrants? Migrant labour in rural Scotland' (*Social Policy and Society*, 2009, with Wright); 'Migrant workers in rural Scotland: going to the middle of nowhere?' (*International Journal on Multicultural Societies*, 2007, with Jentsch and MacDonald); and 'Let's keep our heads down and maybe the problem will go away' (in Agyeman and Neal [eds] *The new countryside*, The Policy Press, 2006).

Kim McKee is Lecturer in Housing/Urban Studies in the School of Geography and Geosciences, University of St Andrews. Prior to taking up her current post she was an Urban Studies Fellow at the University of Glasgow and Associate Lecturer with The Open University in Scotland. Her research interests lie in the interconnections between social, housing and urban policy in a devolved Scotland.

John McKendrick is Senior Lecturer in the School for Business and Society, Glasgow Caledonian University. He is working with the Community Regeneration and Tackling Poverty Learning Network of the Scottish government to provide resources and expert advice to practitioners tackling poverty in Scottish communities and localities. With Stephen Sinclair, he co-authored the Scottish Executive report evaluating Closing the Opportunity Gap, the previous Scottish government's anti-poverty strategy, and a Viewpoints paper on child poverty in Scotland for the Joseph Rowntree Foundation.

Mo McPhail is Head of Social Work (Scotland) with The Open University. She has developed a research and writing profile in the area of service user and carer involvement. She edited *User and carer involvement – Beyond good intentions* (Dunedin Academic Press, 2008), co-authored with a service user and carer.

Gerry Mooney is Senior Lecturer in Social Policy and Criminology, Faculty of Social Sciences at The Open University. Among other publications he is co-author of *Understanding social welfare movements* (The Policy Press, 2009); co-editor of *New Labour/hard labour?* (The Policy Press, 2007); *Community: Welfare, crime and society* (Open University Press, 2009); *Criminal justice in Scotland* (Willan, 2010); and of *Poverty in Scotland 2011: Towards a more equal Scotland?* (CPAG, 2011).

Carlo Morelli is Senior Lecturer in Economics in the School of Business at Dundee University. His research interests are in inequality and poverty, business and economic history.

Jenny Ozga is Professor of the Sociology of Education, in the Department of Education, University of Oxford. Her main research areas are education policy in international comparative contexts, with a focus on governance. Research topics include education and social policy; policy elites and policy communities; and policy networks and policy for the teaching profession, within and across the UK and increasingly in the context of the Europeanisation of education.

Danny Phillips is an independent researcher and writer working mostly in the third sector. He was head of the Child Poverty Action Group (CPAG) in Scotland 1999-2003, and special adviser to the First Minister of Scotland 2003-07.

Lynne Poole is Lecturer in Social Policy at the University of the West of Scotland.

Eurig Scandrett is Lecturer in Sociology at Queen Margaret University, Edinburgh. After an initial career in environmental science research, he spent 15 years in adult education including eight years as Head of Community Action at Friends of the Earth Scotland. He is editor of *Scotlands of the future: Sustainability in a small nation* (Luath Press Ltd, 2003) and *Bhopal survivors speak: Emergent voices from a people's movement* (Bhopal Survivors' Movement Study 2009). He is a Fellow of the Centre for Human Ecology.

Gill Scott is Emerita Professor at Glasgow Caledonian University where she led the Scottish Poverty Information Unit and set up the Master's in Applied Social Sciences. She was the Lead Expert for a European Union (EU) URBACT project that focused on urban regeneration and equalities from 2009-12 and acted as an external expert on poverty and employability for the Scottish government 2003-07. She has written widely on gender equality, social inclusion, social policy and Scottish devolution. Among other publications she was co-author, in 2005, with Gerry Mooney, of *Exploring social policy in the 'new' Scotland* (The Policy Press, 2005).

Paul Seaman is Lecturer in Economics in the School of Business at Dundee University. His research interests include the economics of education and the economics of welfare reform. Together with Carlo Morelli they have published a series of papers examining income inequality, poverty and devolution.

Stephen Sinclair works in the School for Business and Society at Glasgow Caledonian University, where he specialises in research into poverty and social exclusion, with a particular interest in child poverty, financial exclusion and community planning issues. Previously he was Head of the Local Government and Public Services Reform Research Branch in the Scottish Executive.

Sharon Wright is Lecturer in Social Policy at the University of Stirling. Her research has included an ethnographic street-level study of employment services implementation from adviser and user perspectives; a three-year European research project comparing employment advice services for out-of-work adults in five countries; and an in-depth study, based in Australia for six months, comparing welfare reforms and the contracting-out of employment services with the UK. She was Managing Co-Editor of the journal *Social Policy and Society* and member of the UK Social Policy Association Executive Committee (2006-11). Recent publications include: *Contracting out employment services: Lessons from Australia, Denmark, Germany and the Netherlands* (CPAG, 2008); and, with Tess Ridge, *Understanding inequality, poverty and wealth: Policies and prospects* (The Policy Press, 2008).

Acknowledgements

This book is the result of the important and collective effort of many people, both behind the scenes and as contributors. We would particularly like to show our gratitude to Jenny Robertson at the Open University in Scotland in Edinburgh for her patience and support in getting the disparate chapters into a unified product, and to Emily Watt, Jessica Hughes, Jo Morton and Kathryn King at The Policy Press in Bristol for their very practical and professional support to us as editors.

Thanks are due to our referees who provided insightful comments that helped clarify our ideas, as we responded to what has been a fast-changing Scottish context since we first thought of putting the book together. We are also, obviously, very grateful for the efforts and willingness to respond to the central issues of the book that all the contributors have shown, an effort that has proved worthwhile according to our pre-publication readers who provided such glowing testimonials for the book.

A debt of gratitude, less obviously, is owed to our families, colleagues and friends who have allowed and encouraged us to remain committed to a society where change is possible and social justice worth working for. And lastly, we would like to remember, with much love, Gill's late husband Mick, whose painting provides a perfect cover for the book.

ONE

Devolution, social justice and social policy: the Scottish context

Gerry Mooney and Gill Scott

Introduction

> We are committed to promoting social justice and equality of opportunity for everyone in Scotland ... we can build on the commitment to social justice which lies at the heart of political and civic life in Scotland. We need to harness the efforts of many to the greater good of all, and establish social justice as the hallmark of Scottish society. (Dewar, 1999)

> An independent Scotland could be a beacon for progressive opinion south of the border and further afield – addressing policy challenges in ways which reflect the universal values of fairness – and are capable of being considered, adapted and implemented according to the specific circumstances and wishes within the other jurisdictions of these islands and beyond. (Salmond, 2012)

Few students of social policy would dispute that the pursuit of social justice is an admirable goal. However, it is by no means an automatic goal or indeed a constantly pursued one of any government. Certainly social justice is an ambiguous, contested and changeable idea, the focus of many different theorisations, subject to competing claims and used in a myriad of different ways to promote and legitimate government policies, not least social policies (McLaughlin and Baker, 2007; Christie et al, 2008; Craig et al, 2008; Newman and Yeates, 2008; Hattersley and Hickson, 2012). In the context of Scotland, however, social justice has an added presence and impetus. This is partly because of the need to address the very real problem of poverty and inequality. However, it is also because, as highlighted in the comment above from the late Donald Dewar, the First Minister in the first Labour-led Scottish government that was reconvened following devolution in 1999, there are claims that social justice is an essential part of Scottish life, and that this could be pursued far more effectively by a devolved government.

Such a view also informs the other quote, made in January 2012 when debate about independence became more heated.

These claims by Dewar and Salmond, albeit made in very different contexts, go to the heart of long-standing and ongoing debates about the nature of Scottish society – and of Scottish national identity, indeed of 'Scottishness' itself (see Leith and Soule, 2011). They highlight themes that inform the most potent and recurring myths that circulate in Scotland. Central to these are claims that Scotland (and 'the Scots') is imbued with a series of progressive values, notable among which is a sense of, and commitment to, egalitarianism, collectivism and social justice (see Keating, 2007b; EHRC Scotland, 2010). The comments of Dewar and Salmond also demonstrate that despite changes in the political leadership of the government, the concept of social justice plays a central role in the rhetoric of Scottish politics, crossing party lines. Further evidence of this can be seen in the fact that each and every Scottish government since 1999, of which following the May 2011 Scottish Parliament elections there have been four, has made great claim of their commitments to the pursuit of social justice, fairness and equality, and have extended the space in political debate for discussions of fairness, accountability and redistribution. Dorling (2010) claims that within affluent nations, inequality is no longer caused by not having enough resources to share, but by unrecognised and unacknowledged beliefs that actually propagate it and limit policies to reduce it. If Scotland really does have a different set of values then it is important to see whether this is sufficient to produce budget decisions that allow policies of social inclusion to be developed and implemented, policies that would reduce the impact of social inequalities that exist within the UK, and policies to resist the retreat from the welfare state that characterise so many industrialised societies today.

This book is concerned to engage with these issues, such as whether the Scottish government really has such autonomy, whether Scottish government policies have had a positive impact on inequalities, whether developments in specific sites of social policy in Scotland highlight possibilities for Scotland and other countries to resist threats to state welfare in the 21st century.

A repeated claim of those supporting devolution in the late 1990s was that it would allow the development of distinctively 'Scottish solutions for Scottish problems' (see Stewart, 2004; Mooney and Scott, 2005a). To quote Donald Dewar again, then in his pre-devolution role as Secretary of State for Scotland in the 1997 New Labour UK government:

> We have a proud tradition in Scotland of working to tackle social division. We have developed innovative responses to social problems, many of which are now being promoted within the UK as models of good practice. We have a body of people … who are committed to creating a fairer society in Scotland. And in the not too distant future we will have a Scottish Parliament, which will give us the opportunity to develop Scottish solutions to Scottish needs, and to bring the arm of government closer to the needs of the people. Devolution matters. It will let us take the decisions that matter here in Scotland. It is an

end in itself: but it is a means to other ends, and none more important than the creation of a socially cohesive Scotland. (Scottish Office Press Release, 3 November 1998)

From 1999 through to the early days of the fourth Scottish Parliament in 2011, there have been repeated claims to social justice on the part of successive Scottish governments. Further, and importantly, the two largest political parties in Scotland, the Labour Party and the SNP, also make competing claims as the inheritors of Scottish social democracy, infused with the language of social justice (see Keating, 2007b; Hassan, 2009). Devolution itself, and the re-establishment after almost 300 years of a Scottish Parliament, has been viewed as an exercise in social justice, addressing the so-called 'democratic deficit' (that successive Conservative-led UK governments from 1979 to the mid-1990s had been decisively rejected by the overwhelming majority of Scottish voters), and bringing forth a 'new' politics for the 'new' Scotland that was being forged (see Mooney and Scott, 2005b, pp 2-7; Tijmstra, 2009; Keating, 2010, pp 29-33).

The relationship therefore between social policy making in the devolved Scotland and questions and issues of social justice offer up important and potentially insightful ways of understanding the degree to which the oft-stated goals of social justice exist in any meaningful way beyond political rhetoric. How far has social policy in Scotland worked to promote social justice? Is Scotland now a fairer and more just country following a decade and more of devolution? To what extent has inequality been tackled, eroding long-standing issues of significant material inequality and assorted social problems? Does it have lessons for others? Are there alternative ways to address social injustice that have simply not been tried in Scotland? How have changes in the political and economic context of Scottish policy making affected ongoing debates in welfare and social justice? What are the main contestations and controversies around social justice itself as it is deployed in relation to social and public policy more generally, and the competing ways in which social justice has been understood and re-made in the devolved Scotland? These are among the central questions and themes that run through this book.

Setting the scene: the policy making landscape in 2012

Four key factors characterise the landscape of policy in Scotland in 2012 and affect the actual direction of policy: first, the maturing of the institutions of a devolved government; second, changes in the UK government; and third, the economic crisis which developed in late 2008. Fourth, and perhaps most significant, is that the May 2011 Scottish Parliament elections saw a monumental victory for the SNP, emerging as a majority government, an outcome that many political pundits had argued was an impossibility under proportional representation.

In the first edition of this book, *Exploring social policy in the 'new' Scotland* (Mooney and Scott, 2005a), written largely in 2004 and early 2005, Scottish devolution was still in its infant stages. This new edition has been written primarily in 2011, some 12 years since the establishment of devolution for Scotland, Wales and Northern Ireland. A frequently stated claim is that devolution has 'matured' in this time, although it is not always apparent what this means. It still stands true that the Scottish Parliament remains a largely social policy making body, a point we emphasised in the first edition, but the context in which social policies are being made is now somewhat different from that of 2004-05. There are a number of different, although interrelated dimensions to this.

The political map of Scotland is very different from that of the mid-2000s. The May 2007 Scottish Parliament elections saw the SNP emerge as the Scottish government, albeit a minority government with a marginal one seat advantage over its closest challenger, the Labour Party. After the May 2011 elections, the SNP had 69 seats to Labour's 37, and an overall majority of 9 seats with the Conservatives and Liberal Democrats sitting well back in third and fourth places. For Labour it was their worst result in Scotland since 1931.

These results have not only Scottish, but also UK implications. After May 2007, but reinforced following the May 2011 elections, different political parties now form the governments in Edinburgh and in London. The fact that the SNP were a minority government after May 2007 meant that its scope for manoeuvre was extremely limited, but this did not prevent it from introducing a series of policy measures which gained widespread support across Scotland (see Mooney et al, 2008; Maxwell, 2009; Scott and Mooney, 2009). Notable here was the abolition of prescription charges by 2011, a renewed emphasis on the construction of social housing and the promise of smaller class sizes, the last two of which were subsequently threatened or rendered infeasible by the impact of large-scale budget cuts announced by both the Scottish and UK governments during 2010 and 2011 (an issue to which we return in Chapter Fifteen).

There is a further element to the changed political landscape, this time at UK level, although of course that also includes Scotland. The UK Parliament elections in May 2010 had significant implications not only for the future shape and direction of UK politics, but also for the future shape of the UK itself. Briefly, and following 13 years of New Labour rule at Westminster, the 2010 General Election saw the Conservatives emerge as the single largest political party in terms of votes and seats – but without a clear overall majority. For the first time in a generation, the Conservatives and Liberal Democrats formed a coalition government. However, and certainly not for the first time, the political landscape of Scotland following the 2010 UK elections was markedly different from the rest of the UK. The Tories, holding on to their one Scottish seat, performed very poorly, with 16 per cent of the vote. Their new UK Coalition partners, the Liberal Democrats, won 11 seats and 19 per cent of the vote. The SNP gained 6 seats and 20 per cent of the vote, while the Labour Party won 41 seats and 42 per cent of votes cast, reinforcing its position as the most popular party in Scotland, at least as far as UK elections are concerned.

There has been another major change which is also having an impact on the policy making landscape of the contemporary UK, as well as on governments in both Edinburgh and in London. As we prepared this book in 2012, the UK, as is much of the rest of the Western world, is experiencing what most commentators have identified as the deepest financial crisis since the Wall Street Crash and Great Depression of the 1920s and 1930s. The crisis of 2008 has had a massive significance given its far-reaching impact on the world economy, bringing with it repeated pronouncements of a prolonged economic slump. The financial crisis – and the reactions to it by different governments and transnational institutions – has major implications for our understanding of social welfare today and the future shape and direction of social policy in Scotland as well as across the UK (see Bell, 2010).

The UK Coalition government and the Scottish Parliament

Taken together, the election successes of the SNP, the election of a Conservative Liberal Democrat UK Coalition government, and the deep economic and financial crisis of 2008, means that the landscape surrounding Scottish devolution (and devolution for other parts of the UK) is somewhat different in 2011/12 from that of 1998/99 (see Lodge and Schmuecker, 2010). After a decade largely characterised by budget increases, the Scottish government is now in a very different financial position. Not surprisingly, there is a developing debate about how Scotland should be financed in the immediate future.

The UK Coalition government did move to give the Scottish Parliament more control over fiscal powers. In 2009 the Calman Commission on Scottish Devolution (Commission on Scottish Devolution, 2009; see also Chapter Two, this volume) reported on proposals for developing Scottish devolution. Supported by the three main unionist parties, including the Tories, key elements of the Calman proposals were reflected in the Scotland Bill, introduced by the UK Coalition government in 2010 and approved by the UK Parliament in 2011. It was made somewhat irrelevant by the election of the SNP in 2011 but it did open up yet another series of controversies around the issue of 'fiscal accountability'/'fiscal autonomy' (McCrone, 2012). In brief, for critics of the Calman proposals (see for example, Cuthbert and Cuthbert, 2011), Scotland would lose out financially if the Scotland Bill was passed, that is, in the unlikely event that it secured the support it would also need in the Scottish Parliament, as it would both reduce the share of total UK income tax coming to Scotland, as well forcing any Scottish government to significant increases in income tax to make up any shortfall. For the SNP, supporting 'full' fiscal autonomy, the proposals were flawed, as full economic management would not be devolved, only a degree of financial responsibility. The Scotland Bill planned to increase the proportion of revenue raised by the Holyrood Parliament with a corresponding decrease in the level of funding from Westminster, a move rejected by the SNP as working to decrease the Scottish government's overall income. 'Fiscal autonomy' rapidly became yet another political fault line with the SNP demanding more control over finances and taxation, including the devolution of corporation tax (see Trench, 2010). Within days of the May 2011 elections, the SNP leadership were already making noises that the election outcome had given them the mandate to challenge Westminster to further increase the range of financial and economic powers that would be devolved to the Scottish Parliament. In many ways this made the revisions of the Scotland Act increaaingly redundant: independence was back on the agenda!

Disagreements over the Scotland Bill and the vexed issue of the devolution of fiscal powers led to renewed arguments over the SNP's plans for independence more generally. Claiming that 'constitutional uncertainty' was harming the Scottish economy, leading politicians in the UK Coalition government attacked the Scottish government's fiscal demands as well as the economic viability of Scottish independence. In speeches in the early autumn of 2011, the Secretary of State for Scotland and Liberal Democrat MP, Michael Moore, set down 'six questions' (as they subsequently came to be referred) regarding the SNP's ambitions. What would independence mean for bank regulation, currency, European Union (EU) membership, defence, pensions as well as the total costs of independence (Moore, 2011a, 2011b)? This has been followed up with a series of claims and counterclaims about the constitutional route to a referendum on independence (BBC, 2012; Guardian, 2012; Hassan, 2012; Lodge, 2012; McWhirter, 2012) as well as what independence would mean for Scotland and the UK. The run-up to a referendum, for example, saw a number of things contested – the date for the referendum, whether 16- and 17-year-olds should vote and whether devo-max as well as independence should be included as questions. The meaning of independence was also up for debate – with Alex Salmond, for example, claiming that the SNP's commitment to an independent social democratic Scotland would mean a fairer future for all in Scotland (Salmond, 2012) and Ed Miliband arguing that the task is to create a 'more equal, just and fair society' but one where 'separation will not help the working people of Scotland' (Miliband, 2012).

Such attacks on the SNP's goal of an independent Scotland were part of a more 'muscular' approach from the UK government, combined with a more virulent defence of the Union (see Brady, 2011; Gordon, 2011; Macwhirter, 2011). In the context of financial crisis, massive UK debt and budget constraint, the economic basis of Scottish independence has become a major battleground in Scottish politics.

However, these conflicts and the developments highlighted above are not simply about the future of Scottish independence, but also throw into sharp relief questions over the future of some of those key Scottish social policies around which Scottish devolution has been built, notably including free personal care and the funding of further and higher education. How can Scotland continue to fund free personal care and free tuition for students (and, following the example of Wales, from 2011 prescription charges were abolished)? The funding of Scotland's universities in particular has become a major political issue, not least given the plans for reductions in the financing of higher education in England. Scottish public attitudes continually show considerable support for public services and opposition to private and for-profit systems of delivery. But as councils feel the squeeze in budgets (not least following the September 2011 Scottish government budget statement; see The Scottish Government, 2011b), there have been announcements by several local authorities that they will contract out/privatise key services, leaving service users with poorer quality services and public sector workers with poorer wages and conditions. Despite commitments to no compulsory redundancies from Scottish government ministers, there is clear evidence of job losses across the public sector in Scotland, as in other countries where the economic crisis is having an impact (see Theodoropoulu and Watt, 2011).

As a consequence of tightening fiscal constraints, some key SNP policies have gone by the wayside, for instance, in relation to school class sizes and proposals for a new generation of council housing, as the impact of the financial crisis and UK government cuts take their toll. The SNP government has championed itself as the guarantor or protector of 'Scottish social democracy' advocating, and to a limited extent implementing, the kinds of policies that many would see as essentially 'Old Labourist'. However, the economic basis for such policies is now considerably weaker.

In addition to the devolved areas we have focused on thus far, there are the reserved areas of public spending – in the main, welfare benefits. It is estimated that the reduction in welfare spending in Scotland by 2014–15 will amount to around £1.7 billion. It is the disadvantaged sections of Scottish society that will suffer most from the assault on public services. Proposed welfare cuts, too, will have the greatest impact on those living in some of the most deprived communities to be found anywhere in the UK. In the decade of devolution there have been mostly falling levels of poverty in Scotland, especially child poverty, although poverty remains widespread and deep (JRF, 2010; see also Chapter Four, this volume). The interaction of devolved powers and reserved powers (legislative powers controlled by the Westminster government) in a context of relative economic growth played a major part in this, but this is now threatened by the deepening economic crisis, and by the 'austerity' measures and welfare 'reforms' introduced by the UK Coalition government.

Highlighting the wider context to policy making in Scotland in this way is important for our understanding of some of the factors that encourage policy divergence, and which may also promote some policy convergence between the different nations of the UK. Furthermore, examination of some of those directions underlines the similarities and variations in the experience of social justice and social policy within the UK. There are marked differences in terms of the devolution settlement as they apply to Wales, Northern Ireland and Scotland, reminding us once again of the asymmetrical nature of UK devolution.

Social policy divergence within the UK

Exploring social policy in the 'new' Scotland highlighted and explored an issue that has become central to the discussion and analysis of policy making in the devolved UK – the extent to which there has been growing policy divergence across the four UK nations, or contrary pressures towards convergence (see also Stewart, 2004; Adams and Schmuecker, 2005; Kay, 2005; Birrell, 2009; Keating, 2010; Lodge and Schmuecker, 2010). One of the recurring claims made about devolution for Scotland, Wales and Northern Ireland since 1999 is that it has provided the opportunity for significant policy innovation and policy differentiation in relation to social welfare. As is now well-documented, free personal care for older people and the abolition of student fees are just two of the key policy changes in Scotland that have been heralded as marking a growing degree of policy divergence.

It has generally been agreed that, in its first decade, devolution has not produced radically different forms of government across the UK, nor has policy making across the devolved countries and England been as significantly divergent as was anticipated, although of course this is not to rule out this occurring in the near future. Many different reasons have been given for the lack of major policy divergences between Scotland, Wales and England/the UK. Included here are issues as broad as neoliberalism and globalisation through to continuing Treasury control over the level of budgets, and that New Labour was the dominant party in each of the first three Scottish governments, as well as the party forming the UK government. There is also the question of political will, or the lack of it, for far-reaching policy divergence. These are some of the main factors that have been highlighted as playing a role in limiting the scope for policy differentiation, at least of the more radical forms.

Following the May 2007 and 2011 Scottish elections, with the SNP forming the government in Scotland, and Plaid Cymru as coalition partners in Wales between 2007-11, there was a further expectation that a new form of territorial politics would emerge in the UK, characterised not least by a growing divergence in policy making and practice. Such developments were widely regarded as having significant implications for our understanding of social welfare and social policy in the UK, and in particular for questions of citizenship, territorial justice and also for the continuing 'unity' of the UK itself (see also Mooney et al, 2006; Williams and Mooney, 2008; Birrell, 2009; Greer, 2009; Lodge and Schmuecker, 2010). However, with relatively few exceptions, even with the Scottish and Welsh nationalists in power in Edinburgh and Cardiff, their room for manoeuvre has been limited, not least by the fact that the former were in a minority government while the Welsh nationalists were partners in a coalition with the Labour Party in the Welsh Assembly.

In addition to the constraints on divergence, it is also possible to highlight some surprising policy convergences. From the Scottish context, one issue that stands out regards youth justice legislation, which has been characterised by a drift towards a harsher and more punitive regime (moving towards the approach in England

and Wales), demonstrating a relative decline not only in Scottish distinctiveness in this field, but also more significantly an erosion of the more welfarist approach to youth justice policy making that had characterised the period up to the late 20th century (Croall et al, 2010; see also Chapter Eleven, this volume). The fact that criminal justice has always been a matter under Scottish control (it was not only devolved to Scotland in 1999) makes this a more significant case in point.

Further, and importantly, policy divergence has been more noticeable in the context of England, with radical Blairite and New Labour measures for the 'reform' of key heartland policy areas, such as with the NHS and in education. The promotion of 'choice' and consumerist models of governance, engagement and participation in England has not been followed in Scotland and Wales. Divergence here, then, is very much a case of the devolved administrations refusing to depart down a similar route, or at least not to the same extent as in England (see Adams and Schmuecker, 2005; Lodge and Schmuecker, 2010).

However, policy divergence has reached new levels following the May 2010 UK General Election, not least with UK government plans for a further phase of 'reform' for the NHS, and for far-reaching changes in higher education funding and in the management of schools. The fact that these proposals affect the NHS and education in England only, something generally overlooked by sections of the UK media who still talk about the NHS as if it were an undifferentiated UK-wide body, represents yet another way in which policy change is leading to more divergence – at least as far as England is concerned – where the Conservative-dominated Coalition is able to push through a much more radical neoliberal privatisation agenda. By contrast, for some Scotland stands as a bastion of public service:

> Inequality in Britain diminished until the late 1970s, then began to increase until today the gap ... is as wide as it was 90 years ago.... We are travelling backwards, and the current assault on 'the public sector' only makes the slide faster.
>
> Scotland never wanted or needed this. It's not just that nearly a third of employment is in the public sector. It's that the mania for privatising never made sense here, in a country whose tradition is communitarian rather than individualist, deeply suspicious of its own and everyone else's elites, obsessive about equality.
>
> In 'Britain of the cuts', the present Scottish Government has become the last bastion of faith in a public service state. It upholds beliefs which were once shared all over the UK: that health and prescriptions, school meals and university education, care and public transport for the old, should all be free, the state's honouring of the contract between citizen and ruler.
>
> But the Scottish bastion is now isolated, and the waters are rising around its walls.... (Ascherson, 2010)

Such is the somewhat romanticised view that has been a recurring feature of commentary of Scotland since the introduction of devolution in 1999 (see Mooney and Poole, 2004, and Alex Law also engages with Ascherson in Chapter Two, this volume). These views also reflect that for much of its first 12 years, Scottish devolution, and Scottish society more generally, has been triumphed (see, for example, Paterson et al, 2004), with relatively few comprehensive critiques of the impact of neoliberalism, economic change and deep inequalities in Scotland. Arguably, there could have been greater recognition by observers of devolution that in Scotland, as in other parts of the UK, services and jobs are under threat and working conditions are being subjected to far-reaching transformation, which is seeing long-standing conditions of service eroded (see Cumbers and Whittam, 2007; Mooney and Law, 2007; Davidson et al, 2010).

Why does devolution matter for social justice?

> It is a paradox that our new constitution, although promulgated by Labour, exemplifies liberal rather than social democratic values. It limits the incursions that government can make into our civil rights, while implying a preference for diversity over uniformity. It makes it harder for a government of the left to secure equality of conditions in different parts of the kingdom. The welfare state was based on the principle that benefits and burdens would depend on need, not on geography. Devolution negates that philosophy. (Bogdanor, 2003)

As noted above, devolution is widely understood to pose particular questions for those who are interested in issues of social justice in Scotland. However, devolution 'matters' for social justice (*and social justice matters for devolution*) in a wider context, that is, for the entire UK, not only for those countries on the 'Celtic rim' that gained devolution in 1999. Devolution, it has been claimed, is not simply a matter of constitutional change, but 'an important component of the revitalisation of democracy within the UK and represents a significant change to the public policy making process' (Adams and Robinson, 2002, p 198). The process of devolution carries with it UK-wide implications for politics, policy and society and has brought into sharp relief once more questions about social and territorial justice, identity, belongings and exclusions, political mobilisations and social inequalities. Devolution (and decentralisation) was portrayed, not least by New Labour, as a key element in the emergence of a 'new politics' across the UK, a new politics that would help address democratic deficits.

However, while these constitutional developments can only adequately be understood as UK-wide processes, they are also uneven. As remarked earlier, there are significant differences in the terms of the devolution settlement as they apply to Wales, Northern Ireland and Scotland (and there are different devolved/ reserved legislative powers in each country in part reflecting that distinctive policies were pursued therein prior to 1999), reminding us of the asymmetrical nature of UK devolution. Further, as devolution is a process this also means that it continues to provoke questions about the overall shape of the UK, as well as about social policy making and about social justice itself. Morgan (2002, 2006) claims that devolution makes it more difficult for a UK government to secure territorial justice between different nations and regions, while others claim that devolution, as a political process in general, 'upsets' distributive justice (Segall, 2007). This is regarded as having posed an obvious risk to the former New Labour government's commitment to a 'one nation politics' and also a threat to the future unity of the UK.

There are oft-repeated concerns that devolution may erode UK-wide minimum standards. This is, of course, highly contentious, as it suggests that the UK welfare state pre-devolution *was* successful in achieving and delivering such a universal minimum. However, devolution has not taken place against a backdrop of welfare state expansionism, and in times of retrenchment, and the neoliberal onslaught that underpins this, it is plausible to argue that the scope for devolved administrations to markedly 'depart' down different paths is limited (especially given the existence of reserved powers in key areas of social policy such as benefit entitlements). This is not just an issue for Scotland and the UK. Elsewhere in the world, welfare state reduction has led to reductions in the capacity of devolved administrations to provide for the welfare of vulnerable groups. In Canada, for example, the reduction of federal government funds for housing in the 1990s and devolved responsibility for existing stock down to the provincial level of government led to a 65 per cent reduction in social housing construction. The politics of privatisation and liberalisation of markets that characterise neoliberalism were at the base of such a move. They represent a redrawing of the boundaries between the public domain of the state and the private domain of business (McBride, 2009), but at the same time the impacts across Canada in the 1990s vary and reflect the political complexion of the different devolved provinces of Canada. Similarly in Spain, Keating argues that:

> ... there is evidence that spending on social priorities in Spanish autonomous communities varies according to the parties in power. (Keating, 2007a, p 10)

Devolution has not, as yet, challenged the fundamental position of the UK welfare state (arguably it is the 2010 UK Coalition government which offers the most significant threats to such). Holyrood's refusal to pass a legislative consent motion for Iain Duncan Smith's welfare reform programme in December 2011 (BBC, 2011) was the first time the devolved legislation had refused to pass a Westminster measure dealing with devolved powers. It showed a high level of cross-party dissatisfaction with the UK government's programme but perhaps not a realisable desire for radically divergent welfare entitlements in different areas. But devolution has raised some serious questions about the nature of UK citizenship – and of citizenship in the devolved nations – and is of particular importance for those concerned with social and welfare policies, as it generates a renewed, and in some ways novel, concern with the long-standing tensions between uniformity and difference. For Morgan,

> … the biggest challenge in post-devolution Britain: how to strike a judicious balance between subsidiarity and solidarity or more specifically how to secure the holy grail of a devolved polity, namely equality-in-diversity. (Morgan, 2002, p 807)

There is no inevitability that the process of devolution will lead to greater inequalities, at least at a regional level. In the context of UK devolution, while acknowledging the debates that have re-emerged around a 'north–south divide', and territorial differences in general, devolution was elsewhere celebrated as offering a bulwark against the 'race to the bottom'. It should not be forgotten that devolution, in its early stages, took place amidst New Labour's welfare 'reforms', which were UK-wide in impact and consequences. Devolution has certainly not inhibited such reforms but arguably legitimised them in particular ways in the devolved nations. Against this there was a widespread view (and no little hope!) that devolution for Scotland would shape the development of innovative policies that would act as a 'progressive break' on further welfare retrenchment (see Paxton and Gamble, 2005), echoed in Salmond's claim that Scotland could be a 'progressive beacon' (Salmond, 2012).

The fact that Scotland was also viewed (both internally and externally) as a residual bastion of an 'older' egalitarian and collectivist culture meant that at a UK level social democracy would remain on the agenda and that 'social justice' would underpin devolved policy making. Keating is by no means alone in arguing that in Scotland there is a 'sense of shared responsibility and community ethos that challenges the neo-liberal and market driven assumptions of much public policy under successive British governments' (Keating, 2005, p 458). Thus, the commitment of the Scottish government to free personal care for older people and the abolition of (up-front) tuition fees were widely regarded as reflecting such an ethos.

Further, there appears to be considerable evidence that people in Scotland remain committed to a UK welfare state, at least in its Beveridgean shape, although perhaps this is not surprising given the large and widespread reliance on the institutions of the welfare state across large sections of Scottish society, as well as employment. There is also continuing strong support for universalism north of the Border, which opens up the possibility of another clear fault line between the policyscapes of Scotland and England. It remains to be seen how far the tensions around devolution and UK-wide social citizenship will come to be a major political issue, and concerns have been repeatedly voiced as to how permanent and solid UK citizenship and solidarity will prove to be as the process of devolution continues to unfold.

Remaking of social justice and social democracy in Scotland

The significant shifts in the economic and political landscape that surround devolution raise important questions for our understanding of social justice, and of social democracy, as they play out in the context of contemporary Scotland. As highlighted above, there have been repeated claims from leading Scottish politicians and successive Scottish governments that there is a strong commitment to social justice, that social justice is central, to remind ourselves of Dewar's claim, to a Scottish 'sense of self'.

It is a commitment, however, which although since 2007 has increasingly been set within the context of what Arnott and Ozga (in Chapter Nine, this volume) describe as 'the Scottish Government's "project" of achieving greater autonomy and ultimately independence', has largely been in tune with that displayed by the UK New Labour government between 1997 and 2010, a market-driven approach in which any commitment to social justice, not least as a key policy objective, is overwhelmingly tied to the pursuit of economic growth and economic competitiveness. The creation of a dynamic and competitive market economy is regarded as entirely compatible with social justice 'outcomes' ('competition and cohesion'). Speaking at the launch of the Scottish Centre for Research in Social Justice in Glasgow in July 2002, the then Labour First Minister, Jack McConnell, argued that 'sustaining economic growth and prosperity' was crucial to the pursuit of social justice, but went on to add that 'fairness and equality' were also central to his vision of the new 'ambitious Scotland' (quoted in Stewart, 2004, p 17).

In 1999, the Scottish Executive (the title 'Scottish government' replacing 'Executive' was one of the first decisions of the SNP in coming to power in May 2007) set out its first wide-ranging social justice strategy – *Social justice: A Scotland where everyone matters* (Scottish Executive, 1999) – and presented this as 'the most comprehensive framework ever for tackling poverty in Scotland'. Incorporated into policy development was the setting up of a Social Inclusion Network that was supposed to be consulted at various stages of policy development. The idea of empowerment for the socially and economically marginalised was a strong one in the political rhetoric of policy formulation. The principles – of empowerment, social inclusion, fairness and, to a much lesser extent, redistribution – have remained part of the political rhetoric of both Labour in Scotland and the SNP throughout the first 12 years of devolution. In *Achieving our potential: A framework to tackle poverty and inequality in Scotland* (The Scottish Government, 2008a) the SNP government restated the significance of anti-poverty policy for the development of Scotland as a nation (see also Chapters Three and Four, this volume):

> The overarching Purpose of this Government is to create a more successful country, with opportunities for all of Scotland to flourish, through increasing sustainable economic growth. Delivering on that Purpose will mean delivering greater Solidarity in Scotland. (The Scottish Government, 2008a, p 1)

The principle of solidarity is one that holds great resonance elsewhere in Europe. Within the European Community it is claimed as a fundamental principle based on sharing both the advantages, that is, economic prosperity, and the burdens equally and justly among members. The SNP government appeared to have evoked a similar principle with the use of the term in its two key texts *The Government economic strategy* (The Scottish Government, 2007, and since updated for 2011, see The Scottish Government, 2011a) and *Taking forward the Government economic strategy: A discussion paper on tackling poverty, inequality and deprivation in Scotland* (The Scottish Government, 2008b). Of some interest is the reference made to other European countries in these documents, particularly the Nordic countries, as examples of how solidarity can be achieved, highlighting how some European countries are often trying to find the right balance between economic competitiveness and social cohesion, but also emphasising the role of social policy in developing supranational as well as national identity (see Beland and Lecours, 2008). In its approach to social policy in general, and in particular in relation to poverty, the SNP government presented this as part of a wider debate around the future development of Scottish society, and of prosperity for Scotland, with a greater focus on a more essentialist and social democratic notion of 'Scottishness'.

As a number of our contributors develop their arguments about the nature of welfare in Scotland, readers will notice the varied way in which such discourses of economic growth and values of 'fairness' and 'social justice' are invoked in policy development. Many of the chapters provide an insight into the institutional and economic constraints as well as the political debates that are informing current social policy in Scotland. Readers should also be able to identify the ways in which the devolution process is an ever-changing one that needs and benefits from a focused, detailed and critical analysis of policy change.

Structure of social justice and social policy in Scotland

This book does not purport to offer a comprehensive overview of each and every aspect of social policy making in contemporary Scotland. Due to constraints of space, we have been unable to devote the attention that we would have wished on the experiences and protests of workers in the beleaguered public sector, for instance, or to service users and their experiences of public services 'modernisation' and 'reform', as well as to their ongoing struggles for better provision. In comparison with the first edition, however, we have included here additional chapters that focus on income and wealth inequalities, housing policies and provision, policies for younger people, work and employment and environmental justice. These are important areas for any understanding of social justice in Scotland today.

Any discussion of social justice must also take account of social injustice (Dorling, 2010). Yet it can be argued that with relatively few exceptions (Newlands et al, 2004; Cumbers and Whittam, 2007; Morelli and Seaman, 2007; Mooney et al, 2009; Davidson et al, 2010; Parekh et al, 2010; McKendrick, et al, 2011), and as we have highlighted already, the study of Scottish devolution has tended overwhelmingly to neglect the extent of social injustices in Scotland, especially in relation to material inequalities and its devastating impact across society. In some ways, then, this book offers a report card on the extent to which Scottish society has become more socially just during the first 12 years of devolution.

The approach adopted throughout is multi- and interdisciplinary, drawing on theories, insights and arguments not only from social policy, but also from sociology, criminology, human geography, economics, political science and cultural studies. Across the chapters, the interconnectedness of social justice/injustice and social policies is explored in different ways, collectively contributing to a wide-ranging appraisal of the social policy scape in Scotland today.

This chapter and the next largely set the scene for the chapters that follow. In Chapter Two, Alex Law focuses on the question of the form that the state takes in the devolved Scotland. In rejecting claims that Scotland represents a prime case of a 'stateless nation', he considers issues of legitimacy and territorial justice, the latter based, of course, on the idea of a national community, the Scots. He argues, persuasively, that social policy is shaped by the nature of the state through which it is enacted. His key idea is that Scotland represents a transitional state – indeed a liminal state – where a 'critical questioning of the normal is legitimate', where the possibilities to address injustice and inequalities exist; a state, however, where the analysis of whether and how this is happening needs to be undertaken. The chapters in this book do this to considerable effect, highlighting the areas where social policy in Scotland has addressed social injustices but also highlighting the fact that there is still much to be done.

Evidence is provided throughout that underlines the need for policy and interventions for social justice at local and national level, as well as some of the successes and limitations of policy. Evidence of need is presented that shows that the degree of income inequality within Scotland by the mid-2000s was stark; child poverty in Scotland remains three times higher than in Denmark; for many young people schooling is an unproductive experience; Scottish mortality rates are the highest in comparison with the rest of Western Europe; unemployment among young people has been rising steeply since 2007; social services are viewed by many as being in crisis; racism and discrimination continue to shape the lives of minority ethnic groups, travellers and recent migrants; work has become less secure; and gender inequality continues to determine life chances for men and women. All this within the context of deep-seated divisions and inequalities of class (see Cumbers and Whittam, 2007; Davidson et al, 2010).

At the same time chapters show how Scottish devolution has been conceptualised as a means of tackling social injustice. In Chapter Three, Carlo Morelli and Paul Seaman argue that inequality must be understood as a source of social dislocation, and ask whether measures available for action under the current devolution settlement that could reduce inequality have been used to their full. Their conclusion is that they have not. Tax-varying powers, for example, have remained unused even though they could address the problem of inequality to some extent; the Living Wage has been adopted by some cities but not others; and universality in the provision of welfare has been adopted in some areas but not others. Stephen Sinclair and John McKendrick, in Chapter Four, point out how this is perhaps not surprising. Devolution has provided only a limited opportunity for 'path departure' from the approach taken by UK governments and it is important to remember this when considering Scotland's track record in tackling poverty since 1999. Nevertheless they point to the tough conditions confronting policy makers and citizens in the changed economic environment and how this may produce difference in the choices made by government in Scotland and other parts of the UK.

Gill Scott's discussion of urban regeneration (Chapter Five) takes this further, arguing that policy at local level as well as UK and Scottish level needs to be included in any discussion of agents and contexts of policy change. Regeneration policy in Scotland has a distinctive identity and at times when the Scottish government has attempted to decentralise many of the decisions on social policy, an examination of urban regeneration, its changing values and effect on inequalities is essential for how injustices are experienced by different groups within the country, and how access to power at local and national level plays a part in the continuation of injustice.

Certainly inequalities are experienced in a range of ways, not least of which is the world of work. In Chapter Twelve Christine Bertram and Sharon Wright explore paid employment as a key site of inequality in contemporary Scotland, considering how different social groups are positioned, both in relation to paid work, but also in terms of 'being out of work'. Class, 'race', age and gender are major dimensions of inequality that are highlighted in this book. They reappear in much of the analysis provided, and at times are focused on in more detail, as in Chapter Six, where Philomena de Lima shows how issues of 'race' and immigration are strongly connected to labour market rather than to social justice policies. Some of the reasons why addressing such inequalities are vital to the quality of life for many in Scotland are also highlighted in Chapter Seven, where Lynne Poole shows that despite significant divergences between health policies in Scotland, England and Wales, the health of many in Scotland has not improved as much as might be hoped in a devolved system where local needs might be met by local policies. Housing is another area where very distinctive Scottish policies have been developed since devolution began – developments that bring their own problems. In Chapter Thirteen, Kim McKee and Danny Phillips' discussion of social housing and homelessness policies, the unique nature of tenure structure and social landlords in Scotland compared to the rest of the UK, is presented alongside a suggestion that while developments in homelessness legislation have been progressive (and recognised internationally as such), if it is not supported by an increase in the supply of social housing it may create 'ghettoes' of vulnerable households and further marginalise the social rented sector.

One of the key themes to emerge from the book is that questions of social justice are not narrow and that policy decisions actually matter. Policy has and can make a difference. All the authors tackle the different ways in which welfare provision can, or could, address injustice. No perfect blueprint is available and key debates about what constitutes social injustice, as well as social justice, and whether social welfare is actually achieving and how it might be improved, runs through the book. Commonly discussed sites of policy are examined here: education, health, urban policy, anti-poverty policy and social work. However, we also draw attention to some areas that have often been neglected, but which are now arenas of social tension. For example, in Chapter Fourteen, Eurig Scandrett makes a strong claim that environmental justice needs to be considered in any discussion of Scottish social policy and is also a crucial component of any social justice agenda. Environmental policy is likely to be a site for increasing tensions and skirmishes in a war of position between competing interests, albeit often disguised as technical problem solving. In Chapter Eleven the focus is on to another area that has all too often been overlooked in discussions of devolution and its development – criminal justice. Here Hazel Croall highlights the distinctiveness of the Scottish criminal justice system, as well as possible trends towards declining distinctiveness. Crucially she also demonstrates how processes of criminalisation connect with the far-reaching inequalities that characterise contemporary Scottish society.

A persistent thread through all the chapters is that it is worth examining Scottish policy and social welfare if we are to understand how policy does, or does not, address inequality and what works as well as what doesn't. Central to the book too is an attempt to understand how policy develops, and whether 'Scottish solutions to Scottish problems', that is, policy developed in a situation where the relationship between the individual and state is changing, can provide lessons for welfare elsewhere and crucially, whether the types of policies that have emerged in Scotland hold the potential to reduce inequalities.

The scrutiny of education policy, for example, by Margaret Arnott and Jenny Ozga in Chapter Nine, shows how the SNP government attempted to align economic and social justice agendas in education, showing a particular interest in pursuing stronger national identity alongside economic growth. A less distinctively Scottish trend is identified by Sue Dumbleton and Mo McPhail in Chapter Eight. Their scrutiny of social work argues that the overall picture of social services in Scotland at the end of the first decade of the 21st century falls short of what can be seen as a 'coming of age', and amidst severe economic and political threats, a distinctively Scottish approach to social welfare and the aspirations of the social services profession to promote its core values and social justice are under threat.

Drawing on more than Scottish experience and ideas may not necessarily be a threat. In Chapter Ten, Eddy Adams' discussion of policies for young people in contemporary Scotland identifies how learning from wider experiences, such as those of the Organisation for Economic Co-operation and Development (OECD), about investing in the short term to keep young people active during recessionary periods, may be particularly useful if a generation of young people are not to be 'lost'. Similarly, Arnott and Ozga suggest that the openness of policy actors in Scotland will be important if positive European lessons are to be drawn on.

Finally, a key argument of the book is that despite changing political leadership in Scotland affecting policy making as devolution has progressed, a recurrent theme since the setting up of a Scottish Parliament has been the pursuit of social justice. A question worth asking is whether this is because of a long-standing, commonly held belief among Scottish people that equality is a worthwhile aim, or whether it is because there has been recognition that the symptoms of extreme inequality constitute a long-term threat to the economic and political future of an emergent state. But what is also worth asking is whether the rhetoric of social justice has made any difference to policy or its impact. Extreme inequality still remains a problem, educational achievements are not the ones most Scots would want, health improvements are not greater than in England and inequalities remain worse on many measures, despite free care and different health administrations. So has devolution made a difference? Are there other ways of doing things that could be tried? In many chapters the answer is ambivalent but still worth asking.

The outcome of the May 2011 elections – a majority Scottish government – was one which was widely said could never happen, and indeed one that the architects of devolution thought to be impossible. The devolution settlement for Scotland in 1998 and the voting system adopted were designed to ensure that there would never be a majority Scottish government, especially a government of a nationalist persuasion. In the early days of devolution, that looked such a remote possibility anyway, never mind that the SNP would within 12 years of devolution register probably the most significant result in Scottish political history, and one that left the Union looking more perilous than at any time in the 304 years of the United Kingdom.

As we argue throughout, this has UK-wide implications and ramifications. The SNP have promised a referendum on independence for Scotland within the five-year lifetime of the fourth Scottish Parliament, and with a working majority they are sure to go ahead with this. The fact that the majority of voters opted for the SNP in May 2011, does not, however, mean that they necessarily support independence and indeed there is considerable evidence to the contrary. However, the SNP are now in a position to build towards a 'yes' for independence vote, although they are doing so in a period of severe economic and financial constraints, and in implementing cuts in public services they are likely to alienate some sections of the Labour vote which opted for them in 2007 and in particular in 2011.

For the first time in the history of devolution, there is a majority party in the devolved Scottish Parliament that is seriously at odds with the ruling government in Westminster. As we look forward to the next Scottish Parliament it remains to be seen if this will result in the oft-talked-about 'policy laboratory' of devolution becoming much more than mere rhetoric.

Further resources

A special themed section of *Social Policy and Society* (vol 8, no 3, July 2009) contains a series of articles under the theme of 'Social policy in the devolved Scotland:

towards a Scottish welfare state?'. Two of the contributions to this collection, 'Social policy in Scotland since devolution' by Elke Viebrock and 'Some useful sources' by Vikki McCall, together provide a detailed overview of the first 10 years of devolution, and highlight some of the key debates and literature as they pertain to social policy.

A themed issue of *Environment and Planning C: Government and Policy* (vol 30, no 1, 2012) focuses on devolution and the shifting political economic geographies of the United Kingdom.

Journalist Hamish MacDonnell offers an accessible and comprehensive account of the first 10 years of devolution in *Uncharted territory* (Politico's, 2009), while Neil Davidson, Patricia McCafferty and David Miller's edited collection of essays, *Neoliberal Scotland* (Cambridge Scholars Publishing, 2010), provide a detailed and comprehensive critique of many aspects of Scottish economy, politics and society since 1999.

Devolution Matters, a blog with content and analysis about different aspects of devolution across the UK, is to be found at http://devolutionmatters.wordpress. com/

The Institute for Public Policy Research (IPPR) publications site offers details of their ongoing research and reports on devolution, available at: www.ippr.org/

The journal *Scottish Affairs* offers detailed and informed commentary around many different aspects of Scottish devolution and on politics and policy making in contemporary Scotland more generally, and is available at: www.scottishaffairs. org/onlinepub/

Scottish Left Review, as its name suggests, offers commentary on many aspects of Scottish economy, culture and society from a left of centre perspective. This is available at: www.scottishleftreview.org/

Scottish Review provides a platform for discussion and analysis of many aspects of Scottish society, politics and culture. It is available at: www.scottishreview.net/

References

Adams, J. and Robinson, P. (2002) 'Divergence and the centre', in J. Adams and P. Robinson (eds) *Devolution in practice: Public policy differences within the UK*, London: Institute for Public Policy Research, pp 198-227.

Adams, J. and Schmuecker, K. (eds) (2005) *Devolution in practice 2006*, Newcastle: Institute of Public Policy Research North.

Alexander, D. (2011) Speech by the Chief Secretary to the Treasury at the CBI Scotland Annual Dinner, Glasgow, 1 September (www.hm-treasury.gov.uk/speech_cst_010911.htm).

Ascherson, N. (2010) 'Return to Babylon', *Sunday Herald*, 31 October.

BBC (2011) 'MSPs withhold consent from UK Welfare Reform Bill', 11 December (www.bbc.co.uk/news/uk-scotland-scotland-politics-16292327).

BBC (2012) 'Scottish independence: David Cameron in referendum offer', 16 February (www.bbc.co.uk/news/uk-scotland-scotland-politics-17052800).

Beland, D. and Lecours, A. (2008) *Nationalism and social policy: The politics of territorial solidarity*, Oxford: Oxford University Press.

Bell, D. (2010) 'Devolution in a recession: who'd have thought it would come to this?', in G. Lodge and K. Schmuecker (eds) *Devolution in practice 2010*, London: Institute for Public Policy Research, pp 60-82.

Birrell, D. (2009) *The impact of devolution on social policy*, Bristol: The Policy Press.

Bogdanor, V. (2003) 'The elements of a codified British constitution', *Financial Times*, 8 December.

Brady, B. (2011) 'A war of independence: PM squares up to Salmond', *The Independent on Sunday*, 25 September.

Christie, A., McLachlan, H.V. and Swales, J.K. (2008) 'Scotland, devolution and justice', *Scottish Affairs*, vol 65, autumn, pp 107-28.

Commission on Scottish Devolution (2009) *Serving Scotland better: Scotland and the United Kingdom in the 21st century. Final report* (Calman Commission), presented to the Presiding Officer of the Scottish Parliament and to the Secretary of State for Scotland, on behalf of Her Majesty's Government.

Craig, G., Burchardt, T. and Gordon, D. (eds) (2008) *Social justice and public policy*, Bristol: The Policy Press.

Croall, H., Mooney, G. and Munro, M. (eds) (2010) *Criminal justice in Scotland*, Cullompton: Willan Publishing/Routledge.

Cumbers, A. and Whittam, G. (eds) (2007) *Reclaiming the economy*, Biggar: Scottish Left Review Press.

Cuthbert, J. and Cuthbert, M. (2011) 'The Scotland Bill is broken', *Scottish Left Review*, vol 62, January/February, pp 12-13 (www.scottishleftreview.org/li/images/stories/pdf/slri62.pdf).

Davidson, N., McCafferty, P. and Miller, D. (eds) (2010) *Neoliberal Scotland: Class and society in a stateless nation*, Newcastle: Cambridge Scholars Publishing.

Dewar, D. (1999) 'Preface', in *Social justice – A Scotland where everyone matters*, Edinburgh: Scottish Executive.

Dorling, D. (2010) *Injustice: Why social inequality persists*, Bristol: The Policy Press.

EHRC (Equality and Human Rights Commission) Scotland (2010) *Is Scotland worth coming home to?*, Glasgow: EHRC.

Gordon, T. (2011) 'New blows in the battle of the Union', *Sunday Herald*, 16 September.

Greer, S.L. (ed) (2009) *Devolution and social citizenship in the UK*, Bristol: The Policy Press.

Guardian (2012) 'Scotland could raise £30bn energy fund over 20 years, says Salmond' (www.guardian.co.uk/politics/2012/feb/15/independent-scotland-energy-fund-salmond).

Hassan, G. (ed) (2009) *The modern SNP: From protest to power*, Edinburgh: Edinburgh University Press.

Hassan, G. (2012) 'The Battle for Britain has begun', *New Statesman*, 16 January, pp 20-3.

Hattersley, R. and Hickson, K. (2012) 'In praise of social democracy', *The Political Quarterly*, vol 83, pp 5-12.

JRF (Joseph Rowntree Foundation) (2010) *Devolution's impact on low-income people and places*, York: JRF.

Kay, A. (2005) 'Territorial justice and devolution', *British Journal of Politics and International Relations*, vol 7, no 4, pp 544-60.

Keating, M. (2005) 'Policy convergence and divergence in Scotland under devolution', *Regional Studies*, vol 39, no 4, pp 453-63.

Keating, M. (2007a) 'Devolution, policy-making and innovation', Conference Paper, ECPR Conference, Pisa, September.

Keating, M. (ed) (2007b) *Scottish social democracy*, Brussels: P.I.E. Peter Lang.

Keating, M. (2010) *The government of Scotland* (2nd edn), Edinburgh: Edinburgh University Press.

Leith, M. and Soule, D.P.J. (2011) *Political discourse and national identity in Scotland*, Edinburgh: Edinburgh University Press.

Lodge, G. (2012) 'The UK's last chance saloon', *Prospect*, 12 January.

Lodge, G. and Schmuecker, K. (eds) (2010) *Devolution in practice 2010*, London: Institute for Public Policy Research.

MacDonnell, H. (2009) *Unchartered territory*, London: Politico's.

Macwhirter, I. (2011) 'What's the union for ... anyone?', *Sunday Herald*, 18 September.

Maxwell, S. (2009) 'Tackling Scottish poverty – principles and absences', *Scottish Affairs*, vol 67, spring, pp 57-69.

McBride, S. (2009) 'Devolution and neoliberalism in the Canadian welfare state: ideology, national and international conditioning frameworks, and policy change in British Columbia', *Global Social Policy*, vol 9, pp 127-33.

McCall, V. (2009) 'Some useful sources', *Social Policy and Society*, vol 8, no 3, pp 431-6.

McCrone, D. (2012) 'Scotland out of the Union? The rise and rise of the nationalist agenda', *The Political Quarterly*, vol 83, no 1, pp 69-76.

McKendrick, J.H., Mooney, G., Dickie, J. and Kelly, P. (eds) (2011) *Poverty in Scotland 2011: Towards a more equal society?*, London: Child Poverty Action Group.

McLaughlin, E. and Baker, J. (2007) 'Equality, social justice and social welfare: a road map to the new egalitarianisms', *Social Policy and Society*, vol 6, no 1, pp 53-68.

McWhirter, I. (2012) 'An independent Scotland could become a beacon of progressive opinion', *Sunday Herald*, 29 January.

Miliband, E. (2012) 'Our fairest and most just days lie ahead of us', Speech, Glasgow, 30 January (www.scottishlabour.org.uk/the-case-for-a-fairer-country).

Mooney, G. and Law, A. (eds) (2007) *New Labour/hard labour?*, Bristol: The Policy Press.

Mooney, G. and Poole, L. (2004) '"A land of milk and honey"? Social policy in Scotland after devolution', *Critical Social Policy*, vol 24, no 4, pp 458-83.

Mooney, G. and Scott, G. (eds) (2005a) *Exploring social policy in the 'new' Scotland*, Bristol: The Policy Press.

Mooney, G. and Scott, G. (2005b) 'Introduction: themes and issues', in G. Mooney and G. Scott (eds) *Exploring social policy in the 'new' Scotland*, Bristol: The Policy Press, pp 1-20.

Mooney, G., Morelli, C. and Seaman, P. (2009) 'The question of economic growth and inequality in contemporary Scotland', *Scottish Affairs*, vol 67, spring, pp 92-109.

Mooney, G., Scott, G. and Mulvey, G. (2008) 'The "Celtic lion" and social policy: some thoughts on the SNP and social welfare', *Critical Social Policy*, vol 28, no 3, pp 378-93.

Mooney, G., Scott G. and Williams C. (2006) 'Rethinking social policy through devolution', *Critical Social Policy*, vol 26, no 3, pp 483-97.

Moore, M. (2011a) 'Empowering our nation, reaching our potential: the future of Scottish devolution', Speech at the Royal Society of Edinburgh, 31 August.

Moore, M. (2011b) Speech to the Liberal Democrat Conference, Birmingham, 21 September.

Morelli, C. and Seaman, P. (2007) 'Devolution and inequality: a failure to create a community of equals?', *Transactions of the Institute of British Geographers*, vol 32, pp 523-38.

Morgan, K. (2002) 'The English question: regional perspectives on a fractured nation', *Regional Studies*, vol 36, no 7, pp 797-810.

Morgan, K. (2006) 'Devolution and development: territorial justice and the North–South divide', *Publius: The Journal of Federalism*, vol 36, no 1, pp 189-206.

Newlands, D., Danson, M. and McCarthy, J. (eds) (2004) *Divided Scotland?*, Aldershot: Ashgate.

Newman, J. and Yeates, N. (eds) (2008) *Social justice: Welfare crime and society*, Maidenhead: Open University Press.

Parekh, A., Kenway, P. and MacInnes, T. (2010) *Monitoring poverty and social exclusion in Scotland 2010*, York: Joseph Rowntree Foundation/New Poverty Institute.

Paterson, L., Bechhofer, F. and McCrone, D. (2004) *Living in Scotland: Social and economic change since 1980*, Edinburgh: Edinburgh University Press.

Paxton, W. and Gamble, A. (2005) 'Democracy, social justice and the state', in N. Pearce and W. Paxton (eds) *Social justice: Building a fairer Britain*, London: Politico's Publishing, pp 219-39.

Salmond, A. (2012) 'Scotland's place in the world', Hugo Young Lecture 2012 (www.guardian.co.uk/politics/2012/jan/25/alex-salmond-hugo-young-lecture/print).

Scott, G. and Mooney, G. (2009) 'Poverty and social justice in the devolved Scotland: neoliberalism meets social democracy?', *Social Policy and Society*, vol 3, no 4, pp 379-89.

Scottish Executive (1999) *Social justice:A Scotland where everyone matters*, Edinburgh: Scottish Executive.

Scottish Government, The (2007) *The Government economic strategy*, Edinburgh: The Scottish Government.

Scottish Government, The (2008a) *Achieving our potential: A framework to tackle poverty and income inequality in Scotland*, Edinburgh: The Scottish Government.

Scottish Government,The (2008b) *Taking forward the Government economic strategy:A discussion paper on tackling poverty, inequality and deprivation in Scotland*, Edinburgh: The Scottish Government.

Scottish Government,The (2011a) *The Government economic strategy*, Edinburgh:The Scottish Government (www.scotland.gov.uk/Publications/2011/09/13091128/0).

Scottish Government,The (2011b) *Scotland's spending plans and draft budget 2011-12*, Edinburgh: The Scottish Government (www.scotland.gov.uk/Resource/Doc/331661/0107923.pdf).

Segall, S. (2007) 'How devolution upsets distributive justice', *Journal of Moral Philosophy*, vol 4, no 2, pp 257-72.

Stewart, J. (2004) *Taking stock: Scottish social welfare after devolution*, Bristol: The Policy Press.

Theodoropoulu, S. and Watt, A. (2011) *Withdrawal symptoms: An assessment of the austerity packages in Europe*, Working Paper 2011.02, Brussels: European Trade Union Institute (www.etui.org/Publications2/Working-Papers/Withdrawal-symptoms-an-assessment-of-the-austerity-packages-in-Europe).

Tijmstra, S.A.R. (2009) 'Uniquely Scottish? Placing Scottish devolution in theoretical perspective', *Environment and Planning C: Government and Policy*, vol 27, pp 732-46.

Trench,A. (2010) 'Intergovernmental relations and social citizenship: opportunities Labour missed', in G. Lodge and K. Schmuecker (eds) *Devolution in practice 2010*, London: Institute for Public Policy Research, pp 45-59.

Viebrock, E. (2009) 'Social policy in Scotland since devolution', *Social Policy and Society*, vol 8, no 3, pp 419-30.

Williams, C. and Mooney, G. (2008) 'Decentering social policy? Devolution and the discipline of social policy: A commentary', *Journal of Social Policy*, vol 37, no 3, pp 1-18.

TWO

Between autonomy and dependency: state and nation in devolved Scotland

Alex Law

Introduction

Social policy cannot fail but to be shaped by the nature of the state through which it is enacted. It is therefore of central importance to situate questions of social justice and social policy in Scotland within an adequate understanding of the territorial politics of the devolved state. While there have been many learned accounts (see *inter alia* Greer, 2007; Keating, 2010) of devolved constitutional arrangements and the exercise of differential powers between London and Edinburgh, there has been far less sustained sociological exploration of the form that the state takes in Scotland. More than a decade after devolution, the Scottish Parliament occupies an ambiguous position within established sociological models of the state. It has not evolved into a sovereign nation–state and nor has it become a client or supplicant state, wholly dependent on the external authority of the UK state or the European Union (EU).

In 1999 Donald Dewar famously repeated the former Labour leader John Smith's description of devolution as 'the settled will of the Scottish people' (McLean, 2004, p 47). Yet the nature of the Scottish state is more unsettled and incomplete than this verdict might imply. Devolution, as politicians and commentators frequently claim, represents an ongoing process rather than a finished article. On the one side, Scottish nationalists contest the idea that devolution represents some final 'settled will' of the Scottish people. Nationalist politicians routinely frame formal independent statehood as the responsibilities and rights of a *normal* European state, implying that any other constitutional arrangement is that of an abnormal 'stateless' nation. As Scottish National Party (SNP) First Minister Alex Salmond put it in his introduction to the document setting out the case for independent statehood:

> ... our Parliament is incomplete, unfinished. Its voice is muted or silent in many areas vital to our nation. I believe that Scotland cannot fully flourish until it takes responsibility for itself: for its economy, taxes, and spending; for its rich and its poor; for its natural resources and its waste; for its old and its young; for its roads and its seas; for its place in the world, for peace and war, for ties of friendship and common

interest with the other nations of the earth. These are the matters with which *normal*, independent countries deal every day. (The Scottish Government, 2009, p 1; emphasis added)

For them devolution represents a tactical concession by the central UK state rather than the principled expression of the nation's right to self-determination. And while the Conservative Party and certain sections of Scottish society, notably business organisations, vigorously opposed devolution, there are now no demands to abolish the devolved state or to impose limits on its existing powers.

Neither is the devolved state completely defined by its existing powers. It appears to be a transitional form of state, in perpetual motion as it strives to fulfil its apparently inherent potential to mutate into something else: a more comprehensive form of self-government. Over the past decade reviews of the nature and purpose of the Scottish government have come thick and fast. In 2008 the Calman Commission traced the future shape of the Parliament. This resulted in the introduction of the Scotland Bill (Cm 7937, 2010), symbolically presented on St Andrew's Day (30 November). In 2010 a commission was set up by the Scottish government under the former STUC (Scotland's Trade Union Congress) leader Campbell Christie to restructure local government, the NHS, the police and other emergency services (Braiden, 2010; Christie, 2011).

Social policy sits at the heart of the contest of the nationalisms in the UK. Scottish nationalists are concerned to convince 'the nation' that a radically different state architecture will improve the prospects for collective solidarity and territorial justice. A constant effort is made by nationalist and unionist politicians to define the collective identity of the national community, British and/or Scottish, as coinciding with the group interests of the social justice community. In this respect, the language of social policy is routinely attached to discourses of 'the nation'. Insider groups within the nation construct emotive and evidential appeals that the nation collectively possesses more of a certain quality (for example, egalitarian or entrepreneurial) than other groups positioned outside the nation (Billig, 1995). An insider–outsider dialectic is constantly set in motion by the framing of sub-state nationalism in terms of collective justice as a distinguishing and defining attribute of group membership.

The incomplete, transitional nature of the Scottish state has its origins in the politics of devolution. Politicians, academics, commentators and voters may disagree about the degree and extent of the autonomy of the Scottish state, but never about the legitimacy of some form of autonomous state apparatus in Scotland. However, any sense of radical divergence of Holyrood from the Westminster model, either in specific policies or political culture, should not be exaggerated (Keating, 2010). This chapter discusses how devolution was shaped by a crisis of legitimation for the UK state in Scotland. The legitimation of the unitary UK state in Scotland was transformed into a constitutional issue by conflicting ideas of social justice and territorial inequalities. Before devolution, sociologists described Scotland as a 'stateless nation', which, I argue, has limited conceptual coherence. To account for the unfinished and contested relationship between state and nation in Scotland I adopt the idea of liminality from anthropology. This approach is developed further through an examination of three critical aspects of the relationship between state and nation in Scotland: legitimation, autonomy and dependency. While devolution represents a solution to the legitimation crisis of territorial justice, this stands in permanent tension with unresolved political dilemmas of social justice in Scotland.

Stateless in Scotland

Sociological accounts of the state in Scotland stress the institutional autonomy of the Scottish Office and the distinctive institutions of Scottish civil society, principally law, religion and education (Paterson, 1994). Through such autonomy the British welfare state forged an accommodation with the professional classes of Scottish civil society. This autonomy of policy networks led pre-devolution Scotland to be characterised as a 'stateless nation' by David McCrone in his pioneering study *Understanding Scotland: The sociology of a stateless nation* (1992). More recently Marxist writers have used the concept of a 'stateless nation' to describe Scotland (Davidson et al, 2010).

Before devolution Scotland was 'an awkward, ill-fitting case' for sociology, argued McCrone (1992, p 1). Because it lacked a nation-state of its own, Scotland was simply incapable of being conceived as a distinct society worthy of serious sociological analysis. But by the early 1990s, Scotland as a 'stateless nation' now stood, for leading sociologists like McCrone, at 'the centre of the discipline's post-modern dilemma'. At the time, this was an audacious claim. Then fashionable postmodernist sociological theory aimed to de-stabilise privileged ideas about 'the centre' such as the unitary British state, which had long consigned other subjects, like Scotland, to the margins of sociological interest. McCrone's focus was on the changed nature of the real, empirical world of political, economic and social change rather than simply a change in sociological theory, although he also recognised that theories would need to change in order to keep up with developments in a rapidly changing universe.

Of course, as part of the UK, Scotland was never 'stateless' in any absolute sense of the term. By the 1990s the nation-state no longer occupied the centre ground of sociology, as it had since its foundations in the 19th century.

> Because Scotland is a nation which is not a state, conventional
> sociological models – premised on a fusion of nation and state – are
> of limited utility. Nevertheless, as the nation-state loses its *raison d'etre*
> in a world economy, polity and culture, so Scotland seems to provide
> a glimpse into the future rather than the past. (McCrone, 1992, p 33)

As a nation without a state, the serious sociological study of Scotland could no longer be marginalised. Scotland had become more typical of wider global developments than those societies defined by large nation-states. Being 'stateless' was no longer something anachronistic but pointed to the future direction of social development.

However, soon after devolution, McCrone dropped the concept of 'stateless nation' from the second edition of his book, now re-titled *Understanding Scotland: The sociology of a nation*. As he explained: 'Recovering its parliament, albeit a devolved one, after almost 300 years of union means that Scotland is no longer stateless' (McCrone, 2001, p 1). But a few pages later, McCrone seemed less certain that the 'stateless nation' concept had become inadequate:

> There is of course no denying that Scotland has a degree of statehood (a devolved parliament, a governing bureaucracy), but *it is still best described as a stateless nation*, an imagined community with considerable institutional autonomy, and, at least as yet, no sovereign parliament. (McCrone, 2001, p 6; emphasis added)

This definitional ambiguity in characterising the devolved state was accompanied by the shelving by McCrone of postmodernism as a theory and postmodernity as empirical reality (Thomson, 2004). By the turn of the new Christian millennium it had become a realistic possibility that devolution might be a staging post on the road to Scotland becoming an independent sovereign nation-state. However, the prospect of sovereign statehood for Scotland resembled the 'common sense' model of state and society that McCrone (1992, p 1) had previously dismissed as fundamentally 'problematic' and out of date.

More damaging than McCrone's inconsistencies is that the concept of 'stateless nations' arbitrarily accepts the common-sense nationalist definition of the situation. For instance, in the *Encyclopedia of the stateless nations*, James Minahan (2002) selected 350 candidates from potentially 9,000 stateless 'peoples' across the world on the basis of three simple criteria: self-identity as a distinctive group, possession of national symbols (especially a flag), and a political organisation demanding self-determination. This last criterion alone specifies the 'stateless' part of the concept: nations are defined as 'stateless' only if a nationalist political organisation demands a sovereign state on the basis that national identity and self-determination ought to correspond more closely to each other.

In such ways, the concept of a stateless nation accepts the nationalist definition of the political situation. In Scotland, however, political forms of nationalism command the support of only a (sizeable) minority of the national population. It is one thing to characterise nations according to the self-definition of a whole group – in the classical definition people constitute a nation because they subjectively demand to be recognised as such (Anderson, 1991). It is something else to characterise a nation as 'stateless' solely on the basis of a demand for statehood by an organised political minority within the nation. Almost the entire population of Scotland recognises itself as a nation but only a small fraction demand that it become a sovereign state in its own right (Keating, 2007). As a nation, most

Scots, thus far, have made no mass bid to form a state separate from the UK and have, thus far, remained content with some model of devolution as the political expression of national distinctiveness and territorial justice.

While displaced Palestinians can be categorised as a stateless nation, legally secure Scots in no way fall under the same concept. There are few recent examples of so-called stateless nations seceding from an economically advanced nation-state. Instead, ruling groups within small nations like Scotland (as for Québec and Catalonia among others) seem to prefer to secure greater autonomy within a larger state rather than risk outright independence. In this sense, Scottish devolution, as Greer (2007, p 38) argues, represents 'the formalization of pre-existing but threatened elite autonomy'. Classical forms of nation-state sovereignty appear to be permanently suspended for a small nation like Scotland. Instead, its ruling groups demand increased autonomy to negotiate the turbulent waters of global capitalism and the geopolitical networks of the world system from within the protective shell of the larger institutional framework of the UK state.

Liminal state–nation relationship

Instead of the idea of a stateless nation it might prove more fruitful to think of the dialectic between nation and state in devolved Scotland as having a 'liminal' character. As a concept, liminality derives from the Latin word *limen*, which refers to a threshold between spaces or time. In anthropology, the concept of liminality indicates a movement or ritualistic passage between two fixed points or conditions. Liminality for the anthropologist Victor Turner (1985, p 236) operates as a 'time outside time in which it is often permitted to *play* with the factors of sociocultural experience, to disengage what is mundanely connected, what, outside liminality, people may even believe to be naturally and intrinsically connected, and to join the disarticulated parts in novel, even improbable ways'. If liminality is transposed to the level of the state form, devolution might comparably be said to reconstitute 'the disarticulated parts' of the UK state in novel, although not improbable, ways, and break the mundane connection of sovereignty routinely assumed to exist between statehood and nationhood.

Being caught up in a permanent liminal situation can stimulate a critical questioning of what is ordinarily considered 'normal' and legitimate. Liminal nations tend to form along what Turner (1985) termed a 'normative *communitas*', similar to what the major theorist of nationalism Benedict Anderson (1991) called 'horizontal comradeship', rather than the functional or vertical integration of 'community'. A strong sense of equal belonging based on identity and resemblance develops within the *communitas*, often through negative or inverted collective representations. All forms of nationalism, not least Scottish, are constructed as collective representations against what they are not. *Communitas* as an equalising but changeable form of social solidarity is subject to a dialectic interplay with the unequal social structure of community. Demands for social justice emerge in the charged space between the equal belonging of *communitas* and the unequal hierarchical integration of community. Modern societies tend to have a looser 'liminoid' character than the fixed rituals of *communitas*. Turner places modern liminoid phenomena on the margins of political systems as an 'anti-structure' because he mistakenly believes that the state–nation relationship assumes a fully finished, integrated and unitary form, lacking scope for innovation and experimentation.

It might not always be possible or desirable to complete a transition from one fixed structure to another, say, from statelessness to sovereignty. Even though nationalist politicians in Scotland ritualistically lament the lack of an independent state, it is doubtful if this is considered a serious possibility in the near future. Nationalism in Scotland functions as a strategic bargaining gambit for greater autonomy as a constitutional insurance policy for territorial justice, if not always social justice, rather than a go-for-broke gamble on sovereign independence. Nationalists are content to legitimise their rational-legal credentials as 'civic nationalists', imagining national identity in Scotland in terms of the values of social justice – tolerant, pluralist, inclusive and democratic – in contrast to more virulent, illegitimate forms of 'ethnic nationalism' based on blood, soil, violence, xenophobia and sectarianism (Davidson, 2000). Committed to civic legality, the case for greater territorial autonomy, such as full fiscal powers, accepts the procedural confines of an overarching UK state. A purely symbolic appeal is constructed, lacking the mass mobilisation of an insurgent political movement, resulting in a collective representation of Scotland as a 'wee' nation that political nationalists believe could realise its special place in the world if only it was possible, which it isn't, to shake free of the suffocating power of the Goliath-like UK state.

Similar appeals to social justice shape devolved government and social policy decentralisation in multinational states like Canada and Belgium (Beland and Lecours, 2008). Here the inner logic of the 'policy and nation' dialectic represents a powerful force for the decentralisation of social policy in mutually reinforcing ways. Social policy routinely makes contact with people in everyday life and helps establish direct, intimate and tangible links with 'the nation' as a collective frame for common-sense making across otherwise divided social groups. By framing everyday life in various ways, social policy shapes, regulates and directs the meaning and possibilities of collective existence, experienced in national terms as 'a social justice community' (Beland and Lecours, 2008). Political disputes about social policy are readily translated into a presumed consensus about distinctive core national values, principles and collective identity.

Defined in this way, the Scottish state–nation relationship is determined by questions of legitimacy, autonomy and dependency. For Scottish nationalists, the devolved state represents a platform to legitimise claims for an improbable independent statehood, while for unionists the devolved state promises to evolve into a more efficient and responsive manager of a territorially defined population. Both seek to legitimate their claims by conflating the territorial justice of constitutionally defined communitarian groups with demands for social justice arising from structural socioeconomic inequalities, which always threatens to leap over the arbitrary lines of constitutional borders. Since 1999 the constitutional argument has been largely defined by a rather arid and abstract discourse of institutions, mechanisms, committees, procedures and administration. However, as the financial crisis threatened to engulf Scottish society in 2008, debate about the constitution took on renewed vigour, if not always one of relevance to demands for social justice, involving claims and counter-claims over responsibility for the fiscal crisis and the contraction of public services. Even in the eye of the fiscal crisis, this surfeit of political discourse never had cause to ask about the legitimation processes guaranteeing the devolved state's right to continue to rule.

Legitimacy and territorial justice

The question of the legitimacy of the state is significant for all students of social policy, never more so than during a period of economic crisis and welfare cuts. For Max Weber (1978, p 212ff) the legitimation process of a modern democratic state like that of the UK requires that its rule be seen as binding, valid and justified because the correct legal procedures have been followed in electing a government and enacting laws. Clearly, this type of legitimacy is much too formal to account for the loss of political legitimacy where a state denies some part of its citizenry adequate democratic representation, as in pre-devolution Scotland. A more substantive form of legitimation, what Weber (1978, p 699) called 'autonomy', lay behind the democratic demand for devolution in Scotland:

> Unless the word "autonomy" is to lack all precision, its definition presupposes the existence of a group of persons which, though membership may fluctuate, is determinable, and whose members are all, by consent or enactment, under a special law depending on them for its modification.

Objective rule by the state tolerates the subjective right of autonomous citizens, or at least its recognised representatives, to demand social justice but they are, in turn, duty bound to observe the legal-rational authority of the state bureaucracy.

Devolution was an outcome of the growing sense in Scotland over the course of the 1980s and 1990s that the British state ruled Scotland in an increasingly illegitimate way. Scotland was ruled through policies imposed by a Tory government that fewer and fewer people in Scotland actually voted for (McEwen, 2006; Greer, 2007). By the 1990s the presence of the UK state in Scotland was experiencing what might be called a 'legitimation crisis'. A crisis of legitimation occurs whenever the state is no longer able to promote its welfare functions in order to meet demands for social justice and so stimulate support for the 'system' within the existing set-up (Habermas, 1976). This does not mean that Scotland was mobilised as a national mass in order to secede from the rule of the UK as a state. It was less the entire political-economic system that faced the withdrawal of legitimacy than the particular form of governmental power assumed by the

UK state, minority rule by successive Tory governments attempting to impose unpopular neoliberal policies on Scotland.

Devolution addressed the more limited crisis of legitimation in Scotland within the terms of the overall legitimacy of the UK state. The process leading up to devolution operated within and respected the valid legal forms of the UK state at the same time as proclaiming the subjective rights of Scottish society to press demands for territorial justice. At no time did the campaign for Scottish devolution represent an extra-parliamentary challenge to the legal-rational authority of the UK state, as the mass Poll Tax rebellion of the early 1990s had done in conditions where social democratic values of redistributive social justice were flagrantly flouted (Lavalette and Mooney, 2000).

In 1997 a Labour government was returned to office for the first time in 18 years. Expectations ran high that Labour would deliver a Scottish Parliament as a form of democratic protection against social injustices and illegitimate rule by a Westminster government experiencing less and less electoral support in Scotland. The Scottish Labour Party has traditionally been a staunch defender of the UK, although this has been tempered with fluctuating historical support for some form of Home Rule for Scotland (McLean, 2004; McEwen, 2006). In some quarters, however, New Labour had seemed ambivalent about devolution. Its leader, Tony Blair, belittled the prospects for a Scottish Parliament by comparing its powers to that of an English parish council (*The Scotsman*, 4 April 1997). Some attempts were made to de-legitimate the democratic claims for a devolved state beyond the ranks of New Labour. As a prominent Scottish celebrity, the comedian Billy Connolly ridiculed the proposals:

> You always hear them say they speak for Scotland, you know, Scotsmen won't stand for this, the people of Scotland ... well I'm one of the people of Scotland and they don't speak for me.... I don't want a pretendy government in Edinburgh and a rush of carpetbaggers along the M8 to join it. It is just another expensive layer of government. (quoted in Smith, 1997)

Although Connolly's remarks found support in the Conservative Party, the only political party in Scotland to oppose devolution and to openly contest its legitimacy, his views were well out of touch with the mainstream of political developments that saw devolution as a precondition for territorial justice in Scotland.

Labour moved quickly to arrange a referendum on devolution, largely as a tactic to forestall the electoral threat to their core support in urban central Scotland from a nationalist-led opposition. Devolution was considered a better compromise solution to the crisis of political legitimacy than the imponderable risk of the break-up of the UK state (Nairn, 1981). Blair imposed two questions on the referendum held in September 1997. Voters were asked to decide on whether to, first, establish a parliament and, second, allow the Parliament tax-varying powers. A decade later, the power to vary taxation retains political significance as a measure of government autonomy in Scotland. For many commentators, only a large turnout would give the result a degree of popular legitimacy (something that an earlier referendum in 1979 appeared to lack, with just 52 per cent support for devolution from a turnout of 64 per cent, a mere one third of the electorate). As one character puts it in James Robertson's novel about the prehistory of devolution, *And the land lay still*:

> What was to be feared was public indifference or exhaustion, another vote of little or no confidence. A big turnout was needed, an overwhelming affirmation that, whatever else emerged in this new political era, nobody would later be able to say that the Scots had their parliament imposed on them. (Robertson, 2010, p 617)

In the event, around 60 per cent of those eligible to vote took part in the referendum. Of these, three quarters supported the establishment of a Scottish Parliament, around 46 per cent of the electorate at this time, while nearly two thirds backed tax-varying powers (Pattie et al, 1998). For many commentators, this represented an 'overwhelming' endorsement of the legitimacy of the Parliament. For Scottish nationalists, like Robertson's character in the book, this 'overwhelming' turnout was a result of 'the ghosts of history' forcing Scottish people to finally accept that political change was necessary.

At the time of the referendum, the precise powers of the parliament were not spelled out in any detail, except for taxation. The Scotland Act 1998 turned vague inferences about the legal powers of the Parliament into statutory rights. Two sorts of powers were established: devolved powers held in Edinburgh and reserved powers held in London. The reserved powers of the UK Parliament are those thought to be fundamental to sovereign forms of government: defence, foreign affairs, home affairs, macroeconomic policy and social security. Devolved power in Scotland allows some exercise of power normally associated with sovereignty in the areas of law, home affairs and the police. Its main powers, however, are economic, social and cultural (Law and Mooney, 2012). First, devolved *economic* powers include agriculture, fisheries, planning, economic development, training and tourism. Second, devolved *social* powers cover policies in health, social work, housing and local government (Mooney and Scott, 2005). Third, devolved *cultural* powers enable control over policies in education, the arts and sport and the natural and built environment (Scotland Office, 2009). The UK government continued to appoint a Minister for Scotland, which posed little problem when the same parties ruled in both London and Edinburgh, but could result in political tension when different parties ruled the separate parliaments, as was the case with the SNP minority Scottish government from 2007 to 2011 under first a Labour and then from May 2010 a Conservative–Liberal Democrat Coalition UK government. Scotland also acquired a different method of election, a mix of 'first past the post' and proportional representation.

The scope for distinctive policy making in Scotland remains wide, although it is constrained by the fiscal as well as the constitutional reserve powers of the UK government. Michael Keating (2010, p 255ff) identifies five types of policy divergence and convergence from the rest of Britain. First, there are 'non-comparable' policies where Scotland initiates a radical policy departure from the UK, such as policies around land reform. Second, in less unique ways 'policy autonomy' occurs within areas of shared policies across the UK but customised to Scottish conditions, such as education, health and criminal justice. Third, 'concurrent policies' shadow broader patterns of policy making across the UK or Europe, as in much health policy. Fourth, 'policy uniformity' is imposed on Scotland through legal or external constraints, as with ratification of the International Criminal Court. Finally, there is 'policy competition', a special case of policy autonomy, where policy in Scotland reacts to and mimics high profile policy innovations elsewhere in the UK, stimulating reconvergence, as in draconian youth justice policies. Generally, there has been little of the radically distinctive and responsive policy innovation in Scotland that was supposed to be the *sine qua non* of devolution (Mooney and Scott, 2005).

This limited capacity of the Scottish state was exposed for some by the advent of the banking crisis of 2007 and 2008 and the resulting fiscal crisis of the UK state. In the first case, the crisis of Scottish-based banks, Royal Bank of Scotland and HBOS, exposed the limits of the Scottish state's finances. As a constrained state, unionist politicians, such as Labour Party MSP and ex-Minister in the Scottish Executive, Wendy Alexander (2010), claim that devolved Scotland has limited power to raise revenues on the scale needed to refloat the finance and banking sectors. As gigantic financial behemoths, the assets of the two major Scottish clearing banks outstrip the entire revenue of the Scottish state. This fact, combined with the Scottish economy's overdependency on financial services, led unionist politicians to argue that an independent Scottish state is simply untenable. Only the UK state, they assert, can protect Scotland from the ravages of global financial crisis and national fiscal retrenchment (Alexander, 2010).

Others, less ideologically committed to the integrity of the British state, see things differently. In fact, the opposite process may well be under way. As a small, devolved nation, Scotland is only 'half a state' (Ascherson, 2010). The fiscal crisis may force the 'half state' to become 'a whole state' in order to protect collective welfare values. As the UK state withdraws fiscal support for welfare services in order to shore up the financial system conflicting conceptions of social and territorial justice between Scotland and the rest of Britain may become more, not less, acute, propelling the political case for an independent state and a new legitimation crisis for the UK state. Ascherson (2010, p 35) identified a fundamental clash of values between Scotland and Britain:

> It's not just that nearly a third of employment is in the public sector.
> It's that the mania for privatising never made sense here, in a country

whose tradition is communitarian rather than individualist, deeply suspicious of its own and everyone else's elites, obsessive about equality.

In contrast, when Gordon Brown drew up a list of 'British values' he talked about 'fair play' but not about 'equality'. Values of fairness and equality have quite different political implications. As Ascherson continues: 'But "fair play" is just a boo at the ref. "Equality" is a battle cry, a call for the hammer of justice which only a state can wield'. Scotland has become 'the last bastion' of legitimate social welfare values:

> It upholds beliefs which were once shared all over the UK: that health and prescriptions, school meals and university education, care and public transport for the old, should all be free, the state's honouring of the contract between citizen and ruler.

But the problem for Ascherson is that the incomplete Scottish half-state lacks the legal authority to resist the cuts to public services demanded by the British Coalition government and imposed through the blunt instrument of reductions in the block grant.

Autonomy and dependency

In such accounts the Scottish state is legitimated by the values of civil society. This conveniently sidesteps the fact that the defining mark of sovereign state power is bound up with force. For Max Weber (1946, p 78), the state is defined by its exclusive claim on 'the *monopoly of the legitimate use of physical force* within a given territory'. Only the state has the 'right' to use violence. While force is by no means the only capacity of the state, Weber argues that it is the means wholly specific to it. Without a capacity to rightfully organise the exclusive use of violence the state cannot be said to exist in any meaningful sense. Of course, organised violence is not all that there is to state power. With the emergence of the modern state, central authority began to be yoked to exclusive power over and protection of territorially defined populations rather than more geographically dispersed forms of religious or imperial authority.

Weber's definition of the state as possessing the monopoly of legitimate violence appears to have little relevance in Scotland. In the devolved settlement, the organisation of military violence and border control rests exclusively with the UK state. This seems to support the view that Scotland might still be characterised as a 'stateless nation' (McCrone, 1992, 2001). In the absence of a distinctively Scottish capacity for warfare the values of welfare nationalism are magnified. In such ways the violent foundations of the state in Scotland are displaced to the level of the UK. Hence the British state is associated with a history of militarism and imperialism from which the Scottish state and the civic nation are made exempt. Instead of being defined like classical nation-states by possession of a monopoly of legitimate violence, the Scottish state is seen as the undiluted expression of civil society and its values of social justice (Paterson, 1994).

While the Scottish state lacks some of the core instruments of violence, it is not entirely bereft of coercive power. It has a distinctive legislative and criminal justice system covering law, home affairs and the police (Croall et al, 2010; see also Chapter Eleven, this volume). Even here, the role of Scots law in the relations of domination tends to be subordinated to its role as an enlightened rational institution at the core of civil society (alongside distinctively Scottish religion and education). Moreover, the welfarist values of the Scottish criminal justice system are emphasised at the expense of punitive authority, with Scots law reflecting the compassionate values of the nation, graphically illustrated in August 2009 by the controversial release by the Scottish government of the convicted Lockerbie bomber, the Libyan national Abdelbaset Al-Megrahi.

Similarly, the Scottish state is not 'dependent' on the centralised British state in a strong or unilateral sense. Scotland has long been characterised as dependent on external economic and political forces. In more fevered imaginations, Scotland has even been compared to an 'internal colony' of Britain in its belated and distorted form of industrial capitalism (Hechter, 1999). Scotland was 'invited' to develop as an industrial nation only as a subordinate partner in the British imperial project. Long-time critics like Tom Nairn (1981) laid the blame for the lack of militant political nationalism in Scotland on the supposedly anti-modern character of the UK state. As a union of separate nations under a constitutional monarchy, the British state represented a freakish anomaly in an age of modernity and democracy. Politics in a small nation like Scotland was debased by the imperial pretensions of the over-centralised, status-riddled British state. Moreover, Scotland's economic development was badly distorted by the bias of uneven development in favour of South East England, raising claims about territorial justice as proxies for social justice. In such analyses, Scotland's national culture supposedly suffered from an inferiority complex and its social structure retarded by a poverty-soaked culture of labourism.

Arguments about the territorial peculiarities of Scottish dependency are premised on an endlessly circular argument: Scotland lacked internal resources for autonomous development because it was dependent on external sources of economic and political authority (McCrone, 1992). In fact, as Hechter (1999) notes more recently, far from being under-developed lowland Scotland passed through the Industrial Revolution decades before it even began in the US. Nevertheless, this idea of Scottish subordination under British imperial authority had considerable political traction in the years before devolution. 'Oppressed', dependent Scotland formed a central part of the vocabulary of the campaign for devolution, especially among left-leaning Scottish nationalists (Davidson, 2000). The legitimation crisis of the UK state in Scotland was largely constructed through the prism of dependency. For instance, the closure of the Ravenscraig steelworks in 1992 and the introduction of the Poll Tax in 1989 were filtered through a nationalist frame of dependent Scotland suffering under the hostile external power of Tory England.

The Scottish state also appears to be locked in to a relationship of fiscal dependency through the allocation of a block grant from Westminster. Revenues for the Scottish state have been determined since 1979 by a ('temporary') mechanism known as 'the Barnett formula', which calculates the level of the block grant proportionate to public spending in England (House of Lords, 2009). Today, almost all political debate about Scotland fluctuates around the question of just how much fiscal and political autonomy from Westminster the Scottish government ought to acquire. Michael Moore, Scottish Secretary for the UK Coalition, described the Scotland Bill as the greatest transfer of fiscal power in the UK since 1707 (Settle and Dinwoodie, 2010). It proposed to give the Scottish state greater fiscal autonomy and accountability, removing 10 per cent from the block grant, and to allow the Scottish Parliament the power to set a definite rate for income tax. Other taxes like stamp duty and landfill tax become devolved powers but any new taxes require Westminster's agreement. The Scottish state can borrow up to 10 per cent of its capital funding to a maximum debt of £2.2 billion (2010 prices). The Bill also grants additional powers over traffic laws and airguns.

Here the Scotland Bill of 2010 was proposed by a 'consensus' of the UK's largest parties but did not include the nationalist governing party in Scotland. According to established convention the UK Parliament cannot 'normally' legislate on devolved issues without majority support in the Scottish Parliament. Moreover, the governing nationalists in Scotland viewed the fiscal powers granted by the Scotland Bill as far too limited compared to the comprehensive fiscal powers that they claim are more appropriate for an increasingly autonomous Scottish Parliament. They also objected to the condescending tone of unionist politicians introducing the Bill. The Scottish government, of whichever stripe, unionists argued, need to be exposed to increased financial 'accountability' and take 'responsibility' for raising its own revenue rather than simply spending it. Like a scolded child, the ruling Scottish government was told to take responsibility by the grown-up parties at Westminster, neglecting the fact that Labour and the Liberal Democrats formed the government in Scotland for its first eight years.

Critics of the Calman Commission and the Scotland Bill point to flaws in the tax proposals that run contrary to claims about territorial justice (Cuthbert and Cuthbert, 2010). First, if the Scottish government reduced the rate of income tax in order to give capital in Scotland a competitive market advantage then overall total income tax receipts might well rise, but the share returned to the Scottish government would decrease. Second, the Scottish government receives a lower proportion of revenue generated by the higher rate bands, potentially resulting in a decline in the average proportion of revenue flowing back to the Scottish government. They also highlight the different political implications of the adverse effects of the tax proposals for the main political parties in Scotland. Further restrictions on public spending in Scotland will appeal to core Conservative support while the nationalists have publicly spelled out their objections to the proposals. On the other hand, the Labour Party, who were instrumental in setting up Calman, may become trapped in a unionist consensus but have most to lose electorally from any further rounds of public sector austerity.

Conclusion

With devolution, Scotland crossed the threshold from statelessness but did not arrive at full-blown sovereignty. Instead, it acquired a novel, liminal relationship between state and nation. Scotland is neither wholly 'stateless' nor fully sovereign but operates on the threshold between the two ideal models. On the one hand, it lacks the trappings of sovereign power to declare war or to set up independent border controls. On the other hand, it possesses powers over a whole range of functions, particularly social policy, that normally characterise the classical model of democratic citizenship. It is no exaggeration to say that Scotland has some of the widest powers of any devolved state (Keating, 2010). This is not limited to social policy but includes key economic and cultural functions.

Closer to the immediate concerns of this book, the devolved state exercises power over key welfare functions like health, education, social work, housing and local government. It also shapes the cultural field through powers over the arts and sport, and the natural and built environment (Scotland Office, 2009). Indeed, the much vaunted commitment to welfare nationalism in Scotland has been in constant tension with neoliberal forms of competitive nationalism. For some, devolution arrived too late to stop the remorseless march of the neoliberal marketisation of state and society from undermining collectivist values of social justice and state welfare in Scotland. In his novel, James Robertson's characters debate the potential for devolution to preserve the collectivist values of state welfare in Scotland against market encroachments:

> '… just at the point when we've won, when we've got what we worked for aw these years, right at that moment we throw it away because naebody can be bothered ony mair. Thatcher won after all, in spite of everything. That's what I think.'
>
> 'How can you say that?' Mike said. 'Her own party chucked her out. She fought against devolution all the way, and we beat her. And the Tories won't be back in power for years.'
>
> 'They don't have to be. Brown and Blair are gonnae dae it aw for them. It's true. The market is king. So what aboot this parliament of oors? It's like we fought our way tae the bar just in time for the barman tae tell us he's stopped serving.
>
> 'No,' Mike protested. 'I don't feel that. We're at the start of something new and different. It *can't* be like it was before.' (2010, pp 618-19)

As other chapters in this book will make plain, some things in social policy in Scotland have undoubtedly been 'new and different' since devolution.

Considerable policy discretion has been exercised to produce a series of original policy developments, including free personal care for older people and land reform, as well as market-facing neoliberal programmes for public services, urban regeneration and economic strategy measures. The extent of territorial divergence, however, can be overstated, although a more radical divergence cannot be ruled out in the near future, while the shared assumptions across political parties about neoliberal, market-based priorities in Scotland can be overlooked by even the most informed commentators.

Detailed policy developments are amply described and commented upon elsewhere. Here the focus has been on more fundamental questions concerning the nature of the state and nation dialectic in Scotland. To say that the state is devolved and to describe its functions in copious detail is a necessary starting point. On its own, however, it is not very enlightening. I have approached the question of the state in a more sociological vein. Scotland does not fit the ideal-type model of the classical sovereign nation-state. Neither is it a dependent suppliant of the larger body of the UK state. I have also cast doubt on the conceptual adequacy of the idea of Scotland as a 'stateless nation', which, I argue, merely naturalises the nationalist conception of the state, so distorting the concept's explanatory value or descriptive power.

Students of social policy need to address the liminal, in-between spaces in which the Scottish state and nation dialectic operates, with its possibilities for and constraints on social and territorial conceptions of justice. Devolution is not a free-floating ideal, unmoored from the determinants of coercive forms of state power and class domination. It secured a political solution, or rather a breathing space, for the legitimation crisis of territorial justice premised on a national *communitas* as a substitute claim of social justice. Where the communitarian appeal of devolution may have obscured the impermeable fault line of socioeconomic divisions within Scotland, and conflated the claim of social justice with territorial justice, the crisis of neoliberal political economy and public sector retrenchment demands a more critical sociological theory of the relationship between the devolved state, nation and social policy.

Further resources

The Institute of Governance at the University of Edinburgh is a key centre for the study of public policy and territorial identity in Scotland. It has a long record of working closely with the Scottish government, the Scottish Parliament, Scottish and UK civil servants, business and the media, and publishes *Scottish Affairs*, a key journal covering political and social policy issues: www.institute-of-governance. org/

The Centre for Public Policy for Regions at the University of Glasgow specialises in the study of public policy with a particular emphasis on economic and social development in Scotland: www.cppr.ac.uk/

A more critical range of perspectives on social policy and social justice in Scotland is presented in Davidson, N., McCafferty, P. and Miller, D. (2010) *Neoliberal Scotland: Class and society in a stateless nation*, Newcastle: Cambridge Scholars Publishing.

References

Alexander, W. (2010) 'Memo to SNP: times have changed', *Sunday Herald*, 10 October.

Anderson, B. (1991) *Imagined communities* (2nd edn), London: Verso.

Ascherson, N. (2010) 'Return to Babylon', *Sunday Herald*, 31 October.

Beland, D. and Lecours, A. (2008) *Nationalism and social policy: The politics of territorial solidarity*, Oxford: Oxford University Press.

Billig, M. (1995) *Banal nationalism*, London: Sage Publications.

Braiden, G. (2010) 'Public sector shake-up plans', *The Herald*, 19 November.

Christie, C. (2011) *Commission on the future delivery of public services*, Edinburgh: The Scottish Government.

Croall, H., Mooney, G. and Munro, M. (eds) (2010) *Criminal justice in Scotland*, Cullompton: Willan Publishing.

Cuthbert, J. and Cuthbert, M. (2010) 'The Scotland Bill is broken', *Scottish Left Review* (www.scottishleftreview.org/li/index.php?option=com_content&task=view&id=359&Itemid=1).

Davidson, N. (2000) *The origins of Scottish nationhood*, London: Pluto Press.

Davidson, N., McCafferty, P. and Miller, D. (2010) *Neoliberal Scotland: Class and society in a stateless nation*, Newcastle: Cambridge Scholars Publishing.

Greer, S.L. (2007) *Nationalism and self-government: The politics of autonomy in Scotland and Catalonia*, Albany, NY: State University of New York.

Habermas, J. (1976) *Legitimation crisis*, London: Heinemann.

Hechter, M. (1999) *Internal colonialism: The Celtic fringe in British national development* (2nd edn), Piscataway, NJ: Transaction Publishers.

House of Lords (2009) *Select Committee on the Barnett Formula: 1st report of Session 2008-09, Report with Evidence, HL Paper 139*, London: House of Lords.

Keating, M. (2007) *Plurinational democracy: Stateless nations in a post-sovereignty era*, Oxford: Oxford University Press.

Keating, M. (2010) *The government of Scotland: Public policy making after devolution* (2nd edn), Edinburgh: Edinburgh University Press.

Lavalette, M. and Mooney, G. (2000) '"No poll tax here!" The Tories, social policy and the great poll tax rebellion, 1987-1991', in M. Lavalette and G. Mooney (eds) *Class struggle and social welfare*, London: Routledge, pp 155-82.

Law, A. and Mooney, G. (2012) 'Competitive nationalism: state, class and the forms of capital in devolved Scotland', *Environment and Planning C: Government and Policy*, vol 30, no 1, pp 62-77.

McCrone, D. (1992) *Understanding Scotland: The sociology of a stateless nation*, London: Routledge.

McCrone, D. (2001) *Understanding Scotland: The sociology of a nation* (2nd edn), London: Routledge.

McEwen, N. (2006) *Nationalism and the state: Welfare and identity in Scotland and Quebec*, Brussels: Peter Lang.

McLean, B. (2004) 'Labour in Scotland since 1945: myth and reality', in G. Hassan (ed) *The Scottish Labour Party: History, institutions and ideas*, Edinburgh: Edinburgh University Press, pp 34–49.

Minahan, J. (2002) *Encyclopedia of the stateless nations: Ethnic and national groups around the world, Volume I: A-C*, Westport, CT: Greenwood Press.

Mooney, G. and Scott, G. (eds) (2005) *Exploring social policy in the 'new' Scotland*, Bristol: The Policy Press.

Nairn, T. (1981) *The break-up of Britain*, London: New Left Books.

Paterson, L. (1994) *The autonomy of modern Scotland*, Edinburgh: Edinburgh University Press.

Pattie, C., Denver, D., Mitchell, J. and Bochel, H. (1998) 'The 1997 Scottish referendum: an analysis of the results', *Scottish Affairs*, vol 22, pp 1–15.

Robertson, J. (2010) *And the land lay still*, London: Hamish Hamilton.

Scotland Office (2009) 'An outline of the Scottish devolution settlement' (www.scotlandoffice.gov.uk/scotlandoffice/49.33.html).

Scottish Government, The (2009) *Your Scotland, your voice: A national conversation*, Edinburgh: The Scottish Government.

Settle, M. and Dinwoodie, R. (2010) '"The settled will of the Scottish people", Holyrood: powerful blueprint is set to strengthen devolution, the UK government claims', *The Herald*, 1 December.

Smith, K. (1997) 'Big Yin's political sideshow', *The Herald*, 10 February.

Thomson, A.J.P. (2004) 'Phrasing Scotland and the postmodern', in E. Bell and G. Miller (eds) *Scotland in theory: Reflections on culture and literature*, Amsterdam: Editions Rodpoi B.V.

Turner, V. (1985) *On the edge of the bush: Anthropology as experience*, Tucson, AZ: University of Arizona Press.

Weber, M. (1946) *From Max Weber: Essays in sociology*, New York: Oxford University Press.

Weber, M. (1978) *Economy and society*, Berkeley and Los Angeles, CA: University of California Press.

THREE

Income and wealth inequalities in Scotland since 1997

Carlo Morelli and Paul Seaman

Introduction

Inequality is an indication of the polarisation that exists within society. Societies, whether they are poor or (in the case of Scotland) rich, can be either equal or unequal. Decisions on levels of inequality are made by individuals, households, politicians and businesses in varying degrees, and addressing inequalities is a necessity if we want to create a society where a maximum number of individuals are able to thrive. Scottish devolution has been conceptualised as a means of tackling social injustice with inequality understood as a source of social dislocation over and above the problems associated with Scottish poverty (for more on poverty, see Chapter Five, this volume). Thus, Gow (1975, p 68) wrote that devolution would seize power from the hands of the powerful and ensure it was 'given to the people in their local, regional and national variety' in order to redress the over-concentration of power in Scotland. This view rests alongside an idealised set of wider Scottish traditions that focus on religion and education, suggesting 'education [h]as a symbolic kind of Protestant virtue', embedding an ideology that develops equality within Scottish society (Walker, 1996, p 252). Poverty and inequality are certainly not identical and can be understood as separate from one another. In recent Scottish history national identity, tied to a 'democratic' intellectual tradition, was often cited as an explanation for the rise in support for devolution (Devine and Finlay, 1996; Poole and Mooney, 2005).

The most recent examples of this focus on equality can be found in the Scottish National Party (SNP) government's paper *Taking forward the Government economic strategy: A discussion paper on tackling poverty, inequality and deprivation in Scotland* published in January 2008. The Scottish Government set out a solidarity golden rule that would create a target to 'increase overall income and the proportion of income earned by the three lowest income deciles as a group by 2017' (The Scottish Government, 2008, para 15).

This more recent conceptualisation identifies income inequality as the form of inequality to focus on. Of course inequality encapsulates a range of wider social and material inequalities that cannot simply be reduced to income, or more broadly wealth. Nevertheless, it is an important proxy of inequality within society as many of the means by which other social and material disadvantages are overcome is through access to income. It is not therefore surprising that governments, researchers and indeed this chapter's focus is on income and wealth inequalities. However, even at the level of income inequality, the rhetoric and reality within Scotland have all too often been at odds with one another. Levels of income inequality in Scotland, as we show below, are high both in absolute terms and relative to the rest of the UK, and as a consequence inequality matters for the development of the population's economic and general well-being. The need to set an explicit target for a reduction in income inequality derives not simply from the recognition that Scotland is a highly unequal society but recognition that high levels of income inequality impose costs on individuals and society itself. As Wilkinson and Pickett (2009) make clear, income inequality damages all in society, not simply the most poor.

Income and wealth inequalities are recognised to have increased within the UK since the 1970s. Dorling et al summarise the consensus by suggesting that 'in the UK this inequality has remained at obstinately high levels. From the late 1970s to the mid-1990s, income inequality grew at a faster rate in the UK than even within the US' (Dorling et al, 2007, p 3). Indeed we have seen the return to levels of income and wealth inequalities that had not been evident for a generation (see also Dorling, 2010). Figure 3.1 below highlights that the proportion of total wealth accrued by the top 1 per cent of the population now exceeds the levels that existed before the Second World War, that is, prior to the emergence of a welfare system which aimed at eradicating the 'five giants' of poverty that were associated with income inequality (want, disease, ignorance, squalor and idleness). This chapter seeks to show that this picture for the UK as a whole can also be identified in Scotland. Income inequality within Scotland has continued at high levels, and this persistence of inequality is associated with high levels of social deprivation and social injustice.

The nature of this inequality needs to be recognised. The period from the 1980s onwards was one in which not only were the very poorest in society faced with falling real incomes but for those a little above the very poorest, although their incomes rose, they were not rising at the rates of the very richest. Thus, the defining feature of income distribution during this period was the development of a long, thin tail emerging with the very richest moving ahead very rapidly, and a resultant sharp increase in measures of inequality.

This chapter examines income inequality in Scotland and its changes since devolution. High levels of persistent income inequality have been a feature of Scottish society since the 1990s. While Chapter Five examines in depth the specific issue of poverty, we seek in this chapter to contextualise this persistence of poverty within the wider framework of income inequality. As we now go on to show, the pattern of rising income inequality was evident, and indeed worse, in Scotland in the early 1990s before it returned to levels close to the UK average at the time of devolution. We show that this inequality has a definite geographical component such that higher income areas are associated with higher levels of income inequality. We then go on to show that the impact of this inequality was also seen in associated high levels of social deprivation, and that this social deprivation is highly responsive to changes in income inequality. This evidence then enables us to indicate areas of action where inequality could be addressed and Scottish society as a whole could benefit. We conclude that for inequality to be addressed we need both anti-poverty measures, aimed at workless and working-poor households, and redistribution policies aimed at ensuring Scottish society becomes more inclusive and solidarity focused. Only by addressing these questions, and providing a means by which they can be addressed, can social justice and some of the alternative futures identified within this volume be brought into being.

Figure 3.1: Share of all income received by the richest 1 per cent in Britain, 1950–2005

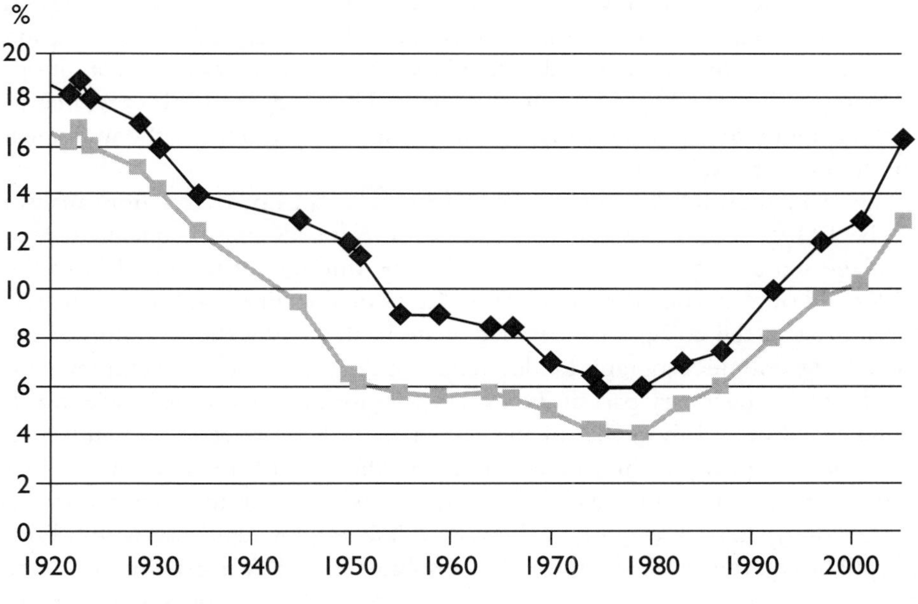

Source: Dorling (2010, Figure 14)

Counting inequality

In order to undertake an examination of income inequality and to link it to changes in social deprivation we require a dataset that permits a detailed examination of inequalities between households. Here social scientists face their first stumbling block. Data on personal income and wealth is far from complete. Despite the fact that government routinely measures individual income and wealth for taxation purposes this data, even in an anonymous form, is rarely made available for research. Extensive official government datasets are available for a wide range of health, educational and social indicators yet linking these to income and wealth is extremely difficult. Insofar as income data is available it is most detailed for those at the bottom of the income distribution and wealth data, that is, inherited and saved income, is extremely sparse. One of the few datasets available for this form of study is the British Household Panel Survey (BHPS), a government survey of households undertaken annually since 1991. It provides social science researchers with a unique data source to examine changes in households. While its sample of between 10,000 and 15,000 households makes it significantly smaller than some other government surveys, it has at least two unique advantages over other official government survey data. First, the panel nature of the dataset means that to a large extent the households covered remained constant throughout the survey period; thus it provides a genuinely unique dataset for those interested in inter-temporal change.[1] Second, it combines detailed income data with detailed information on household composition and the social condition of the household and the individual members within it; thus, it provides not only details of age and income for each individual but this is linked to educational and health data, and importantly this information is also then linked to social questions on conditions of living, security and participation in society.[2] Therefore the BHPS provides us with an ability to uniquely match income to social conditions at the individual and household level over time.

Figure 3.2 shows the changing levels of income inequality derived from analysis of the BHPS dataset.[3] As can be seen, the level of income inequality within Scotland significantly exceeded that of the UK throughout the first half of the 1990s. Although beyond the scope of the discussion contained within this chapter, the impact of the collapse of manufacturing in the 1980s, the recession of the early 1990s and the geographical differences in the location of new employment would form a necessary part of the explanation for understanding why Scottish inequality diverged from that of the rest of the UK. Between 1997 and 2002 changes in inequality within Scotland mirrored those for the rest of the UK, albeit with a lag until after 2002 at which point Scottish levels of inequality followed more closely those of the rest of the UK. While employment rose within both the public and the private sector, and in absolute terms by a larger amount in the private sector, the importance of the public sector has been growing in Scotland since devolution (Bell et al, 2007). By the second quarter of 2010 total public sector employment had increased by 79,100 (15.0 per cent) since the second quarter of 1999. Total public sector employment now accounts for 24.7 per cent of total employment in Scotland, up from 23.1 per cent in the second quarter of 1999 (The Scottish Government, 2010a). Thus, Bell et al conclude that employment growth within Scotland since 1997 has been highly reliant on the public sector. Scotland's catching up in terms of equality with the rest of the UK has much to do with the development of public sector employment over time. This rise and importance of the public sector also combines an important gender component. As Killingsworth and Heckman note, the rise in married women's participation rates within the labour market has been one of the key features of changes in employment in advanced economies. Further they suggest this 'substantial increase in participation among women, particularly married women, stands in sharp contrast with the secular decline in male participation rates' (Killingsworth and Heckman, 1986, p 107). The importance of public sector employment comes not simply in terms of the quantity of jobs increasing but also the multiplier effect on private sector employment. The widely quoted PricewaterhouseCoopers assessment of the impact of government cuts from the government Comprehensive Spending Review in October 2010 suggested that while up to half a million public sector jobs could be lost, a further half a million private sector jobs could also be lost (PwC, 2010). Thus attempts to reduce employment and introduce a pay freeze within the public sector will all be likely to have a disproportionate impact on Scotland, relative to the UK as a whole, to have a disproportionate impact on women and thus set back recent improvements in both gender and income equality.

Figure 3.2: Changing inequality within the UK (Gini coefficients 1991–2007)

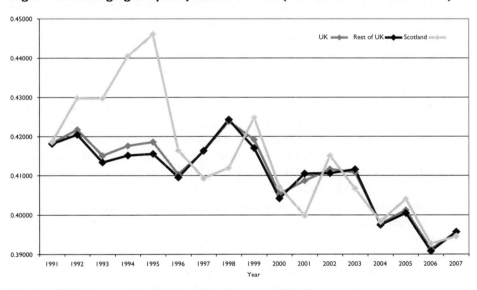

Source: British Household Panel Survey 1991–2007; authors' estimates

Despite the recent record of declining inequality as evidenced by the downward trends of the three series presented in Figure 3.2, it nonetheless remains the case that the current levels of income inequality in the UK remain high relative to their historical levels. The degree of income inequality within Scotland by the mid-2000s was stark. BHPS data for 2005 highlighted that the richest 1 per cent of households had an annual income over 70 times that of the poorest 1 per cent. Indeed, the richest 1 per cent had incomes over four times that of even the median income. Does this matter? Yes. More so for the UK than many other countries in Europe, higher income/wealth is the means by which the rich can separate themselves off from the rest of society. It is a means of 'preferential' exclusion. And this matters to the whole of society since the cost of provision of universal services to society then falls on the least well off. If those with wealth do not benefit from 'universal' provision, they are likely to object to paying for it. Thus, universal services are likely to be underfunded, of poor quality and stigmatised. Further, since the effects of wealth on health and education is transmitted over time, current inequality levels are more likely to reinforce inequality for the next generation, with social mobility declining and a reduction in social justice.

Scottish government statistics covering the period 2007-08 also provide some insight into the patterns and extent of income inequality at the local authority level (The Scottish Government, 2010b). In Table 3.1 below, local authority-level data has been used to show the differences in mean annual income levels (before housing costs) for the third quartile (the second richest 25 per cent) of households of the population as a percentage of the first quartile (the poorest 25 per cent) of households. As can be seen, Scotland's average household income level was £25,600 and the third quartile, before housing costs, had an income of 280 per cent of that of the poorest quartile. Even once we take into account differing household types, a process referred to as equivilising,[4] the ratio of third quartile to poorest quartile mean household annual income levels are typically over 200 per cent.

A number of patterns emerge from closer inspection of this data. Table 3.1 provides evidence of the extent of income inequality by measuring the income of the third quartile of the population as a proportion of the first quartile and evidence of poverty by assessing mean income. Thus above-average income inequality in rural areas (high Q3/Q1 percentages) and high levels of widespread poverty in urban areas (low means) are evident. Within certain rural areas poverty sits side by side with pockets of considerable, but concentrated, wealth giving rise to above-average levels of mean income and above-average inequality, such as in Aberdeenshire and Shetland. Alternatively, rural equality is to be found in certain areas where there are generally low income levels and few of the significant pockets of wealth that can increase mean income levels and income inequality; examples include Dumfries and Galloway. For urban areas we find evidence of below-average levels of inequality (low Q3/Q1 percentages) combined with higher levels of poverty (low means). Cities such as Glasgow and Dundee are associated with the presence of high levels of urban poverty and the ability of higher earners to move into private housing in rural/suburban areas while using good transport links to commute to their work in the cities. 'Fiscal flight' is the term used to describe this squeezing of a city's funding as richer households move outwith the tax boundary yet utilise the services within the city's boundaries (Whittam and Danson, 2007).

This same data can be presented in graphical form (see Figure 3.3), to demonstrate one further finding. Figure 3.3 shows there is a positive correlation between income inequality and mean household income.[5] Thus the greater the

Table 3.1: Third quartile net annual income as a percentage of first quartile net annual income

	Mean	Q3:Q1 % net household	Mean	Q3:Q1 % equivalised households
Aberdeen City	28,700	273.4	27,800	211.9
Aberdeenshire	32,400	290.7	28,600	222.8
Angus	23,800	276.3	22,300	209.4
Argyll & Bute	24,100	270.6	23,200	209.9
Clackmannanshire	26,400	271.2	24,300	219.1
Dumfries & Galloway	22,500	263.2	21,200	202.3
Dundee City	21,300	246.3	20,900	193.2
East Ayrshire	25,700	255.0	23,700	205.8
East Dunbartonshire	31,400	286.2	27,800	228.1
East Lothian	26,700	260.0	25,000	202.0
East Renfrewshire	32,000	309.9	28,200	209.2
Edinburgh City	26,300	279.8	25,900	216.8
Eilean Siar	24,200	321.5	21,600	226.8
Falkirk	25,000	275.4	23,900	198.7
Fife	24,400	279.8	23,100	212.3
Glasgow City	22,200	268.2	22,100	212.2
Highland	26,000	260.2	24,200	210.2
Inverclyde	23,500	274.8	21,900	218.4
Midlothian	27,000	250.4	24,400	197.3
Moray	25,700	284.9	24,000	223.0
North Ayrshire	23,800	268.4	22,200	202.9
North Lanarkshire	25,500	275.0	23,400	216.8
Orkney Islands	26,000	282.0	23,900	218.5
Perth & Kinross	28,200	277.2	26,100	206.3
Renfrewshire	25,500	280.3	23,700	198.0
Scottish Borders	25,000	275.2	23,800	205.4
Shetland Islands	33,500	259.6	33,700	205.8
South Ayrshire	24,700	299.1	23,100	217.9
South Lanarkshire	25,500	292.3	23,500	220.4
Stirling	28,100	267.2	25,700	221.8
West Dunbartonshire	24,600	259.2	22,600	188.8
West Lothian	26,100	285.7	23,600	204.7
Scotland	25,600	279.5	24,100	213.4

Source: Derived from The Scottish Government (2010b, Table 2)

Figure 3.3: Q3 : Q1 % (net of housing costs, unequivalised income data) versus mean income

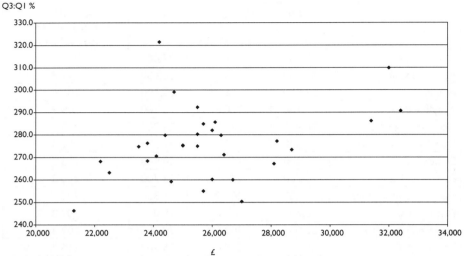

Source: Derived from The Scottish Government (2010b, Table 2)

mean income the more likely it is that income inequality is also high, that is, the richer local authority areas are also the most unequal suggesting that increases in average prosperity have not had the 'trickle-down' effect neoliberal economic thinking suggests would be expected to take place.

Although we have seen that income inequality is significant within Scotland (and the UK generally), the disparity is not as great as when we consider inequality in wealth – wealth is much more concentrated in the hands of the rich than income. Unfortunately, comprehensive data on wealth is not widely available, and most analysis on wealth must utilise some proxy for wealth (or a measure of a subset of it). In the BHPS individuals were asked to provide details of their *income* from financial wealth ('investment income'). In normal circumstances (for example, in the period prior to the current banking-induced financial crisis) the income from financial wealth would correlate fairly closely with the quantity of financial wealth – all other things being equal, the greater the stock of financial wealth an individual holds the more non-earned income ('investment income') flows they would receive. In the analysis we present below we use data from the 2006 and 2007 waves of the BHPS, and therefore from a period before the onset of the current financial crisis. The results are for the UK as a whole (since the sample size for some of the groups would be too small to be reliable were the analysis conducted on Scottish households only).

Table 3.2 illustrates the concentration of investment income in the rich within society, with separate results for the top 5 per cent (compared to the bottom 95 per cent) and the top 1 per cent (compared to the bottom 99 per cent). Taking the top 5 per cent results first, we can see that in 2006 this group had an average level of investment income (£13,142.05 per annum) that is more than 38 times that of the bottom 95 per cent (£342.24 per annum); despite being outnumbered by a ratio of 19:1 it is nonetheless the case that they receive 66.61 per cent of all of the nation's investment income. This inequality would be bad enough were everyone to be assured of their 'day in the sun', but the final column in Table 3.2 shows that there is a marked degree of persistence in terms of who is in receipt of the nation's investment income – 38.1 per cent of the top 5 per cent in 2006 find themselves in the top 5 per cent a year later (2007), and only 2 per cent of the (much larger) bottom 95 per cent group will enter into the top 5 per cent to replace those that leave.

But then there is rich, and there is super rich, and for that we turn to the results that compare the top 1 per cent against the bottom 99 per cent. Since these results transfer those in the 95th to 99th percentiles from the top group to the bottom group, this rearrangement will serve to increase the average income figures for both groups (the top group will lose its 'poorest' members while the bottom group will gain members that are richer than its current members). As a result the average income figures become £29,168.67 per annum and £693.17 per annum respectively (a ratio of more than 42). Despite the loss of these relatively rich members to the bottom 99 per cent group, the top 1 per cent group still accounts for 29.57 per cent of all of the investment income accrued during that year.

But perhaps the most striking result concerns the persistence of this super rich group's membership – the final column of Table 3.2 reveals that 46.7 per cent of the top 1 per cent group in 2006 were still in the top 1 per cent group come 2007; furthermore, other analysis (not presented here) indicates that a further 33 per cent of the top 1 per cent had fallen out of the top 1 per cent by 2007, but were still in the top 5 per cent that year (they were 'merely' rich, rather than super rich). Only 20.3 per cent of the top 1 per cent in 2006 had fallen completely out of the top 5 per cent by 2007. What these results strongly suggest is that the concentration of wealth is more persistent than the concentration of income and that this persistence becomes ever stronger as the focus narrows higher up the income distribution (see also Morelli and Seaman, 2009). Thus any attempt to address social justice must also address levels of both income and wealth inequality.

A fundamental conclusion to be drawn from these data is that income inequality is endemic in and across Scottish society, not just at the national level (comparing rich and poor regions), but also within regions themselves. Poverty and inequality are both important problems within Scottish society but they are not identical to one another. And as the following section will argue, this means that Scotland's inequality will be a cost for *all* Scots, no matter where they live or which part of the income distribution they lie in.

Costs of inequality

Unequal income distributions within society come at a cost of increased social injustice. Wilkinson and Pickett (2009) have examined the correlation between income inequality and several dimensions of social deprivation, including health

Table 3.2: Concentration in wealth income

Results for 'Top 5%'					
Group	Sample size	Average annual investment income in 2006 (£)	Total annual investment income in 2006 (£)	Share of total annual investment income in 2006 (%)	Percentage remaining in group one year later (2007)
Bottom 95%	7,217	342.24	2,469,946.08	33.39	98.0
Top 5%	375	13,142.05	4,928,268.75	66.61	38.1
Results for 'Top 1%'					
Group	Sample size	Average annual investment income in 2006 (£)	Total annual investment income in 2006 (£)	Share of total annual investment income in 2006 (%)	Percentage remaining in group one year later (2007)
Bottom 99%	7,517	693.17	5,210,558.89	70.43	99.5
Top 1%	75	29,168.67	2,187,650.25	29.57	46.7

and well-being, social inclusion, educational attainment, crime and violence. They conclude that advanced societies with higher levels of income inequality also exhibit (in almost all cases) higher levels of social deprivation and that 'these relationships are so strong that we can be confident that they are not due to chance' (Wilkinson and Pickett, 2009, p 53).

Their results are demonstrated with a dramatic figure showing the cross-country comparison, reproduced in Figure 3.4 below, which demonstrates the strength of this relationship and the degree to which the UK lies towards the most unequal end of the distribution, with both high income inequality and high incidences of a range of social deprivations. Wilkinson and Pickett argue that while this research demonstrates a correlation (that is, a statistical association), the relationship they have identified also has a causal linkage – that is, income inequality is responsible for the preponderance of social deprivations. Thus, their conclusion that these relationships 'cannot be dismissed as some statistical trick done with smoke and mirrors' (p 23) implies very strongly a process of causation. In looking for a causal linkage they suggest that an individual's relative position within society can lead to changes in chemical and biological conditions in human physiology that then has an impact on our well-being. That Wilkinson and Pickett limit themselves to correlations rather than examine causation is perhaps most linked to the problem of suggesting deterministically that a change in income inequality leads to an exact change in the level of deprivation. Human beings are complex biological beings and there are many mediating social factors that may act to limit or intensify the degree to which direct causation takes place. Nevertheless, the consistency of Wilkinson and Pickett's results indicates that there is indeed a degree of causation and not simply correlation between income inequality and social deprivation.

Figure 3.4: Health and social problems are worse in more unequal countries

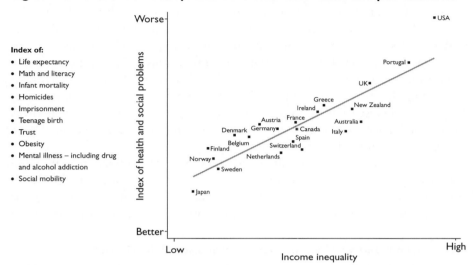

Source: Wilkinson and Pickett (2009)

To what extent is this link between higher income inequality levels and higher levels of social deprivation consistent with Scotland since devolution? Table 3.3 presents results derived from the BHPS for the years 1997 and 2007, using Gini coefficients for the UK, Scotland and the rest of the UK previously used in Figure 3.2. A Gini coefficient is a widely used measure of inequality providing a measure of inequality between 0 and 1 that permits comparisons between income distributions. The lower the figure the more a population can be said to be equal.

By looking at the results contained in the third row we see that in all three cases the Gini coefficient has declined between 1997 and 2007, suggesting that Scotland's experience of improving equality has been a shared experience across the UK.

Subsequent rows show the response to questions contained within the BHPS relating to crime, health and well-being. So, for example, in row 5 respondents are asked 'How safe do you feel walking alone in this area after dark?'. Their response is scored on a 1-5 scale with 5 being the most unsafe.[6] As we can see, between 1997 and 2007 respondents across the UK on average felt safer, with the score falling from 2.41 to 2.28. The corresponding average scores in Scotland were 2.40 and 2.19 respectively.

Examining the other rows in Table 3.3 we find a fairly consistent pattern – the decline in income inequality seen in Scotland, and across the UK, over the period 1997 to 2007, has occurred at the same time as improvements in crime, health and well-being (see Chapters Seven and Nine, this volume). Thus in rows 6 and 7 we have two further questions which examine aspects of individuals' concern over crime. Here again we see a similar decline in the Gini coefficient for each area of the UK between 1997 and 2007. Row 9 includes a question reflecting individuals' feeling of trust and loneliness and here again we see a decline in the degree to which individuals consider themselves to be isolated. Finally, in rows 11, 12 and 14 we have questions regarding aspects of health and mental well-being. Both the questions on improvement in physical health (row 11) and improvement in mental health (row 14) demonstrate the same results as highlighted above – improvement in all areas between 1997 and 2007. Only in responses to the question concerning the extent to which health limits the opportunity to work (row 12) do we see little discernible improvement over the period. This itself may perhaps reflects the long-term health costs of inequality combined with the limited 'yes/no' response permitted to the question.

The significance of these results is that they provide Scottish and UK-wide evidence reinforcing Wilkinson and Pickett's central conclusion – higher levels of income inequality are bad for society generally and are associated with poor outcomes for a wide range of social indicators. And as Table 3.1 has clearly

Table 3.3: Link between income inequality and social deprivation

	1997			2007		
	UK	Rest of the UK	Scotland	UK	Rest of the UK	Scotland
Gini coefficient	0.416	0.416	0.409	0.396	0.396	0.395
Crime questions						
How safe do you feel walking alone in this area after dark? (1–5)	2.41	2.41	2.40	2.28	2.30	2.19
How common: Teenagers hanging around in streets (1–4)	1.69	1.69	1.72	1.52	1.51	1.56
Do you ever worry about the possibility that you, or anyone else who lives with you, might be the victim of crime? (1–2)	1.63	1.63	1.58	1.48	1.48	1.46
Trust/social network questions						
Is there anyone who you can really count on to help you out in a crisis? (0–2)	0.42	0.43	0.41	0.34	0.35	0.31
Physical health questions						
Over the last 12 months, how has your health been relative to people of your own age? (1–5)	2.20	2.20	2.19	2.17	2.18	2.16
Does your health limit the type of work or the amount of work you can do? (0–1)	0.20	0.20	0.23	0.20	0.20	0.19
Mental health questions						
Have you recently been feeling unhappy or depressed? (1–4)	1.93	1.93	1.92	1.89	1.90	1.87

indicated, income inequality is pervasive throughout Scotland's local authorities. Whether we are looking at the poorest areas (Dundee City, £21,300 per annum) or the richest areas (Shetland Islands, £33,500 per annum), Scotland is beset by income inequality and the social problems that it ushered in.

While it is necessary to develop policy proposals that address the impact of these inequalities on specific groups in society (the subject of Chapter Five on poverty, Chapter Six on 'race' and racism, Chapter Seven on health and Chapters Eight and Nine on social work and education), the above evidence leads us to suggest that a more far-reaching approach to redistribution is required. Poverty, racism and health inequalities are the social injustices of the underlying association between income inequality and social deprivation and it is these associations that must also be addressed.

At a time of austerity and welfare cuts brought on by the banking crisis of 2008 it would be helpful to consider not simply the threats but the opportunities that such a crisis creates. The Scottish government has a choice between permitting increases in income inequality to develop as welfare spending, public sector employment and economic policy are framed by limits on government expenditure, or to promote social justice through the protection of welfare and employment framed by an economic policy which promotes income equality, or seeks to limit the rise in income inequality. The current economic circumstances call for a reconfiguration of welfare that may provide an opportunity to move in a decisive manner towards the more egalitarian societies that Wilkinson and Pickett's evidence suggests provide better outcomes. These approaches are commonly identified with Scandinavian models of state provision of welfare rather than the Anglo-American model of increasingly market-driven welfare provision (Henrekson et al, 1995). Whichever choice is made will have a lasting impact on Scottish society.

Conclusion: policy proposals for a more egalitarian Scotland

This book seeks to develop an understanding of the importance of the relationship between social policy making and issues of social justice within Scotland. Any conceptualisation of social justice requires recognition of the importance played by income and wealth equality. In order to move to a more egalitarian society what measures might be available to the Scottish government?

Universality as a principle for the delivery of welfare has had an uneasy balance alongside means testing in the welfare state in Britain since its inception. Whether in health, education or pension provision, universality has been central to the conception of provision, yet means testing has increasingly encroached on areas of universal provision. The most recent example is the move to abolish the current system of universal Child Benefit for higher rate tax payers. As a result, in debates on the reconfiguration of welfare the extent to which universality of provision is provided has always been a key area of debate. Arguments against universality revolve around cost and equity. Cost is suggested to be prohibitive and equity is suggested to be undermined by the better-off receiving welfare. The arguments in favour of universality have always centred on three points: first, the extent to which means testing incurs additional costs for administration and generates high marginal taxation rates at the boundary where means testing has an impact. Second, the advantages of generating social solidarity and support for the provision of welfare; and, third, the importance of progressive taxation as a redistribution policy. The evidence provided earlier implies that there are real gains to generating equality and these gains spread beyond simply benefits of equalising income. Thus, the first step towards committing to equality could be made through moving decisively towards universality in the provision of welfare where the Scottish government maintains control. In certain policy areas, such as health and education, universality is already existing practice. However, even here there are threats to its protection and limits to its coverage. The provision of free personal care within social services is one area under threat and the limitation of free school meals to primary schools are both indications that the principle of universality is not yet embedded into Scottish welfare thinking.

Addressing income inequality requires action at both ends of the income distribution. We have already suggested that public sector employment has been an important feature of the reduction of inequality in Scotland since devolution. The London Living Wage campaign, a minimum wage that would cover the essential costs of living without having to receive in-work benefits, has been an increasing demand of trades unions and campaign groups. Trades unions such as the public sector UNISON have argued for the acceptance of the Living Wage in wage bargaining since the 1990s (London Living Wage, 2009a). A Living Wage has a progressive impact on those sections of the labour force trapped into low-waged, low-skilled work, in particular those facing discrimination in terms of age, gender or 'race' (Wills, 2001, p 3). The success of the Living Wage campaign in London is suggested to have won pay increases for some 6,000 workers in London across the private and public sectors, ensuring increased income to poor households totalling over £30 million by 2009 (London Living Wage, 2009b). In 2010, the STUC (Scottish Trades Union Congress) called for a living wage. The success of these demands is highlighted by the fact that in 2009 Glasgow City Council was the largest of 130 employers across the city to support the introduction of a £7 per hour Living Wage (Glasgow Living Wage, 2010) and both the SNP and the Labour Party committed to its introduction after the 2011 election (*The Scotsman*, 2010a, 2010b). Thus, here again, is a small step where equality can become further embedded into Scotland's economic and political system.

A third area for action lies with addressing the concentration of wealth at the top of society. One proposal that has already been subject to debate within Scotland is the replacement of the Council Tax with a local income tax, referred to as a Scottish Service Tax. The regressive nature of the Council Tax compared to the earlier Rates form of taxation is widely understood. The old Rates system, still based on household valuations, retained a ratio of 14:1 between the highest and lowest payments, whereas with the Council Tax the ratio is only 3:1 (Cooper et al, 2007, p 107). A local income tax has demonstrably been shown to generate sufficient tax revenue, despite being set at levels which are historically low, to cover expenditure and to generate increases in equality (Whittam and Danson, 2007).

Finally, we might turn ourselves to the question of the devolved Parliament. The three policy examples above are chosen not because they are the only ones available, nor necessarily the most far reaching in their impact on income inequality. Instead they are chosen because they are all available for action under the current devolution settlement. That none are enacted to date suggests that the problem of inequality within Scotland does not lie primarily with the devolution settlement, but rather the political will of those in power throughout the whole of the period of devolution since 1997. Indeed some of the tax-varying powers available to the Scottish Parliament since 1997 have remained unused throughout the period, that is, the income tax-varying powers. We could easily have suggested more far-reaching changes, including progressive income tax, a more enlightened public accounting system that takes equality into consideration not to mention addressing the extent to which corporate taxation lies far below that of personal taxation. Similarly, we have restricted ourselves to consideration of earned income and not given consideration to accumulated wealth. Accumulated wealth and unearned income is even less evenly distributed than earned income in the UK and even more so in Scotland (Morelli and Seaman, 2009).

Of course the 2011 election victory for the SNP raises the possibility of making good earlier promises, and voters' expectations, on equality. The SNP government will now be tested more severely than ever before by all those campaigning for greater equality. With a clear majority in Parliament there are no longer obstacles or excuses for inaction on inequality. Perhaps most worryingly in this respect was the absence of comment from the SNP administration in the six months following the May 2011 election. This is in stark contrast to the first SNP administration where announcements on free school meals among other initiatives flowed almost immediately. If the SNP government now places the independence referendum above all other policy agendas then action on inequality will be dropped until after an independence referendum is secured. To do so would not only amount to a missed opportunity, but also a political betrayal of all those who face inequality and poverty in Scotland.

Notes

[1] The BHPS has used a boosted sample for Scotland and Wales since 1999, and introduced a Northern Ireland sample in 2001.

[2] Even in the BHPS dataset income is limited for high earners with the maximum earnings identified as those earning over £100,000 per annum.

[3] A Gini coefficient is a score running from 0 (perfect equality) to 1 (perfect inequality). Therefore, the general downward trend in the three series in Figure 3.2 suggests a move towards less inequality over the time period considered.

[4] Raw household income data is adjusted such that households with more members, or more expensive types of member, have their income data adjusted downwards to reflect their higher costs of living, so that the new adjusted (or equivalised) income constitutes a better measure of standard of living.

[5] A correlation coefficient measures the extent to which a linear relationship exists between the two variables of interest – in this case we are examining mean income and income inequality. For income net of housing costs the correlation with income inequality has a coefficient of 0.347, while for the equivalised version of that income it is 0.314. We have excluded one outlier in the data – the Shetland Islands. Including this data point does not alter the positive relationship but does reduce the extent of correlation somewhat.

[6] Whatever the original coding of variables in the BHPS dataset, subsequent recoding of the data used in the analysis presented in Table 3.2 has ensured that a 'high' number corresponds to a 'bad' outcome.

Further resources
Morelli, C.J. and Seaman P.T. (2007) 'Devolution and inequality: a failure to create a community of equals?', *Transactions of the Institute of British Geographers*, vol 32, issue 4, pp 523–38.

Scottish Government, The (2008) *Taking forward the Government economic strategy: A discussion paper on tackling poverty, inequality and deprivation in Scotland*, Edinburgh: The Scottish Government.

Williamson, R. and Pickett, K. (2009) *The spirit level: Why more equal societies almost always do better*, London: Allen Lane.

Social and Spatial Inequalities Group: www.sasi.group.shef.ac.uk/

The Equality Trust: www.equalitytrust.org.uk/

References
Bell, D.N.F., Elliott, R., Ma, A. and Scott, A, (2007) 'The pattern of geographical wage differences in the public and private sector in Great Britain', *Manchester School* (July), pp 386-421.
Cooper, C., Danson, M. and Whittam, G. (2007) 'Tackling poverty through local taxation', in J.H. McKendrick, G. Mooney, J. Dickie and P. Kelly (eds) *Poverty in Scotland in 2007*, London: Child Poverty Action Group, pp 106-10.

Devine, T.M. and Finlay, R.J. (eds) (1996) *Scotland in the 20th century*, Edinburgh: Edinburgh University Press.

Dorling, D. (2010) *Injustice: Why social inequality persists*, Bristol: The Policy Press.

Dorling, D., Rigby, J., Wheeler, B., Ballas, D., Thomas, B., Fahmy, E., Gordon, D. and Lupton, R. (2007) *Poverty, wealth and place in Britain, 1968 to 2005*, York: Joseph Rowntree Foundation.

Glasgow Living Wage Campaign (2010) (www.glasgowlivingwage.co.uk/Glasgow_living_wage_employers/).

Gow, D. (1975) 'Devolution and democracy', in G. Brown (ed) *The Red Paper on Scotland*, Edinburgh: EUSPB, pp 58-68.

Henrekson, M., Jonung, L. and Stymme, J. (1995) 'Economic growth and the Swedish model', in N.F.R. Crafts and G. Toniolo (eds) *Economic growth in Europe since 1945*, Cambridge: Cambridge University Press, pp 240-79.

Killingsworth, M.R. and Heckman, J.J. (1986) 'Female labor supply: a survey', in O.C. Ashenfelter and R. Layard (eds) *Handbook of labour economics*, vol 1, London: Elsevier.

London Living Wage Campaign (2009a) *A chronology of the London Living Wage campaign*, London: Queen Mary, University of London (www.geog.qmul.ac.uk/livingwage/chronology.html).

London Living Wage Campaign (2009b) 'Clean living: new report shows economic and ethical benefits to paying cleaning staff "living wage" at Queen Mary', Friday, 18 December.

Morelli, C.J. and Seaman, P.T. (2007) 'Devolution and inequality: a failure to create a community of equals?', *Transactions of the Institute of British Geographers*, vol 32, issue 4, pp 523-38.

Morelli, C.J. and Seaman, P.T. (2009) 'Devolution and entrenched household poverty: is Scotland less mobile?', *Social Policy and Society*, vol 8, no 3, pp 367-77.

Poole, L. and Mooney, G. (2005) 'Governance and social policy in the devolved Scotland', in G. Mooney and G. Scott (eds) *Exploring social policy in the 'new' Scotland*, Bristol: The Policy Press, pp 21-52.

PwC (PricewaterhouseCoopers) (2010) *Spending cuts: The impact on regions and industries*, London, PwC (http://psrc.pwc.com/pdf/impact_of_fiscal_squeeze.pdf).

Scotsman, The (2010a) 'Tackling policing: a fine first step to public sector reform', 18 October.

Scotsman, The (2010b) 'Iain Gray to pledge living wage', 27 September.

Scottish Government, The (2008) *Taking forward the Government economic strategy: A discussion paper on tackling poverty, inequality and deprivation in Scotland*, Edinburgh: The Scottish Government.

Scottish Government, The (2010a) *Public sector employment in Scotland: Statistics for 2nd Quarter 2010* (www.scotland.gov.uk/Topics/Statistics/Browse/Labour-market/PublicSectorEmployment/OverallPSE).

Scottish Government, The (2010b) *Relative poverty across Scottish local authorities*, Edinburgh: The Scottish Government, table 2.

Walker, G. (1996) 'Varieties of Scottish Protestant identity', in T.M. Devine and R.J. Finlay (eds) *Scotland in the twentieth century*, Edinburgh: Edinburgh University Press, pp 250–68.

Whittam, G. and Danson, M. (2007) 'Using the tax system under devolution to address the effects of poverty in Scotland', in A. Cumbers and G. Whittam (eds) *Reclaiming the economy: Alternatives to market fundamentalism in Scotland and beyond*, Biggar: Scottish Left Review Press, pp 187–94.

Wilkinson, R. and Pickett, K. (2009) *The spirit level: Why more equal societies almost always do better*, London: Allen Lane.

Wills, J. (2001) *Mapping low pay in East London*, London: UNISON.

FOUR

From social inclusion to solidarity: anti-poverty strategies under devolution

Stephen Sinclair and John H. McKendrick

Introduction

> We have a proud tradition in Scotland of working to tackle social division....We have a body of people ... who are committed to creating a fairer society in Scotland. And in the not too distant future we will have a Scottish Parliament, which will give us the opportunity to develop Scottish solutions to Scottish needs, and to bring the arm of government closer to the needs of the people. Devolution matters. It will let us take the decisions that matter here in Scotland. It is an end in itself: but it is a means to other ends, and none more important than the creation of a socially cohesive Scotland. (Donald Dewar, Secretary of State for Scotland, 17 October 1997)

Reducing poverty and enhancing social inclusion were regarded as priorities for the devolved Scottish administrations even before the Scottish Parliament was reconstituted in 1999 (Parry, 1997). It was also anticipated that devolution throughout the UK would create 'policy laboratories' and enable the different UK nations to develop strategies that addressed their particular circumstances or expressed their distinctive political cultures (Jeffrey, 2004). The devolution settlement granted Scotland 'one of the widest ranges of competences of any devolved or federated government in Europe' (Keating, 2005). It conferred control over health, social services, education and training, local government, housing, environmental quality and regeneration to the Scottish Parliament. Significantly, these devolved powers did not include control over the key policy levers in relation to poverty and social exclusion. The most important policy areas for tackling poverty were reserved to the UK government: the Treasury retained control over tax credits and most areas of taxation, while the Department for Work and Pensions remained responsible for social security benefits. Even the bulk of employability or welfare-to-work programmes have been outside the direct control of the Scottish Executive or government.

It is therefore important to remember when considering Scotland's track record in tackling poverty since 1999 that devolution has provided only a limited opportunity for 'path departure' from the approach taken by UK governments. This chapter discusses measures introduced by the devolved authorities in Scotland since 1999 to reduce poverty and income deprivation directly, rather than actions to address social exclusion more generally. It focuses on policies to increase household incomes or reduce expenditures through enhancing access to services, and does not discuss such wider poverty-related issues as healthcare, social services or education.

Scotland's track record on poverty

One of the national performance indicators of the current Scottish government is to 'decrease the proportion of individuals living in poverty' (The Scottish Government, no date, a). This objective uses a relative definition of poverty – 60 per cent of UK equivalised net disposable median household income before housing costs (The Scottish Government, no date, b). Data drawn from the Department for Work and Pensions' Households Below Average Income analyses of the Family Resources Survey are used to assess progress towards this objective. There are three issues to consider about this definition and source. First, an obvious feature of a relative poverty target is that the incomes of the poorest households must increase more than median income for the level of recorded poverty to fall. Second, defining poverty before housing costs counts Housing Benefit as income, which substantially reduces the numbers of certain low-income groups estimated to be in poverty, notably lone parents (Palmer, 2010). The poverty figures referred to throughout this chapter are measured after housing costs, unless otherwise stated. Finally, these data sources provide insufficient evidence about wider social justice and equality issues, such as the scale and nature of poverty among religious groups, sexual orientation and gender reassignment groups, and those living in rural areas (The Scottish Government, 2009).

Overall, poverty in Scotland fell in the first decade of devolution. This fact holds true whether using official relative or absolute definitions, or measured before or after housing costs. In 2009/10 there were 870,000 people in relative poverty in Scotland (after housing costs), amounting to 17 per cent of the population (The Scottish Government, 2011a). This compares with 1,200,000 individuals in 1999/2000 (24 per cent of the population) (see Figure 4.1).

The fall in poverty in Scotland varies between different types of household (see Figure 4.2).

Figure 4.2 illustrates the significant reduction achieved in poverty among retired people in Scotland throughout the period since devolution. This matches a UK-wide trend, and poverty among pensioners is at its lowest level in 50 years (Jin et al, 2011, p 69). The number of pensioners in relative poverty in Scotland fell from 230,000 (27 per cent of all pensioners) in 1998/99 to 110,000 (11 per cent) in 2008/09, before increasing again to 13 per cent in 2009/10.

Figure 4.1: Relative poverty in Scotland, 1998/99–2009/10

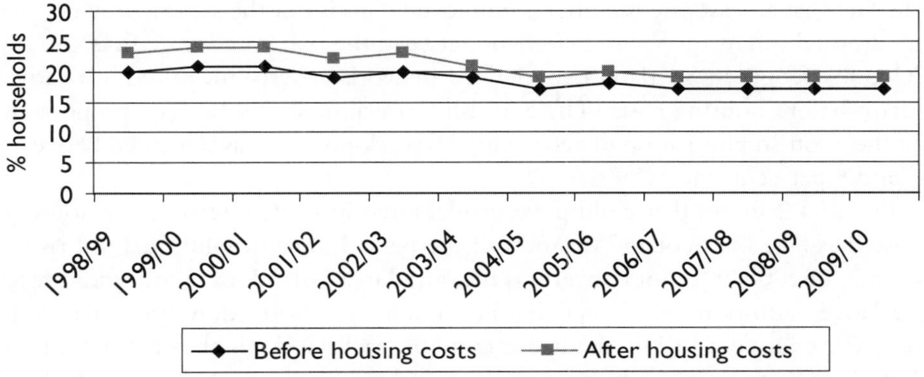

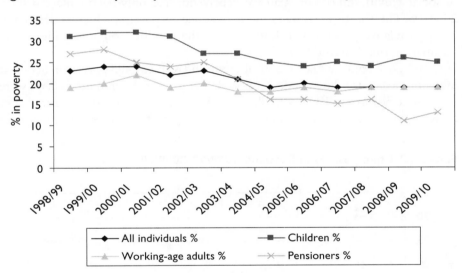

Source: The Scottish Government (2011a)

Figure 4.2: Relative poverty in Scotland, 1998/99–2009/10, by household type

Source: The Scottish Government (2011a)

Partly reflecting the decline in poverty among pensioners, more than half of those in poverty in Scotland are of working age, and the risk of poverty among working-age adults is now higher than that among those who are retired. Within working-age households in poverty in Scotland, the proportion of those without children has risen. This reflects the fact that the value of social security benefits for claimants without dependent children has not increased relative to inflation for at least two decades, so that this group has fallen further behind the general increase in living standards (Kenway et al, 2008). Another relevant factor in this case is the increase in 'in-work' poverty, that is, households in relative poverty despite the fact that at least one member is employed. This is not the same as low pay *per se*, although there are obvious overlaps between the two conditions. In 2009/10, 330,000 people in Scotland experienced in-work poverty, measured in relative terms before housing costs (The Scottish Government, 2011a). The proportion of the Scottish population experiencing in-work poverty has remained between 6 and 8 per cent since 1999.

Figure 4.2 shows that child poverty, measured in relative terms after housing costs, has fallen in Scotland for most of the period since devolution, until rising slightly in 2008/09. Child poverty is measured in Scotland using four indicators: a relative definition (numbers living in households whose equivalised income is below 60 per cent of UK median income in each year), an absolute definition (numbers living in households whose equivalised income is below 60 per cent of the inflation-adjusted British median income in 1998/99), and in terms of combined low income and material deprivation (using questions selected from the Family Resources Survey about whether households with children and living below 70 per cent of median income can afford to participate in certain leisure or social activities). Data on material deprivation has only been collected since 2004/05. The fourth measure is the persistence of poverty, which is defined as living in relative poverty in at least three of the previous four years. Figure 4.3 summarises trends in the first three measures.

There was a significant fall in both absolute and relative child poverty in Scotland in the first 10 years following devolution: 31 per cent of children in Scotland were in absolute poverty in 1998/99, falling to 25 per cent in 2009/10, measured after housing costs (the corresponding before housing cost figures were 28 per cent

Figure 4.3: Child poverty in Scotland, 1998/99–2009/10

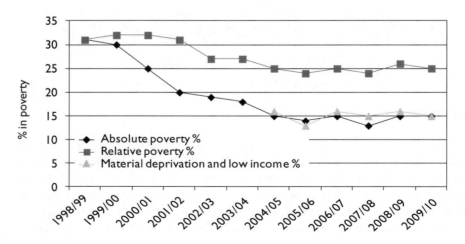

Source: The Scottish Government (2011a)

and 20 per cent respectively). Data on material poverty has only been available from 2004/05, and has remained largely unchanged, at 15-16 per cent since then. There has been slightly more movement in persistent poverty among children in Scotland in the last 10 years: 22 per cent of children in Scotland were estimated to be in persistent poverty (after housing costs) between 1999 and 2002 compared to 18 per cent between 2005 and 2008 (The Scottish Government, 2011a).

Since devolution child poverty has fallen further in Scotland than in most other parts of the UK, so that by 2009/10 the child poverty rate in Scotland was among the lowest in the UK (see Table 4.1).

Table 4.1: Proportion of children on low income, by region, 1996/97–1998/99 to 2007/08–2009/10 (before housing costs)

	Average of 1996/97 to 1998/99 (%)	Average of 2007/08 to 2009/10 (%)
London	34.1	26.7
West Midlands	27.4	28
North East England	30.5	20.4
North West England	30.7	22.9
Wales	25.1	19.7
East Midlands	24.2	21
Yorkshire & Humber	28.5	21.4
Northern Ireland	-	23.3
South West England	24.7	17.9
Scotland	26.4	17.4
East England	20.8	17.2
South East England	19.7	16.9

Note: Regional price indices for 2004/05 are used here to approximate variations in regional living costs. Three-year averages are used to ensure adequate Family Resources Survey sample sizes.

Source: Jin et al (2011, p 68, Table 4.11a), and Family Resources Survey

The relative success in reducing child poverty in Scotland may initially appear impressive, but Scotland's performance is broadly similar to that in the three regions of northern England (Barham, 2011). One reason why child poverty seems to have fallen further in Scotland than the British average is because the relative lack of progress in London and the West Midlands raises the average. In fact, in terms of meeting the UK child poverty target, the real issue to consider is continuing under-performance in parts of England rather than the apparent success of Scotland (Sinclair and McKendrick, 2009).

The current Scottish government's 'solidarity' target commits it to 'increase overall income and the proportion of income earned by the three lowest income deciles as a group by 2017'. This is a demanding target, given the lack of significant change in the income share of the bottom 30 per cent of households in Scotland in recent years (Parekh et al, 2010). Over the last decade, the poorest three deciles in Scotland have shared approximately 13-14 per cent of overall income, while the richest three deciles possessed about 50-54 per cent of total income (see also Chapter Three, this volume). Almost half (46 per cent) of those in the lowest income quintile also possess no assets or savings (The Scottish Government, 2011a).

In summary, there has been progress in reducing poverty in Scotland since 1999, but as with the UK more generally (and with the exception of poverty among pensioners), success has been relatively modest, particularly in comparison to the scale of the problem and in comparison to the picture in some other parts of Europe (McCormick, 2009). The period of greatest impact was in the first five or so years of devolution, but whether devolution itself and the policies introduced by the Scottish Executive were responsible for these results requires further examination.

Social inclusion policy in Scotland, 1999–2007

Despite the expectations of some, the social inclusion policies of the first two Scottish Executives after devolution did not differ significantly from those of the UK government (Scott and Mooney, 2009). In some respects, this is unsurprising, given the structural and political pressures discouraging policy divergence (see also Chapter One, this volume). For one thing, the Labour Party did not relish the potential awkwardness of defending contrasting welfare policies in different parts of the UK, although their Liberal Democratic Coalition partners in Scotland obliged them to do so in the case of student tuition fees and long-term care for older people. What did distinguish these first two Scottish Executives from the UK government were, first, the UK policy developments that were not followed, and related to this, the style of policy making and governing. Some of the most significant divergences in social inclusion policy were due not to Scotland breaking new ground so much as policies introduced by the UK government in England departing from what happened elsewhere in the UK. For example, the devolved governments in both Scotland and Wales were significantly less enthusiastic about New Labour's so-called 'choice agenda' which regarded service users as individual consumers rather than social citizens (Jordan, 2005) and used market mechanisms and quasi-privatisation of public welfare to enact this (Adams and Schmuecker, 2006). Consequently, Scottish social policy in the first few years after devolution has been described as 'UK policy diluted a bit, with the edges taken off' (Gallagher, 2007).

It has been suggested that the suspicion within Scotland towards the more market-oriented welfare experiments undertaken in England reflects a stronger public sector or collectivist ethos in Scotland 'that markedly distinguishes it from New Labour aspirations and policies and, perhaps, from the currently dominant value system in England' (Stewart, 2004, p 143). There is little evidence from public opinion surveys that this is the case (Sinclair et al, 2009), but there are other political and institutional factors that account for this relative aversion to certain aspects of New Labour's welfare reform agenda. The small size of Scotland gives a certain 'village-life' quality to political culture (McConnell, 2004, p 216). Scotland has been described as a 'small associative society' with dense networks between key political figures and policy makers, many of whom have worked together for several years and know one another personally (Fawcett, 2005). These established relationships can shorten and accelerate communications between institutions, and ensure that the Scottish policy and legislative systems are more open to the influence of those outside party politics than Westminster and Whitehall (Keating, 2004). However, this intimacy may also contribute to a tendency to seek consensus and lead to a certain institutional conservatism and policy inertia. The absence of a significant right wing political party and media also reduced demand for some of the public sector and policy reforms introduced in England since 1999, at least until the economic recession of 2007–08 and fiscal austerity which followed.

These tendencies are evident in the successive social inclusion strategies introduced in the first years of the Scottish Executive following devolution. These measures came in three phases: the Scottish Social Inclusion Network (SSIN) in the early years of devolution; the social justice strategy which succeeded it; and the Closing the Opportunity Gap (CtOG) programme which operated until the election of the Scottish National Party (SNP) minority government in May 2007.

The SSIN was 'an institutional response to the aspiration for a new politics associated with the establishment of the Scottish Parliament' (Fawcett, 2005). It was an advisory body that included members from public, voluntary and community sectors. It was a short-lived experiment in drawing on input from outside government to formulate social inclusion policy, and served a number of functions. Among these were signalling a new, inclusive approach to policy making which would distinguish the Scottish Executive from the UK government. A second reason for the Network was recognition of the limited policy making capacity which existed in the new Executive, as the old Scottish Office had little experience or expertise in developing anti-poverty and social inclusion policy. For a short time, the SSIN appeared to represent an innovative approach to policy making; for example, its policy making capacity extended beyond that of the Social Exclusion Unit created in the UK Cabinet Office at a similar time. However, the influence of the Network appeared to wane as the Scottish Executive matured and ministers grew in experience.

The Scottish Executive's first fully developed social inclusion strategy – *Social justice: A Scotland where everyone matters* (1999) – bore a strong resemblance to the UK government's *Opportunity for all* report (DWP, 1999) launched about the same time. Both initiatives highlighted the importance of joined-up policy responses to cross-cutting problems of social exclusion. Each outlined an extensive set of policy targets and indicators, and published annual progress reports to monitor performance. The social justice strategy set out the Scottish Executive's vision for achieving social inclusion by pursuing 29 'milestones' organised into 10 targets across four thematic areas: child poverty, support for young people; enabling employment for those of working age; provision for older people; and a policy for deprived communities (Scottish Executive, 1999). However, over time, the value of this vision and strategy appeared to wane, partly due to a lack of significant progress towards some of the milestones in the short term and partly because several went beyond the capacity of the Scottish Executive to deliver. Following the May 2003 Scottish parliamentary elections, the social justice strategy was replaced by a new social inclusion programme that concentrated more on devolved issues within the control of the Scottish Executive.

The Scottish Executive's main social inclusion strategy from 2004 until the election of the Scottish government in 2007 was known as Closing the Opportunity Gap (CtOG). The Scottish Executive specified three aims for CtOG: to prevent poverty, provide routes out of poverty and to sustain people in poverty-free lives. To accomplish these aims, six broad objectives and ten more specific targets were identified. These included increasing sustained employment (targets A and C); improving the confidence and skills of disadvantaged young people (targets B, E, F and G); reducing financial exclusion and debt (target K); regenerating the most disadvantaged neighbourhoods (target J); improving health in deprived communities (target D); and improving access to services in remote and disadvantaged areas (target H).

An evaluation of the strategy concluded that while progress was evident in some areas (for example, overall poverty rates), these trends pre-dated not only CtOG but in some cases devolution itself (McKendrick et al, 2007). CtOG could claim a degree of success for four targets: A (increasing employment), C (employment in the NHS), D (reducing health inequalities) and K (financial inclusion). However, there was little evidence of success in the six other targets, and it was too early to assess the impact of CtOG on the six broader objectives at such an early stage in its implementation. Shortly after this evaluation reported, the newly elected Scottish government replaced CtOG with its own social inclusion strategy.

One reason why CtOG appeared to have a minimal impact in certain areas was due to how success was defined and measured. As Hills and Stewart point out, 'there is an (often unacknowledged) conflict between raising standards for all and reducing differences between disadvantaged groups and others' (2005, p 24). For example, CtOG target F committed the Scottish Executive to improving by 5 per cent the educational attainment of the worst performing quintile of 16- to 17-year-old school pupils. Even if the qualification results of these pupils improved (which they did not), this could be negated by a greater improvement in the qualifications of higher achieving pupils. The phrase 'Closing the Opportunity Gap' suggests reducing those disadvantages that contribute to differential access to opportunities and subsequent unequal outcomes; that is, reducing unearned advantages and inherited privileges. In reality, the CtOG strategy made no attempt to do this, even to the extent that this was within the capacity of the Scottish Executive to deliver. Like almost all social inclusion policy in the UK, CtOG concentrated on the circumstances of disadvantaged groups and sought to address certain deprivations they experienced rather than address their causes. In this respect CtOG was characteristic of the social inclusion strategy pursued by the New Labour government in London (Driver, 2009).

To summarise, while the Scottish Executive between 1999 and 2007 may have adopted a distinctive terminology of social *inclusion* that contrasted with that of the UK government, the substance of their social inclusion measures did not depart markedly from those developed elsewhere in the UK at that time. There were some successful policy innovations introduced by the first two Scottish Executives, such as the Working for Families employment support programme (McQuaid et al, 2009), and financial inclusion initiatives, but these were not in themselves sufficient to deal with large-scale problems of poverty and social exclusion. During the first two terms of the reconstituted Scottish Parliament, the Labour-Liberal Democratic Coalition chose to follow the same general policies as the UK government and, as a result, reductions in poverty were less marked than some might have anticipated or hoped. However, the election of the SNP, initially as a minority government in May 2007 and subsequently with a majority in 2011, removed several of the political constraints on policy divergence, and raised the possibility of a new direction for social inclusion policy in Scotland.

Scottish government social inclusion policy since 2007: solidarity and cohesion?

Launching a consultation on the Scottish government's strategy to tackle social exclusion, the Deputy First Minister, Nicola Sturgeon, declared that 'making poverty history in Scotland will be central to everything we do' (The Scottish Government, 2008a). The Scottish government moved quickly to rebrand the social inclusion policy to distinguish it from its predecessors: terms such as 'social justice' and 'Closing the Opportunity Gap' were replaced with 'solidarity' and 'cohesion'. However, it is questionable how far differences of substance underlie this image makeover. Part of the reason for this was that in its first term (2007–11) the SNP did not command a majority in the Scottish Parliament. Equally important is that there is no significant ideological divide between the SNP and Labour or Liberal Democratic parties in the area of social inclusion policy in Scotland, aside from freezing Council Tax rates, and an initial SNP proposal to replace Council Tax with a local income tax, which has since been postponed, if not abandoned.

The resemblance appears particularly striking in the priority that the Scottish government attaches to economic growth and employment in its social inclusion programme (see Chapters One, Two and Three, this volume). The Scottish government stated that increasing sustainable economic growth is its over-arching purpose. The centrality of employment in tackling poverty was made clear in the government's *Economic strategy* published in November 2007 (The Scottish Government, 2007) and reiterated one year later in the framework to tackle poverty and income inequality, *Achieving our potential*, which summarised the approach as 'encouraging work by removing barriers to employment; supporting those who cannot work for example through income maximisation; and making work pay' (The Scottish Government, 2008b, p 1). Furthermore, the Scottish government has repeatedly stated that reducing poverty and income inequality would be achieved without reducing the incomes of higher earners, and none of its social inclusion policy statements refer to direct income redistribution. This focus on employment and rejection of overt redistribution are central principles of the Scottish government's social inclusion policy that it shares both with the previous UK Labour government and the UK Conservative-Liberal Democrat Coalition government elected in May 2010.

Another similarity between the current Scottish government's approach to tackling poverty and that of its predecessors is the hierarchy of aims, rules and targets used to coordinate policy. One of the 'golden rules' governing social and economic policy has already been mentioned: the solidarity rule which aims to 'increase overall income and the proportion of income earned by the three lowest income deciles as a group by 2017' (The Scottish Government, no date, c). Accompanying this, the cohesion rule aims to 'narrow the gap in participation between Scotland's best and worst performing regions by 2017'. These are two (of seven) 'purpose targets' in the National Performance Framework, which are supported by 15 national outcomes and 45 national indicators. Among the national outcomes are 'We have tackled the significant inequalities in Scottish society', and Indicator 14 is to 'Decrease the proportion of individuals living in poverty'. None of these ambitions, or the monitoring systems established to track progress towards them, indicate that the Scottish government has embarked on a distinctive approach to tackling poverty.

However, one way in which the Scottish government has gone further than its predecessors has been the degree of consultation in the development of policies and significance it has attached to partnership arrangements to implement these. This was particularly notable in the first SNP administration, and perhaps reflected the government's pragmatic acknowledgement of its relative lack of power and policy capacity. Whatever the motivation, the SNP government has been more active in consulting stakeholders and using cross-sectoral partnerships to develop and deliver social inclusion policy than at any time since the decline of the SSIN. Examples of this approach include the Tackling Poverty Board[1] and broader Tackling Poverty Stakeholder Forum, launched in autumn 2009 to assist in the development and assess the impact of the *Achieving our potential* strategy.

The most important expression of this consultative and partnership approach is the relationship which the Scottish government has forged with local government. This was formalised in a Concordat signed in 2007, which gave local government a shared responsibility for developing and enacting the poverty strategy. Under the terms of the Concordat, the Scottish government pledged to 'stand back from micro-managing service delivery', remove most of the ring-fenced funding allocated to local authorities, and not undertake any major reforms of local government (COSLA, 2007). In return, local authorities agreed to freeze

Council Tax rates at 2007/08 levels and extend provision of free school meals for all school children in primary years 1 to 3. The Convention of Scottish Local Authorities (COSLA) was closely involved in the development of the *Achieving our potential* strategy, and local authorities committed to set out how they would deliver the measures to achieve it in Single Outcome Agreements (SOAs) which they agreed with the Scottish government. In effect, between 2007 and 2011 social inclusion policy was not determined and directed by central government, but a joint responsibility of the Scottish government and local authorities and the Community Planning Partnerships (CPPs) that they lead. It is not clear whether the majority SNP government elected in May 2011 intend to persist with this partnership approach. The SNP's election manifesto made no reference to the Concordat and instead echoed the 'localism' agenda that has become a staple policy of most UK parties.

Unsurprisingly, local authorities initially welcomed their increased involvement to policy making. However, the situation appears less wholesome in terms of delivering effective measures that actually reduce poverty and social exclusion. Despite the role which Scottish local authorities have in addressing poverty, the UK Child Poverty Act places a duty on local authorities in England to tackle child poverty – including undertaking local strategic needs and childcare provision assessments – which is stronger than any obligation involved in the Concordat and SOAs in Scotland (Ben-Galim, 2010). The vagueness of the commitments to tackle poverty and the lack of effective systems to monitor performance in many local authorities' SOAs have also been criticised by anti-poverty organisations; only four out of 32 SOAs included an explicit commitment to tackling child poverty as a priority (End Child Poverty in Scotland, 2009). Furthermore, anti-poverty campaigners have not universally welcomed the removal of some funding constraints. In particular, concerns have been expressed that some of the anti-poverty policies previously supported by the Fairer Scotland Fund (such as the successful Working for Families employment support initiative) would no longer be prioritised once the protection of earmarked funding was removed (Fyfe et al, 2009).

Perhaps the most conspicuous strain in the relationship between central and local government in Scotland in relation to tackling poverty has been over the expansion of free school meals for primary school children, which ran into funding problems even before the introduction of spending cuts by the UK government in 2010. The Scottish government was forced to dilute its previous commitment to introduce free school meals for all primary year 1–3 school children from August 2010. Instead local authorities have 'flexibility' to prioritise free school meals for children in the most deprived areas. Local authorities have claimed that the obligation to freeze Council Tax – initially for three years, and now extended to 2016 – undermined their ability to finance the free school meals policy, although the Scottish government denied this. This disagreement put strain on the Concordat agreed between the Scottish government and local authorities, and highlights how expensive is the commitment to freeze Council Tax – estimated by one opponent at £700 million – and a measure which does not particularly benefit lower-income households (Scottish Parliament, 2010, col 2796).

The anti-poverty measures outlined in the *Achieving our potential* strategy are accompanied by two related policy statements: the *early years and early intervention* policy aimed at preventing deprivation in childhood causing subsequent social exclusion, and the *Equally well* framework to address health inequalities. Among the measures proposed in these documents are intermediate labour market initiatives involving partnerships with third sector organisations to create transitional placement opportunities for those outside the labour market. The Scottish government also committed to encouraging more flexible and accessible working environments to enable caring responsibilities to be combined with employment. Recognising that two fifths of households in poverty have a member in paid employment (Palmer et al, 2005), the Scottish government has expressed 'support [for] the aspirations of the campaign' for a living wage in Scotland (The Scottish Government, 2011b, p 21). However, its analysis of the impact of this reform does not suggest that the living wage rate called for by campaigning groups is likely to be implemented in the near future (The Scottish Government, 2010).

All of the principal political parties in Scotland endorsed the commitment made by the UK government in 1999 to eradicate child poverty by 2010, and the Scottish government is required by the UK Child Poverty Act 2010 to develop a strategy to accomplish this. The first Scottish *child poverty strategy* was launched in March 2011 and espoused three guiding principles: (i) early intervention and action to prevent poverty; (ii) building on individual and community assets; and (iii) putting children's needs at the centre of service design and delivery (The Scottish Government, 2011b). Perhaps unsurprisingly the policies proposed to enact these principles are a consolidation of existing practice rather than any significant departure from what the Scottish government was already doing. The main measures outlined in the strategy include increasing parental employment, reducing household expenditure (for example, the Council Tax freeze, ending prescription charges and assisting with heating costs), and supporting early years development and 'positive parenting'. The Scottish child poverty strategy shares the focus of the UK government's child poverty strategy on increasing employment, improved childcare provision and emphasising the importance of the 'foundation years' for young children (DWP/DfE 2011). The Scottish strategy provides more detail than the UK strategy about proposed action in these areas, but it does not express the same ambition as the Welsh Assembly Government, which committed to reduce child poverty to 5 per cent or less by 2020, half the official UK target. It has been suggested that the Welsh Assembly Government is perhaps being over-ambitious (Parekh and Kenway, 2011) particularly in view of the constraints of devolved powers and the estimated impact of the welfare expenditure cuts announced by the UK government in the 2010 Budget and Spending Review. However, the Scottish Tackling Poverty Board (2011) is right to insist that 'Poverty and current rates of income inequality are not inevitable and we must not be fatalistic about our ability to make transformational change, even in challenging economic times'. Child poverty across the UK was reduced during the initial period of the 2008 recession, demonstrating that effective action can make a difference when there is political will.

Poverty is significantly lower in several countries across Europe than in the UK. This has been achieved by addressing some of its structural causes: low pay and employment which provides little security or progression, low levels of benefits and a lack of support for parents and carers (TÁRKI Social Research Institute, 2010). The powers currently held by the Scottish government do not enable it to take action on all of these, but it has scope to act in three important areas: supporting employment, particularly among parents; tackling low pay and reducing in-work poverty; and recognising that poverty is caused by structural limits to opportunities, not the behaviour of those with low incomes.

Both the UK and Scottish governments recognise the importance of employment in reducing vulnerability to poverty, and have taken action to increase employment. However, neither has introduced the family-friendly employment required to enable parents to increase their earnings, for example, generous maternity benefits and parental leave, affordable and accessible childcare provision and active labour market policies that increase skills and help overcome barriers to employment. The Working for Families initiative already provides the Scottish government with a successful model to follow and extend. This provides integrated active employment support and is likely to be more successful than the narrow 'work-first' approach of the UK government's Work Programme (Wright and Haux, 2011).

The principal causes of low pay and in-work poverty – and the measures required to address these – were outlined some time ago in the Harker Review (2006) but have still to be acted on in full. A national living wage is required to address the continuing problem of low pay, although effective enforcement of existing national minimum wage regulations is also necessary (Croucher and White, 2007). Some parents need further support (including training) to maintain and progress in employment so that they do not become trapped in low-paid entry-level jobs. Similarly, households relying on a single earner or on part-time employment are vulnerable to poverty and need additional help to increase the security of jobs or hours worked, including access to childcare that corresponds to actual working patterns. The recent recession increased the problem of enforced under-employment across the UK, and particularly in Scotland: two thirds of those working part time in Scotland would prefer a full-time job (Parekh et al, 2010). It is important in such conditions to resist neoliberal measures to further deregulate labour markets, which reduce working conditions, employment security and earnings, and exacerbate the low-pay no-pay cycle which is a major cause of recurrent poverty in the UK (Shildrick et al, 2010).

The UK Coalition government has correctly argued that poverty 'goes beyond a narrow focus on income'; however, it does not mean by this multidimensional forms of social exclusion but what it regards as cultural and behavioural deficiencies among some lower-income groups, including 'family breakdown' 'educational under-attainment' and low aspirations, a lack of 'personal responsibility' and a benefits 'hand-out culture' (DWP/DfE, 2011). The UK government has declared that poverty must be tackled by changing the behaviour of those who experience it and that poverty is not reduced 'through simply throwing money at the perceived symptoms' (p 4). This is the language of 'tough love', 'compassionate conservatism' and the shibboleth of blaming the victim; it does not have an impressive record of success in reducing poverty or increasing social inclusion but can be politically attractive (Ryan, 1971). So far this approach has not featured in the Scottish policy discourse, and the main political parties have publicly endorsed a campaign to challenge language that stigmatises those experiencing poverty (The Poverty Alliance, no date). This is an encouraging feature of the debate over poverty in Scotland, but it could be improved on by extending measures to widen and democratise participation in developing responses to poverty, particularly at the community level; as the Poverty Truth Commission noted, 'poverty will never be truly addressed until those who experience it first hand are at the heart of the process' (2011, p 3).

Conclusion: social inclusion policy since devolution

The first 10 years of devolution took place in uniquely benign circumstances of continuous economic growth and relative political harmony (Bell, 2010). Despite these favourable conditions progress in reducing poverty and social exclusion in Scotland was moderate. Conditions undoubtedly improved on several fronts, and more so in Scotland than in most other parts of the UK (McCormick and Harrop, 2010), and it could be argued that some social inclusion policies will take more than a decade to show their full benefit. Nevertheless, despite experiencing similar levels of economic growth over the last 10 years, the child poverty rate in Scotland remains over 20 per cent compared to less than 10 per cent in Denmark (Brewer et al, 2009; McCormick, 2009). In international terms, poverty and social exclusion remain stubbornly persistent in Scotland.

One reason for this is that devolved social inclusion policy was not as bold or innovative as might have been expected, particularly given conventional beliefs about Scottish attachment to the principles of social democratic citizenship (Mooney and Poole, 2004). While a small number of high profile reforms were introduced in the early years of the Scottish Parliament (such as free social care for the over-65s), overall devolution 'has not been seen to bring significant change to the poverty agenda in Scotland' (Jarvis and Gardner, 2009, p 36). Fundamentally, there has been no challenge from any of the main political parties in Scotland to the market-oriented orthodoxy that has recently distinguished UK social policy. Social inclusion policy in Scotland expresses the belief that poverty should be addressed indirectly through encouraging economic growth and strengthening national competitiveness by means of labour activation and training programmes. International experience and evidence suggests that such an approach risks widening rather than narrowing inequalities (Alcock and Craig, 2009), and the lack of progress towards the Scottish government's solidarity target is not encouraging. During their initial period in office, some Scottish government ministers expressed an interest in developing social welfare policies more in line with mainstream European principles or even Scandinavian models: the *Achieving our potential* strategy suggested that the Scottish government was keen on 'Learning from our neighbours' and proposed developing stronger links with such countries as Finland and Norway (The Scottish Government, 2008b, p 18). These aspirations did not survive the recession of 2008 and subsequent period of retrenchment, and poverty policy in Scotland remains firmly within the family of English-speaking welfare regimes (Castles, 2008).

The 2010 UK General Election saw significant political divergence between Scotland and the rest of Britain, with the Labour Party losing votes and constituencies in England but retaining its position in Scotland. The election of a majority SNP government in May 2011 was the clearest evidence yet of diverging political cultures and allegiances between Scotland and England (if not the other UK nations). Devolution in Scotland continues to evolve, with cross-party support for the recommendations of the Calman Commission that extend the range of powers available to the Scottish Parliament, albeit not significantly in those policy areas most closely related to poverty (Commission on Scottish Devolution, 2009).

The first 10 years of Scottish devolution demonstrated that devolved government itself only provides opportunities for policy innovation but that it requires political will or compelling pressures for these opportunities to be taken and lead to significant policy divergence. Until recently neither of these conditions existed; however, the tough economic conditions since 2008 and the divergence between the political landscapes of Westminster and Holyrood have removed some of the constraints on divergence. It is more likely that the next 10 years of devolution will see the emergence of a distinctive Scottish approach to the problem of poverty.

Note
[1] See www.scotland.gov.uk/Resource/Doc/1135/0095401.doc

Further resources
Lodge, G. and Schmuecker, K. (eds) (2010) *Devolution in practice 2010: Public policy differences in the UK*, London: Institute for Public Policy Research.

McKendrick, J.H., Mooney, G., Dickie, J. and Kelly, P. (eds) (2011) *Poverty in Scotland 2011*, London: Child Poverty Action Group.

Parekh, A., Kenway, P. and Machines, T. (2010) *Monitoring poverty and social exclusion in Scotland, 2010,* York: Joseph Rowntree Foundation, New Policy Institute: www.jrf.org.uk/publications/mopse-scotland-2010

Social Policy and Society, vol 8, no 03, July 2009: themed edition.

Scottish Index of Multiple Deprivation: www.scotland.gov.uk/Topics/Statistics/ SIMD/

The Scottish Government income and poverty statistics:/www.scotland.gov.uk/ Topics/Statistics/Browse/Social-Welfare/IncomePoverty

The Poverty Site, Scotland indicators:/www.poverty.org.uk/summary/scotland. htm

References

Adams, J. and Schmuecker, K. (eds) (2006) *Devolution in practice 2006: Public policy differences within the UK*, London: Institute for Public Policy Research.
Alcock, P. and Craig, G. (eds) (2009) *International social policy* (2nd edn), Basingstoke: Palgrave.
Barham, E. (2011) *Differences in decline: Relative child poverty in Scotland and England 1998-99 to 2008-09*, Edinburgh: The Scottish Government.
Bell, D. (2010) 'Devolution in a downturn', in G. Lodge and K. Schmuecker (eds) *Devolution and practice 2010*, London: Institute for Public Policy Research.
Ben-Galim, B. (2010) 'Eradicating child poverty: what next', *Scottish Anti Poverty Review*, Spring /Summer, pp 12-14.
Brewer, M., Browne, J., Robert, J. and Sutherland, H. (2009) *Micro simulating child poverty in 2010 and 2020*, London: Institute for Fiscal Studies.
Castles, F. G. (2008) 'What welfare states do: a disaggregated expenditure approach', *Journal of Social Policy*, vol 38, no 1, pp 45-62.
Commission on Scottish Devolution (2009) *Serving Scotland better: Scotland and the United Kingdom in the 21st century*, Calman Commission, Edinburgh: Commission on Scottish Devolution.
COSLA (Convention of Scottish Local Authorities) (2007) *Concordat with the Scottish Government* (www.cosla.gov.uk/attachments/aboutcosla/concordatnov07.pd0).
Croucher, R. and White, G. (2007) 'Enforcing a national minimum wage: the British case', *Policy Studies*, vol 28, no 2, pp 145-161.
Driver, S. (2009) 'Work to be done? Welfare reform from Blair to Brown', *Policy Studies*, vol 30, no 1, pp 69-84.
DWP (Department for Work and Pensions) (1999) *Opportunity for all: Tackling poverty and social exclusion*, London: DWP.
DWP/DfE (Department for Education) *A new approach to child poverty: Tackling the causes of disadvantage and transforming families' lives*, London: TSO.
End Child Poverty in Scotland (2009) *Single Outcome Agreements 2009: An analysis by members of the campaign to End Child Poverty in Scotland*, (www.cpag.org.uk/ scotland/downloads/ECPSOAreport231109final.pd0).
Fawcett, H. (2005) 'Social exclusion in Scotland and the UK: devolution and the welfare state', ESRC Devolution Briefing No 2. (March).

Fyfe, A., Macmillan, K., McGregor, T. and Reid, S. (2009) *Informing future approaches to tackling multiple deprivation in communities: Beyond the Fairer Scotland Fund*, Edinburgh: The Scottish Government.

Gallagher, J. (2007) 'Public policy in a different Scotland'; Research Unit for Research Utilisation seminar, 'Policy Making and Research', Edinburgh, 16 May (www.ruru.ac.uk/PDFs/Public%20Policy%20in%20a%20Different%20Scotland.pdf).

Harker, L. (2006) *Delivering on child poverty: What would it take?*, London: Department for Work and Pensions.

Hills, J. and Stewart, K. (2005) *Policies towards poverty, inequality and exclusion since 1997*, York: Joseph Rowntree Foundation.

Jarvis, A. and Gardner, P. (2009) *Poverty and inequality in Scotland: Report of expert seminars and stakeholder feedback on the relationship between equality and poverty*, Glasgow: Equalities and Human Rights Commission.

Jeffrey, C. (2004) 'Devolution: what difference has it made?', Interim findings from the ESRC Devolution and Constitutional Change Research Programme (www.devolution.ac.uk/interim_findings.ht0).

Jin, W., Joyce, R., Phillips, D. and Sibieta, L. (2011) *Poverty and inequality in the UK: 2011*, London: Institute for Fiscal Studies.

Jordan, B. (2005) 'New Labour: choice and values', *Critical Social Policy*, vol 85, pp 427-446.

Keating, M. (2004) 'How distinctive is Holyrood? An analysis of legislation in the first Scottish Parliament', ESRC Devolution and Constitutional Change Research Programme (www.devolution.ac.uk/pdfdata/keating_2004_policy_paper.pdf).

Keating, M. (2005) 'Policy making and policy divergence in Scotland after devolution', ESRC Devolution Briefing No 21, March (www.devolution.ac.uk/pdfdata/Briefing%2021%20-%20Keating.pdf).

Kenway, P., Machines, T. and Palmer, G. (2008) *Monitoring poverty and social exclusion in Scotland 2008*, York: Joseph Rowntree Foundation.

McConnell, A. (2004) *Scottish local government*, Edinburgh: Edinburgh University Press.

McCormick, J. (2009) 'Overview of poverty in Scotland – the scale of the challenge', Tackling Poverty Stakeholder Forum, September, Edinburgh.

McCormick, J. and Harrop, A. (2010) Devolution's Impact on Low-Income People and places, York: Joseph Rowntree Foundation.

McKendrick, J.H., Sinclair, S., Mason, D., Smith, N., Gillespie, M., Bivand, P., Moley, S. and Tyler, D. (2007) *Closing the opportunity gap programme: Phase 1 evaluation*, Edinburgh: Scottish Executive (www.scotland.gov.uk/Publications/2007/12/07105255/0).

McQuaid, R., Bond, S. and Fuentes, V. (2009) *Evaluation of the Working for Families Fund*, Edinburgh: The Scottish Government (www.scotland.gov.uk/Publications/2009/04/20092521/0).

Mooney, G. and Poole, L. (2004) 'A land of milk and honey'? Social policy in Scotland after devolution', *Critical Social Policy*, vol 81, pp 458-483.

Palmer, G. (2010) *The impact of devolution: Indicators of poverty and social exclusion*, York: Joseph Rowntree Foundation.

Palmer, G., Carr, J. and Kenway, P. (2005) *Monitoring poverty and social exclusion in Scotland 2005*, York: Joseph Rowntree Foundation.

Parekh, A. and Kenway, P. (2011) Monitoring poverty and social exclusion in Wales, York: Joseph Rowntree Foundation.

Parekh, A., Kenway, P. and Machines, T. (2010) Monitoring poverty and social exclusion in Scotland 2010, York: Joseph Rowntree Foundation.

Parry, R. (1997) 'The Scottish Parliament and social policy', *Scottish Affairs*, vol 20, May, pp 14-21.

Poverty Alliance, The (no date) *Stick your labels! Challenge the stigma of poverty* (www.povertyalliance.org/campaigns_detail.asp?camp_id=11).

Poverty Truth Commission (2011) *Nothing about us without us is for us*(www.povertytruthcommission.org/uploads/doc_16351614042011_30031_Poverty_Truth_Commission_A5_report_-_small.pdf).

Ryan, W. (1971) *Blaming the victim*, Oxford: Blackwell.

Scott, G. and Mooney, G. (2009) 'Poverty and social justice in the devolved Scotland: neoliberalism meets social democracy?', *Social Policy and Society*, vol 3, no 4, pp 379-89.

Scottish Executive (1999) *Social justice: A Scotland where everyone matters*, Edinburgh: Scottish Executive (http://scotland.gov.uk/Publications/1999/11/4174/File-0).

Scottish Government, The (no date, a) *National indicators* (www.scotland.gov.uk/About/scotPerforms/indicators).

Scottish Government, The (no date, b) *Social and welfare – Income and poverty statistics – Methodology* (www.scotland.gov.uk/Topics/Statistics/Browse/Social-Welfare/IncomePoverty/Methodology).

Scottish Government, The (no date, c) *Scotland performs: Performance at a glance* (www.scotland.gov.uk/About/scotPerforms/performance).

Scottish Government, The (2007) *The Government economic strategy*, Edinburgh: The Scottish Government (www.scotland.gov.uk/Resource/Doc/202993/0054092.pdf).

Scottish Government, The (2008a) 'Targets to tackle poverty', News release, 31 January (www.scotland.gov.uk/News/Releases/2008/01/31112502).

Scottish Government, The (2008b) *Achieving our potential: A framework to tackle poverty and income inequality*, Edinburgh: The Scottish Government.

Scottish Government, The (2009) *The experience of poverty in rural Scotland: Qualitative research with organisations working with people experiencing poverty in rural areas*, Edinburgh: The Scottish Government.

Scottish Government, The (2010) *Low pay and income inequality in Scotland – A living wage* (www.scotland.gov.uk/Publications/2010/07/livingwageanalysis).

Scottish Government, The (2011a) *Poverty and income inequality in Scotland, 2009-10* (http://www.scotland.gov.uk/Publications/2011/05/povertystats0910).

Scottish Government, The (2011b) Child poverty strategy for Scotland, Edinburgh: The Scottish Government.

Scottish Parliament (2010) Poverty framework debate, *Official Report*, 17 June, (www.scottish.parliament.uk/business/officialReports/meetingsParliament/or-10/sor0617-02.htm#Col27480).

Shildrick, T., MacDonald, R., Webster, C. and Garthwaite, K. (2010) *The low-pay, no-pay cycle: Understanding recurrent poverty*, York: Joseph Rowntree Foundation.

Sinclair, S. and McKendrick, J.H. (2009) *Child poverty in Scotland: Taking the next steps*, York: Joseph Rowntree Foundation.

Sinclair, S., McKendrick, J. H. and Kelly, P. (2009) 'Taking the high road? Media and public attitudes toward poverty in Scotland', *Scottish Affairs*, vol 68, pp 7-92.

Stewart, J. (2004) *Taking stock: Scottish social welfare after devolution*, Bristol: The Policy Press.

Tackling Poverty Board (2011) Statement, January (www.scotland.gov.uk/Resource/Doc/304557/0112578.do1).

TARKI Social Research Institute (2010) *Child poverty and well being in the European Union*, Brussels: Report for the European Commission DG Employment, Social Affairs and Equal Opportunities Unit.

Wright, S. and Haux, T. (2011) *On the receiving end: Perspectives on being out of work and claiming benefits*, London: Child Poverty Action Group.

FIVE

Regeneration policy and equalities issues

Gill Scott

Introduction

Scotland's capacity to address issues of social exclusion and withstand the chills of economic crises relies on government policy as well as the twists and turns of the global economy and political environment. So, while social exclusion owes much to global economic restructuring, there can be little doubt (as a number of chapters in this volume show) that social exclusion and environmental injustices have a spatial dimension in Scotland and that local policy can play a part in reducing the impact of wider change. It is this that urban and area-based regeneration policy takes as its starting point. It has been an important part of the policy lexicon drawn on to address the challenges of social exclusion that have marred significant parts of Scotland and the UK as a whole, but also represents a strategy for economic growth, innovation and change.

Area regeneration is not solely focused on cities but it does tend to be the main focus. So while pockets of poverty and disadvantage exist in both urban and rural areas (McKendrick, 2011), and a growing acknowledgement of the rural as well as urban poverty of Scotland is evident in government reports such as the 2010 *Speak up for rural Scotland* (Scottish Government, 2010), a regeneration focus on cities rather than rural areas and small towns has been much more evident in Scotland, as in the UK and Europe as a whole. Cities, especially their disadvantaged districts, have borne many of the social costs of past economic and political change, including inadequate housing, poor health, crime, long-term unemployment and social exclusion. Regeneration policy has been seen as a way to address such social and economic inequalities. Central and local government as well as community and voluntary sector organisations in Scotland, England and Wales have been major drivers in the evolution of policy, but a further dynamic derives from an approach encouraged and funded by the European Commission (EC) through its regional and cohesion policies, where the focus is on economic development and reducing economic and social disparities in cities and city regions. Although there is no legal base for urban policy in the treaties establishing the European Union (EU), the EC has a long tradition of being active in the field of urban development and regeneration, especially through its cohesion policy, where strengthening the economic prosperity of towns and cities and promoting social inclusion and equality have been seen as critical to the achievement of the renewed Lisbon Strategy (EC, 2005, 2006). The funds attached to such programmes are not inconsiderable for Scotland. From 2000–06 European Structural Funds were a significant source of funding for economic development and social regeneration in Scotland. They provided over £1.1 billion of support for Scotland and supported the Scottish government's aims of boosting economic growth and improving productivity in Scotland while reducing economic and social disparities. The 2007–13 Structural Fund allocation amounts to over €800 million and the new JESSICA initiative (Joint European Support for Sustainable Investment in City Areas) includes €24 million ERDF (European Regional Development Fund) investment to be spent in 13 ERDF eligible local authority areas. Although funds will be reduced post-2011, it is an important funding stream with considerable power to affect regeneration policy in Scotland.

How to address issues of economic and social disadvantage in a way that reduces inequalities, increases social cohesion and increases opportunities and social justice are key themes in discussions of regeneration, themes that immediate commentators to the August 2011 riots in England reminded us remain vital to social cohesion (Connolly, 2011; Cowley, 2011; Livingstone, 2011). In practice, regeneration is a concept with many meanings. Some see it as a set of development activities that attempt to promote economic growth by supporting business growth in an area or increasing training to improve poor employment opportunities. Others see it as comprising interventions to improve social cohesion and improve the quality of life of neighbourhoods (Roberts and Sykes, 2000). Certainly it has moved beyond the urban renewal policies of the 1970s in the UK where the aims, aspirations and achievements were largely focused on physical improvement. Attachment to the more social and economic understanding of regeneration is a strong one in Scotland. In 2011 the Scottish government, in its review of regeneration policy, *Building a sustainable future*, stated that,

> Regeneration contributes directly to the Government's overall purpose – sustainable economic growth. Investing in Scotland's deprived communities generates growth and employment and can help to tackle the poverty and deprivation that still holds back too many of Scotland's people and stops them fulfilling their potential. It is a shared agenda across central and local government, the wider public, private and third sectors and communities themselves. (The Scottish Government, 2011a, p 3)

It is an important area to examine for any book on social policy in contemporary Scotland. Decisions and resources for many of the areas of urban regeneration policy come under areas of responsibility devolved to the Scottish government, for example, adult skills and training, housing, public health and local economic development. It is also the case that policy divergence exists between the different parts of the UK (Roberts, 2004). We see a range of strategies, varied funding regimes and different models of delivery existing between Scotland, Wales, Northern Ireland and England (Adamson, 2010). The experience of Scotland differs from that of England partly because of different relationships between local authorities and government since devolution. Different goals in the devolved nations of the UK also play a part in allowing divergence in policy direction. The pattern has been different, with, for example, a greater stress on partnership working and earlier integration between economic and social regeneration agencies in Scotland and a greater stress on community development (Fyfe, 2009). Regeneration policy in Scotland has a distinctive identity that students of social policy and social justice can engage with.

Time for change

Despite evidence of regeneration policy having an impact on economic growth and local employment, improving training, physical infrastructure and environment, and empowering underrepresented groups participating in development processes, the evidence is not overwhelmingly positive (Hutchinson, 2000). Much of regeneration policy has received criticism: as too targeted at opportunity rather than need, paying insufficient attention to areas outside large cities, encouraging competition rather than cooperation between areas and regions, too focused on physical restructuring, too short term and experimental and insufficiently integrated (Oatley, 1998; Buck et al, 2005; Cochrane, 2007; Coaffe, 2008; Mooney and Neal, 2009). The criticisms highlight how balancing economic and social justice issues is far from easy. The criticisms also draw attention to a situation where, despite the last two decades of focus on a more 'bottom-up' approach in which community engagement and partnership have been stressed in regeneration rhetoric, significant groups continue to remain excluded in the regeneration process (Brownhill, 2000; Gosling, 2008). Indeed McWilliams and Johnstone (2005) argue that Scottish urban policy has often pursued economic growth at the expense of meaningful sustainable regeneration.

> The result was entrepreneurial economic policies designed to 'glamourise' city centre regeneration and an under funded, fragmented social policy designed for problem areas. (McWilliams and Johnstone, 2005, p 172)

Gray and Mooney's analysis of regeneration in Glasgow's East End (one of the most deprived areas of Scotland) via the Clyde Gateway project and Commonwealth Games in 2014 similarly argues that regeneration strategy is not automatically positive for the poorest. In examining how the project has an impact on regeneration in the area, they argue that opening up investment opportunities for capital in the model adopted by the Gateway project may actually legitimise punitive and market-led policy changes in welfare, environment and housing that can further stigmatise areas and groups who have borne the legacy of past disinvestment (Gray and Mooney, 2011).

The balance of social versus economic and national versus local in regeneration strategy are major issues for debate at any time, but at a time of economic slowdown and political change, these sorts of criticisms are worrisome. The Scottish government's *Building a sustainable future* discussion paper recognises the greatly changed context of regeneration policy when it reports 'the economic crisis has meant that many traditional models of regeneration are fractured' (The Scottish Government, 2011a, p 7). Similarly the Scottish Urban Regeneration Forum (SURF) has argued that it is not only that the UK government's response to the financial crisis is resulting in loss of services to the most vulnerable, it is also that even the previous property-based models of funding regeneration via rising property values are no longer possible (SURF, 2011).

It is a problem throughout Europe. Despite this, however, it is possible to identify a potential for regeneration policy to produce positive change even in the face of economic crisis (Mulgan and Salem, 2009). A research report, *Cities facing the crisis*, produced by the European URBACT Programme (URBACT, 2010), for example, highlights how city authorities have and can develop strategies in complex, locally focused and varied ways to address both economic growth and social inclusion in a post-crisis situation. The report highlights and exhorts greater coherence and long-term planning to ensure cities and communities within them plan and benefit from longer-term integrated planning. The OECD (Organisation for Economic Co-operation and Development) goes further (Froy and Giguere, 2010) when they argue that policies at city and regional level have a strong role to play in developing a more sustainable economic future, but only if attention is paid to local assets and integration between local, regional and national needs. Research with local stakeholders in a number of OECD regions in 2008 led the OECD to develop a set of principles for such a role (the Barcelona Principles). These include providing proactive and collaborative leadership at local level; making the case for continued public investment and public services; building local economic strategies that align with long-term drivers; and taking steps to ensure the sustainability and productivity of public works and infrastructure. Their point is that actions at the local level are key to creating better coordinated responses to the economic crisis and its aftermath: local actions and city administrations are as important as national ones.

Some evidence of a willingness to a recovery strategy is evident among all political parties in Scotland. The government's *Building a sustainable future* represents a welcome step in the development of a national regeneration strategy in Scotland. It has been welcomed as a step in the right direction, but we have to recognise that it can only be a partial solution in the light of wider UK changes in welfare, low pay and employability strategies. The responses from key agencies to the Scottish government's discussion paper (SURF, 2011; SCVO, 2011; Shelter, 2011) stress that community-led regeneration, asset-based programmes, early intervention and prevention in housing decay, employment and employability programmes need to be seen as part of any future strategy. Many of the responses also highlight the point that many of the 'innovative approaches to funding development' outlined in the government paper are only suited to areas with a recognisable potential for market return, and a long period of disinvestment in community development has reduced the capacity of many residents to develop community assets that would merge with larger structural change and the needs of people.

Is Scotland going in the right direction?

The Scottish government's *Building a sustainable future* discussion paper is by no means the first foray into regeneration policy in Scotland and it is only a consultative paper. Drawn up by the SNP government, prior to the Scottish parliamentary elections in May 2011, nevertheless it shows commitment to mainstream regeneration issues. Furthermore, with the SNP newly elected in 2011, it means that the process of developing a national policy can continue. It could build on previous policies developed and funded by the Scottish government to direct resources to areas of greatest need, but there is no guarantee. Regeneration policies that have preceded the current review include the pre-devolution Priority Partnership Areas (1996–99) and earlier New Life for Urban Scotland (1989–99), as well as the post-devolution Social Inclusion Partnerships (1999–2006), Better Neighbourhood Services Fund (2001–05), People and Place: Regeneration Policy Statement (2006) and Community Regeneration Fund and Regeneration Outcome Agreements (ROAs) (2005–08) (Roberts, 2004; Fyfe, 2009). These innovations from government often worked side by side with local authority interventions and innovations, often encouraging new ways of working and adding to local authority work (Roberts, 2004). Gradually they also began to be more focused on the economic and social health of cities and regions as a whole rather than small local area intervention. Following the establishment in 2007 of the Concordat between the Scottish government and the Convention of Scottish Local Authorities (COSLA), there has been an additional change in the relationship between government and local authority that could allow this more strategic approach to develop. Even before *Building a sustainable future* the 2007–11 minority SNP Scottish government stated:

> Regeneration is the lasting transformation of places to benefit those who live and work there. The Scottish Government works to do this sustainably through enabling targeted action in the most disadvantaged areas and by devolving power locally. (The Scottish Government, 2009, p 11)

Fine words, and following the Concordat each local authority and its partners in Community Planning Partnerships (CPPs) were obliged to set out the strategic priorities in their CPP area – the Single Outcome Agreements (SOAs) – and show how these outcomes would contribute to the Scottish government's national outcomes (Scottish Government, 2007a). Summarised, these objectives were to develop a Scotland that was: wealthier and fairer; healthier; safer and stronger; smarter; and greener. This looks like an attempt to match economic growth with social inclusion, but it was started before the economic crisis really started to bite and the assumption that economic growth would, with a little government help, trickle down to all was put to the test. Supporting the work of the CPPs on social regeneration was the Fairer Scotland Fund (a relatively new fund in 2007 that consolidated a range of previous social regeneration funds but which was phased out from 2011). The end result was a double devolution, more localism, where more comprehensive city policies and greater local authority freedom from ring-fenced funding could be expected to produce change. Unfortunately the end of the Fairer Scotland Fund has tended to coincide with local authority funding cuts. In reality the sums involved in supporting regeneration work were always too limited to make a real impact on the capacity of communities to weather wider economic change or to generate the base for community-led change, but the withdrawal of ring-fenced funding for regeneration makes such funding even more vulnerable.

With the danger of local authorities becoming more financially constrained, there is an increased danger of cuts in regeneration activity. There is much to be gained by all in effective regeneration ... and there is also much to lose. Even before the riots of August 2011, opinions had been voiced that the lack of long-term investment in partnership with people and communities meant the potential for violence existed in parts of England:

> Millions spent in the wake of the 1981 riots – largely on physical environment and employment schemes for young people resulted in many areas becoming less impoverished and gross discrimination against ethnic groups diminishing. Regeneration has helped protect communities from further disadvantage and exclusion but high levels of inequality, poverty and disaffection remain and the potential for violence remains. (Goff, 2010, p 20)

Equality, equity and regeneration

It is not just violence or the potential for violence, however, that can shift the focus from place to people. Poor health, poor job prospects, lack of real partnership between people and public authorities occur within areas of deprivation and highlight a real need for a focus on people as well as place. When we look at communities and the capacity of regeneration policies to address the needs of people, and specific groups within them, we enter into a further debate that has engaged regeneration analysts and policy makers for a considerable time. Not all people will benefit from economic growth or regeneration measure. Nor is it the case that all local authorities will maintain or be able to maintain the commitment to the sort of social regeneration measures that the Fairer Scotland

Fund encouraged. New approaches are needed if the impact of regeneration policies on traditionally disadvantaged groups is to be improved. Equalities as well as regeneration strategies are needed.

It is an issue that we see recognised in EC-led and funded regeneration where horizontal themes of equality are included in regeneration and cohesion approaches. There are four political objectives involved in EC initiatives and programmes to support urban regeneration: strengthening economic prosperity in towns and cities; promoting equality in urban areas; protecting the environment; and contributing to good governance. Not least among these, then, is 'Promoting equality, social inclusion and regeneration in urban areas' (EC, 2009). An EC review of urban policy across nation-states in 2009 concluded, *inter alia*, that cities can and do achieve more if they create equal opportunities for all citizens within projects. Furthermore the review concluded that taking action against discrimination, enhancing the integration of people with disabilities and improving opportunities for women and men can help cities to face the challenges linked to globalisation *and* changing social realities. In fact, all activity funded by the 2007–13 Structural Fund programmes in Scotland must address three horizontal themes linked to this political objective: environmental sustainability, equal opportunities and social inclusion (ESEP, 2011). In practice this means any regeneration activity funded by European Social Funds must demonstrate a focus on individuals most at risk of exclusion or under-represented in the workforce, training or business start-up as well as a focus on place. People as well as place are thus identified as key elements of regeneration. For the EC the groups who are key priorities are women, younger people, people with disabilities and older workers.

The picture in Scotland

In Scotland, mainstreaming social inclusion and equalities considerations into regeneration is a stated aim of ESEP Ltd, the organisation responsible for Structural Fund allocation related to regeneration in Scotland, and the Scottish government. It is seen as a key measure for tackling the experience of disadvantage among minority ethnic groups, younger people, people with disabilities and women in cities. Achieving it, however, will be difficult for a number of reasons. First, the way that current poverty indicators are constructed and the way that the impact of regeneration is measured mean information about the experience of distinct social groups is relatively scarce and this makes impact assessments as well as pre-policy assessment more difficult (Scottish Government, 2005; Loots, 2006). Despite this, research does show that the experience of inequality and the impacts of regeneration differ. Single parents, younger people, people of minority ethnic heritage, people with disabilities are, for example, likely to have more community disadvantage, poorer health and fewer overall formal resources to overcome their disadvantage. Chapters on poverty, work, ethnicity and on youth in this volume highlight some of the disadvantages accruing to groups, but a few examples here indicate why people as well as place need to be recognised in the regeneration agenda:

- Between 2002/03 and 2009/10 the proportion of individuals in relative poverty (before housing costs) was higher in disabled than in non-disabled households in Scotland. In 2009/10, 19 per cent of individuals in disabled households were in relative poverty. For non-disabled households the figure was 16 per cent (The Scottish Government, 2011b).
- People from minority ethnic (non-white) groups in Scotland are around twice as likely to be in relative poverty (before housing costs) compared to those from the 'White – British' group (32 per cent and 16 per cent respectively) (McPherson and Bond, 2009; Netto et al, 2011).
- Twenty-seven per cent of female single pensioners in Scotland are in poverty, compared to 19 per cent of males (McPherson and Bond, 2009).
- Women represent two thirds of all low-paid workers in Scotland (paid less than £7 an hour and the recession is now hitting women hard; see New Policy Institute, 2009; Rake and Rotheroe, 2009; The Poverty Alliance, 2010; TUC 2010).
- Lone parents tend to be concentrated in deprived areas: they represent 52 per cent of families in the poorest 10 per cent of areas in Scotland, but only 9 per cent in the least deprived areas .The poverty rate for single women with children is 36 per cent compared with 18 per cent of all households in urban areas (The Scottish Government, 2011b).
- In 2009, 13.8 per cent of 16- to 19-year-olds in Scotland were not in employment, education or training (NEETs). Young people aged 16 to 19 living in the 15 per cent most deprived areas in Scotland are less likely to be in education, employment or training than those in more advantaged areas. One quarter of young people aged between 16 and 19 in poorer areas are NEETs compared to 11 per cent in Scotland as a whole (The Scottish Government, 2011c). The ILO (International Labour Organization) youth unemployment rate (16–19) for January 2010-December 2010 in Scotland was 25.3 per cent (Skills Development Scotland, 2011).
- People aged 16–24 are by far the most likely to experience violent crime: 17.6 per cent of young men and 8.6 per cent of young women report being victims of crime (The Scottish Government, 2007c).

Unfortunately there is evidence of a lack of positive response to this picture of people-based disadvantage from regeneration agencies. For example, the formal investigation in 2007 of regeneration and the Race Equality Duty carried out by the Commission for Racial Equality across England, Wales and Scotland prior to its merger into the Human Rights Commission demonstrated very clearly that such considerations have simply not reached regeneration agencies or policy. The report shows that regeneration bodies at every level were failing to meet their 'race' relations obligations and concluded:

Failure to recognise the relevance of racial equality in physical regeneration may be costly. But we also need to move away from the notion that action to promote racial equality is just another hurdle to jump over before one can get on with the real business of regeneration. It is imperative that those responsible for the projects that are reshaping our landscapes and communities see racial equality and good race relations as central to all regeneration activity. (CRE, 2007, p 125)

In relation to Scotland the report shows, moreover, that the Scottish government's approach to mainstreaming the Race Equality Duty was inconsistent and a source of confusion for those trying to understand the government's priorities.

A review in Scotland in 2005 (Maguire and Riddell, 2005), of the extent to which equalities issues had been embraced by CPPs in their ROAs, is also not encouraging for the issue of equalities as a whole. It highlighted the following:

- In the majority of cases, the ways in which equalities and regeneration policies and strategies interrelate are only partially articulated.
- Most ROAs do not have an explicit policy of mainstreaming equalities, and their ROAs do not exemplify a clear understanding of the concept.
- Young people were by far the most frequently targeted group in relation to the national priorities for community regeneration but gender, disability and ethnicity were seldom mentioned as targets (Maguire and Riddell, 2005).

Similarly in a review (Fyfe, 2009) of the SOAs that replaced the ROAs, this point is reiterated. It was reported that,

Regeneration Outcomes Agreements were generally weak on statutory equalities issues, despite guidance being given on this. With less guidance on this issue since their replacement, equalities issues are understated. There is a need to keep equalities issues at the front of people's minds. (Fyfe, 2009, p 13)

Keeping it at the front of people's minds also means giving greater power to those affected by regeneration policy, but this means a recognition and respect for the most disadvantaged. A Joseph Rowntree report in 2003 (McGregor et al, 2003) pointed to distinct benefits for bringing the parallel worlds of regeneration and social inclusion policies together. Ruth Lister (2004) provides a more theoretical argument when she argues that social justice depends on a culture of equal respect. She argues forcefully for a relational politics of social justice – for a form of respect and caring that sustains and promotes equality in income and wealth and access to services and neighbourhood quality, an approach that recognises how group and individual issues are inextricably related to the organisation and structure of society. With such an argument the specific relationship to city life and urban policy of, for example, women and minority ethnic groups, needs to be recognised. Transferring these ideas to mainstream equalities and social inclusion into urban policy means we need to examine a further issue – whether those who suffer the greatest inequalities are adequately represented in policy making.

Before Communities Scotland was disbanded in 2008 the organisation claimed that:

> Pivotal to the long-term success of community planning and regeneration work is engagement with communities. A key principle of community engagement is ensuring that all groups and communities are equally involved in the community planning process. (Communities Scotland, 2006, p 18)

Such engagement has not always been successful in Scotland. In a review of women and regeneration work in four cities in Scotland, for example (Scott, 2000), it was found that women-specific targets were often seen as unnecessary or counterproductive. Significant resources were directed into activities of value to women, but there was no evidence that their development was based on any systematic gender analysis or strategy. The report also found that a general assumption of regeneration officers was that since most community representatives on partnership boards were women, issues affecting women were thereby addressed; women community representatives on partnership boards, however, reported barriers to their effective participation in partnership governance.

Since 2000 much has happened in this field, particularly in Scotland. Across the UK the Gender Equality Duty was supposed to make it mandatory for public sector organisations to make a more explicit consideration of gender in planning decisions and process and carry out a gender impact assessment of planning and legislation (Greed, 2005). In addition, even though the power to legislate on equal opportunities is reserved to the UK Parliament, the Scottish Parliament can encourage equal opportunities. Equal opportunities requirements and duties can be imposed on Scottish public authorities and cross-border public authorities in relation to their Scottish functions, and the Scottish government was, for a while, active in developing plans for its implementation in the area of regeneration. By 2007, prior to the change in administration, a Gender Equality Duty Action Plan had been developed covering the housing and investment programme, service improvement, regeneration policy and community engagement to which the Scottish government appears to have been committed (The Scottish Government, 2007b, 2007c).

In many ways devolution had the potential to bring the issue of gender into local authority and community planning again. Greater representation of women was, after all, an important issue in the setting up of the Scottish Parliament in 1999 and gender budget analysis into committee work (McKay, 2010). Nevertheless, as we have seen above, at municipal/local authority level there are few examples of strategic planning for equality. It is not impossible to achieve. Elsewhere in Europe, change in the ways that municipalities are approaching equalities issues can be identified. In Berlin, for example, gender considerations have been incorporated into all procurement decisions by the municipality for the last 10 years. In Vienna, gender mainstreaming has been incorporated into all departments since 2007. Other indications of change can be found in the European Charter for Equality of Women and Men in Local Life that was launched by the Council of European Municipalities and Regions (CEMR, 2006) and has over 500 cities, regions and municipalities as signatories. In Glasgow the employability programme Glasgow Works has an equality and diversity coordinator to help develop work on equality with the projects funded by the Local Regeneration Agencies in the city (Glasgow Works, 2011).

It is, however, unwise to expect equalities issues to be prioritised in Scotland or the UK in the near future. According to the Centre for Local Economic Strategies (CLES, 2011), a number of reasons exist for such pessimism. First, the future role of the Equalities and Human Rights Commission is not clear, there appears to be a weakening of regulatory structures and public bodies are already failing to comply with public sector equalities duties that existed even before the Single Equality Duty came into place in April 2011. Second, funding regimes for voluntary and community sector bodies that promote equalities are being constrained; with increasing pressure to do 'more with less', services may focus on those who already successfully access their services and may not have time to engage with the more disadvantaged or in any equalities-based advocacy work. Most importantly the CLES report argues that at UK level leadership from the government in relation to equalities issues has shown a retreat and this is particularly the case when it comes to regeneration and policies related to areas of deprivation.

The lack of leadership on integration between equalities issues and regeneration is not a surprise. According to Cochrane:

> ... a concern with area is often a coded way of referring to a concern about the particular social groups which are believed to be concentrated in it. (Cochrane, 2007, p 3)

When this is the case issues of equality tend to take a back seat. Regeneration policy comes to be targeted on particular populations as 'problem' populations rather than individuals with rights enshrined in equality legislation. Nowhere do we see this more clearly than in the response to the riots of 2011. Riot hot spots were also unemployment hot spots (ONS, 2011; Stewart, 2011), with unemployment being particularly high among minority ethnic youth and women in those areas. However, the response to the riots from the UK government was not one of attempting to understand or address the growing economic and social exclusion of people in those areas but included statements highlighting the 'moral decay' of people in those areas, exhortations to the justice system to be 'rigorous' in the use of deterrent sentences and threats of withdrawal of benefits to those involved. At the same time there were announcements about investment in private sector enterprise zones in areas of cities involved in the riots, but all were outwith the 'riot zones', confirming the view of Hastings et al (2009) that investment tends to go to affluent rather than poorer areas. Combine this with cuts in funding to services for the most disadvantaged (Local Futures, 2010; Yeates et al, 2011) and there is little evidence of understanding how 'race', age, disability as well as place can produce disenchantment. Scotland was not subject to rioting in 2011 but the failure to effectively engage with the equalities issues outlined above carries the potential risk of exacerbating established inequalities, particularly if the SNP emphasis on private sector growth leads to regeneration agencies losing interest in equalities issues.

Conclusion

Reimagining cities as places of both economic growth and social cohesion has been a significant part of urban and regeneration policy in Scotland. Addressing poverty and social exclusion at the same time as restructuring local economies, however, is not without its problems. The spatial focus, process and impact of regeneration are characterised by continual negotiation where power and structural inequalities affect what and who are the focus and beneficiaries of urban policy. Often social regeneration, with its promise of improved services and opportunities for those areas and groups most affected by economic restructuring, competes with grand schemes for economic growth in city regions. Results can be negative even when an economy is growing for those with the least power either because they are stigmatised as part of a 'broken society' that needs to be moulded to neoliberal needs or because the area they live in is seen as unworthy of investment. But at times when the UK and Scottish economies are relatively static and public resources are increasingly restricted, the picture is even more problematic.

What this chapter has also shown is that, even though responses at city level can be more flexible than in the past because of the increasing decentralisation of urban policy in Scotland, there appears to be strong resistance to change and to a recognition of not just class inequalities but also those of disability, age, gender and ethnicity. Localisation has been increasingly evident since the SNP government developed its Concordat with local authorities in 2008, but integrating social regeneration and equalities policy has been far less evident. The potential to address the challenges of mainstreaming equalities issues in Scotland by publicly funded organisations is one that does exist. Pursuing equality has been a feature of the Scottish Parliament since its inception. The existence of both the Race and the Gender Equality Duty appeared to offer a push in this direction but cuts in public funding, increasing reductions in the powers of the Equality and Human Rights Commission, the replacement of the duties with a wider but in some ways less specific Equality Duty and a shift in welfare policy towards a stigmatising of the long-term unemployed who tend to be in areas of deprivation are all combining to increase rather than reduce inequalities.

So despite the high level discussion of a more strategic approach to regeneration in *Building a sustainable future*, those discussions need to be further developed into policy. The issues cannot be shelved. The use of what are increasingly limited resources alongside more nuanced and integrated equalities strategies at local level is needed. Only in this way can local economic strategies that will see the creation of solid, well-paid jobs, maintain decent health services and ensure decent housing and childcare services, at the same time as capturing and developing community assets, be grown and a quality of living for all in a city be assured.

Further resources
Adamson, D. (2010) *The impact of devolution: Area-based regeneration policies in the UK*, York: Joseph Rowntree Foundation.

Glasgow Works (2010) *Working with ethnic minority clients: Toolkit for employability partnerships* (www.glasgoworks.eu/).

Gosling, V. (2008) 'Regenerating communities: women's experiences of urban regeneration', *Urban Studies*, vol 45, no 3, pp 607-26.

Scottish Government, The (2011) *Building a sustainable future: Regeneration discussion paper*, Edinburgh: The Scottish Government.

The Fawcett Society is an independent UK campaign organisation for equality between women and men: www.fawcettsociety.org.uk/

The Community Regeneration and Tackling Poverty Learning Network is a cross-Scottish government initiative that supports CPPs: www.scotland.gov.uk/Topics/Built-Environment/regeneration/pir/learningnetworks/cr

Scottish Urban Regeneration Forum (SURF), Scotland's Independent Regeneration Network: www.scotregen.co.uk/index.asp

References
Adamson, D. (2010) *The impact of devolution: Area-based regeneration policies in the UK*, York: Joseph Rowntree Foundation.
Brownhill, S. (2000) 'Regen(d)eration: women and urban policy in Britain', in J. Darke, S. Ledwith and R. Woods (eds) *Women and the city: Visibility and voice in urban space*, Basingstoke: Palgrave, pp 114-30.
Buck, N., Gordon, I., Harding, A. and Turok, I. (eds) (2005) *Changing cities: Rethinking urban competitiveness, cohesion and governance*, Basingstoke: Palgrave.

CEMR (Council of European Municipalities and Regions) (2006) *European Charter for equality between men and women at local level*, Brussels: CEMR.

CLES (Centre for Local Economic Strategies) (2011) *The implications of government policy for equality issues*, Manchester: CLES.

Coaffe, J. (2008) 'The search for policy innovation in urban governance: lessons from community-led regeneration partnerships', *Public Policy and Administration*, 1 April, vol 23, pp 167-87.

Cochrane, A. (2007) *Understanding urban policy: A critical approach*, Oxford: Blackwell.

Communities Scotland (2006) *National standards for community engagement*, Edinburgh: Communities Scotland (www.communitiesscotland.gov.uk/stellent/groups/public/documents/webpages/lccs_008411.pdf).

Connolly, M. (2011) 'Are the tensions of earlier decades still smouldering?', *The Guardian*, 17 August.

Cowley, J. (ed) (2011) 'Don't mention the family', *New Statesman*, 22 August, pp 23-9.

CRE (Commission for Racial Equality) (2007) *Regeneration and the Race Equality Duty: A formal investigation in England, Wales and Scotland*, London: CRE.

EC (European Commission) (2005) *Communication to the Spring European Council, Working together for growth and jobs – A new start for the Lisbon Strategy*, Brussels: EC.

EC (2006) *Cohesion policy and cities: The urban contribution to growth and jobs*, Directorate-General for Regional Policy, Brussels: EC.

EC (2009) *Promoting sustainable urban development in Europe: Achievements and opportunities*, Directorate-General for Regional Policy, Brussels: EC.

ESEP (2011) *Horizontal themes in the 2007–2013 Structural Fund programmes* (www.esep.co.uk/01-esf-programmes-intro.html).

Froy, F. and Giguere, S. (2010) *Putting in place jobs that last: A guide to rebuilding quality employment at local level*, Paris: Organisation for Economic Co-operation and Development/Local Economic and Employment Development.

Fyfe, A. (2009) *Tackling multiple deprivation in communities: Considering the evidence*, Edinburgh: The Scottish Government (www.scotland.gov.uk/Publications/2009/06/01092951/0).

Glasgow Works (2011) *Working with ethnic minority clients: A toolkit for Employability Partnerships*, Glasgow: Glasgow Works.

Goff, C. (2010) 'Better equipped: why regeneration must change to avoid a return to social unrest', *New Start*, July/August, pp 17-21.

Gosling, V. (2008) 'Regenerating communities: women's experiences of urban regeneration', *Urban Studies*, vol 45, no 3, pp 607-26.

Gray, N. and Mooney, G. (2011) 'Glasgow's new urban frontier: "civilising" the population of "Glasgow East"', *City*, vol 15, no 1, pp 4-24.

Greed, C. (2005) 'An investigation of the effectiveness of gender mainstreaming as a means of integrating the needs of women and men into spatial planning in the United Kingdom', *Progress in Planning*, vol 64, pp 239-321.

Hastings, A., Bailey, N., Bramley, G., Croudace, R. and Watkins, D. (2009) *Street cleanliness between deprived and better off neighbourhoods: A clean sweep*, York: Joseph Rowntree Foundation.

Hutchinson, J. (2000) 'Urban policy and social exclusion', in J. Percy-Smith (ed) *Policy responses to social exclusion*, Buckingham: Open University Press, pp 164-83.

Lister, R. (2004) *Poverty*, Cambridge: Polity Press.

Livingstone, K. (2011) 'Once peace is restored, we have to talk about the causes of violence', *New Statesman*, 14 August, p 15.

Local Futures (2010) *Barometer: The geography of public sector cuts*, London: Local Futures (http://mainsitedemo.localknowledge.co.uk/Assets/3949/public%20sector%20employment%20barometer.pdf).

Loots, F. (2006) *Using evidence to mainstream equalities in regeneration*, Edinburgh: Communities Scotland.

Maguire, R. and Riddell, S. (2005) *The treatment of equalities in draft regeneration outcome agreements: Final report to Communities Scotland*, Edinburgh: University of Edinburgh.

McGregor, A., Glass, A., Higgins, K., Macdougall, L. and Sutherland, V. (2003) *Developing people – Regenerating place: Achieving greater integration for local area regeneration*, York: Joseph Rowntree Foundation.

McKay, A. (2010) *Recession and recovery: Who will pay the price? Women in Scotland's economy*, Glasgow: Glasgow Caledonian University.

McKendrick J. (2011) 'Rural poverty', in J. McKendrick, G. Mooney, J. Dickie and P. Kelly (eds) *Poverty in Scotland 2011*, London: Child Poverty Action Group.

McPherson, S. and Bond, S. (2009) *Equality issues in Scotland: A review of research 2000-08*, Edinburgh: Equality and Human Rights Commission.

McWilliams, C. and Johnstone, C. (2005) 'Urban policy and the city', in G. Mooney and G. Scott (eds) *Exploring social policy in the 'new' Scotland*, Bristol: The Policy Press.

Mooney, G. and Neal, S. (eds) (2009) *Community: Welfare, crime and society*, Maidenhead: Open University Press.

Mulgan, G. and Salem, O. (2009) *Fixing the future: Innovating more effective responses to recession*, London: Young Foundation (www.youngfoundation.org/fixing-future).

Netto, G., Sosenko, F. and Bramley, G. (2011) *A review of poverty and ethnicity in Scotland*, York: Joseph Rowntree Foundation.

New Policy Institute (2009) *Scotland, low pay by gender* (www.poverty.org.uk/s51/index.shtml).

Oatley, N. (ed) (1998) *Cities, economic competition and urban policy*, London: Paul Chapman Publishing.

ONS (2011) *Labour market statistics August 2011*, Newport: ONS.

Poverty Alliance, The (2010) *Briefing on low pay in Scotland*, Glasgow: The Poverty Alliance.

Rake, K. and Rotheroe, A. (2009) *Are women bearing the costs of the recession? A Fawcett Society report*, London: The Fawcett Society.

Roberts, P. (2004) 'Urban regeneration in Scotland: context, contribution and choices for the future', in D. Newlands, M. Danson and J. McCarthy (eds) *Divided Scotland: The nature, causes and consequences of economic disparities within Scotland*, Aldershot: Ashgate, pp 137-55.

Roberts, P. and Sykes, H. (eds) (2000) *Urban renewal: A handbook*, London: Sage Publications.

Scott, G. (2000) *Women's issues in local partnership working*, Edinburgh: Scottish Executive.

Scottish Government, The (2005) *Equality and diversity impact assessment toolkit*, Edinburgh: The Scottish Government.

Scottish Government, The (2007a) *Concordat between the Scottish government and local government*, Edinburgh: The Scottish Government.

Scottish Government, The (2007b) *The National Performance Framework, published as part of The Scottish Budget Spending Review 2007*, Edinburgh: The Scottish Government.

Scottish Government, The (2007c) *Gender equality scheme, Part 13*, Edinburgh: The Scottish Government.

Scottish Government, The (2009) *What we do: Scottish Government Housing and Regeneration Directorate*, Edinburgh: The Scottish Government.

Scottish Government, The (2010) *Speak up for rural Scotland* (www.scotland.gov.uk/publications/2010/07/22091602/2).

Scottish Government, The (2011a) *Building a sustainable future: Regeneration discussion paper*, Edinburgh: The Scottish Government.

Scottish Government, The (2011b) *Income and poverty: Main analysis* (www.scotland.gov.uk/Topics/Statistics/Browse/Social-Welfare/IncomePoverty/CoreAnalysis).

Scottish Government, The (2011c) *More choices, more chances: High level summary of statistics* (www.scotland.gov.uk/Topics/Statistics/Browse/Labour-Market/TrendNEET).

SCVO (Scottish Council for Voluntary Organisation) (2011) *SCVO response to 'Building a sustainable future'*, Edinburgh: SCVO (www.scvo.org.uk/policy/community-news/response-building-a-sustainable-future/).

Shelter (2011) *Consultation response to 'Building a sustainable future'* (http://scotland.shelter.org.uk/professional_resources/policy_library/policy_library_folder/consultation_response_building_a_sustainable_future_discussion_paper).

Skills Development Scotland (2011) *Labour market information: Monthly unemployment update, July 2011*, Edinburgh: Skills Development Scotland.

Stewart, H. (2011) 'Riot hotspots among hardest hit by jobless rise', *The Guardian*, 18 August.

SURF (Scottish Urban Regeneration Forum) (2011) *A SURF response to the Scottish Government's regeneration discussion paper: 'Building a sustainable future'*, Edinburgh: SURF.

TUC (Trades Union Congress) (2010) *The gender impact of the cuts: November 2010*, London: TUC.

URBACT (2010) *Cities facing the crisis: Impact and responses*, Paris: URBACT.

Yeates, N., Haux, T., Jawad, R. and Kilkey, M. (eds) (2011) *In defence of welfare: The impact of the Spending Review*, Lavenham: Social Policy Association (www.social-policy.org.uk).

SIX

Migration, 'race' equality and discrimination: a question of social justice

Philomena de Lima

Introduction

Despite the positive discourses by policy makers on encouraging migration into Scotland, evidence suggests that 'race' and racism continue to be significant factors in shaping the lives of minority ethnic groups. Some minority ethnic groups, for example, continue to be vulnerable to disproportionate levels of poverty, inequalities and racial discrimination (Rolfe and Metcalf, 2009; Netto et al, 2011). Racialised frames of reference, used interchangeably with 'ethnicity' to emphasise cultural differences, continue to exert influence on people's lives and experiences (Omi and Winnant, 2002; Gunaratnam, 2003; Bloch and Solomos, 2010). Hence, an understanding of the impact of discrimination on specific groups, and within specific national contexts and social structures, is an essential element of any discussion about social justice, as well as an important prerequisite for devising appropriate social policy responses. The focus of this chapter is on the Scottish devolutionary context, while also making appropriate links to wider contexts, for example, the UK Parliament, as well as European Union (EU) policies.

While recognising the diversity within and between ethnic groups, the focus here is on long established minority ethnic groups (for instance, Asian, African, etc) and more recent migrant workers from Eastern and Central Europe, with a brief discussion of asylum seekers and refugees. The latter groups and Gypsy/Travellers are highly discriminated and the prevalence of 'anti-English' sentiments and religious sectarianism does complicate the issue of racism in Scotland (Lomax et al, 2000; Bruce et al, 2004). However, lack of space precludes the possibility of giving these issues, as well as the complex interaction of 'race' or ethnicity with other social identities (for instance, class, age, gender, disability, sexual orientation and faith, etc) the due consideration they deserve (Arber, 2000; Anthias, 2001).

This chapter starts by providing a brief overview of concerns about population trends in Scotland and their perceived impact on the Scottish economy, as these concerns have provided the backdrop for discourses on migration in Scotland and have implications for the existing and new minority ethnic groups in Scotland.

This is followed by a discussion of relevant continuities and discontinuities that have emerged since devolution began, including:

- the legislative and policy context in relation to immigration and 'race' equality and discrimination;
- an overview of demographic trends in Scotland, focusing on minority ethnic groups, recent migrant and asylum seekers and refugees in Scotland;
- a discussion of the policy–practice gap in relation to migration, 'race' equality and discrimination.

The chapter concludes by arguing that positive policy discourses on immigration and the role of migrants are not enough. If discrimination of Scotland's minority ethnic groups is to be addressed, migration policies need to foreground social justice considerations as well as economic stability. These are essential prerequisites not only for minority ethnic groups, but also for those members of Scottish society who feel that minority ethnic groups threaten their livelihoods because of their own precarious economic circumstances (Ormston et al, 2011).

Population trends, the Scottish economy and emerging policy

Scotland's population trends – an ageing population and declining fertility rates – are not unique, but a phenomenon affecting most of the Westernised world (UN, 2007). However, in Scotland, these demographic trends have led to immigration receiving significant policy attention as a means of addressing concerns about the consequences of such trends for the sustainability of the economy and society (ESRC, 2007; Wright, 2006; The Scottish Government, 2007). Scottish government policy has been based on the assumption that population growth is 'a key contributor to, and consequence of, a more vibrant society and a more dynamic economy' (The Scottish Government, 2007, p 16), and that immigration can contribute to this process. The fundamental assumption that a successful economy and society is predicated on having a growing population and vice versa is deeply embedded in Scottish policy discourses. This contrasts with the UK government where the policy discourses have focused predominantly on reducing immigration.

Influencing fertility rates and encouraging migration into Scotland have come to occupy a salient place in Scottish policy discussions on population and the economy. However, there is little reference within these discourses on addressing ongoing concerns about the ways in which 'race' and racism continue to be significant in shaping the lives of new and more established minority ethnic groups in Scotland (Netto et al, 2011). Migration, 'race' equality and discrimination provide a useful lens through which to explore both the specificity of social justice issues in Scotland and the potential to effect change in these areas. This is especially relevant in a context where the legislation related to immigration and equality are reserved to Westminster Parliament, as well as being shaped by EU legislation. These issues are discussed next.

Legislative and policy context

Addressing immigration and migration within a devolved context

Matters related to nationality, immigration, asylum seekers as well as equalities and anti-discrimination legislation remain 'reserved powers' to the Westminster Parliament. Following the Labour Party victory in the UK General Election in 1997, Somerville et al (2009) argue that:

> The direction of policy has been one of "selective openness" to immigration, with a commitment to economic migration on one hand and development of a tough security and control framework on the other.

In a context where the focus of immigration is mainly driven by utilitarianism, that is, an emphasis on the economic benefits of immigration which is expected to accrue to the receiving society and security concerns, social justice considerations seem absent. In the context of this chapter social justice is perceived as encompassing multiple dimensions, including, *inter alia*, policies that promote recognition and redistribution, with an emphasis on equality of opportunities and outcomes and treatment and the reduction of disparities between groups (Craig et al, 2008).

Between 1997 and 2009 the New Labour government passed six major pieces of legislation on immigration and asylum (see Somerville et al, 2009). Throughout this period, the emphasis on economic migration has led, on the one hand, to policies encouraging international students, the introduction of a points-based system in relation to recruitment of labour for applicants outside the EU and the decision to allow citizens from the recently enlarged EU to access the UK labour market. A focus on security, on the other hand, following the September 11 2001 attacks in the US, and the 2007 London bombings, has led to a greater emphasis on visa controls, countering 'illegal' immigration and reducing the number of asylum seekers. The Labour government embarked on developing a 'firm-but-fair' approach to managing the migration system using a points-based system (EHRC, undated a, pp 9-11).

Within this evolving legislative and policy context, to what extent has it been possible for Scotland to influence immigration policy and migration to meet its objectives of increasing population and addressing skills shortages? The then Scottish Executive, under the leadership of the First Minister Jack McConnell, launched the Fresh Talent Initiative in 2004 in an attempt to address Scotland's declining population and skill shortages. Fresh Talent included a number of strategies to attract and retain primarily overseas labour migrants to Scotland:

promoting Scotland as a destination for migrants as well as the Scottish diaspora; a one-stop relocation advice service to assist potential migrants and Scottish employers in navigating through the immigration system; and finally, but most importantly, it enabled foreign students at Scottish universities and further education colleges to live and work in Scotland for two years after their study and subsequently move into other legal migration categories (Scottish Executive, 2004a). The latter scheme was subsumed into the UK Border Agency's revised immigration scheme (Tier 1 Post-Study Work), which allowed international students who studied in the UK to remain and look for work. However, at the time of writing, in September 2011, this is under review by the UK Conservative-Liberal Democrat Coalition government (for the latest information, see www.ukvisas.gov.uk/en/doineedvisa/).

A study undertaken by Cavanagh et al (2008, pp 15-16) of the Fresh Talent Initiative estimated that 8,181 individuals had gained Fresh Talent Working in Scotland Status by April 2008. Just over half were male, a third were Indian, a quarter were Chinese and just over one in ten was Nigerian. The success or otherwise of this scheme in addressing labour skills shortages or a declining population is difficult to assess in the light of a lack of clear criteria and evidence (EHRC, undated a). Furthermore, apart from the question of whether immigration is the appropriate strategy to address Scotland's population decline, there are also social justice implications that emerge in this context: the ethics of 'poaching' skilled talent from countries where their labour and skills may be essential; and concerns about the capacity of Scotland's labour market to absorb highly skilled labour at the appropriate rate of pay and conditions (EHRC, undated a, p 15). The latter not only reinforces doubts raised about Scotland's ability to compete with other nations in attracting immigrants (Crawford, 2004), but also raises questions as to whether enough is being done to address the circumstances of existing minority ethnic groups who are qualified but cannot access work commensurate with their qualifications (EOC, 2007; Netto et al, 2011).

While responsibility for asylum seekers and refugees remains with the UK government, Glasgow is one of the primary dispersal areas in the UK for asylum seekers, following the Immigration and Asylum Act 1999. This led to increased numbers of asylum seekers in Scotland. Scottish government policies and activities have evolved in response to their needs and diverged in some respects from the rest of the UK. For example, in Scotland funding of integration programmes is provided for all asylum seekers when they arrive, rather than when they are given leave to remain or granted refugee status. This contrasts with the approach taken by the Home Office which funds integration activities only to those granted refugee status, discretionary leave or humanitarian protection. The Integration Fund in Scotland has provided opportunities for a variety of organisations to work with asylum seekers, refugees and local communities to promote their integration, since 2001 (www.scotland.gov.uk/Topics/People/Equality/Refugees-asylum/support). Furthermore, in contrast to the rest of the UK where those granted refugees status can only apply for social housing within a dispersal area, in Scotland those granted refugee status can apply for social housing outside the dispersal area, which in this case is Glasgow (EHRC, undated a).

The examples cited above suggest that the devolved Scottish government has managed to make small policy changes in relation to immigration and asylum seekers and refugees. However, the dialogue on Scotland's ability to influence immigration continued under the 2007–11 minority Scottish National Party (SNP) government and will surely further continue under the 2011–16 administration. The thrust of the argument has centred round regional/national flexibility in the allocation of extra points to provide an incentive for individuals to migrate to Scotland, following similar policies in countries such as Canada (EHRC, undated a, pp 24-9; Wright, 2006). What is unclear and difficult to assess is how the conflicting discourses of an instrumentalist approach to migration on the one hand – primarily to meet labour skills and market shortages – will work with the Scottish government's wider objective of stemming population decline on the other hand. On the question of whether greater devolved powers on migration would lead to an increase in population growth, the Equality and Human Rights Commission (EHRC) in Scotland (undated a, p 31) concludes:

> ... targeting the right groups and linking them into the labour market is likely to be more important for successful outcomes than the level of government at which this occurs. Variations within the immigration rules could give Scotland a competitive advantage over the rest of the UK in attracting migrants, but, unless Scotland then manages to capitalise on that advantage, by offering migrants the economic opportunities and welcoming environment that will induce them to stay, retention will prove difficult.

In other words, attracting migrants to Scotland is not enough; equally important are retention strategies that address wider quality of life and social justice issues including access to employment commensurate with their qualifications (Danson, 2007; de Lima and Wright, 2009).

Addressing 'race' equality and discrimination in Scotland

Turning to issues related to 'race' equality and anti-discrimination, both the UK and the European Commission (EC) have significant roles to play in determining policy and legislation in these areas (see European Commission Justice, 2010a, 2010b). The present EC measures on equal treatment and discrimination which member states have to adhere to can be traced to the Treaty of Amsterdam in 1999. The latter brought together existing and new provisions, including a ban on discrimination based on nationality (Article 12) and a new Article 13 adopted in 2000 which '... empowers the EU to *combat all discrimination based on sex, racial or ethnic origin, religion, disability, age and sexual orientation*' (European Commission Justice, 2010a, Part 1; original emphasis). In addition to defining direct and indirect discrimination, the Directive prohibits discrimination in a number of areas including employment, social security, education, healthcare, housing and provision of goods and services. Alongside attempts and initiatives by the EC to address discrimination, there has also been an emphasis on member states adopting a European framework on integration, based on some common principles considered essential to integrating migrants:

> ... employment; basic knowledge of the host society's language, history, and institutions; education; and 'access to institutions, as well as to public and private goods and services, on an equal basis to national citizens and in a non-discriminatory way'. (Watt and McGaughey, 2006, p 31)

While UK anti-discrimination and equalities legislation has to take into account changes initiated by the EC, the legislative context and the mechanisms for the delivery of equalities and human rights have been undergoing changes since 2004. The core of these changes have been about extending legislation to cover new areas, such as, for example, age, sexual orientation, transgender, faith or belief – while also rationalising both institutional structures and legislation on different aspects of equalities.

The passing of the Equality Act in 2006 and the establishment of the EHRC in October 2007 led to a new commission incorporating the work of the then existing three commissions: the Equal Opportunities Commission, the Commission for Racial Equality and the Disability Rights Commission. It also took on responsibility for new protected equality areas: sexual orientation, transgender status, religion or belief and age, as well as assuming responsibilities for building good relations and the promotion of human rights. The EHRC, although a UK body, has a Scottish and Welsh EHRC respectively, whose work one commissioner in each country oversees. Working with a committee comprising of seven individuals in Scotland, the commissioner has responsibility across all equalities.

Following extensive consultations, a single Equality Act came into force on 1 October 2010, which subsumes previous 'race' equality (for example, the Race Relations Act 1996 and the Race Relations [Amendment] Act 2000) and other equalities legislation, and according to the EHRC:

> ... brings together over 116 separate pieces of legislation into one single Act. Combined, they make up a new Act that will provide a legal framework to protect the rights of individuals and advance equality of opportunity for all. The Act will simplify, strengthen and harmonise the current legislation to provide Britain with a new discrimination law, which protects individuals from unfair treatment and promotes a fair and more equal society. (EHRC, undated b)

In the devolved context, although matters related to equality and anti-discrimination legislation remain reserved powers, the Scottish Parliament has the authority to encourage and ensure the observance of equal opportunities, and to 'impose duties on Scottish public authorities and cross-border public authorities in relation to their Scottish functions' (Scottish Executive, 2000, p 31). The Scottish Parliament established an Equal Opportunities Committee in 1999 – one of eight mandatory committees – to report and monitor equal opportunities (www.parlamaid-alba.org/s3/committees/equal/index.htm). The Scottish Parliament can, and has on occasion, used its powers to place more specific duties on some bodies with regard to aspects of housing, education, care and social services (Fitzgerald, 2009). There is also a requirement that all proposed legislation is assessed to ensure that equal opportunities considerations are taken into account. However, it would appear that limited progress has been made by the Scottish Parliament and Scottish government in using the equal opportunities powers granted under the Scotland Act 1998. A review undertaken in 2009 suggested that although equality considerations were to be found in public policy discourses, lack of progress was attributed to a number of factors which included a limited understanding of the equality opportunities powers available through the Scotland Act and 'a perceived lack of scrutiny and leadership from the Scottish Government' (Fitzgerald, 2009, pp iv-v).

Given some of the challenges and opportunities presented by the legislative and policy context in relation to Scottish discourses on migration and equalities, who are Scotland's minority ethnic groups and what is their profile?

Migration and demographic trends: minority ethnic groups

Statistics from the Office for National Statistics (ONS) suggest that the population of the UK was 62.3 million and net migration for the year ending December 2010 was 239,000. While emigration is at its lowest since June 2005, at 336,000, immigration remained fairly steady, at 575,000. The most common reason for migration to the UK was study (228,000), and 78 per cent of these were from outside the EU. The number of those migrating to the UK for a definite job was reported to be at its lowest since March 2004, at 110,000, possibly related to the economic downturn (ONS, 2011, p 1).

The estimated population of Scotland on 30 June 2010 was 5,222,100, an increase of 0.5 per cent in the previous 12 months (GROS, 2011, p 15). While predicting future demographic trends and behaviour is difficult, the General Register Office for Scotland (GROS) (2011, p 23) predicts that Scotland's population is likely to rise by 7.3 per cent between 2008 and 2033, thus in part countering some of the pessimistic claims about longer-term population decline. This is higher than the 5.1 per cent projected increase in Europe (EU-27) and lower than that predicted for the rest of the UK, and countries such as Ireland, which 'are projected to have much bigger increases'. Overall the ageing of the population continues, with a decrease in population aged 16 and under and an increase in those aged 45 and over (GROS, 2011, p 17).

While much of the increase in population in Scotland is attributed to net migration, more births than deaths have also been an important factor. Net migration gain was around 25,000, comprising of approximately 3,300 from other parts of the UK to Scotland and around 21,500 from overseas, including asylum seekers (GROS, 2011, p 15). Obtaining accurate data on migration is fraught with difficulties (for further discussion, see GROS, 2011, pp 48-9). However, recent information and media discourse has identified the most significant increases as being among the Polish population as well as increases in the number of Indian and German migrants (Macnab, 2011).

Undoubtedly one of the main contributors to increased migration from overseas in recent years has been the accession of eight Central and Eastern European Countries (Accession 8 [A8] countries) in May 2004, joined by two more (Accession 2 [A2]) in 2007: Romania and Bulgaria. The migration of A8 (since May 2004) and A2 (since January 2008) nationals into the UK is considered to be one of the most significant phenomena in contemporary migration into the UK, both in terms of its scale, characteristics and composition (Pollard et al, 2008). Although there are serious concerns about the accuracy of data on A8 migrants (Rolfe and Metcalf, 2009; GROS, 2011), it is widely acknowledged that migration from the A8 states in particular was both without precedent and unexpected. It is estimated that around 1.5 million Accession 8 nationals have come to the UK since 2004, and approximately 700,000 are resident in the UK (Sumption and Somerville, 2010, p 5). Of the estimated 427,095 successful applicants to the Worker Registration Scheme (WRS) in the UK between 1 May 2004 and 30 June 2006, 32,135 were registered in Scotland (COSLA, 2007; Home Office, 2006, cited in de Lima et al, 2007, p 22). The Convention of Scottish Local Authorities (COSLA) (2007) reports that there were 34,931 National Insurance numbers also allocated to A8 nationals in Scotland over the same period. More recently COSLA (undated a) reported declining numbers of migrants registering for work; for instance, in 2010 the total number of migrants who registered for work was 8,890, which was 1,425 down on the previous year. Data sources for the UK consistently show that applications from Poles formed the majority (58 per cent) of WRS applications, followed by Lithuanians (14 per cent) and Slovaks (11 per cent) (Gilpin et al, 2006, p 14). Similar trends are also evident in Scotland (de Lima et al, 2005, 2007; Macnab, 2011).

Obtaining accurate statistics on asylum seekers and refugees is also bedevilled with problems. The Refugee Council (2003, cited in Charlaff et al, 2004, p 9) estimated that there were 10,000 refugees and asylum seekers living in Scotland, representing at least 50 different nationalities, the majority of whom were concentrated in Glasgow. According to a Home Office report (2009, p 21), the number of UK asylum applications received in 2009 was 24,485, 6 per cent less than in 2008 (25,930). At the end of December 2009, 2,470 asylum seekers were dispersed in Scotland and a further 50 received 'subsistence only' support (Home

Office, 2009, pp 29, 69). More recently COSLA (undated b) reported that there were over 2,450 asylum seekers living in five different Scottish local authorities.

Although, the 2001 Census is increasingly outdated until new statistics become available following the 2011 Census, it continues to be the main source of data available on minority ethnic groups in Scotland and the UK. The minority ethnic population comprised 7.9 per cent of the total UK population, making up 2 per cent (around 100,000) of the Scottish population (of just over 5 million) (Scottish Executive, 2004b). The majority (70 per cent) of the Scottish minority ethnic population were Asian. Pakistanis were the largest minority ethnic group followed by Chinese, Indians and those from 'Mixed Backgrounds' (Scottish Executive, 2004b). However, since 2004, the position may have changed and it is highly possible that the Polish community figure in the top three or four minority ethnic groups.

Despite the variations in size and ethnic composition, the minority ethnic populations across the UK shared some similarities with regard to, for instance, age distribution, patterns of ethnicity, settlement trends, economic activity rates and vulnerability to poverty and inequalities (for example, poor access to services and employment). Overall the age distribution among minority ethnic groups revealed a younger age profile. More than 20 per cent of all minority ethnic groups, except the Caribbean group, were less than 16 years old, with the 'Mixed' group having the youngest age structure (Scottish Executive, 2004b, pp 6-7). The profile of A8 migrants also suggests a predominance of younger age groups, ranging from 18 to 34 years of age (COSLA, 2007).

According to the 2001 Census, all local authority and health board areas in Scotland had recorded a presence of minority ethnic groups. Sixty per cent of minority ethnic people lived in Scotland's four largest cities – Glasgow, Edinburgh, Aberdeen and Dundee – with the rest dispersed across Scotland (Scottish Executive, 2004b, pp 24-7). In contrast to the longer established minority ethnic communities, A8 migrants were more likely to be dispersed across urban and rural areas (EHRC, undated a). The majority of asylum seekers and refugees are based in Glasgow with small numbers dispersed across Scotland (COSLA, 2007).

Overall, immigrants into the UK are mainly from the EU and former Commonwealth countries, with India, Australia and Western European countries continuing to be the main labour source countries. However, allocation of National Insurance numbers (an indication of those taking up employment for the first time) in 2007-08 showed a major shift in favour of Eastern European countries such as Poland, Lithuania, Slovakia and Romania in the top ten, replacing countries such as the Philippines, Ireland and Afghanistan (Sumption and Somerville, 2010, p 10).

Having identified trends in migration and some of the demographic features of minority ethnic groups, the next issue to be addressed is the impact of policies and positive discourses, discussed earlier on in this chapter, on minority ethnic groups living in Scotland.

Policy and practice gaps: 'race' equality and discrimination

Devolution, together with the Race Relations Amendment Act 2000 and the duties it placed on public bodies, undoubtedly led to a greater focus on the need to address 'race' equality and to the involvement of stakeholders from minority ethnic communities which previously was absent with a Westminster-based government (Scottish Executive, 2002; The Scottish Government, 2008). A plethora of activities also emerged following devolution, which included: establishing advisory groups, such as the Race Equality Advisory Forum (REAF) and the Scottish Refugee Integration Forum; commissioning research to address research gaps; the 'One Scotland Many Cultures' campaign launched in 2002; funding of organisations such as the Black Ethnic Minority Infrastructure in Scotland (BEMIS) and the Council for Ethnic Minority Voluntary Organisations (CEMVO); and funding of specific initiatives such as 'Race, Religion and Refugee Integration' and work with Gypsies/Travellers (see Williams and de Lima, 2006; The Scottish Government, 2008).

Nevertheless, despite these activities and the production of numerous policy documents there is as yet no clear 'race' equality strategy for Scotland (see, for example, The Scottish Government, 2008). Despite successive governments in Scotland since 1999 acknowledging the need to challenge racism, much of what exists in policy documents is repetitious. There is little or no evidence of policy that has evolved and developed systematically or monitoring of policies for impact, and messages about which groups are the targets of policy are confusing.

Looking beyond government to the role of local authorities in addressing 'race' equality and discrimination issues, an Audit Scotland report (2010), while acknowledging that a wide range of initiatives had been undertaken by local authorities to address issues of 'race' equality, also argued that:

> ... the duty [the Race Equality] has not yet had a significant impact on the delivery of services on people from minority ethnic communities. We conclude that councils need to build a better understanding of the needs of their minority ethnic communities; mainstream their approach to race equality by ensuring it is integral to their routine management arrangements; and give more priority to race equality in delivering services. (Audit Scotland, 2010, p 3)

On the positive side, there has been an increase in recruitment of minority ethnic individuals in the Scottish Executive/government and to non-governmental departmental bodies (Scottish Executive, 2005). There are reported to be around 14 elected councillors from minority ethnic groups following the 2007 council elections (GARA, 2008, p 94). However, the lack of a significant minority ethnic presence in senior executive positions across the public sector and the lack of Members of Scottish Parliament (MSPs) from minority ethnic groups suggest that Scotland is still a long way off from achieving real social justice, as minority ethnic groups continue to lack an effective voice at the highest levels.

Despite the positive Scottish policy discourses (for example, the idea of Scotland as a 'welcoming nation'), in sharp contrast to the UK government discourse, minority ethnic groups in Scotland, as in the rest of the UK, are more likely to experience poverty, unemployment, racial harassment, poor health and inadequate housing (Rolfe and Metcalf, 2009; Netto et al, 2011). While it is important to recognise the heterogeneous nature of minority ethnic groups and that there are issues related to social justice that apply to both minority and majority ethnic groups, a review of evidence undertaken by Netto et al (2011) identified some persistent trends. For example, low pay is a significant feature among many minority ethnic groups including recent migrant workers, and some minority ethnic groups experience higher unemployment than the majority Scottish population. This was also reflected in the 2001 Census, where minority ethnic groups were twice as likely to be unemployed than 'White' groups, and a much higher proportion of minority ethnic females of working age had never worked. This was especially evident among Asian groups, with Pakistani and Bangladeshi women more likely to be in this situation (Scottish Executive, 2004b, pp 37-8). Lack of understanding and awareness of their employment rights can potentially exacerbate the exploitation of minority ethnic groups and migrant workers in the workplace, and long working hours can have an impact on others aspects of their lives, for example, family, social life and engaging in education/training and civic activities (de Lima et al, 2007; Rolfe and Metcalf, 2009).

While there are suggestions that the gap between minority ethnic groups and the rest of the Scottish population may have been narrowing in the last few years, data suggests that the employment gap widened again during and since the recession of 2008 (Communities Analytical Services et al, 2010). In contrast to the more established minority ethnic communities, Rolfe and Metcalf (2009) suggest that the unemployment rate among the A8 was not significant – whether this continues to reflect the current situation given the economic recession is difficult to say. They also cite evidence of gender-based discrimination in recruitment and allocation of work in relation to migrant workers, which is also confirmed by an Equal Opportunities Commission (EOC) study of 'visible minority ethnic' women in Scotland (EOC, 2007).

Overall, for those minority ethnic individuals and recent migrants who are employed, the evidence suggests that they tend to be employed in a narrow range of occupational sectors with little career progression prospects (Netto et al, 2011). An analysis of 2004–06 WRS data in relation to A8 workers (Home Office, 2006, cited in de Lima et al, 2007, p 21) showed that, for the 32,135 registered workers in Scotland, hospitality, agriculture and food/fish/meat processing accounted for 60 per cent of A8 employment, in contrast to 15 per cent employed in administration, business and management services. While there are differences between long-term established minority ethnic groups in terms of sector of employment, they also tend to be concentrated in a fairly limited range of industries: wholesale and retail trade; manufacturing; health and social work; and real estate, renting and business activities. The groups with the highest rate of self-employment are those from the Pakistani, Chinese and Indian communities; the extent to which this is out of choice or an alternative route to employment is not known (Scottish Executive, 2004b, pp 38, 42–3; Netto et al, 2011).

Although it is important to recognise the heterogeneity of minority ethnic groups, being employed in jobs for which they are overqualified, non-recognition of overseas qualifications and language barriers are consistent themes that emerge not just in Scotland, but also across the UK (de Lima and Wight, 2009; Netto et al, 2011). While there is a recognition by the Scottish government of the need to address the issue of overseas qualifications (SCQF, 2010), in the meantime some minority ethnic groups continue to experience barriers in accessing employment that is commensurate with their qualifications, consequently ending up in semi-skilled and unskilled work (Charlaff et al, 2004; de Lima and Wright, 2009; Rolfe and Metcalf, 2009). In addition, even if overseas qualifications were recognised, the question as to whether Scotland's economy has the capacity to provide skilled jobs at competitive rates of pay and conditions for all (majority and minority ethnic groups) remains doubtful (Danson, 2007; EHRC, undated a).

Conclusion: continuities and changes

Encouraging migration in the context of Scotland's demographic trends provides a useful illustration of how the discourses on 'race' and ethnicity are shaped by the specific needs of the different countries that make up the UK as well as by policies set in the UK, European and global contexts. Each has a part to play in setting the direction and tone of policies and discourses and constrains what can realistically be achieved in a devolved Scotland.

Devolution has, undoubtedly, provided new opportunities in Scotland to address both migration issues suited to its circumstances, and 'race' equality and discrimination in ways that did not occur previously. It has opened up new spaces for debate and discussion on issues of identity and belonging. However, evidence on the extent to which these activities have made a real difference to the lives of minority ethnic groups in Scotland is mixed, both in relation to policy implementation and with regard to the vulnerability of minority ethnic groups and migrants to discrimination (Netto et al, 2011).

In contrast to the rest of the UK, the Scottish government has used its devolved powers to respond to the needs of asylum seekers and refugees more flexibly. However, on migration, the ability of the Scottish government to shape immigration policy has been limited and short-lived; for example, the 2004 Fresh Talent Initiative has now been overtaken by UK-wide changes to immigration rules. Overseas migration is an important contributor to stemming population decline. However, even if there was greater scope for negotiating on immigration matters with the UK government, evidence on whether migration can contribute to stemming Scotland's population decline is ambivalent and complex. Evidence appears to suggest that highly skilled migrants (this also applies to Scots-born people) are unlikely to stay in Scotland because of the limited capacity of the Scottish economy to provide well-paid employment and career progression prospects (EHRC, undated a).

Scottish discourses on migration have privileged instrumentalist considerations, with an emphasis on addressing labour market skill gaps and shortages in order to contribute to Scotland's 'sustainable economic growth' (The Scottish Government, 2007). This is not much different from the way in which UK immigration policies are developing using a points-based system. The ubiquitous presence of 'sustainable economic growth' as an overarching objective has led to it being perceived as the end, rather than as a means for achieving other equally important goals, such as social justice (an issue picked up in several other chapters in this book). The absence of strong social justice considerations – reflected in the continued discrimination of minority ethnic groups and migrants in employment, for example – is reinforced by the evidence that suggests there is a lack of leadership and limited understanding of the equal opportunities powers already available through the Scotland Act (Fitzgerald, 2009). Consequently, much of the debate on migration, racial equality and discrimination has continued to be underpinned by contradictory discourses and policies.

The re-election in May 2011 of the SNP, this time as the majority party in government in Scotland, may provide opportunities for moving from what Williams and de Lima (2006) have called a 'politics of recognition' to a 'politics of redistribution', where people from all ethnic backgrounds (minorities as well as the members of the 'White Scottish' communities) are treated equitably and fairly. What is needed is a strong emphasis on anti-discrimination as well as immigration policies that are clearly thought out and where social justice considerations are foregrounded.

Further resources

de Lima, P. and Wright, S. (2009) 'Welcoming migrants? Migrant labour in rural Scotland', *Social Policy and Society*, issue 8, no 3, pp 391-404.

Netto, G., Sosenko, P. and Bramley, G. (2011) *A review of poverty and ethnicity in Scotland*, York: Joseph Rowntree Foundation (www.jrf.org.uk/publications/review-poverty-and-ethnicity-scotland).

Williams, C. and de Lima, P. (2006) 'Devolution, multicultural citizenship and race equality: from laissez faire to nationally responsible policies', *Critical Social Policy, Special Issue – Devolution and Social Policy*, vol 26, no 3, pp 498-522.

Equalities and Human Rights Commission (EHRC): www.equalityhumanrights.com/

General Register Office for Scotland (GROS): www.gro-scotland.gov.uk/

The Scottish Government: www.scotland.gov.uk/Home

References

Anthias, F. (2001) 'The concept of "social division" and theorising social stratification: looking at ethnicity and class', *Sociology*, vol 35, no 4, pp 835-54.

Arber, R. (2000) 'Defining positioning within politics of difference: negotiating spaces "in-between"', *Race, Ethnicity and Education*, vol 3, no 1, pp 46-62.

Audit Scotland (2010) *The impact of the Race Equality Duty on council services* (www.audit-cotland.gov.uk/docs/local/2008/nr_081113_equalities.pdf).

Bloch, A. and Solomos. J. (eds) (2010) *Race and ethnicity in the 21st century*, Basingstoke: Palgrave Macmillan.

Bruce, S., Paterson, I., Rosie, M. and Glendinning, T. (eds) (2004) *Sectarianism in Scotland*, Edinburgh: Edinburgh University Press.

Cavanagh, L., Eirich, F. and McLaren, J. (2008) *Fresh talent: Working in Scotland scheme: An evidence review*, Scottish Government Social Research, Edinburgh: Scottish Executive (www.scotland.gov.uk/Resource/Doc/235857/0064664.pdf).

Charlaff, L., Ibrani, K., Lowe, M., Marsden, R. and Turney, L. (2004) *Refugees and asylum seekers in Scotland: A skills and aspirations audit*, Edinburgh: Scottish Executive Social Research.

Communities Analytical Services, with contributions from the Scottish Centre for Social Research (ScotCen), Glasgow Council for the Voluntary Sector and Napier University Employment Research Institute (2010) *Coping with change and uncertainty: Scotland's equalities groups and the recession*, Edinburgh: Scottish Government (www.scotland.gov.uk/Publications/2010/11/15095850/10).

COSLA (Convention of Scottish Local Authorities) (2007) *Asylum and migration statistics* (www.asylumscotland.org.uk/asylumstatistics.php).

COSLA (undated a) *A8 migrants in Scotland* (www.migrationscotland.org.uk/migration-info-centre/migration-statistics/asylum-seekers-scotland).

COSLA (undated b) *Asylum seekers in Scotland* (www.migrationscotland.org.uk/migration-info-centre/migration-statistics/asylum-seekers-scotland).

Craig, G., Burchardt, T. and Gordon, D. (eds) (2008) *Social justice and public policy*, Bristol: The Policy Press.

Crawford, A. (2004) '"Fresh Talent" won't come to Scotland: the Executive's hope of attracting skilled workers to boost the economy faces a big hurdle: persuading potential immigrants', *Sunday Herald*, 29 February, p 7.

Danson, M. (2007) 'Fresh or refreshed talent: exploring population change in Europe and some policy initiatives', *IJMS: International Journal on Multicultural Societies*, vol 9, no 1, pp 13-34 (www.unesco.org/shs/ijms/vol9/issue1/art1).

de Lima, P. and Wright, S. (2009) 'Welcoming migrants? Migrant labour in rural Scotland', *Social Policy and Society*, issue 8, no 3, pp 391-404.

de Lima, P., Jentsch, B. and Whelton, R. (2005) *Migrant workers in the Highlands and Islands*, Inverness: Highlands and Islands Enterprise.

de Lima, P., Chaudhry, M.M., Whelton, R. and Arshad, R. (2007) *A study of migrant workers in Grampian*, Edinburgh: Communities Scotland.

EHRC (Equalities and Human Rights Commission) (undated a) *Room for manoeuvre?*, Glasgow: EHRC (www.equalityhumanrights.com/uploaded_files/room_for_manoeuvre.pdf).

EHRC (undated b) *What is the Equality Act?* (www.equalityhumanrights.com/legal-and-policy/equality-act/what-is-the-equality-act/).

EOC (Equal Opportunities Commission) (2007) *Moving on up? The way forward. Final Report on the investigation into visible minority ethnic (VME) women at work in Scotland*, Manchester: EOC (www.vhscotland.org.uk/library/misc/BME_GFI_Scotland_final_report.pdf).

ESRC (Economic and Social Research Council) (2005) *Why is Scotland's population shrinking and ageing?* (www.eurekalert.org/pub_releases/2007-12/esr-sec120407.php).

European Commission Justice (2010a) *Fighting all forms of discrimination in the European Union – Part 1* (http://ec.europa.eu/justice/policies/rights/discrimination/policies_rights_discrim_en.htm#part_1).

European Commission Justice (2010b) *Fighting all forms of discrimination in the European Union – Part 2* (http://ec.europa.eu/justice/policies/rights/discrimination/policies_rights_discrim_en.htm#part_2).

Fitzgerald, R. (2009) *Equal opportunities and the Scottish Parliament: A progress review*, EHRC (www.equalityhumanrights.com/.../equal_opportunities_and_the_scottish_parliament_-_a_progress_review.pdf).

GARA (Glasgow Anti-Racist Alliance) (2008) *State of the Nation report* (www.gara.org.uk/index.php?option=com_content&view=article&id=255&Itemid=108).

Gilpin, N., Henty, M., Lemos, S., Portes, J. and Bullen, C. (2006) *The impact of free movement of workers from Central and Eastern Europe on the UK labour market*, DWP Working Paper No 29, London: Department for Work and Pensions.

GROS (General Register Office for Scotland) (2011) *Scotland's population 2010*, Edinburgh: Scottish Executive (www.gro-scotland.gov.uk/statistics/at-a-glance/annrev/2010/index.html).

Gunaratnam, Y. (2003) *Researching 'race' and ethnicity*, London: Sage Publications.

Home Office (2009) *Control of immigration: Statistics United Kingdom 2009* (www.homeoffice.gov.uk/publications/science-research-statistics/research-statistics/immigration-asylum-research/hosb1510/hosb1510?view=Binary).

Lomax, D., Lancaster, S. and Gray, P. (2000) *Moving on: A survey of travellers' views*, Edinburgh: Scottish Executive Central Research Unit.

Macnab, S. (2011) 'Number of migrants to Scotland doubles', *The Scotsman*, 26 August (http://ukblog.y-axis.com/?p=2137).

Netto, G., Sosenko, P. and Bramley, G. (2011) *A review of poverty and ethnicity in Scotland*, York: Joseph Rowntree Foundation (www.jrf.org.uk/publications/review-poverty-and-ethnicity-scotland).

Omi, M. and Winant, H. (2002) 'Racial formation', in P. Essed and D.T. Goldberg (eds) *Race critical theories*, Oxford: Blackwell Publishers, pp 123-45.

Office for National Statistics (ONS) (2011) *Migration Statistics Quarterly Report August 2011* (www.ons.gov.uk/ons/dcp171778_223724.pdf).

Ormston, R., Curtice, J., McConville, S. and Reid, S. (2011) *Scottish Social Attitudes Survey 2010:Attitudes to discrimination and positive action*, Edinburgh:The Scottish Government Social Research (www.scotland.gov.uk/Resource/Doc/355716/0120166.pdf).

Pollard, N., Latorre, M. and Sriskanarajah, D. (2008) *Floodgates or turnstiles? Post-EU enlargement migration flows to (and from) the UK*, London: Institute for Public Policy Research.

Rolfe, H. and Metcalf, H. (2009) *Recent migration into Scotland: The evidence base*, Edinburgh: The Scottish Government (www.scotland.gov.uk/Publications/2009/02/23154109/0).

Scottish Executive (2000) *Equality strategy*, Edinburgh: Scottish Executive.

Scottish Executive (2002) *Committing to race equality*, Edinburgh: Scottish Executive.

Scottish Executive (2004a) *New Scots: Attracting fresh talent to meet the challenge of growth*, Edinburgh: Scottish Executive (www.scotland.gov.uk/Publications/2004/02/18984/33666).

Scottish Executive (2004b) *Analysis of ethnicity in the 2001 Census – Summary report*, Edinburgh: Office of the Chief Statistician, Scottish Executive.

Scottish Executive (2005) *Review of race equality work in Scotland:A summary of the review and the way forward* (www.scotland.gov.uk/Publications/2005/11/1881943/19435).

Scottish Government,The (2007) *The Government economic strategy* (www.scotland.gov.uk/Publications/2007/11/12115041/0).

Scottish Government,The (2008) S*cottish Government Race Equality statement* (www.scotland.gov.uk/Topics/People/Equality/18934/RaceEqualityStatement).

SCQF (Scottish Credit and Qualification Framework) (2010) *Scoping study on support mechanism for the recognition of the skills, learning and qualifications of migrant workers and refugees – Final report*, Glasgow: SCQF.

Somerville, S., Sriskandarajah, D. and Latorre, M. (2009) *United Kingdom: A reluctant country of immigration*,Washington DC: Migration Policy Institute (www.migrationinformation.org/feature/display.cfm?ID=736).

Sumption, M. and Somerville, S. (2010) *The UK's new Europeans,* Manchester: EHRC (www.equalityhumanrights.com/uploaded_files/new_europeans.pdf).

UN (United Nations) (2007) *World population prospects: The 2006 revision*, Highlights andWorking Paper No ESA/P/WP.202, NewYork: UN Department of Economic and Social Affairs, Population Division.

Watt, P. and McGaughey, F. (2006) *Improving government service delivery to minority ethnic groups* (www.ofmdfmni.gov.uk/nccrireport2.pdf).

Williams, C. and de Lima, P. (2006) 'Devolution, multicultural citizenship and race equality: from laissez faire to nationally responsible policies', *Critical Social Policy, Special Issue: Devolution and Social Policy*, vol 26, no 3, pp 498-522.

Wright, R. (2006) *Devolved immigration policy:Will it work in Scotland?*, Strathclyde: Department of Economics, Strathclyde Business School, November (www.gla.ac.uk/media/media_51213_en.pdf).

SEVEN

Health policy and health inequalities

Lynne Poole

Introduction

This chapter examines the issue of health inequalities in Scotland with reference to the evidence on mortality and morbidity rates, the emerging specificities of the Scottish NHS and policy options relating to the distribution of social determinants of health, including income, wealth and cultural capital, which, it is argued, continue to have a marked impact on health and longevity across the UK. In doing so, this chapter suggests that while health policy and the shape of health services matter, restructuring the NHS in Scotland with a view to improving the access of the most disadvantaged on the one hand, and resetting the priorities of health service intervention to target the principle causes of early death and chronic ill health among that population on the other, are *not* sufficient strategies *on their own* to tackle persistent health inequalities. Indeed, insofar as policy makers have sought to address health inequalities principally through an elevation of health service 'solutions', alongside an increased responsibilisation of individuals with regard to healthy lifestyle choices, they have failed to deliver a more socially just society in health terms. This is because such an approach neglects that significant body of evidence which suggests that tackling poverty and inequalities in income, wealth and opportunity, for example, have a far greater potential to deliver better health for the most disadvantaged; as Macintyre (2007, p 5) notes, 'most of the major drivers of the distribution of health in the population lie outside the NHS'. As a result, the poorest and most deprived in society have seen improvements in their life expectancy over time, but not to the extent of wealthier individuals, leaving them at greater risk of premature death and escapable morbidity even in the early 21st century (Graham, 2007, 2009; Leyland et al, 2007).

This chapter begins by charting the persistence of health inequalities both across the UK and within Scotland. It goes on to discuss the divergence of health policy and service delivery north and south of the border, particularly since the Scotland Act 1998, with a view to highlighting those developments within the Scottish NHS which may work towards the delivery of better health for the poorest sections of society, before going on to consider the limits of the Scottish approach to health inequalities. Here the focus is on the broader social determinants of health, which, while being recognised as crucial by successive governments in Scotland (Scottish Executive, 2000; The Scottish Government,

2007, 2008), have not been sufficiently acted on. The chapter ends with a brief discussion of key factors that may help to account for that failure, a failure that has resulted in poorer, more disadvantaged sections of the population continuing to suffer from avoidable early death and chronic limiting long-term illness (LLTI), with the aim of highlighting what else needs to be done.

Persistence of health inequalities in Scotland

Focusing on health within a contemporary Scottish context with a view to addressing issues of social justice immediately raises the question of health inequalities, as evidenced across the UK, within Scotland *and* in an international context. Figures from the Office for National Statistics (ONS) for the period 2006–08 show significant variations in life expectancy across the UK. For example, for males the highest life expectancy was in South East England (79.2 years) and the lowest in Scotland (75.0 years), while for females the highest was in South West England (83.1 years) with the lowest, once again, recorded in Scotland (79.9 years). However, within that general picture, the ONS figures also reveal that particular areas of Scotland are associated with lower life expectancy in relative terms, whether measured at birth or at the age of 65. For example, life expectancy for men and women living in Kensington and Chelsea was 84.3 and 88.9 years respectively at birth and 23.1 and 26.3 years respectively at 65, but just 70.7 and 77.2 years in Glasgow at birth and 13.8 and 17.4 years at 65. The picture is further complicated within the Scottish context by generally higher levels of life expectancy in the East than in the West, with Glasgow City, West Dunbartonshire and Inverclyde faring particularly poorly, especially in relation to men's health (ONS, 2009). That said, geographical inequalities of health status and mortality rates in the East of Scotland are also in evidence, with marked contrasts between parts of Fife and Edinburgh, for example. Similarly, not all deprived people or households live in deprived areas, suggesting that area–based initiatives would need to be supplemented by additional measures if inequalities are to be fully addressed (McLoone, 2001). Moreover, if the picture relating to socioeconomic status, gender and place is complex, it is made even more so once the variables of racial/ethnic identity and age, for example, are added into the equation (Evandrou, 2000; Karlsen and Nazroo, 2010).

Crucially, inequalities in health have not only been a persistent feature of UK society as a whole and Scotland in particular, they have also *widened* as life expectancy has increased everywhere over time (Graham, 2007, 2009). This clearly indicates that some have benefited more than others from general improvements in the UK (and Scottish) nation's health, with the most significant increases in longevity being in areas that were already relatively advantaged.

According to Whyte (2006), in international terms, it is in the working-age population (measured in this study as 15–74 years) that Scottish mortality rates are highest in comparison with other Western European nations and, once again, the persistent nature of health inequalities, this time in a European context, is evident. Indeed, despite an overall decrease in mortality rates in the latter half of the 20th century, the rate of reduction in Scotland has not matched that elsewhere and, as a result, its relative mortality ranking has worsened, recording the highest mortality rates in Europe for working-age men since 1978 and for working-age women since 1958.

In morbidity terms, despite the methodological difficulties associated with measuring sickness rates and the numbers living with LLTI, there is a growing body of evidence, not least generated by the census, to support the claim that it too is patterned, with LLTI prevalence increasing with decreasing socioeconomic position. Moreover, as Shaw et al (2007, p 242) note, 'local authorities with high LLTI prevalence tend to have lower life expectancy rates, and the association between the two is strong and linear'. Hence, in the Scottish context, 'in 2001, 21% of women living in disadvantaged areas reported they had a limiting long-standing illness or disability, compared to 8% of women in the most affluent areas. The corresponding figures for men were 21% and 9%' (Scottish Executive, 2005a, p 22).

Tackling health inequalities: elevating the role of the NHS and health policy in political discourse

While the problem of health inequalities is now something that not even politicians are able to deny, the reasons for their persistence over time has been the focus of much contestation and debate. Nevertheless, many sociologists and social policy commentators researching health inequalities have highlighted the enduring importance of socioeconomic position, both as a structural location and as actively produced (Graham, 2007). Here, the work of Bourdieu (1986) is cited as crucial in highlighting 'the processes through which people produce the unequal positions in which they are located' (Graham, 2007, p 43), and moving us beyond a simple structural explanation through the attention given to social agency and, arising out of that, the importance of childhood and our experiences of family life. The concepts of cultural and social capital are important here in illuminating how our health is, at one and the same time and in complex and dynamic ways, influenced by our socioeconomic position *and* our access to cultural and social resources. In the words of Bourdieu and Wacquant (1992, p 119), 'acknowledging that capital can take a variety of forms is indispensable to explain the structure and dynamics of differentiated societies'. Indeed, as Abel (2008, p 3) notes, both material and non-material resources have been associated with population health and risk of disease. Here not only economic but also social and cultural capital have been shown to have an impact on the health and well-being of communities and have explanatory power in relation to the *social reproduction* of health inequalities and 'the translation of social disadvantage into poor health'. The relationship between the three is one of interdependency and complexity, with access to cultural resources affecting the use of economic and social capital for health and vice versa. Nevertheless, recent research in the field of social epidemiology suggests, for example, that 'cultural resources such as the capacity for active information seeking and critical consumer behaviour contributed significantly to the explanation of social class differences in patients' behaviour' (see Noiesen et al, 2004, cited in Abel, 2008, p 1).

While recognising the need for further work on the development of meaningful indicators of cultural capital and on how we understand and integrate other social factors such as gender and 'race'/ethnicity into the equation, Abel (2008, p 3) suggests that acknowledging 'people's culture-based health resources as part of their health-relevant capital ... places cultural determinants firmly in the discourse of structurally based health inequalities'. He goes on to conclude that cultural capital needs to be considered as a 'non-monetary form of capital that interacts with economic and social capital to constitute people's health chances and choices', and thus the concept of cultural capital 'links structural and behavioural determinants of health by explaining how people's behavioural options and preferences are constrained and structured by their cultural, social and economic resources' (Abel, 2008, p 3).

Notwithstanding the complex picture painted by those researching health inequalities, a high degree of consensus seems to exist between the different party political players that reflects a rather selective and simplistic approach to tackling the problem of health inequalities. This approach is marked by the elevation of those explanatory aspects which emphasise the role of the individual, and to a lesser extent communities, in combating 'unhealthy lifestyle choices', and suggest a subsequent focus on improving mortality rates and meeting specific morbidity-focused targets (for example, chronic heart disease) when in government. However, none seem willing to fully engage with the evidence base that suggests inequalities in income and wealth, as well as in social and cultural capital, continue to have a significant impact on inequalities in health (Acheson Report, 1998; Marmot and Wilkinson, 2006; Graham, 2007, 2009). Indeed, while government policy documents and reports often acknowledge the role that poverty and deprivation, for example, play in the persistence of health inequalities, intervention strategies nevertheless emphasise improving the outcomes of and access to the NHS, which may involve targeting behavioural risk factors through health education strategies (see below). In the Scottish context, importance is also placed on constructing a different sort of NHS north of the border with a greater focus on mutuality, cooperation and collaboration (Scottish Executive, 2007; Keating, 2009) as a means of tackling poor health more effectively. As Graham (2007) notes, the emphasis is overwhelmingly on medical or 'downstream' interventions at the expense of interventions that focus on 'upstream' factors, that is, those social determinants which shape people's health, particularly their living and working environments in the broadest sense (see also Macintyre, 2007). This is clearly evident in Scotland where, in *Our national health*, it was acknowledged that 'poverty, poor housing, homelessness and the lack of educational and economic opportunity are the root causes of major inequalities in health in Scotland. We must fight the causes of illness as well as illness itself' (Scottish Executive, 2000, pp 14-15); but in *Delivering for health*, five years later, it was argued that,

> ... the most significant thing we can do to tackle health inequalities is to target and enhance primary care services in deprived areas. Strengthening primary care teams and promoting anticipatory care in disadvantaged areas will reduce health inequalities by: targeting health improvement action and resources at the most disadvantaged areas; building capacity in primary care to deliver proactive, preventative care; providing early interventions to prevent escalation of health care needs. This approach will ensure that people at greatest risk of ill health are actively identified and offered opportunities for early detection, advice and treatment, enabling earlier identification, prevention and treatment for conditions such as high blood pressure, type 2 diabetes and high cholesterol. Strengthening primary care services in these communities can improve health outcomes through preventive medicine, changing the focus to 'anticipate' and prevent....We believe that NHS Scotland can do more itself to break the link between deprivation and poor health. We need not only a sustained effort to promote good health and good health care, but also to target our resources at areas of greatest need. (Scottish Executive, 2005a, pp 24-5)

Here, the emphasis is on health service 'solutions' (which, as we shall see, have been accompanied by various behavioural change strategies) with the broader social determinants of health inequalities all but falling from view at the stage of shaping the policy response and setting priorities.

Indeed, in Scotland, politicians have made much of the emergent differences between the NHS north and south of the border, which have built on those Scottish specificities already in evidence before 1999, including a non-market-driven orientation. This has been particularly clear since the election of the minority Scottish National Party (SNP) government in 2007. For example, launching the new Scottish government's strategy for a healthier Scotland, *Better health, better care* (2007), Nicola Sturgeon, Deputy First Minister, emphasised the principle of mutualism and the need to see the NHS in Scotland as co-owned by NHS staff and the Scottish public (Sturgeon, 2008). Similarly, Sturgeon has emphasised the Scottish government's commitment to reducing the role of private sector involvement in the Scottish NHS, arguing that there was 'a real battle of ideas between different parts of the UK about the future directions of health care. It is a battle between the values of the market, internal competition and contestability on the one hand and the values of public ownership, cooperation and collaboration on the other' (Sturgeon, 2008, p 1, quoted in Birrell, 2009, p 157).

So, to what extent have developments in the Scottish NHS and health policy north of the border given rise to a divergence of organisation, guiding principles, priorities and outcomes?

The NHS in Scotland

While the organisational structure and funding arrangements of the NHS north and south of the border have always been characterised by a degree of difference (Stewart, 2004; Greer and Trench, 2010) – albeit never adding up to 'a systematic differentiation' or distinct Scottish model (Keating, 2009) – it was not until the introduction of devolved governance that these became marked (Crinson, 2009). In particular, given that health policy became the responsibility of the Scottish Parliament, devolution brought with it an explicit rejection of the market as the primary coordinating mechanism for healthcare (although significant inroads were made by the private sector, not least in relation to the use of private finance in capital rebuilding programmes, as noted by Pollock, 2004). Arguably, this reflects a more sceptical stance on both the value of competition in healthcare delivery and the reduction of healthcare to a 'set of clearly defined procedures' (Harrison and McDonald, 2008, p 158), itself related to the nature of the devolution settlement and the different political cultures, parties, policy networks and electoral system in Scotland, where coalition and minority SNP governments have been the order of the day since 1999 (see Baggott, 2007). Given that this remains the stated view of the SNP, returned to government with a clear majority following the May 2011 Scottish elections, we can reasonably assume that this will continue to be the case, at least in the short to medium term. Of course, the marketisation strategies embodied in the NHS and Community Care Act 1990 had been resisted at the level of local implementation in Scotland, particularly by the medical profession but also by NHS managers who were reluctant to abandon collaborative ways of working established prior to devolution. Nevertheless, the fact of devolution means that there is now clear scope to mark out a divergent path in policy terms too. Consequently, in place of the elevation of market–type mechanisms, successive Scottish governments have sought to build on the more hierarchical structure inherited by the Scottish Parliament, emphasising the principles of collaboration and consultation. Here, Keating (2009) notes that the move away from 'old' NHS structures and organising principles by successive Conservative and New Labour governments was increasingly seen to be out of line with elite preferences. Indeed, Greer and Trench (2010, pp 9-10) highlight that 'a much greater elite consensus on the value and structure of the welfare state' exists in Scotland which was a significant driver in the push to protect the principles of universalism and collaboration and hence the Scottish NHS from those English policies that threatened to 'change or erode citizenship rights'.

Hence, in place of the rampant marketisation, managerialisation and consumerisation of the NHS in England, Scottish policy makers reasserted the principle of cooperation and collaboration with professional groups and public sector workers (Keating, 2009). These principles were institutionalised in the form of integrated Managed Clinical Networks on the one hand, and Community Health Partnerships on the other. Together these 'structures' seek to link different groups of health professionals with primary, secondary and tertiary care organisations in both the voluntary and public sectors. The objective is to ensure an integration of health and social care services and that services are delivered in an equitable and effective manner to meet local needs. Indeed, more recently in August 2011, following the SNP's victory at the May elections, Nicola Sturgeon embraced the call of the Christie Commission on the Future Delivery of Public Services for a 'radical, new collaborative culture' (Public Services Commission, 2011, p ix) as a mechanism for preventing many of the social problems, including poor health status and health inequalities, that were consuming the shrinking budgets available to tackle them in a context of sustained economic crisis. The main thrust of her response was to emphasise the benefits of a rapid pooling of health and social care budgets as a means to increasing the efficiency of preventative and early intervention services and thus refocusing resources on preventing as opposed to responding to health problems once they are established. In essence, these networks and partnerships are seen as an effective way of supporting work across the boundaries between the different tiers of the NHS, groups of health professions and the health and social care divide with the aim of delivering the national health improvement agenda within the constraints of increasingly limited budgets and growing demand.

In effect, those mechanisms seen to be potentially damaging to equity and effectiveness (Scottish Executive, 1999) have been abandoned in favour of unified local health boards charged with the responsibility for planning and delivering primary and secondary care with the key objective of employing primary preventative and health promotion strategies as mechanisms for improving the health of the nation (Scottish Executive, 2000).

This process of divergence has been even more marked since the election of both minority and majority SNP governments (and the election of a UK Coalition government in 2010) who have clearly been under significantly less pressure to follow Westminster's lead than the New Labour/Liberal Democrat Coalition governments before them, and who are keen to magnify the distinctiveness of the Scottish NHS in terms of increasing their government credentials in the eyes of the Scottish population (see The Scottish Government, 2007, 2009).

In relation to the general health of the Scottish population and the problem of health inequalities, particular emphasis is placed on tackling specific conditions and, hence, responding in a focused way to those known causes of death which feed into high relative mortality rates through dedicated treatments and increased service entitlements. This is illustrated, on the one hand, by the setting of targets, for example, for reducing the rates of death from coronary heart disease, cancer and stroke and for decreasing levels of smoking, alcohol consumption and obesity, all identified as key risk factors in early death and high levels of LLTI, especially in more deprived communities; and on the other hand, by the introduction of free eye tests in 2006, free dental check-ups in 2007 and, more recently, the phasing out of all prescription charges in 2011 (The Scottish Government, 2007), all with the explicit aim of increasing access to healthcare.

Regarding the availability of new treatments, there is also evidence to suggest that some have become available earlier to Scottish patients than their English counterparts and, further, that some may also become available *only* in Scotland as a result of institutional differences, specifically the setting up of the Scottish Medicines Consortium in 2001. This body seeks to rapidly review the evidence on new treatments and provide speedy guidance to the Scottish NHS, in contrast to the National Institute for Health and Clinical Excellence (NICE), its English counterpart, which offers its guidance based on a later, more extensive review of the evidence, thus delaying patient access to some new treatments that may be beneficial (Cairns, 2006; Watts, 2006). At the interface of health and social care, it should also be noted that the 'majority' recommendations of the 1999 Sutherland Inquiry were adopted in Scotland resulting in the provision of free long-term 'personal care' since 2002. So, in all, there are several ways in which the Scottish NHS has begun to look significantly different from the health service in England and to deliver different outcomes.

Also significant is the limited emphasis placed in Scotland on decreasing waiting times and increasing consumer choice, both primary objectives in England. Indeed, while there has been more interest recently in reducing waiting times as a specific objective of the Scottish government, given the unfavourable comparative data on Scottish and English outcomes and the recommendations of the Kerr Report on the future of the NHS in Scotland (Scottish Executive, 2005b; Baggott, 2007), it has not been constructed as a principal driver of policy north of the border. Moreover, as noted briefly earlier, consumerist discourses and the extension of patient choice, particularly through increased private sector provision, for their own sake, have been seen not only as potentially damaging to the idea of the NHS as a 'public' service, accountable to the Scottish people and accessed as a right of citizenship, but also as an attack on social justice in terms of undermining the principle of universalism and hence the commitment to the provision of equal entitlement, equal access and equal treatment within and between social groups and geographical contexts.

That said, while alternative strategies have been employed to increase NHS capacity – for example, in 2002 Scotland's largest private hospital was taken into state hands – contracts with the independent sector *have* also been used, albeit as a means of reducing waiting times. Similarly, Hellowell and Pollock (2009a) highlight the introduction of a different method of financing capital building projects in the Scottish healthcare sector. In doing so, they claim that the standard private finance initiative (PFI) model used by both the Scottish Executive and Westminster governments since 1992, in line with HM Treasury preferences (HM Treasury, 1997, 2000), has been supplanted by a 'non-profit-distributing' model, a shift that sought to ensure a more cost-effective method of procurement whereby any surpluses generated are passed to a designated charity as opposed to being paid out as dividends to consortia members. However, the general principle of drawing on private finance has not been abandoned in Scotland despite the evidence that it has not delivered value for money (Hellowell and Pollock, 2009b). Clearly, the political capital gleaned from keeping such public service investments off the balance sheet is still seen to outweigh the economic costs of non-traditional forms of procurement and the potential political costs of enabling an increased role for the private sector.

Similarly, while the Kerr Report called for the Scottish Parliament to clarify policy relating to consumer choice within the NHS, it too has not enjoyed the same status in Scotland as in England. Indeed, the 2006 British Medical Association's Scottish survey of doctors' priorities for health found that the overwhelming majority believed that increased patient involvement and empowerment with a view to helping them make meaningful choices about the treatment options available to them was more important than offering them a choice about where they receive treatment. Moreover, the respondents felt that patients and the general public should be given a voice in the development of local services and the setting of priorities. In line with this, the Scottish government has introduced the Health Boards (Membership and Elections) (Scotland) Act 2009 that provides for members of the public to be elected onto health boards as paid members, following a pilot of the scheme which is now under way.

So, in drawing up a balance sheet, care must be taken not to overstate the differences between health policy, service procurement and the organisational structure of the NHS north and south of the border, while at one and the same time recognising the divergence of the two systems in important ways and acknowledging the potential impact this has on social justice in terms of equal entitlement, access and treatment.

Having charted the different paths that the health service has taken in England and Scotland, it is now possible to consider in a little more detail how that has translated into a Scottish strategy for tackling health inequalities.

Tackling health inequalities: the medical model, individual responsibility and health service 'solutions'

As noted above, at the heart of recent strategies to combat health inequalities in Scotland are explicit national performance targets of which, according to Audit Scotland (2009), 10 out of 13 due for delivery in 2008/09 were met, resulting in a fall in mortality rates for key causes of death including cancer, coronary heart disease and stroke. In addition, as implied earlier, successive governments across the devolved UK have also focused policy on behavioural change in relation to known health risks. Most obviously, governments have sought to engage in both 'carrot' and 'stick' interventions to decrease the numbers engaging in 'unhealthy behaviours'. For example, in relation to smoking, governments have embarked on a sustained health education campaign, often accompanied by very graphic anti-smoking messages and increased access to counselling and practical support in a quest to help smokers quit successfully, as well as increasing taxes on cigarettes, penalties for those found to be selling cigarettes to underage smokers and finally, banning smoking in public places, confined or otherwise, in 2006. Similarly, in relation to heavy and binge drinking, governments have increased taxes, attempted to raise awareness through targeted education campaigns and, more recently, have even flirted with the notion of imposing a minimum price on a unit of alcohol in Scotland. The latter proposal, a key policy objective for the SNP, provoked considerable debate between political actors and stakeholders but was voted down by Parliament in late 2010 (BMA, 2010).

Similar campaigns have been played out in relation to obesity, particularly among children, with a view to educating and, indeed, shocking people into behaviour modification. Here the emphasis has been firmly placed on changing individuals' lifestyle choices by drawing on a combination of strategies that give responsibility to the individual and increase the role of an 'enabling' government. But while there is a clear focus on helping individuals to help themselves, rather less attention is paid to the evidence suggesting that what may appear to be apparently free, rational choices made by individuals, which can in turn be influenced by increased information, are actually socially, materially and culturally influenced in important ways.

Effectively then, the Scottish government has committed itself to monitoring health inequalities by tracking what it has called 'indicators of inequality' between the most deprived and most affluent areas (as identified by the Measuring Inequalities in Health Working Group) in its 2003 policy document *Improving health in Scotland – The challenge* (Scottish Executive, 2003). However, its targets have not focused explicitly on the multiple causes of health inequalities, as recognised, for example, in *Our national health*, but rather on improving mortality rates relating to particular causes of death. Of course, insofar as the poorest sections of society are more at risk from these particular causes, such a strategy may well have a disproportionately positive impact on their health status and mortality rates, but, nevertheless, the overall impact on health inequalities is likely to be limited given the complex causality.

Similarly, responding to the 2008 report of the Ministerial Taskforce on Health Inequalities, *Equally well*, the minority SNP government at the time launched a detailed action plan to take forward its recommendations that also made too little of the multiple causes of health inequalities (The Scottish Government, 2008a, 2008b). Interestingly, the 2010 *Equally well review* noted that the overall picture of health inequalities remained stable, while some indicators, for example, those relating to premature mortality, suggested that the relative gap between the most and least deprived had widened. Of course, the review itself recognises, quite rightly, that in the short term little change is likely to be recorded given the long timescales required to influence persistent health inequalities. However, it also recognised the importance of the recession in the lack of progress achieved to date, but crucially, said nothing about the uneven impact of that recession on the most and least deprived sections of the population, nor did it propose any specific action to ameliorate this uneven impact (The Scottish Government, 2010). Evidence thus suggests a strong continuity between SNP and Labour governments, certainly in terms of their failure to respond directly and explicitly to many of the broader social determinants of health inequalities when it comes to shaping the policy response and setting priorities for action.

In essence then, the continued application of a medical model of inequalities, despite a recognition of non-medical causes in selected policy documents and statements, is effectively limiting the impact that government policy and practice can potentially have, irrespective of the differences in the Scottish and English NHS. Indeed, drawing on their critical discourse analysis of national policy statements relating to health inequalities, Smith et al (2009, p 219) note that to date there has been little to distinguish the approach to health inequalities taken north and south of the border (and in Wales), and that 'the similar ways in which health inequalities have been conceptualized and framed in the three policy contexts, combined with the dominance of a medical model of health, are likely to have played an important role in constraining policy responses'.

The point here, then, is not to suggest that the shape of the NHS, its priorities, levels of access to services and increased equity in terms of the distribution of services are of no consequence; clearly, resisting the English-led, Conservative and New Labour-fuelled rush to the market, with its emphasis on performance management and consumerisation, will go some way to protecting the Scottish people from a breakdown of universalism. As Greer and Mätzke (2009) note, in the context of devolution, the people of Scotland are now making their healthcare claims on a different government, one that more likely than not has different politics and favours a different set of policies to its Westminster counterpart but which can be implemented so long as resources continue to be allocated in the form of largely unconditional Block Grants arising out of the application of the Barnett formula. In that context, politics and policy clearly matter in terms of the social rights of citizenship enjoyed by a population, not least in relation to health and healthcare. But crucially, the additional problem of significant and persistent health inequalities cannot be adequately addressed without recognising the inextricable connections between health, poverty, wealth, cultural factors and the unequal distribution of power. To deny this is to ignore the now abundant evidence showing higher levels of mortality and morbidity among people experiencing poverty and deprivation relative to their more wealthy counterparts, and indicating that health inequalities have grown over time, mirroring growing inequalities in income and wealth in Scotland (see Chapters Three and Five, this volume), despite the improvement of health service provision across the UK throughout the 20th century.

Beyond the NHS: health contexts and policy frameworks

While explaining health inequalities has been and continues to be the focus of much debate across both academic research and writing and the policy-making arena, of particular interest here is the question of why, in a society where the NHS provides largely universal services free at the point of use, health inequalities persist. Several discrete explanatory models have been used in an effort to highlight structural/social, individual/behavioural/cultural and psychosocial causes (see Bartley, 2004), although this has tended to mean a privileging of one explanatory model over another at particular points in time when in effect they may all shed light on what is an extremely complex social problem with multiple causes. However, more recently some researchers and commentators have focused their attention on the value of a lifecourse approach that grapples with the question of accumulated advantage and disadvantage across the lifecycle and its impact on long-term health status with reference to a whole host of social and cultural determinants (Benzeval and Judge, 2001; Shaw et al, 2007). As such, then, a policy response that acknowledges the part a whole range of factors and actors might play in creating and reproducing health inequalities over time – in short, that views health inequality as a multifaceted issue – is more likely to deliver.

However, herein lies one of the key challenges: the Scottish government does not currently have control over all of the policy areas that have an impact on the production and reproduction of health inequalities. For example, fiscal and social security policy are reserved to Westminster, so power here lies in the hands of the Treasury and Department for Work and Pensions and not the Scottish government. Of course, the 1998 devolution settlement made provision for varying the general rate of taxation in Scotland by up to three pence in the pound, but this power has not so far been used. Moreover, according to Nicola Sturgeon, being interviewed on Radio 4's Today Programme on 15 October 2010, the minority SNP government had no plans to change that. If, as Mooney and Wright (2009, p 363) note, the SNP pursues proposals to replace the Council Tax with a form of local income tax following success at the May 2011 election, they could, at least in theory, bring a different model of redistribution to the table.

However, as they also note, successive governments in Scotland have not taken a significantly different route to tackling accumulated advantage and disadvantage despite engaging in a 'more social democratic language of solidarity' (Mooney and Wright, 2009, p 363). Here, as in England, the emphasis has been on reducing unemployment, the numbers of households on a low income and the numbers of children living in poverty (Scott et al, 2005; McKendrick et al, 2011). Insofar as such a strategy begins to tackle the passing on of social and thus health disadvantage across generations through a focus on early years intervention in particular, it is a welcome development. However, given the persistence of inequalities, it is insufficient on its own – there must be additional efforts focused on what Graham (2007, p 163) calls the 'unequal distribution of determinants across the wider socio-economic hierarchy' if improvements in the health of the poorest in society are not to be outpaced by those in wealthier groups. Indeed, as Graham (2007, p 164) goes on to argue, a reduction in broader social inequalities such as income, wealth and opportunity may well be a 'precondition for progress in reducing inequalities in proximal factors', for example, smoking. Moreover, given the Comprehensive Spending Review outlined by Chancellor George Osborne on 20 October 2010, even this limited strategy is now under significant threat, especially when PFI payments, which must be made whatever the circumstances, are factored in, further reducing the options available to government. For instance, a growth in levels of unemployment among poorer households, threats to the value of benefits for the most impoverished in society and cuts to early intervention strategies having a disproportionate impact on the nation's most vulnerable children will all have consequences for inequalities in income, wealth and opportunity that are already a chronic feature of society and, irrespective of the priorities of individual governments, cannot be offset by redirecting resources ring-fenced for PFI payments.

Finally, ongoing debates – for example, those being had by the Calman Commission (Commission on Scottish Devolution, 2009) and as part of Scotland's 'National Conversation' – focus not only on public expenditure as a whole but the share of total resources transferred to the Scottish government via the Barnett settlement, in the context of a growing perception in England that Scotland gets more than its fair share. As McLean et al (2009) argue, the SNP 'vision' of delivering universal welfare services while pursuing a relatively low taxation strategy seems untenable if the Barnett formula is abandoned and the Scottish government has to finance its own settlement.

In sum, the answer is not as simple as challenging the limits of the devolution settlement with a view to transferring more power into the hands of the Scottish government given that none of the larger Scottish parties have so far demonstrated a commitment to a significant redistribution of resources through their actions (see also Chapter Three, this volume). Indeed, while there has been a clear discourse around inequality in Scotland since 2007, the SNP have also been keen to engage with the language of a 'national interest' that works to further obscure and minimise the perceived relevance of a highly socially differentiated Scottish population to opportunities and outcomes, which in turn have an impact on health inequalities and act as additional barriers to the adoption of a more social and cultural model of causation and intervention.

Without a commitment to engaging with the 'problem' of excessive wealth and the concentration of power in the hands of an already well-served minority through the enactment of a wide-reaching redistribution strategy that works in parallel with anti-poverty strategies focused on those at the very bottom of the social scale, governments of any colour or combination will not be able to deliver on social justice agendas, even with more devolution, nor are they going to reduce health inequalities to the extent that the widening gap is halted, let alone reversed over time. It is not, then, enough for the report of the Ministerial Task Force on Health Inequalities, *Equally well*, to state that: 'Difference in income is not the only factor to blame for inequalities. Health may also vary according to people's age, disability, gender, race, religion or belief, sexual orientation and other individual factors. These interact with socioeconomic status and low income' (The Scottish Government, 2008, Executive Summary), when it does not go on to include tackling differences in income in its list of priority recommendations. Indeed, to claim as it does that 'some examples of important policy and action where the Scottish Government does not have enough powers for maximum impact ...

should be pursued as part of discussions about Scotland's constitutional future' may score a political point, but it both obscures the power already in the hands of the Scottish government, some of which has not yet been mobilised, and effectively abdicates responsibility for the health inequalities that persist in modern Scotland.

Conclusion

As noted above, in *Our national health* (2000) the Scottish Executive explicitly acknowledged the broader social determinants of health, arguing that it must not only fight illness but also its causes in the widest of senses. The Scottish government reinforced that message in its 2007 action plan, *Better health, better care*, and in its responses to *Equally well*. Yet, with the emphasis still firmly placed on lifestyle determinants of health and the assumption that tackling specific causes of disease through the setting of targets will improve the health of the population as a whole and reduce health inequalities in particular, given that poorer groups are more at risk of the key targeted causes of death, it is likely that an inherently limited set of outcomes with respect to reducing health inequalities will result. Indeed, even where the Scottish government has recognised the need to tackle those factors in the physical and social environment which reduce positive health outcomes, for example, by improving access to decent housing, regenerating urban environments and building resilience and capacity in individuals and communities (The Scottish Government, 2007), without a specific, focused commitment to redistributing resources, the strategy is unlikely to deliver real improvements in terms of health inequalities. In practice, this has been the reality to date.

Where the notion of 'joined-up solutions' to complex problems has been employed as a political tool to mark out successive New Labour/Liberal Democrat and SNP governments as different from those Conservative administrations of the 1980s/1990s in particular, in practice this seems to have translated into little more than employing a range of strategies to improve working across departmental and professional boundaries in the field of health and social care. It has not extended to improved joint working across government departments and sites of governance, in part due to the shared reluctance to embark on a more radically progressive policy of redistribution in relation to income, wealth, opportunity and access to cultural resources.

With reference to a growing evidence base and increased claims from government policy makers that the application of that evidence base is at the heart of efficient and effective governance, recent developments in the field of social epidemiology, with their increased focus on the impact of social and economic factors on health status and inequality, networks, cultural and social capital and the relationship between racism and health, for example, clearly have the potential to increase our understanding of health inequalities (see, for example, Kawachi and Berkman, 2000; Marmot and Wilkinson, 2006). But unless there is the political will to grapple fully with its implications in such a way as to change direction and rethink the thrust of health and welfare strategies, it seems unlikely that governments will be able to make significant inroads into the problem of health inequalities.

Further resources

Graham, H. (2007) *Unequal lives: Health and socioeconomic inequalities*, Maidenhead: Open University Press.

Greer, S.L. (ed) (2009) *Devolution and social citizenship in the UK*, Bristol: The Policy Press.

The Scottish Government policy documents: www.scotland.gov.uk/Topics/Health

Scottish Public Health Observatory (ScotPHO): *www.scotpho.org.uk*

References

Abel, T. (2008) 'Cultural capital and social inequality in health', *Journal of Epidemiology and Community Health*, vol 62, no 7, e13, pp 1-5.

Acheson Report (1998) *Independent inquiry into inequalities in health*, London: The Stationery Office.

Audit Scotland (2009) *Overview of Scotland's health and NHS performance 2008/09* (www.audit-scotland.gov.uk/docs/health/2009/nr_091210_nhs_overview.pdf).

Baggott, R. (2007) *Understanding health policy*, Bristol: The Policy Press.

Bartley, M. (2004) *Health inequality: An introduction to theories, concepts and methods*, Cambridge: Polity Press.

Benzeval, M. and Judge, K. (2001) 'Income and health: the time dimension', *Social Science and Medicine*, vol 52, pp 1371-90.

Birrell, D. (2009) *The impact of devolution on social policy*, Bristol: The Policy Press.

Bourdieu, P. (1986) *Distinction*, Cambridge: Polity Press.

Bourdieu, P. and Wacquant, L.J.D. (1992) *An invitation to reflexive sociology*, Cambridge: Polity Press.

BMA (British Medical Association) (2010) *Briefing paper for Alcohol etc (Scotland) Bill, Stage 1 debate* (www.bma.org.uk/lobbying_campaigning/scottish_parliament/alcoholdebatebriefing.jsp).

Cairns, J. (2006) 'Providing guidance to the NHS: the Scottish Medicines Consortium and the National Institute for Clinical Excellence compared', *Health Policy*, vol 76, no 2, pp 134-43.

Commission on Scottish Devolution (2009) *Serving Scotland better: Scotland and the United Kingdom in the 21st century* (Calman Commission) (www.commissiononscottishdevolution.org.uk).

Crinson, I. (2009) *Health policy: A critical perspective*, London: Sage Publications.

Evandrou, M. (2000) 'Ethnic inequalities in health in later life', *Health Statistics Quarterly*, vol 8, pp 20-8.

Graham, H. (2007) *Unequal lives: Health and socioeconomic inequalities*, Maidenhead: Open University Press.

Graham, H. (2009) 'The challenge of health inequalities', in H. Graham (ed) *Understanding health inequalities* (2nd edn), Buckingham: Open University Press, pp 1-21.

Greer, S.L. and Mätzke, M. (2009) 'Introduction: devolution and citizenship rights', in S.L. Greer (ed) *Devolution and social citizenship in the UK*, Bristol: The Policy Press, pp 1-19.

Greer, S.L. and Trench, A. (2010) 'Intergovernmental relations and health in Great Britain after devolution', *Policy & Politics*, vol 38, no 4, pp 509-29.

Harrison, S. and McDonald, R. (2008) *The politics of healthcare in Britain*, London: Sage Publications.

Hellowell, M. and Pollock, A.M. (2009a) 'Non-profit distribution: the Scottish approach to private finance in public services', *Social Policy and Society*, vol 8, no 3, pp 405-18.

Hellowell, M. and Pollock, A.M. (2009b) *The private financing of NHS hospitals: Politics, policy and practice* (www.allyson-pollock.com/uploads/2/3/5/5/2355176/economicaffairs_2009_privatefinancingnhs_hellowell.pdf).

HM Treasury (1997) *Partnership for prosperity: The private finance initiative*, London: The Stationery Office.

HM Treasury (2000) *Public private partnerships, The government's approach*, London: The Stationery Office.

Karlsen, S. and Nazroo, J. (2010) 'Religion, ethnicity and health inequalities', in H. Graham (ed) *Understanding health inequalities* (2nd edn), Buckingham: Open University Press, pp 103-24.

Kawachi, I. and Berkman, L.F. (2000) *Social epidemiology*, New York: Oxford University Press.

Keating, M. (2009) 'Social citizenship, devolution and policy divergence', in S.L. Greer (ed) *Devolution and social citizenship in the UK*, Bristol: The Policy Press.

Leyland, A.H., Dundas, R., McLoone, P. and Boddy, F.A. (2007) *Inequalities in mortality in Scotland, 1981-2001*, Medical Research Council (MRC) Social and Public Health Sciences Unit (SPHSU) Occasional Paper No 16, Glasgow: MRC-SPHSU.

Macintyre, S. (2007) *Inequalities in health in Scotland: What are they and what can we do about them?*, Occasional Paper No 17, Glasgow: Medical Research Council Social and Public Health Sciences Unit (MRC-SPHSU).

Marmot, M. and Wilkinson, R. (2006) *Social determinants of health* (2nd edn), Oxford: Oxford University Press.

McKendrick, J.H., Mooney, G., Dickie, J. and Kelly, P. (eds) (2011) *Poverty in Scotland 2011: Towards a more equal Scotland?*, London: Child Poverty Action Group.

McLean, I., Lodge, G. and Schmuecker, K. (2009) 'Social citizenship and intergovernmental finance', in S.L. Greer (ed) *Devolution and social citizenship in the UK*, Bristol: The Policy Press, pp 137-60.

McLoone, P. (2001) 'Targeting deprived areas with small areas in Scotland: population study', *British Medical Journal*, vol 323, pp 374-5.

Mooney, G. and Wright, S. (2009) 'Introduction: social policy in the devolved Scotland: towards a Scottish welfare state?', *Social Policy and Society*, vol 8, no 3, pp 361-5.

ONS (Office for National Statistics) (2009) *Life expectancy at birth and at age 65 by local areas in the United Kingdom, 2006-08* (www.statistics.gov.uk/pdfdir/liex1009.pdf).

Pollock, A. (2004) *NHS Plc: The privatisation of our health care*, London: Verso.

Public Services Commission (2011) *Commission on the Future Development of Public Services* (Christie Commission), Edinburgh: Public Services Commission.

Scott, G., Mooney, G. and Brown, U. (2005) 'Managing poverty in the new Scotland', in G. Mooney and G. Scott (eds) *Exploring social policy in the 'new' Scotland*, Bristol: The Policy Press, pp 85-110.

Scottish Executive (1999) *Introduction of managed clinical networks within the NHS in Scotland*, NHS MEL10, Edinburgh: Scottish Executive Health Department.

Scottish Executive (2000) *Our national health: A plan for action, a plan for change*, Edinburgh: The Stationery Office.

Scottish Executive (2003) *Improving health in Scotland – The challenge* (www.scotland.gov.uk/Publications/2003/03/16747/19929).

Scottish Executive (2005a) *Delivering for health* (www.scotland.gov.uk/publications/2005/11/02102635/26372).

Scottish Executive (2005b) *Building a health service fit for the future: A national framework for service change in the NHS in Scotland* (The Kerr Report) (www.scotland.gov.uk/publications/2005/05/23141307/13171).

Scottish Executive (2007) *Choosing Scotland's future: A national conversation: Independence and responsibility in the modern world* (www.scotland.gov.uk/publications/2007/08).

Scottish Government, The (2007) *Better health, better care: Action plan* (www.scotland.gov.uk/Publications/2007/12/11103453/4).

Scottish Government, The (2008) *Equally well* (www.scotland.gov.uk/Resource/Doc/254248/0075274.pdf).

Scottish Government, The (2009) *Health Boards (Membership and Elections) (Scotland) Act* (www.scottish.parliament.uk/business/bills/63-healthBoard/b63s2-introd-en.pdf).

Scottish Government, The (2010) *Equally well review* (www.scotland.gov.uk/Resource/Doc/924/0100414.pdf).

Shaw, M., Galobardes, B., Lawlor, D.A., Lynch, J., Wheeler, B. and Davey-Smith, G. (2007) *The handbook of inequality and socio-economic position*, Bristol: The Policy Press.

Smith, K.E., Hunter, D.J., Blackman, T., Elliott, E., Greene, A., Harrington, B.E., Marks, L., McKee, L. and Williams, G.H. (2009) 'Divergence or convergence? Health inequalities and policy in a devolved Britain', *Critical Social Policy*, vol 29, no 2, pp 216-42.

Stewart, J. (2004) *Taking stock: Scottish social welfare after devolution*, Bristol: The Policy Press.

Sturgeon, N. (2008) *Future of the NHS in Scotland* (www.scotland.gov.uk/news/releases/2008).

Watts, G. (2006) 'Are the Scots getting a better deal on prescribed drugs than the English?', *British Medical Journal*, vol 333, p 875.

Whyte, B. (2006) *Scottish mortality in a European context 1950-2000: An analysis of comparative mortality trends*, Edinburgh: Scottish Public Health Observatory (ScotPHO).

EIGHT

The coming of age of Scottish social services?

Sue Dumbleton and Mo McPhail

Introduction

The 'coming of age of social work' was the lofty claim made by a devolved Scottish government in response to the report of the 21st-century review of social work, *Changing lives:*

> It will mark social work's coming of age as a mature profession, focusing services on promoting wellbeing, rather than the more paternalistic welfare model underpinning current legislation. (Scottish Executive, 2006b, p 14)

What do mature ('coming of age') social services look like? What do they do and how can we recognise them? The Scottish government (Scottish Executive, 2006b, p 14) defines a mature social work profession as one which: embraces more personalised services; is focused on outcomes subject to performance management; manages risk and promotes 'excellence'; enshrines the position of service users and carers in service design and delivery; and is subject to public service reforms. The definition of 'coming of age' and 'mature' is contentious and open to debate because the profession itself has not agreed the definition. For example, the international definition of 'social work' (IFSW and IASSW, 2004), based on ethical principles of human rights and social justice, provides an alternative perspective on 'maturity' in social services.

This definition, however, does propose indicators that focus on concrete actions and it is these that we examine here, particularly in relation to services for children and young people and services for people who have a learning disability. Social work is, of course, far wider than these two service domains. These are referred to here as illustrative and representative examples of the broader profession. The idea that devolution in 1999 strengthened Scotland's autonomy in social work and social care in the context of UK pressures that continue to shape social policy is also discussed. It is argued that the overall picture of social services in Scotland at the end of the first decade of the 21st century falls short of what can be seen as a 'coming of age'. Amidst severe economic and political threats, which echo

UK-wide welfare and public sector reforms, the distinctively Scottish approach to social welfare and the aspirations of the social services profession to promote its core values and social justice are under threat.

Changing lives report of the 21st-century social work review

The *Changing lives* report was published in 2006 (Scottish Executive, 2006a). The explicit government rationale for commissioning the review identified factors such as reported uncertainty, lack of clarity and confidence in social work, increased expectations from the public and what is described as 'a series of critical reports following tragic incidents' (Scottish Executive, 2006b, p 4). The contention was that social services were in crisis and radical solutions needed to be found.

Major drivers of the review were two social work inquiries: one into the death of a young child (Edinburgh and Lothian's Child Protection Committee, 2003) and the other into the neglect and sexual exploitation of a young woman with learning disabilities (Scottish Executive, 2004). Both were under supervision of social work agencies at the time of the abuse. These two inquiries are considered separately in the following section to illustrate the consequences now reflected in contemporary Scottish social services policy and provision. Different media and government responses to perceived crises in social services in England and Scotland in recent times are also explored.

A pivotal child abuse inquiry

The 2003 inquiry identified missed opportunities for the sharing of professional information which may have prevented the death of 11-week-old Caleb Ness (Edinburgh and Lothian's Child Protection Committee, 2003) at the hands of his father, a man with a history of drug-related offences and a behaviour-affecting brain injury. The baby's mother also posed substantial risks due to her own drug use and involvement in the sex industry. One conclusion from this report was that the child protection process was flawed, and there was confusion between the rights of parents and the rights of the child. This highlights concerns identified since the case of the death of Jasmine Beckford (London Borough of Brent, 1985), that there are substantive differences in the rights and needs of different family members that need to be thoroughly attended to in child protection situations.

Others had different views of the underlying problems and by implication in the response to these problems. Trades union officials and opposition councillors raised major concerns about the resource issues facing staff in all the key agencies (MacGreggor, 2004). Concerns were expressed that there was an acute shortage of skilled social workers, morale was low and pressure high among existing social workers. Some children on the at-risk register did not have an allocated social worker. This event gathered considerable political momentum and acted as a significant spur to a radical overhaul of social work as a profession in Scotland.

Similar debates can be detected in media and political responses to the child abuse tragedy of 'Baby P', where individual social workers were vilified and demonised. In the English context there was a vigilante response, led by *The Sun* newspaper, calling for the sacking of individual front-line social work practitioners, a directive for a fundamental restructuring of social work education and the establishing of a social work college by government (Ferguson and Lavalette, 2009). In Scotland, in response to the Caleb Ness inquiry (Edinburgh and Lothian's Child Protection Committee, 2003), the director of Edinburgh City Council social work resigned his post, the call for the overhaul of social work was strengthened and a new requirement, *Key capabilities in child care and protection* (Scottish Executive, 2006c), was introduced to the four-year honours qualifying social work degree. There has been resistance to the latter policy, in challenge of the assumption that solutions to social problems such as child abuse are best addressed by increased standardisation of qualifying education (Mackay and Woodward, 2010). It is argued here that this reflects a much wider context of standardisation of social work education, increasing departure from social work values and critical analysis of structural roots of discrimination, disadvantage and social injustice.

Exploitation of a woman with learning disabilities

A further trigger for the 21st-century review of social work were events in the Scottish Borders Council and NHS Borders (Petch, 2007, p 48) where people who were considered to have a learning disability were being cared for by a convicted offender. The abuse and exploitation that they experienced was brought to light when one woman was admitted to hospital with multiple injuries resulting from physical and sexual abuse. Concerns about the conditions in which these people lived were known by social services and the health service but had not been acted on. The report into the events (Scottish Executive, 2004) identified numerous longstanding failings on the part of the statutory authorities, including a failure to share or act on information, to coordinate services and to assess, plan, record and monitor.

The events in the Scottish Borders were only one in a long line of scandals and revelations of gross and 'low-level' abuse and ill treatment of people with learning disabilities in Scotland and further afield (see, for example, HMSO, 1969; Healthcare Commission, 2007). It was partly in response to concerns about conditions which allow such abuse to continue that the 21st-century review was commissioned.

Birth of social work and social care in Scotland?

If *Changing lives* was the 'coming of age' of social services, the much earlier Social Work (Scotland) Act 1968 is often regarded as its birth (Scottish Executive, 2006b, p 14). It deserves attention as it represents a major landmark in Scottish social services and is seen by some as determining the nature of services for much of the last 40 years. However, Fabb and Guthrie (1992) suggest that it was not as far reaching as it appears, describing the powers of local authorities to promote social welfare in the 1968 legislation as 'very vague'. They regard the main achievement as bringing together a number of disparate services. For example, although powers for assistance to be made by payments in cash or kind were allowed by this legislation (thus recognising the impact of material factors for a person in need), this was subject to a wide range of interpretations.

While recognising the strengths of the 1968 legislation, Ferguson (2005) claims that there were similar forces at play in England at the time, of fragmentation of services, poor coordination and geographical unevenness of services. He argues that it was not the landmark some claim, and that the Scottish system is based on similar assumptions to the contemporary English review, where poverty is seen as residual and individual, as opposed to as a result of structural factors associated with a particular socioeconomic system (Mooney, 2008). However, as Ferguson also comments, despite these assumptions, there was a prevailing view at the time that social change and social justice were legitimate concerns of social work. In the context of social work, 'social justice' was later reflected in a statement of principles agreed by the International Association of Schools of Social Work (IASSW) and the International Federation of Social Workers (IFSW) in 2004. Social justice is defined here as: challenging negative discrimination; recognising diversity; distributing resources equitably; challenging unjust policies and practices; and working in solidarity – accompanied by a commentary that 'Social workers have an obligation to challenge social conditions that contribute to social exclusion, stigmatisation or subjugation, and to work towards an inclusive society' (IFSW and IASSW, 2004, para 4).

Despite its limitations, the 1968 Act highlighted Scotland's distinctive approach to social work, for example, the system of Children's Hearings. This was introduced as a result of the Kilbrandon Committee (Scottish Office, 1964; see also Ferguson, 2005) to replace the more punitive approaches of juvenile courts. It was hailed as an exemplary approach. Much has, however, changed since its introduction: a review of the Children's Hearings system in 2004 warned that a more punitive approach towards offending behaviour is likely to lead to an increase in re-offending and a greater identification with a criminal lifestyle (NCH Scotland, 2004; see also Chapter Eleven, this volume). While Scotland led the way in the UK in embedding the United Nations (UN) Convention on the Rights of the Child (UN, 1989) in the Children (Scotland) Act 1995, sadly, as Aldgate (2009) comments, the implementation has proved inconsistent, and definitions of 'children in need' are applied differentially across Scotland, interpreted and influenced according to the availability of resource.

The international and UK context of Scottish social services

When *Changing lives* was published the impact of global economic crisis of the early 21st century was unimagined, and probably unimaginable. As political responses to it unfold, it becomes increasingly clear that many welfare systems across the world are experiencing and facing the most severe budget reductions for generations. In a study of global influences on Australian social services, Mendes (2006) found that while global financial market policies clearly have an impact on welfare systems at the national level in terms of rates of poverty and inequality, each country responds to those challenges on the basis of its own distinctive political and cultural context. In Scotland the response can be seen as affected by the culture and politics of the nation, but there are additional limitations to what can be achieved with devolved powers as a result of the continuing and substantial impact of UK-wide and global economic policies, particularly in relation to the benefits system and general taxation (Stewart, 2004; Mooney and Scott, 2005; Mooney et al, 2006).

The Scottish government's response to the impact of the recession on public services in Scotland (even before the full impact of the 2010 UK Comprehensive Spending Review is known) is, as expected, a re-evaluation of spending intentions. An acknowledgement is made in a Scottish government briefing paper (Scottish Parliament, 2009) that there will be a likely increase in demand for social work and health services, due to the physical and psychological impact of increased unemployment, but also an admission that key social policy targets are likely to be missed. These include social inclusion, child poverty (despite the passing of a UK-wide Child Poverty Act 2010), equality, health and homelessness targets (issues that are explored in other chapters in this volume). The link between a global banking crisis (and subsequent UK and Scottish government 'austerity' measures) and the impact on those in the most vulnerable situations in Scottish society has been widely voiced.

Additionally, Scott and Mooney (2009, see also Chapter One, this volume) consider other UK-wide issues such as constraints on citizenship, immigration and welfare entitlements, and their impact on effectively tackling social justice issues from a Scottish base. They argue that given the reserved powers of the Westminster Parliament on the level of welfare benefits and the minimum wage and taxation, there is a limit to what a Scottish government can do to change what remains a deeply divided and unequal society (see also Chapter Three, this volume).

In his analysis of policy divergence across the UK, Birrell (2007, 2009) finds that although there is a high degree of control by the devolved administrations, there are common tendencies away from separate social work departments and towards greater integration of public services. A key policy difference is that criminal justice services remain in the domain of local authority social work services in Scotland. Significant policy divergence relates to free personal care of older people in Scotland, whether in community or residential contexts, on a universal service basis. What are often called 'flagship' policies such as these are, however, threatened by recession-driven budget reduction.

The changing nature of the relationship between state and citizen is also important. An emphasis on increased regulation, centralised control, consumerist discourse and the narrative of 'choice' and 'control' can all be seen in policy position papers prior to *Changing lives* (Scottish Executive, 1999, 2000a, 2001, 2003). Such approaches may be seen to undermine principles of democracy and accountability (Mooney and Scott, 2005). They represent a shift that is part of a broader move from the mid-1970s onwards, in the UK, SA and in some other European countries. Jessop (1990) outlines this as a move away from a 'Keynesian welfare state' to a new model of welfare services based on assumptions about the role of government as facilitator of conditions for economic success rather than a promoter of social justice or the provision of welfare.

Devolution as an ongoing process: social services with children and young people

Aldgate (2009) argues that a greater clarity and autonomy of welfare policy in relation to social work with children and young people in Scotland has emerged since 1998, with the exception of the benefits system, which has had a significant impact upon the Scottish government's anti-poverty strategy. One view is that recent policies for children may reflect the growing confidence of the devolved government in Scotland (Stewart, 2004). Another view reflects the importance of the welfare principle established by the Social Work (Scotland) Act 1968. This is seen to lay the basis for a more integrated, child-centred approach to children's services across both universal services and specialised services, such as social work and social care. Aldgate (2009) argues that this principle, a distinctly Scottish welfare principle, was the precursor to a holistic and inclusive approach to children and young people, based on the children's rights agenda, an emphasis on social justice and a drive for early intervention, later articulated in the policy documents, *'It's everyone's job to make sure I'm alright'* (Scottish Executive, 2002) and the policy of *Getting it right for every child* (Scottish Parliament, 2008). High aspirations of children's well-being coupled with strong statements about collective societal responsibility for children are contained in these policies, tempered, however, by the impact of enduring poverty on children's well-being and curtailment of life chances (see Chapter Five, this volume).

A report on monitoring poverty and social exclusion in Scotland in 2010 by Parekh (2010) illustrates this enduring challenge concluding that although Scotland had a lower unemployment and child poverty rate than England at the start of the recession in 2008, Scotland has subsequently fared worse. Unemployment is at its highest level since 1996. Child poverty rose by 2 per cent in 2009 in Scotland, compared to a 1 per cent decrease in England. Further risks to these proud aspirations are identified by Aldgate (2009) in the wake of the SNP Concordat arrangements, implemented from 2008 al locas authoritiee were given an enhanced responsibility for a devolved budget in return for an agreement not to raise Council Tax.

Theories and explanations of poverty do not figure in the 21st-century review of social work, which presents some difficulty in assessing the under-theorised solutions proposed. Underlining this policy approach is a world view that seeks to explain welfare problems in individual terms, rather than through a structural analysis. Other researchers have found that children who are referred to a Children's Panel are disproportionately from social backgrounds where families are dependent on benefits and social housing (Waterhouse et al, 2000).

It is difficult to make absolute assertions about the links between child maltreatment and poverty, although there is some evidence of a link between stress and poverty and social deprivation, drug use and mental health issues (Dyson, 2008; Devaney, 2009). While acknowledging the complexity of interrelated factors, Dyson calls for a greater awareness of the impact of financial hardship and other forms of deprivation and that the resultant stress can lead to an increased risk of maltreatment by parents living in poverty.

Despite a proliferation of policy and legislation, the words of Asquith and Stafford (1995) continue to resonate, that: 'In short the development of policies and practices that impact on families and children which ignore basic social inequalities in the distribution of wealth and life chances may offer little by the way of attempts to ameliorate the conditions in which families find themselves'. (Asquith and Stafford, 1995, p 4).

Devolution as an ongoing process: social services with people with learning disabilities

Contemporary Scottish policy in relation to learning disability services was set out shortly after the re-establishment of the Scottish Parliament in 1999 and well before *Changing lives* in 2006. In 2000, the publication of *The same as you? A review of services for people with learning disabilities* by the Scottish Executive (2000b) was the first learning disability policy initiative in Scotland for over 20 years. It sought to quicken the pace of change in service provision and support people with learning disabilities to take greater control over their lives. The extent to which *The same as you?* has fulfilled its promise is being reviewed in 2010–12, a decade and more from its publication. The review seems likely to confirm that there has been slower progress over the intervening decade than the original report recommended. *The same as you?* is not a social services report. However, the influence of the social model of disability on learning disability services (although heavily critiqued in relation to people with a learning disability) and the report's stated commitment to social inclusion, equality and fairness (Scottish Executive, 2000b, p iii) ensure that social services workers, among many other groups, play an important role in realising its aims.

As long ago as 2000, the Scottish Executive (2000b, p 96) recommended that, 'Everyone with a learning disability, who wants to, should be able to have a "personal life plan"'. *Changing lives* not only welcomed increasingly 'personalised' services but saw them as inevitable (Scottish Executive, 2006a, p 32). Originally embraced by the New Labour governments of the early 21st century, the term 'personalisation' has become prominent in many aspects of social policy – and no more so than in policies associated with social work and social care (Duffy,

2010). The 'personal' in 'personalisation' creates the impression of an individualised, carefully crafted and decidedly not institutionalised approach to services. Although, as Ferguson notes, there is no formally accepted definition of the term, it carries with it connotations of a positive approach to providing support (2007, p 389). For who would not wish to receive support that is personalised in what Ferguson calls the 'common-sense definition' of services tailored to meet individual need? History, for people who have learning difficulties, in the form of institutional care, still casts a long and bleak shadow over current service provision. Accounts, personal testimony and academic research of institutional care abound (see, for example, Anderson and Langa, 1997; Atkinson et al, 1997, 2005; Ingham, 2002), and are cast almost entirely in a negative light.

A current aim of policy and services is to promote the 'social inclusion' of people with learning disabilities and 'social justice' in relation to them (Macintyre, 2008). *Changing lives* makes numerous references to 'social inclusion', seeing its promotion as a key role of social work. This focus on social inclusion in relation to people with learning disabilities places *The same as you?* and *Changing lives* in the broader policy context of devolved Scotland. Most people wish to feel part of the society in which they live. Beyond the 'warmly persuasive' words (Raymond Williams, 1975, cited in Ferguson, 2007, p 389), what this actually means for people who have learning disabilities is less clear. People with learning disabilities experience bullying, harassment, poverty and physical or mental ill health in far greater measure relative to the general population (Enable, 1999, 2007; Stalker et al, 1999; Emerson, 2007; Macintyre, 2008; Parckar, 2008; Chih et al, 2009), and to this extent their marginalisation is endemic in Scottish society, as it is in most Western countries.

Furthermore, as Quarriers (2008, p 3) discovered, 'People with learning disabilities living in the family home (12,625 people, over 50% of the adults with a learning disability known to local authorities) have become the invisible', and quotes a local authority representative as saying, 'we don't know if people [with learning disabilities] are dead or just not getting a service'. The implication that people known to local authorities and receiving a service are 'socially included' is debatable. Nonetheless it is important to hear the views of people who require services but do not, for whatever reason, receive them. The underlying philosophy for this is described as a new type of partnership between the individual and the state (Scottish Executive, 2006a, p 34), promoting well-being rather than the paternalistic welfare model of the past. A paradox of such policy is that people who are in some circumstances described as 'vulnerable' are somehow to be empowered as 'citizen leaders' to shape the development of services. Identities of vulnerability suggest passivity, powerlessness and dependence, and continue to convey a paternalistic view of people who use social services of the kind that the Scottish Executive sought to eliminate (2006a). As Ager and McPhail (2008) comment:

Their experience and insight of services is acknowledged, but there is little recognition of the transfer of power required that will equip those who are vulnerable to exert "real influence". (Ager and McPhail, 2008, p 9)

The self-advocacy movement has had considerable influence in ensuring that the voices of people who have a learning disability are heard in decisions, policies and practices that affect them, but the extent to which their voices are *really* heard is contested.

One of the recommendations of *The same as you?* and a measure to promote the inclusion of service user and carer voices was the introduction of a system of local area coordination (LAC). Originating in Western Australia, LAC is designed to build personal and community supports around individuals with learning disabilities and their families. The focus on individuals resonates with the drive to provide more personalised services. LAC, however, is not a service provider; rather, it is a system for developing community supports and increasing 'social capital' (Stalker et al, 2007) and for brokering relationships that can develop such supports. Through the promotion of these networks and the interventions of LAC, *The same as you?* proposed that the social inclusion of people with learning disabilities would be increased. But the development of LAC has been patchy and uneven across Scotland. Problems exist with its role, status and funding. In some areas it is both welcome and effective; in others less so, and in some it does not exist at all (Stalker et al, 2007). Despite its vision of being a universal service, access to LAC is limited by factors such as geography and local priorities diminishing the opportunities for increased social inclusion that it was introduced to develop. LAC has a strong value base and is committed to working in person–centred ways to promote social inclusion. In this respect it is difficult to distinguish between LAC and social services. One difference is that LAC is supposed to be a universal service that can be accessed without assessment.

Despite the recommendations of *The same as you?* and *Changing lives*, the introduction of new legislation, the regular overhaul of service provision, increased regulation, training and surveillance of the workforce and the overarching service delivery principles of 'choice' and 'control', the lives of people with learning disabilities in contemporary Scotland remain impoverished. Because the lives of many, although by no means all, people with a learning disability were blighted by historical approaches to institutional care, the tendency to view current service provision 'in the community' as better prevails. However, in times of economic stringency, people with learning disabilities are 'disproportionately affected through a period of tightening public expenditure' (Learning Disability Alliance Scotland, 2010, p 1).

So, many people with learning disabilities in Scotland today experience little in the way of social justice, which results in their continued marginalisation. Johnson and Walmsley (2010) explore an inherent contradiction in the realisation of a 'good life', as proposed by Western philosophy (of which inclusion in a society's most basic principles is one aspect; Nussbaum, 2006, cited by Johnson and Walmsley, 2010, p 59), for people with learning difficulties. Contemporary policy tends to focus, as this chapter has discussed, on the individual. For people with a learning disability this usually results in a practice focus on individual deficits and outputs such as 'independent travel training', single tenancies with visiting support, and a round of 'community-based' activities such as visiting shopping centres or bowling alleys. For Johnson and Walmsley this ignores the Western philosophical position that possession of reason and the capacity to reflect are constituents of a 'good life'. A lack of reason is, they contend, one of the defining characteristics of a person with a learning disability. Because of this people with learning disabilities are not only discriminated against but the very goal of a good life, as it is seen through Western eyes, is difficult, if not impossible, to attain.

Further, a focus on individual rather than collective responses leaves people already marginalised at risk of further exclusion. In the anxiety not to repeat now discredited historical 'collective' approaches, have opportunities to focus on structural inequalities been lost? Expressions of collective approaches, such as adult training centres or long-stay hospitals, were run counter to 21st-century public policy directives. However, in the view of some service users, not every aspect of such services was negative (see, for example, exhibitions from Sense Scotland, 2009; see also Open University, 2008). Rather, a complex picture of the importance of attachment and sense of belonging emerges.

Social services workers grapple constantly with dilemmas and competing rights and demands. Is Johnson and Walmsley's view compatible with contemporary Scottish social work practice with people who have learning disabilities? For widely accepted contemporary reasons, and in keeping with the law, current practice recognises the human rights of people who have a learning disability and tends to emphasise positive personal capacities. Is the mark of a mature profession, one which has 'come of age', however, not an openness to considering points of view such as Johnson and Walmsley's even if they run counter to the prevailing policy and practice landscape, are challenging, possibly pessimistic and perhaps distasteful?

Conclusion: have Scottish social services come of age?

This chapter refers to many social policy achievements, both pre-devolution and since 1999 in Scottish social services, of which Scotland can be proud. A shining example is the policy *Getting it right for every child* (Scottish Parliament, 2008), whose foundations can be largely attributed to a distinctively Scottish approach in the mid-1960s to the welfare of children and young people who offend or are offended against. The argument presented here is that this enlightened thinking some 50 years ago has helped to shape and inform an integrated and holistic approach to supporting the well-being of children, underpinned by social justice perspectives of equality and human rights.

In social services with people with learning disabilities there has been enduring activity to promote meaningful involvement in service provision and in wider social debates. This contemporary policy imperative (see, for example, Levin, 2004; Duncan, 2007) has been implemented to a greater or lesser extent with people who have learning disabilities throughout the UK and internationally (see, for example, Mitchell et al, 2006). Many people welcome the personalisation agenda in contrast to the oppressive regimes of institutional care, whether in a care home or in 'the community'. Local authority services for adults with learning disabilities have for some years been provided by 'integrated' teams of social work, health and sometimes other professionals (Slevin et al, 2008). This practice is likely to increase as the government responds positively to the recommendations of the Christie Report (The Scottish Government, 2011).

Thus, social services provision for people with learning difficulties in contemporary Scotland shares many aspirational characteristics with that of other nations: a commitment to the involvement of people who use services and their carers in decisions affecting their lives, a move to more 'personalised' services, statutory regulation of services and the increased involvement of the independent sector in service provision. The extent to which these aspirations are realised is debatable but they do fit with the Scottish Executive's vision of a sector that has 'come of age'.

On the face of it, and in relation to these policies, Scotland could be deemed to be well on the way to a fine and wise old age. On the one hand, the call is for collective social responsibility for the well-being of children, and people are to be involved in the development of care services tailored to their individual need. Both, however, are threatened by the combination of non-ring-fenced local authority budgets, the impact of the global financial crisis and the UK and Scottish government responses.

Furthermore, if the impact of poverty and inequality are not acknowledged when a tragedy involving social services occurs, the response tends to be focused on a demonisation of individual workers and the subsequent strengthening of a managerial agenda of standards, regulation and inspection, as opposed to solutions based on an understanding of the social and material aspects of the situation (Ferguson and Lavalette, 2009). We concur with the views expressed by Ritchie and Woodward (2009), which are even more compelling in the political and ideological context at the end of the first decade of the 21st century, that *Changing lives* simply does not fully reflect the social and political reality of Scotland, and that:

> ... [a] lack of concern of broader social justice issues increases the likelihood that there is a transfer of risk to poor communities and to individuals. (Ritchie and Woodward, 2009, p 527)

Social work's own international definition, itself quoted in the 21st-century review, reflects a preferable emphasis to the then Scottish government's definition of a mature social services sector. In our view the language of the international definition of social work reflects a narrative of social justice and human rights, which contrasts favourably with a managerial discourse of performance management, welfare reform and consumerisation of service users and carers contained in the *Changing lives* report. A briefing paper commissioned for the review highlights a common concern expressed by social services workers, that 'Regulation has become more important than promotion of core values' (The Scottish Government, 2005). Regrettably this statement is not fully developed in the review's findings. Internationally agreed and accepted standards are, in our view, better measures by which the maturity of contemporary social services can be measured, given that they reflect the stated value base of the international community of social services workers.

Further resources

Emejulu, A. and Shaw, M. (eds) (2010) *Community empowerment: critical perspectives from Scotland, The Glasgow Papers*, Edinburgh: Community Development Journal, September, www.povertyalliance.org.uk/ckfinder/userfiles/files/research/TheGlasgowPapers.pdf.

Ferguson, I. and Woodward, R. (2009) *Radical social work in practice*, Bristol: The Policy Press.

Hothersall, S. (2010) *Social work with children, young people and their families in Scotland* (2nd edn), Exeter: Learning Matters (www.learningmatters.co.uk).

Johnson, K. and Walmsley, J. with Wolfe, M. (2010) *People with intellectual disabilities: Towards a good life?*, Bristol: The Policy Press.

Macintyre, G. (2008) *Learning disability and social inclusion*, Edinburgh: Dunedin Academic Press.

Social Work Action Network: www.socialworkfuture.org

Child Poverty Action Group (CPAG) in Scotland: www.cpag.org.uk/scotland

Scottish Consortium for Learning Disability: www.scld.org.uk

People First (Scotland): www.peoplefirstscotland.org

Learning Disability Alliance Scotland: www.ldascotland.org

References

Ager, W. and McPhail, M. (2008) 'Issues of power in service user and carer involvement: partnership, process and outcomes', in M. McPhail (ed) *Service user and carer involvement: Beyond good intentions*, Glasgow: Dunedin Press, pp 7-22.

Aldgate, J. (2009) *The impact of devolution for children in Scotland*, K802 'Critical practice with children and young people', Milton Keynes: The Open University.

Anderson, N. and Langa, A. (1997) 'The development of institutional care for "idiots" and "imbeciles" in Scotland', *History of Psychiatry*, vol 8, no 30, pp 243-66.

Asquith, S. and Stafford, A. (1995) *Families and the future*, Edinburgh: HMSO.

Atkinson, D., Jackson, M. and Walmsley, J. (1997) *Forgotten lives: Exploring the history of learning disability*, Kidderminster: BILD Publications.

Atkinson, D., Nind, M., Rolph, S. and Welshman, J. (2005) *Witnesses to change: Families, learning difficulties and history*, Kidderminster: BILD Publications.

Birrell, D. (2007) 'Devolution and social care: are there four systems of social care in the United Kingdom?', Paper presented at the Social Policy Association Conference, University of Birmingham (www.sochealth.co.uk/news/birrell.htm).

Birrell, D. (2009) *The impact of devolution on social policy*, Bristol: The Policy Press.

Chih, H.S., Hedges, A., Cook, C., Mguni, N. and Comber, N. (2009) *Disabled people's experiences of targeted violence and hostility*, Research Report 21, Manchester: Office for Public Management.

Devaney, J. (2009) 'Chronic child abuse: the characteristics and careers of children caught up in the child protection system', *British Journal of Social Work*, vol 39, no 1, pp 24-45.

Duffy, S (2010) 'The citizenship theory of social justice: exploring the meaning of personalisation for social workers', *Journal of Social Work Practice*, vol 24, no 3, pp 235-67.

Duncan, B. (2007) 'Inspecting for improvement in Scotland', *Journal of Care Services Management*, vol 2, no 1, pp 17-27.

Dyson, C. (2008) *Poverty and child maltreatment, NSPCC child protection* (www.nspcc.org.uk/Inform/research/briefings/poverty_wda56897.html).

Edinburgh and Lothian's Child Protection Committee (2003) *The report of the Caleb Ness Inquiry*, Edinburgh, Edinburgh and Lothian's Child Protection Committee.

Emerson, E. (2007) *The mental health of children and adolescents with learning disabilities in Britain*, Lancaster: Institute for Health Research.

Enable (1999) *Stop it! Bullying and harassment of people with learning disabilities*, Glasgow: Enable.

Enable (2007) *Speak up! The bullying of children with learning disabilities*, Glasgow: Enable.

Fabb, J. and Guthrie, T.G. (1992) *Social work and the law in Scotland*, Edinburgh: Butterworths.

Ferguson, I. (2005) 'Social work and social care in the "new" Scotland', in G. Mooney and G. Scott (eds) *Exploring social policy in the 'new' Scotland*, Bristol: The Policy Press, pp 221–38.

Ferguson, I. (2007) 'Increasing user choice or privatizing risk? The antinomies of personalisation', *British Journal of Social Work*, vol 37, no 3, pp 387–403.

Ferguson, I. and Lavalette, M. (eds) (2009) *Social work after Baby P*, Liverpool: Liverpool Hope University.

Healthcare Commission (2007) *Investigation into the service for people with learning disabilities provided by Sutton and Merton Primary Care Trust*, London: Healthcare Commission.

HMSO (Her Majesty's Stationery Office) (1969) *Report of the Committee of Inquiry into allegations of ill-treatment of patients and other irregularities at the Ely Hospital Cardiff*, Cmnd 3975, London: HMSO.

IFSW (International Federation of Social Workers) and IASSW (International Association of Schools of Social Work) (2004) *Ethics in social work, Statement of principles*, Bern (www.ifsw.org/p38000324.html).

Ingham, N. (ed) (2002) *Gogarburn lives*, Edinburgh: Living Memory Association.

Jessop, B. (2002) *The future of the capitalist state*, Cambridge: Polity Press.

Johnson, K. and Walmsley, J. with Woolfe, M. (2010) *People with intellectual disabilities. Towards a good life?*, Bristol: The Policy Press.

Learning Disability Alliance Scotland (2010) *Written submission to the Scottish Government Equal Opportunities Committee* (www.scottish.parliament.uk/s3/committees/equal/Budget%20process%202011-12/subs/BSP08LDA.pdf).

Levin, E. (2004) *Involving service users and carers in social work education*, London: Social Care Institute for Excellence.

London Borough of Brent (1985) *A child in trust, Panel of Enquiry into the circumstances surrounding the death of Jasmine Beckford*, Wembley: London Borough of Brent.

MacGreggor, F. (2004) 'Vulnerable youngsters remain at risk in city', *Edinburgh Evening News*, 14 August.

Macintyre, G. (2008) *Learning disability and social inclusion*, Edinburgh: Dunedin Academic Press.

Mackay, K. and Woodward, R. (2010) 'Exploring the place of values in the new social work degree in Scotland', *Journal of Social Work Education: The International Journal*, vol 29, issue 6, pp 633–45.

Mendes, P. (2006) 'Welfare lobby groups responding to globalization – a case study of the Australian Council of Social Service', *International Social Work*, vol 49, no 6, pp 693–704.

Mitchell, D., Traustadòttir, R., Chapman, R., Townson, L., Ingham, N. and Ledger, S. (eds) (2006) *Exploring experiences of advocacy by people with learning disabilities: Testimonies of resistance*, London: Jessica Kingsley Publishers.

Mooney, G. (2008) 'Explaining poverty, social exclusion and inequality: towards a structural approach', in T. Ridge and S. Wright (eds) *Understanding inequality, poverty, wealth*, Bristol: The Policy Press, pp 61–78.

Mooney, G. and Scott, G. (eds) (2005) *Exploring social policy in the 'new' Scotland*, Bristol: The Policy Press.

Mooney, G., Sweeney, T. and Law, A. (eds) (2006) *Social care, health and welfare in contemporary Scotland*, Paisley: Kynloch and Blaney.

NCH Scotland (2004) *Where is Kilbrandon now? Report and recommendations from the Inquiry*, Glasgow: NCH (www.actionforchildren.org/search-results?q=Kilbrandon).

Nussbaum, M. (2006) *Frontiers of justice. Disability nationality species membership*, Cambridge: Harvard University Press.

Open University (2008) *Days gone by. The history of day centres for people with learning disabilities in Croydon*, Croydon: Museum of Croydon.

Parckar, G. (2008) *Disability poverty in the UK*, London: Leonard Cheshire Disability.

Parekh, A. (2010) *Monitoring poverty and social exclusion in Scotland*, York: Joseph Rowntree Foundation (www.jrf.org.uk/publications/mopes-scotland-2010).

Petch, A. (2007) 'Care citizenship and community in Scotland', in S. Balloch and M. Hill (eds) *Care community and citizenship research and practice in a changing policy context*, Bristol: The Policy Press.

Quarriers (2008*) Missed out: Missing out adults with learning disabilities who live in the family home and their right to recognition and resources*, Bridge of Weir: Quarriers.

Ritchie, A. and Woodward, R. (2009) '*Changing lives*: critical reflections on the social work change programme for Scotland', *Critical Social Policy*, vol 29, no 3, pp 510-32.

Scott, G. and Mooney, G. (2009) 'Poverty and social justice in the devolved Scotland: neoliberalism meets social democracy?', *Social Policy and Society*, vol 8, no 3, pp 379-89.

Scottish Executive (1999) *Aiming for excellence: Modernising social work*, Edinburgh: Scottish Executive.

Scottish Executive (2000a) *The way forward to care: A policy position paper*, Edinburgh: Scottish Executive.

Scottish Executive (2000b) *The same as you? A review of services for people with learning disabilities*, Edinburgh: Scottish Executive.

Scottish Executive (2001) *Changing for the future, social services for the 21st century*, Edinburgh: Scottish Executive.

Scottish Executive (2002) *'It's everyone's job to make sure I'm alright', Report of the Child Protection Audit and Review*, Edinburgh: Scottish Executive.

Scottish Executive (2003) *Partnership for a better Scotland*, Edinburgh: Scottish Executive (www.scotland.gov.uk/Publications/2003/05/17150/21952).

Scottish Executive (2004) *Investigations into Scottish Borders Council and NHS Borders Services for people with learning disabilities: Joint statement from the Mental Welfare Commission and the Social Work Services Inspectorate* (www.scotland.gov.uk/Publications/2004/05/19333/36719).

Scottish Executive (2006a) *Changing lives: Report of the 21st century social work review*, Edinburgh: Scottish Executive.

Scottish Executive (2006b) *Scottish Executive response to the report of the 21st century social work review: Changing lives*, Edinburgh: Scottish Executive.

Scottish Executive (2006c) *Key capabilities in child care and protection*, Edinburgh: Scottish Executive.

Scottish Government, The (2005) *The role of the social worker in the 21st century: A literature review* (www.scotland.gov/Publications/2005/12/1994633/46338).

Scottish Government, The (2011) *Commission on the Future of Public Services* (The Christie Report), Edinburgh: Crown Office.

Scottish Office (1964) *The Kilbrandon Report, children and young persons, Scotland, Report by the Committee appointed by the Secretary of State for Scotland*, Edinburgh: HMSO.

Scottish Parliament (2008) *Getting it right for every child* (www.scotland.gov.uk/Topics/People/YoungPeople/childrensservices/girfec).

Scottish Parliament (2009) *SPICe briefing, UK budget 2009*, Edinburgh: Scottish Parliament (www.scottish.parliament.uk/business/research/briefings-09/SB09-26.pdf).

Sense Scotland (2009) *In our own voices: Leaving New Craigs*, Glasgow: Sense Scotland.

Slevin, E., Truesdale-Kennedy, M., McConkey, R., Barr, O. and Taggart, L. (2008) 'Community learning disability teams: developments, composition and good practice', *Journal of Intellectual Disabilities*, vol 12, no 1, pp 59-79.

Stalker, K., Cadogan, L. and Petrie, M. (1999) *'If you don't ask you don't get': Review of services to people with learning disabilities: The views of people who use services and their carers*, Edinburgh: Scottish Executive.

Stalker, K., Malloch, M., Barry, M. and Watson, J. (2007) *Evaluation of the implementation of local area co-ordination in Scotland*, Edinburgh: Scottish Executive.

Stewart, J. (2004) *Taking stock, Scottish social welfare after devolution*, Bristol: The Policy Press.

UN (United Nations) (1989) *UN Convention on the Rights of the Child*, Geneva: UN.

Waterhouse, L., McGhee, J., Whyte, W., Loucks, N., Kay, H. and Stewart, R. (2000) *The evaluation of Children's Hearings in Scotland*, Edinburgh: Scottish Executive Central Research Unit.

Williams, R. (1975) *Keywords: A vocabulary of culture and society*, Glasgow: Fontana.

NINE

Education policy and social justice

Margaret Arnott and Jenny Ozga

Introduction

This chapter looks at the ways in which education, as a policy field, has been connected to the wider concern of social justice. Since 2007 this agenda has been set within the context of the Scottish government's 'project' of achieving greater autonomy and ultimately independence (The Scottish Government, 2010), a 'project' that has entered a new phase following the Scottish National Party's (SNP) success at 2011 Scottish Parliament elections. By winning 69 seats the SNP secured a majority in the Scottish Parliament and ensured that for the first time the devolved Scottish government would be able to secure a working majority in the Scottish Parliament (Herbert et al, 2011). The scale of the party's victory in May 2011 has undoubtedly changed the political context of territorial politics and governance in the UK. For the SNP government its electoral success in the devolved 2011 election has added legitimacy to its 'project' of securing both enhanced powers for the Scottish Parliament and also its wider goal of independence. The SNP government has argued that this project has entered a new stage:

> We [the SNP] have won their trust and we will not abuse it. We know they are listening, keen to hear the positive story we have to tell about the future – their future as parents, students, workers, pensioners, carers, entrepreneurs and professionals. They share our excitement about the project at hand – to build a better nation. The people are ready to move on to the next chapter of Scotland's story. (Salmond, 2011a)

Another related intriguing question raised by the 2011 result is how the party responds in terms of its approach to governing. In this chapter we explore how the SNP approached governing as a minority government in its first term of office (2007–11). As a majority government the SNP will have an enhanced position vis-à-vis the devolved Parliament, but we caution against assuming this will lead the party to undertake a wholesale change in its approach to governing. Early indications are that the experience of governing as a minority administration both within and, perhaps even more pertinently, beyond the Parliament will continue to influence how the new majority devolved government approaches policy making. This approach was crucial to the party's attempts to build a record of competence in government. There are two important related factors that might suggest we are likely to see important continuities with the approach to governing as a minority administration. First, while the party secured a historic victory in the 2011 devolved Scottish election, building support for its wider goal of independence remains crucial to the party. To secure support among the wider Scottish public for its vision of independence in advance of a referendum the SNP government will need to continue to 'build consensus'. Much of the party's strategy in government since 2007 has been to view independence as a process. Frequent reference was made in the 2011 party manifesto to Scotland 'being on a journey' (SNP, 2011). Second, much was made by the Scottish government in its first term of office of the move towards outcomes-based policy making. We discuss this in more detail below, but again, early indications are the SNP majority government would wish to continue with this broad approach to governing.

However, while the Scottish government may argue that its approach will remain one of looking 'to build consensus' (Salmond, 2011b), the economic pressures facing the Scottish Parliament are of such an order that a highly charged political environment seems inevitable (Audit Scotland, 2011a, 2011b). Reform of the public services is likely to be one of the most contentious areas facing the SNP majority administration. Shortly before the 2011 Scottish Parliament election the Scottish government established the Commission on the Future Delivery of Public Services to consider how public services could be delivered in the context of reducing public expenditure and rising demand. The Commission's report, issued in June 2011, argued that 'Scotland's public services are in need of urgent and sustained reform to meet unprecedented challenges' (The Scottish Government, 2011). Public expenditure reductions was one pressure for change but the Commission also stressed that, 'Despite a series of Scottish Government initiatives and significant growth in public spending post devolution, on most key measures social and economic inequalities have remained unchanged or become more pronounced' (The Scottish Government, 2011). Preventative measures to tackle social and economic inequalities have been identified as a priority area for the new majority administration (Gourtsoyannis, 2011; Salmond, 2011a). Education, especially in terms of early intervention reforms, will feature prominently in the government's response to the Christie Commission (Russell, 2011).

This chapter is not a comprehensive review of education policy since May 2007; rather, we focus on an analysis of selected issues in education that have a bearing on our understanding of how governing education relates to social justice. Our argument, put briefly, is this, that, as a minority administration the SNP government of 2007–11 was heavily dependent on discourse, that education as a policy field offers resources that can be discursively mobilised to enable the projection of the Scottish government as a 'learning' government that combines a focus on education as a source of economic recovery and independence with an agenda of fairness and inclusion (Arnott and Ozga, 2010a). The practicalities of minority government in Scotland meant that the SNP had to govern on the basis of cooperation and consensus, which created a space for debate about governance and policy making, their best forms and processes and their purposes (see, for example, the National Conversation [a consulation on Scotland's future constitutional arrangements) (The Scottish Government, 2007a). We believe that the SNP will continue to adopt this approach post-May 2011. Discursive strategies will continue to be used by the SNP government in its attempts to build a consensus around its vision for the future of Scotland. Discourse will continue to be a key resource to shape both policy and the style of governance. In making this argument, we are drawing on an Economic and Social Research Council (ESRC)-funded study of 'Education and nationalism: the discourse of policy in Scotland' (RES-000-22-2893) which we carried out between 2008 and 2009, as well as on more recent research on the relationship between knowledge and policy in education in Scotland (EU FP6 IP 028848-2). Both of these research projects involved extensive interviewing of government officials and policy makers, and we draw on these unattributed interviews throughout this chapter. In the interviews, we asked SNP politicians about how they 'crafted the narrative' (as one of them put it) that both reflected and promoted their policy directions as a minority administration, and we asked officials about the sources of information that were being used in policy, and the kinds of expertise that were mobilised.

Based on these data, we concluded that interdependencies between the layers of governance have been used by the SNP administration in its attempts to build trust and credibility with policy makers and wider policy actors. Growing financial pressures facing the devolved government will place increasing pressure on relationships between government and policy actors. The government presented governing discursively as co-dependent, based on partnership, and negotiated, thus turning their minority position into a source of strength. It is too early to say whether the new majority administration will be able to continue with this strategy with the same degree of success as before 2011. A related argument presented here is that education policy in Scotland has in recent years become increasingly 'Europeanised'. Whatever their political complexion, devolved governments in Scotland have to respond to the increasing significance of Europe in social policy. After some background on developments in education/learning in the wider European and global context, we review some key developments in education policy from this perspective.

Education as a policy field in the contemporary context

Education is an arena of social and public policy that has often been associated with social justice (Gewirtz and Cribb, 2009), although sometimes with unrealistic expectations that education is capable of overcoming the effects of poverty and prejudice, that it can, despite Bernstein's famous and trenchant argument, 'compensate for society', despite much evidence to the contrary (see, among many others, Bernstein, 1971). The relationship between education, or rather education/learning policy, and social justice (however that is defined) is at a particularly interesting juncture not only in Scotland but more widely, as education becomes more important within the UK and Europe, and increasingly connected to other social policy areas, including health (Grek et al, 2009). The growth in significance follows from the central place that education/learning occupies as the vehicle of economic growth (and now of recovery) in a context in which the European Community (EC) is striving to create the most competitive knowledge economy and society in the world. Education/learning is now seen by policy makers across Europe and beyond as a key arena of social policy, not only in terms of economic regeneration but also to help combat social exclusion and build 'well-being'. This is a substantial shift away from a situation where, in Europe: 'education is, by definition, the space for the construction of national identity' (Nóvoa, 2000, p 46). That close bond has been loosened in the 21st century, as education is required to serve a globally ordered knowledge economy and enable the development of a knowledge society, transcending national frontiers (Ozga and Lingard, 2007). The consequence is increased homogeneity in policy in education, as Ball (1998) has put it, the emergence of 'big' policies for a 'small world', or of a global education policy field, dominated by transnational agencies (like the Organisation for Economic Co-operation and Development, OECD) that tend to ignore national traditions and practices. There may be tensions between nationally embedded social and cultural constructions of education and the strong economically driven agendas for 'modernisation' and lifelong learning that are promoted by transnational agencies, including the OECD and the European Union (EU), and that have been highly influential in UK, especially in policy making in education in England (Ozga et al, 2011).

In this situation, the policy field is subject to considerable pressure, pressure to deliver the knowledge economy, which has intensified since the financial crisis, as well as pressure to support social solidarity, perhaps especially through inclusive education policies for migrants and the avoidance of a 'residual category' of underperforming young people, whose lack of qualifications correlates with their low socioeconomic status. Economic improvement is assumed to follow from raising performance in education, which often creates a regime of competitive testing (Grek et al, 2009), while inclusion policies are inhibited by the emphasis on 'hard' indicators and the consequent 'cooling out' of many young people for whom schooling is an unproductive experience, as the OECD report noted with reference to Scotland (OECD, 2007). It is against that context, of considerable tensions in policy across Europe and the UK, with systems reshaping themselves in order to promote diversity of provision (for example, through the so-called 'free schools' advanced by the UK Conservative/Liberal Democrat government and with increasing concern about the 'vocationalisation' of education and its possible consequences) that this discussion of selected features of the education policy is set.

From 2007 the SNP government attempted to manage tensions in education policy through working with global economic 'travelling' policy but combined in distinctive ways with 'embedded' references to fairness and direct prioritisation of action to break the link between poverty and educational failure (Arnott and Ozga, 2010a). The embedded references are mobilised through invocation of 'shaping myths' (McPherson and Raab, 1988) of fairness and egalitarianism that position Scotland in a social democratic policyscape alongside the Nordic social democracies. The official discourse drew on and simultaneously fostered this positioning while clearly referencing global economic priorities. The policy discourse supports the creation of 'new' Scots who are 'better educated, more skilled and more successful, renowned for our research and innovation', and young people are expected to be and to become 'successful learners, confident individuals, effective contributors and responsible citizens' (Hyslop, 2007a). Yet even in this rather direct translation of OECD priorities into education policy, there was an attempt to mobilise public support through the use of key terms that resonate with traditions and mythologies of education in Scotland. We develop this argument in more detail in the next section.

Education policy and the devolved government since 2007

Education has played a particularly strong role historically in the shaping and support of national identity (McCrone, 1992; Keating, 2010). The SNP government drew on key discursive resources to draw out and promote elements that were already implicit in much education discourse, that connect to ideas of fairness and equality. They were able to draw on established myths and traditions that reference the 'public' nature of schooling and its role in both the construction of 'community' and in driving economic progress. In his speech to the SNP conference in March 2011, for example, Alex Salmond argued:

> And this nation pioneered free education for all, which resulted in Scots inventing and explaining much of the modern world. We called this the Scottish Enlightenment. And out of educational access came social mobility as we reached all the talents of a nation to change the world for the better.
>
> We can do so again.... The rocks will melt with the sun before I allow tuition fees to be imposed on Scottish students – upfront, or backdoor....
>
> This is part of the Scottish Settlement, our social contract with the people. In the course of this coming week the Scottish Government intends to move forward again with that contract. (Salmond, 2011c)

Of course education as a policy field had been referenced long before 2007 as marking off difference from England, a trend accentuated during the Conservative UK administrations of 1979–97. Neoliberal principles of system redesign had less impact in Scotland, and this is attributed to the tradition of central regulation there, and the strong sense of civic identity that can be traced to the loss of national sovereignty in 1707, and the consequent central role played by its core institutions

– the church, law and education (Arnott and Menter, 2007). Throughout the 1980s, we can trace the history of the attempted introduction of market-driven, performance management policies in Scotland that were either resisted or adapted so that they were introduced in diluted forms, for example, with no national testing regime or system of performance-related pay for teachers; and nor has parental choice of school operated to anything like the same extent as it has in England. In Scotland these policies were also widely seen as a threat to the distinctive Scottish education system from a Conservative government that was perceived as not having democratic legitimacy in Scotland (Arnott, 2005). On one aspect of Conservative policy – national testing of pupils in primary schools – the opposition of parents and the policy community in Scotland was mobilised to the extent that the government had to withdraw its policy (Paterson, 1997). The UK Labour governments of 1997–2010 continued to emphasise improving standards and performance through competition and these directions were echoed, in a rather muted form, by the Labour-dominated administrations in Scotland from 1999 to 2007. In other words, although the overall direction of policy was shared across England and Scotland, in terms of prioritising testing and improving performance, policies on the ground in Scotland were not so market-driven, with less emphasis on competition between schools, and without the performance management and inspection regimes that were adopted in England (Croxford et al, 2002). Resistance to testing and competition in Scotland was explained by reference to the public nature of provision and its importance as a collective good (Arnott and Menter, 2007).

In the first months of the SNP administration in 2007, there seemed to be a high degree of continuity with both the UK government's education policy agenda and that of the previous administration in Scotland – most references were to the knowledge economy and its imperatives. This is evident in the First Minister's presentation of the strategic objectives of the new government to the Scottish Parliament in both 2007 and 2011 (Salmond, 2007, 2011a). Here the need for an education and skills strategy to support economic development is presented with little reference to education as a resource for fairness or new forms of national identification. Early statements by the Cabinet Secretary for Education, Fiona Hyslop, also stress the need to tie education to the promotion of sustained economic growth (Hyslop, 2007b). However, there is a shift towards incorporating education's capacity to address problems of poverty. The key discursive shift is that of referencing poverty alongside wealth creation in setting the agenda for education: while the need for improved performance is stressed, it is framed by discussion of the obstacles to success encountered by children and young people who lack material and other resources. The findings of the recent Christie Commission alongside ministerial statements following the 2011 election suggest this approach will remain key to the government's strategy in education. In September 2011 the Cabinet Secretary for Education and Lifelong Learning, Michael Russell, argued:

We will continue to implement 'Getting It Right For Every Child' – ensuring the resources deliver for all, including the most vulnerable children. For our most vulnerable children, we will see a greater focus on early intervention to achieve stability and improved outcomes. There are hard-edged economic benefits to early intervention. Early and effective intervention can significantly reduce costs to the state, both in the short and long term, and deliver better results for the individuals involved.

We set out clearly our commitment to supporting children in their earliest years and have talked about the need for a fundamental shift in philosophy and approach. A shift away from intervening only when a crisis happens to prevention and early intervention. (Russell, 2011)

There are examples of policy interventions that are harnessed explicitly to the 'fairer' agenda: for example, long-term investments to be made in young people who do not achieve examination success are now described as targeted at those who need 'more choices and more chances' (MCMC) rather than those 'not in' the system (the previous descriptor carried exclusionary messages about 'those not in education, employment or training, NEET; see also Chapter Ten, this volume). In redefining this group, the Scottish government worked discursively by placing the discussion in the context of descriptions of a system that was successful and worked well for most, thereby underlining Scotland's tradition of meritocratic egalitarianism (Grek et al, 2009) while simultaneously underlining the obligation to help particular groups overcome their material disadvantages, and making links to knowledge economy priorities. The previous Labour/Liberal Democrat Coalition administration had prioritised investment in both early years and the NEET group (Croxford et al, 2002), and so we wish to emphasise that we are not suggesting that the SNP developed a new policy direction. What is important for our purposes is to illustrate the new way in which this policy was promoted. It is harnessed more explicitly to the 'fairer' agenda and a significant issue here is the long horizon – the minority SNP Scottish government positioned itself as strategic despite its minority position. Three main strategic areas were identified in terms of education policy: the early years agenda; 'Curriculum for Excellence' (CfE); and the skills strategy.

A further point, stressed by the Scottish government members in our interviews, was that policy differed from the previous administration because of its scope (looking across the lifecourse and all policy areas) and its means of development and delivery. Policy makers stressed that in both development and delivery of education policy 'social partners' played a key role and saw this as consistent with social democratic policy.

At the same time as increasing the frequency of international referencing, and focusing on key comparators in the Nordic states, the Scottish government began to extend the *principles* of comparison so that they were extended beyond education performance and more generalised across social policy areas, thus offering an agenda that placed education in the wider framework of social policy and social issues. OECD data on a range of indicators, not just educational performance, were used to create an independent research report – the Index of Children's Well-being in Scotland. Categories included suicide rates, dental health, child poverty, teenage pregnancy rates and so on, and Scotland came almost last of 24 OECD comparator 'Western' countries. This selection of data showed severe poverty-related problems in Scotland and the need for a more considered approach to children's services as a whole. This attention to the social indicators of health, wealth and well-being enabled the further development of a modernised nationalist narrative, one that takes some embedded myths or ideals about Scotland and brings them into relationship with continuing social problems, and thus creates a narrative of urgency within Scotland that closely aligns wealth creation with 'fairness'. The two strands of the discourse were combined in December 2007 when the Cabinet Secretary for Education used these data to support the SNP government's policy towards investment and intervention in early education. The speech illustrates the SNP's focus, combining attention to the economy and addressing problems of poverty and society, and illustrating a shift in emphasis towards provision for the 'whole' child, rather than focusing on education as a separate policy sphere:

> Finally, only yesterday, the programme for international student assessment – PISA – report was published. It showed that Scotland's reading and maths scores have experienced one of the highest drops of all the Organisation for Economic Co-operation and Development countries. Scotland also has one of the biggest gaps in performance, which can be identified as related to poverty and deprivation. If we are to tackle Scotland's challenges as identified in the international PISA survey and to climb back up the international tables, we must deal with poverty at its roots and tackle the impact that it can have on families. (Hyslop, 2007b)

The focus on the 'whole' child, in order to better understand and address problems of poverty and underachievement, is referenced by a number of the devolved government officials who were interviewed for the research projects on which this text is based. Most of them put emphasis on the strategic use of data that the SNP government was pursuing, which was often contrasted with the policies and practices of the previous coalition administration. According to one interviewee, the new policies had 'liberated' public servants to "... collaborate to deliver some improvement in some form of public service".

Collaboration and further integration was not only about joining up government; interviewees suggested that partnerships ensured safer transitions for children and young people, where the focus of the service was not only on the service itself at the time of its delivery but crucially on the progression of young people through to the next stages in their lives as well:

"We are shifting that emphasis and we have now got better partnership working with people. Also the idea that you are responsible for the progression of that young person as much as you are when the young person is with you. And that looks to be improving policy delivery for young people and that I think is a good example. And we know from the feedback we are getting from our partners in local government, colleges and young people as well.'" (Interview with a policy officer)

Policy makers suggested that the steer towards outcomes rather than inputs is central in education. There was a tension between those predominantly input-driven targets set out in the 2007 SNP manifesto such as teacher numbers, nursery places and class sizes, with the outcomes or outputs set out within the National Performance Framework. The objective from the Scottish government's viewpoint was to convey a sense of the ways in which government can promote a cultural shift in the governing of Scotland, in the field of education, in such a way as to interweave strategic direction, deregulation, the active participation of partners and the combined purposes of improving performance and fairness of outcomes.

Education policy and the 'learning government'

In this section, we look in more detail at the relationship between policy for education and learning and the context of wider changes in the governing and management of public sector services. One of the key developments in education policy since 2007 has been to change the approach to policy making (Arnott and Ozga, 2010b). These changes were designed to increase devolution of responsibility away from the centre, and to signal a clear move away from target setting and central surveillance.

The National Performance Framework, which was adopted in 2007, exists:

> ... to focus Government and public services on creating a more successful country, with opportunities for all of Scotland to flourish, through increasing sustainable economic growth. (The Scottish Government, 2007b)

It consists of seven purpose targets, 15 national outcomes and 45 national indicators, and it not only exemplifies a new relationship with local government, but also offers a good example of the deployment of discursive resources to shift culture and behaviour in Scottish government. The framework is driven by a narrative that has an overarching theme: the pursuit of economic prosperity (now recovery) in order to achieve a wealthier and fairer, healthier, safer and stronger, smarter and greener Scotland. As is evident from other chapters, this framework is easily understood and referenced across the different social and public policy fields. It links wealth and fairness and so defines economic growth as a public good. The text conveys direction and clarity, claiming and exhibiting the authority of the government through its statement of purpose.

The production of wealth and fairness are linked in the framework; economic growth is defined as a public good. Government is positioned as strategic, and improvement in performance is discursively aligned with quality of life for 'people in Scotland'.

> Purpose and all performance management systems will therefore be aligned to a single, clear and consistent set of priorities. (The Scottish Government, 2007b, p 12)

The Scottish government's purpose is stated directly: as 'to focus the Government and public services on creating a more successful country, with opportunities for all of Scotland to flourish, through increasing sustainable economic growth' (The Scottish Government, 2007b, p 2), and the key national outcomes mix economic and social justice outcomes with a considerable emphasis on issues of poverty and inequality.

National outcomes

- We live in a Scotland that is the most attractive place for doing business in Europe.
- We realise our full economic potential with more and better employment opportunities for our people.
- We are better educated, more skilled and more successful, renowned for our research and innovation.
- Our young people are successful learners, confident individuals, effective contributors and responsible citizens.
- Our children have the best start in life and are ready to succeed.
- We live longer, healthier lives.
- We have tackled the significant inequalities in Scottish society.
- We have improved the life chances for children, young people and families at risk.
- We have strong, resilient and supportive communities where people take responsibility for their own actions and how they affect others.
- We take pride in a strong, fair and inclusive national identity.
- Our public services are high quality, continually improving, efficient and responsive to local people's needs.

(The Scottish Government, 2007b, p 46)

The framework was an initial step in a wide-ranging Scottish government review of policy making in 2008 that advocated a further move towards more collaborative approaches, especially in a new relationship, described as a 'Concordat' with local government in the co-production of policy. There is considerable emphasis, in the documentation produced for this review, on the need to free up knowledge through more experimentation and on ensuring more system learning at all levels. In this the role of evidence, alongside and in relationship with evaluation, are seen as critical drivers of learning (Sanderson, 2009). There is a more strategic approach to developing evaluation capacity reflected in the doubling in the number of economists, social researchers and statisticians working in government and their greater integration and closer working with policy officials to increase analysis and evidence. A further important development is signalled in the Crerar Report of Regulation, Audit, Inspection and Complaints handling of Public Services in Scotland (Crerar, 2007).

This is linked to the changing political landscape in Scotland. Since the establishment of the Scottish Parliament in 1999 there has been a growing awareness of the need for new forms of accountability that strengthen democratic scrutiny (Commission on Scottish Devolution, 2009). This has been evident in education policy through requiring scrutiny bodies (such as the Inspectorate) to account for their activities and costs to Parliament as well as to ministers. The Crerar Report also called for more involvement of service users and the public in the process, to respond to the government's devolution of responsibility for managing and monitoring services to front-line providers. The report recognised, and endorsed, the Scottish government's aim of reducing 'the centrally imposed bureaucracy associated with planning, performance reporting and funding' (Crerar, 2007, p 15), but also underlined the need created by this shift for providers to 'take greater responsibility for monitoring and evaluating their own performance and tackling poor performance when it occurs' (p 15). It suggests that this development had been held back by poor baseline information about performance, which has now been improved, along with 'a wider lack of trust between the Scottish Government and service providers' (p 16).

It is recognised that performance management arrangements are moving towards an outcomes focus, and with a greater degree of self-assessment. For example, the report noted that the performance management framework for local government was being developed in conjunction with Audit Scotland, the Convention of Scottish Local Authorities (COSLA) and the local government Improvement Service. It goes on to note the development of self-assessment in education, where HM Inspectorate of Education (HMIE) is working closely with providers to develop self-assessment. In summary, they suggest that ministers are promoting a culture of continuous improvement for all public services and wish to reduce unnecessary bureaucracy, but in return providers must take greater responsibility for monitoring and evaluating their own performance. New performance management arrangements are developing, which will – apparently – mean that more reliance can be placed on the capacity of service providers to manage services and account for performance (Crerar, 2007, p 16). There is, then, evidence of an attempted shift in the governing culture in Scotland, promoted discursively through the presentation of government as strategic and as working in collaboration with its partners to generate new knowledge leading to continuous improvement. Indeed the culture of government, we argue, is shifted discursively towards that of continuous learning.

School self-evaluation is a particularly instructive example of this larger shift. It moves away from the regulation of performance associated with external mechanisms to a focus on the school, and on engendering in the school a commitment to the constant production and review of knowledge about performance that defines a 'learning organisation' (Senge et al, 1999). Indeed it could be said that school self-evaluation reflects the knowledge economy paradigm in its most developed form: that is, as not simply pre-occupied with ensuring improved performance, but as transforming organisations (whether schools or businesses) into learning institutions that, through their constant production of knowledge about what and how they know, become sites of competitive advantage and also of 'governing knowledge' (Ozga, 2009; Ball, 2011).

Thus the shift towards self-evaluation fits within the wider agenda of economising schooling/learning, and indeed draws on contemporary developments in the 'economics of knowledge' (Foray, 2004) that sees members of learning organisations as contributing added value through their continuous learning, which generates new, productive, knowledge not for the individual learner, but for the organisation (OECD, 2007). This approach, it is argued, also reduces costs, because it is less reliant on external mechanisms to monitor performance, while engendering relations of trust, transparency and openness within the organisation, that are conducive to 'real' learning. As the key school self-evaluation text *How Good is our School?* (HMIe, 2007) makes clear, self-evaluation is used as a tool to encode school knowledge, create consensus and promote specific values that relate to the creation of self-managed and self-sufficient individuals (both teachers and pupils). In other words, schools and their teachers and pupils become members of learning organisations, embedded within the larger learning organisation of the local authority and of government itself.

> The evaluative activities involved are similar to those which we encourage pupils to engage in as part of their own learning process. Taking part in them creates a community of learners. (HMIe, 2007)

School self-evaluation, where HMIe work closely with providers, signalling a move away from their previous judgemental role towards one of support and development, is an example of the discursive construction of a culture of continuous improvement for all public services in which providers must take greater responsibility for monitoring and evaluating their own performance. School self-evaluation and the role of the Inspectorate as 'teachers' of good practice is presented as enabling greater autonomy in schools and local government, thus supporting better outcomes. Service providers manage services and account for performance while learning from self-evaluation, not only in schools and schooling, but also across government. This strategy of promoting an image of collective learning incorporates public and professionals in governing practices and relations: it is considerably cheaper than externally driven performance monitoring systems, and it also builds a sense of collective identification with the 'project' of increased autonomy aligned with improvement.

This 'freeing up' of energy and initiative in education is discursively linked by members of the SNP government to growing political maturity and to independence – for pupils, teachers and local government, and, by extension, to the members of an independent nation. It was framed in terms of both policy makers and students in Scottish education being required to take responsibility and initiative, rather than accepting a top–down approach to decision making. The SNP government's approach to curricular reform has echoes of the same approach.

Reforming the school curriculum has been a key part of devolved education policy since 2003. Both the Labour/Liberal Democrat Coalition government during 2003–07 and the SNP minority government during 2007–11 have regarded the CfE as a landmark reform (Scottish Executive, 2006; The Scottish Government, 2007c, 2008). The rationale of the reform was to move away from a centrally determined curriculum to one that emphasised professional autonomy in the classroom and learners' responsibility for learning. Elsewhere we have argued that there has been a subtle but significant shift in the policy context in which the CfE has been presented. For the Coalition administration a key driver of curricular reform was 'modernisation' of the knowledge economy, whereas the SNP administration has sought to show how curricular reform can be part of addressing wider social inequalities:

> CfE was promoted as an example of a European – even global – policy agenda for increased 'personalisation' of learning with attention to building learners' confidence, enterprise and a range of intelligences in order to better align schooling with KE [knowledge economy] requirements for self-managing, responsible entrepreneurs. The SNP administration does not neglect the economic imperatives, far from it, but it aligns the delivery of CfE more directly to ideas of using education to challenge inequalities. (Arnott and Ozga, 2010a, p 345)

Conclusion

We have tried to show how the SNP government has attempted to align economic and social justice agendas in education, and we have also discussed the importance of the Nordic social democratic states as models to which reference may be made. In terms of education policy making, we suggest that North American, rather than European, models dominate UK policy, despite the UK Coalition government's references to Finland. We suggest that, especially since the formation of the Conservative–Liberal Democrat UK Coalition government in 2010, the landscape of education provision in England is being moved closer to that of the US than to continental Europe. It is likely that this acceleration of diversity and 'choice' in provision will produce a greater gap between the haves and the have-nots in education. The raising of tuition fees and the abolition of Education Maintenance Allowances in England seem to suggest a reduction in the importance of social justice agendas in education at UK government level, as well as a rejection of the top-down regulation of the system by the central state department and its Inspectorate (Ozga, 2009). Indeed, 'ideologies of the market', along with adherence to the principles of new institutional economics, have driven policy initiatives such as diversity in school provision, the adoption of parental choice, the adherence to competition as the basis of improvement and the substantial growth of private sector involvement in education in England since the 1990s (Ball, 2006, pp 70-1).

In contrast, Europe is, and continues to be, an important reference point for SNP education policy, and its significance is increasing. The UK/England governance of education is characterised by an emphasis on policy outcomes and is not congruent with the practices and processes of the European education policy space which works through the setting of agendas and formulation of problems, but where formal policy decisions and implementation remain in the hands of national/state governments. This may help to explain why Scottish policy actors seem to be much more aware of and at home with such policy processes that work through finding common meanings and sharing ideas and practices (Grek and Ozga, 2010).

This argument also suggests some explanations of the fact that Scottish policy actors seem more open to policy exchange and learning, even under conditions of fluidity and negotiation. As well as being more at home with interdependencies, another element of the explanation may lie in the way in which Euroscepticism in Scotland was replaced by support for Europe as a means of encouraging the devolution agenda. Europe became an alternative point of reference for Scotland: UK policy developments could be challenged or mediated through reference to the EU. As Brown, McCrone and Paterson (1998) argue, the growing significance of the EU was an important factor in the politics of Scottish self-government between 1979 and 1999. They point to four aspects: first, Europe was attractive to the SNP as an alternative framework of external security and trading opportunities; second, the EU favoured subsidiarity, an argument that could be used in favour of devolution in the UK; third, Europe, and especially small social democratic states, became the source of modernising and progressive ideas, rather than England; and lastly, in the years of the Conservative government's 'rolling back the state', Europe seemed to favour a social partnership model which had been rejected in Westminster. Hearn suggests that Scottish nationalism was reinforced by Europeanisation because 'the steady growth of the European Union has both eaten into the sovereignty of the British state, and made the viability within the EU seem more plausible, and Scottish independence less isolationist' (2000, p 5). Europe offers Scotland a resource for the recognition of its difference from the larger, more powerful and more visible UK system of England. In fact, while the UK is the EU's 'reluctant partner', Scotland is arguably building an identity between two unions, one in the UK and one in Europe (Dardanelli, 2005).

Here it is also worth noting that education in Scotland has played a particularly strong role historically in the shaping and support of national identity (McCrone, 1992; Paterson, 1997), as one of the 'holy trinity' (Paterson, 1994) of institutions – law and the church being the others – that encapsulated Scotland's 'stateless nationhood' from 1707 to 1999. Since the election of the SNP government in 2007, and the end of shared party political control across the UK and Scottish governments, there are strong incentives for the Scottish government to signal positions (including on Europe) that are independent of policy direction in England, and that do not take England or the UK as the natural reference point but instead highlight Scotland's similarities to small, continental European countries like Denmark and Finland within Europe. These are systems where social justice agendas in education remain broadly intact, and sustain public support for public provision (Ozga et al, 2011).

Further resources
For a useful overview of post-devolution education policy see Bryce, T. and Humes, W.H. (eds) (2008) *Scottish education: Post devolution* (3rd edn), Edinburgh: Edinburgh University Press.

For developments since 2007, the Scottish Parliament Information Centre (www.scottish.parliament.uk/business/research/index.htm) is a valuable resource. Research Briefings on education and related policy areas are provided regularly. In addition, the Scottish government's websites are an invaluable archive of news releases, consultations and statistical data on schools: www.scotland.gov.uk/Topics/Education; www.scotland.gov.uk/Topics/Statistics/Browse/School-Education

Paterson, L. (2003) *Scottish education in the twentieth century*, Edinburgh: Edinburgh University Press, provides a useful insight into the historical development of Scottish education.

More general commentary and analysis of education issues can be found at the journal *Scottish Educational Review*: www.scotedreview.org.uk/

For the wider post-devolution policy environment, see Keating, M. (2010) *The government of Scotland* (2nd edn), Edinburgh: Edinburgh University Press.

References
Arnott, M.A. (2005) 'Devolution, territorial politics and the politics of education', in G. Mooney and G. Scott (eds) *Exploring social policy in the 'new' Scotland*, Bristol: The Policy Press, pp 239-62.

Arnott, M.A. and Menter, I. (2007) 'The same but different? Post-devolution regulation and control in education in Scotland and England', *European Educational Research Journal*, vol 6, no 3, pp 250-65.

Arnott, M.A. and Ozga, J. (2009) *Education policy and the SNP government*, CES Briefing Paper, University of Edinburgh, no 50 (www.ces.ed.ac.uk/PDF%20 Files/Brief050.pdf).

Arnott, M.A. and Ozga, J. (2010a) 'Education and nationalism: the discourse of education policy in Scotland', *Discourse*, vol 31, no 4, pp 335-1.

Arnott, M.A. and Ozga, J. (2010b) 'Nationalism, governance and policy making in Scotland: the SNP in power', *Public Money and Management*, March, vol 30, no 2, pp 91-6.

Audit Scotland (2011a) *Scotland's public finances: Addressing the challenges*, Edinburgh: Audit Scotland.

Audit Scotland (2011b) 'Scotland's public sector needs to focus on the long-term financial sustainability of public services', News Release, 25 August (www.audit-scotland.gov.uk/media/article.php?id=174).

Ball, S.J. (1998) 'Big policies/small world: an introduction to international perspectives in education policy', *Comparative Education*, vol 34, no 2, pp 119-30.

Ball, S.J. (2006) *Education policy and social class*, London: Routledge.

Ball, S.J. (2011) 'Academies, policy networks and governance', in H. Gunter (ed) *The state and education policy*, London: Continuum, pp 146-58.

Bernstein, B. (1971) 'Education cannot compensate for society', in B. Cosin et al (eds) *School and society*, London: Routledge and Kegan Paul.

Brown, A., McCrone, D. and Paterson, L. (1998) *Politics and society in Scotland*, Basingstoke: Macmillan.

Commission on Scottish Devolution (2009) *Serving Scotland better: Scotland and the UK in the 21st century, Final report* (Calman Commission), Edinburgh: Commission on Scottish Devolution.

Crerar, L. (2007) *The Crerar Report: The Report of the Independent Review of Regulation, Audit, Inspection and Complaints Handling of Public Services in Scotland*, Edinburgh: The Scottish Government.

Croxford, L., Iannelli, C., Shapira, M., Howieson, C. and Raffe, D. (2002) *Education and youth transitions across Britain 1984-2002*, CES Special Briefing No 32, Edinburgh: Centre for Educational Sociology, University of Edinburgh.

Dardanelli, P (2005) *Between two unions: Europeanisation and Scottish devolution*, Manchester: Manchester University Press.

Foray, D. (2004) *Economics of knowledge*, Cambridge, MA: MIT Press.

Gewirtz, S. and Cribb, A. (2009) *Understanding education: A sociological perspective*, Cambridge: Polity Press.

Gourtsoyannis, P. (2011) 'Swinney hails "Scottish dimension" of Christie Commission reform plans', *Holyrood Magazine*, 17 October (www.holyrood.com/articles/2011/10/17/9164).

Grek, S. and Ozga, J. (2010) 'Governing education through data: Scotland, England and the European education policy space', *British Educational Research Journal*, vol 36, no 6, pp 937-52.

Grek, S., Lawn, M., Lingard, B., Ozga, J., Rinne, R., Segerholm, C. and Simola, H. (2009) 'National policy brokering and the construction of the European Education Space in England, Sweden, Finland and Scotland', *Comparative Education*, vol 45, no 1, pp 5-23.

Hearn, J. (2000) *Claiming Scotland: National identity and liberal culture*, Edinburgh: Edinburgh University Press.

Herbert, S. et al (2011) *SPICe Briefing: Election 2011*, Edinburgh: Scottish Parliament.

HMIe (Her Majesty's Inspectorate of Education) (2007) *How Good is our School? The journey to excellence*, Edinburgh: HMIe.

Hyslop, F. (2007a) 'Debate on making Scotland smarter', Speech, Scottish Executive Debate, 20 June (www.scotland.gov.uk/News/Speeches/Speeches/smarter/classsizes).

Hyslop, F. (2007b) Evidence to 2nd Meeting of Scottish Parliament Education, Lifelong Learning and Culture Committee, 27 June (www.scottish.parliament.uk/s3/committees/ellc/mop-07/edmop07-0627.htm).

Keating, M. (2010) *Government of Scotland: Public policy after devolution* (2nd edn), Edinburgh: Edinburgh University Press.

McCrone, D. (1992) *A sociology of a stateless nation*, London: Routledge.

McPherson, A. and Raab, C. (1988) *Governing education: A sociology of policy since 1945*, Edinburgh: Edinburgh University Press.

Nóvoa, A. (2000) 'The restructuring of the European educational space: changing relationships among states, citizens and educational communities', in T.E. Popkewitz (ed) *Educational knowledge: Changing relationships between the state, civil society and the educational community*, Albany, NY: State University of New York Press.

OECD (Organisation for Economic Co-operation and Development) (2007) *Quality and equity of schooling in Scotland*, Paris: OECD (http://213.253.134.43/oecd/pdfs/browseit/9107211E.PDF).

Ozga, J. (2009) 'Governing education through data in England: from regulation to self-evaluation', *Special Issue of Journal of Education Policy*, vol 24, no 2, pp 149-63.

Ozga, J. and Lingard, B. (2007) 'Globalisation, education policy and politics', in B. Lingard and J. Ozga (eds) *The Routledge reader in education policy and politics*, London: Routledge, pp 65-82.

Ozga, J., Dahler-Larsen, P., Segerholm, C. and Simola, H. (eds) (2011) *Fabricating quality in education: Data and governance in Europe*, London: Routledge.

Paterson, L. (1994) *The autonomy of modern Scotland*, Edinburgh: Edinburgh University Press.

Paterson, L. (1997) 'Policy-making in Scottish education: a case of pragmatic nationalism', in M. Clarke and P. Munn (eds) *Education in Scotland: Policy and practice from pre-school to secondary*, London: Routledge, pp 138-55.

Russell, M. (2011) 'Scottish Parliament education debate', Speech, 19 September (www.scotland.gov.uk/News/Speeches/Education-16-06-11).

Salmond, A. (2007) 'Strategic objectives of new government', First Minister's Speech to Scottish Parliament, 23 May (www.scotland.gov.uk/News/This-Week/Speeches/Speeches/First-Minister).

Salmond, A. (2011a) 'Programme for government 2011-12', First Minister's Speech to Scottish Parliament, 7 September (www.scotland.gov.uk/News/Speeches/ ProgrammeforGov-2011-12).

Salmond, A. (2011b) 'Election 2011: Alex Salmond', *Holyrood* (www.holyrood. com/articles/2011/05/16/building-on-success/).

Salmond, A. (2011c) Address to Spring SNP Conference, March (http://politics. caledonianmercury.com/2011/03/12/first-minister-alex-salmonds-speech-to-the-snp-spring-conference/).

Sanderson, I. (2009) 'Intelligent policy making for a complex world: pragmatism, evidence and learning', *Political Studies*, vol 57, no 4, pp 699-719.

Scottish Executive (2006) *Building the Curriculum 1: The contribution of curriculum areas*, Edinburgh: Scottish Executive.

Scottish Government, The (2007a) *Choosing Scotland's future: A national conversation: Independence and responsibility in the modern world*, Edinburgh: Scottish Executive.

Scottish Government, The (2007b) *Scottish Budget Spending Review 2007* (www. scotland.gov.uk/Publications/2007/11/13092240/0).

Scottish Government (2007c) *Building the Curriculum 2: Active learning in the early years*, Edinburgh: Scottish Executive.

Scottish Government, The (2008) *Building the Curriculum 3: A framework for learning and teaching*, Edinburgh: The Scottish Government.

Scottish Government, The (2010) *Scotland's future: Draft Referendum (Scotland) Bill consultation paper*, Edinburgh: The Scottish Government.

Scottish Government, The (2011) *Commission on the Future Delivery of Public Services*, Edinburgh: The Scottish Government.

Senge, P. et al (1999) *The dance of change: The challenges of sustaining momentum i learning organisations*, New York: Doubleday/Currency.

SNP (Scottish National Party) (2011) *Re-elect: SNP manifesto 2011*, Edinburgh: SNP.

TEN

Policies for young people in contemporary Scotland: a 'lost generation'?

Eddy Adams

Introduction

Ensuring that all young people feel they have a stake in society and that they can make a successful progression to adulthood are important priorities for all communities. Yet, through recent economic cycles, a significant number of young Scots have struggled to make this transition. In the early 2010s economic uncertainty – combined with austerity measures – have raised the spectre of a 'lost generation'[1] of young Scots, cut off from a life of regular employment and consigned to a lifetime of churn between welfare and low-paid work.

The past decade has seen a growing policy focus on supporting young people to make the transition from education to the labour market. In particular, the issue of young people aged 16–19 not in employment, education or training (NEET)[2] has scaled the policy agenda. The preoccupation with NEETs, however, is not peculiar to Scotland, and the underlying causes of the phenomenon are shared with the rest of the UK (Social Exclusion Unit, 1999), and indeed by other developed industrial economies (Bradley and Nguyen, 2004). In this chapter we examine the social and economic factors contributing to the issue in Scotland, and the extent to which the policy response has been distinctive from that of the rest of the UK, particularly under successive Scottish National Party (SNP) administrations. Within this we explore the concerns relating to a 'lost generation' in Scotland and the effectiveness of the measures taken to address these.

Youth labour market transitions in Scotland

Fortunately, a large majority of young people in Scotland make a successful transition from secondary education to the labour market. In 2010, 86 per cent of school leavers entered a positive destination on leaving school, and between the ages of 16 and 19 a high proportion of young people are engaged in education, employment and training. However, for around 10 per cent of the age group, this is not the case, and there is now a strong body of evidence (Coles et al, 2010) showing the damaging and far-reaching effects of young people who are

NEET, particularly those who have this experience over prolonged periods or in multiple episodes.

Data from the 1970 British Birth Cohort Study indicated that being NEET for six months is likely to mean that by the age of 21 a young man is more than four times more likely to be out of work; three times more likely to have depression and mental health issues; five times more likely to have a criminal record; and six times less likely to have any qualifications. (Bell and Blanchflower, 2010)

In addition, there is evidence (Arulampalam, 2001; Gregg and Tominey, 2005; Bell and Blanchflower, 2009) that youth unemployment creates permanent scarring effects on these individuals. As well as decreased earning power and lower levels of job satisfaction in later life, being NEET has also been found to contribute to lower levels of happiness and poorer overall health.

However, these disadvantages are not just rooted in the labour market: there are a number of established risk factors which make some young people more likely to experience periods of being NEET and all that it brings. As we might expect, there is a strong correlation between levels of socioeconomic disadvantage and being NEET aged 16–19. The phenomenon is clearly linked to wider social justice issues, as key NEET risk factors include having parents with low levels of education; having parents who are workless; and living in deprived neighbourhoods with schools which have poor attainment levels (Social Exclusion Unit, 1999). In addition, this and other studies show that young people are more likely to become NEET if they have grown up in care; have an offending background;[3] have a chronic health problem or disability; or are a young carer or a teenage parent.

However, life does not begin at 16 and many of the young people who become NEET are already disengaged and disaffected in the early years of secondary school. For those excluded from school – and those who exclude themselves by truanting – the risks of becoming NEET are statistically higher. The cost to these individuals is significant, as it is to wider society, with research indicating that the societal cost of an excluded child is £64,000 and that of a persistent truant £45,000 (Brookes et al, 2007).

Unfortunately throughout the 2000s, the challenge of tackling the NEET issue and meeting the needs of young people affected by it has been hampered by the prevalence of negative attitudes towards them – particularly adolescents. Two visible drivers underpinned this in Scotland. One was the high profile political campaign adopted by the UK Labour government and by the 2003 Labour/Liberal Democrat Coalition in Holyrood in relation to youth anti-social behaviour. Prominent features of this were the introduction of curfews and ASBOs (Anti-Social Behaviour Orders), which magnified perceptions of the dangers posed by young people. These fears were further fuelled by the media, particularly the popular press, where tabloids have simplified the issue into that of NEET = ned (a derogatory term used in Scotland broadly equivalent to the term 'chav') (Ipsos MORI, 2004).[4] These negative messages relating to young people are discussed further in Chapter Eleven of this volume.

Although evidence suggests that young offenders are more likely to be unemployed (Social Exclusion Unit, 2002),[5] this is not a direct causal relationship. It is misleading and unhelpful to portray the NEET group as a homogeneous one consisting of hooded delinquents, as the media and policy makers have often done. For example, it includes some of society's most vulnerable young people – such as those with learning disabilities – and also includes young people with a wide range of abilities, including very able children who have been bullied out of the school system, teenagers with chronic health problems and young people who struggle with the academic conformity of the Scottish education system.

Young people NEET in Scotland: a changing picture

The proportion of young people who were NEET in Scotland fell for much of the 2000s but, as Figure 10.1 shows, it started rising after 2007, returning to the 10 per cent figure in 2009. In terms of numbers of young people, this means that in 2010 there were 25,170 young people in this category in Scotland. Of these, just over 70 per cent were over 18 years of age and therefore eligible to claim welfare benefits. The remainder, aged 16–18, were young people leaving school into negative destinations.

Figure 10.1: NEET rates in Scotland (%)

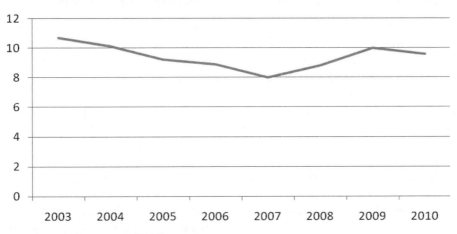

Source: Scottish Government (2011)

Given the links between deprivation levels and being NEET, as we would expect there is a strong correlation between the most deprived parts of the country and levels of NEET. The areas with the highest rates of NEET in 2010 were as follows (see Table 10.1).

Table 10.1: National and highest area NEET rates, by % of 16–19 age group

	2003	2004	2005	2006	2007	2008	2009	2010
Scotland	10.7	10.1	9.2	8.9	8	8.8	10	9.6
Clackmannanshire	17.2	13.3	10.9	12.4	11.2	12.9	12.8	13
East Ayrshire	14.6	13.1	13.9	12.9	10.6	11.7	13.1	12
North Ayrshire	13.6	12.9	11.6	12.8	11.2	12	13.9	13.1
West Dunbartonshire	12.1	12.8	12.1	12.8	11.2	13	13.5	12.3
North Lanarkshire	12.9	12.2	10.1	9.7	9.5	10.3	12.5	12.1

Table 10.1 shows the regional spread of the problem, but the focus on percentage rates, rather than numbers, suggests that solving it is a bigger challenge in mixed urban/rural local authority areas formerly dependent on heavy industry than in Scotland's cities. However, this is rather deceptive, as the percentage rates mask the fact that cities account for some of the most significant volumes – for example, Glasgow accounts for one out of every seven NEET young people in Scotland (The Scottish Government, 2011).

Underlying structural problems affecting NEET levels

In Scotland, as in other developed industrial countries, the past 20 years have brought significant structural changes to the labour market (see also Chapter Twelve, this volume). The key features of this have been an overall decline in the number of threshold-level jobs requiring low skill levels, combined with a sharp drop in the number of opportunities requiring manual skills. This period has also coincided with the decline of the traditional craft apprenticeship system in the UK. As has been well documented (Brynner et al, 2002), this has had a particularly big impact on those communities where the established pattern – primarily for young men – was to enter the labour market via this route.

Changing labour market structures have also seen a growing rise in the qualifications required to access employment. As well as reflecting the growing complexity of many occupational areas – often driven by ICT (information and communication technology) developments – we have also witnessed the phenomenon of *credentialism* whereby in an increasingly competitive labour market entry-level qualifications continually rise for positions at every level (Canning, 1999; Smyth and McCoy, 2011).

These structural changes are evidenced in the dramatic decline in the proportions of Scottish school leavers going directly into the labour market. In 1980, two thirds of Scottish pupils left school at the age of 16 and, of these, 65 per cent progressed directly into employment (Howieson, 2004). By 2009 the proportion leaving school at the age of 16 had halved, and stood at 33 per cent. Of those leaving school that year, only 18.4 per cent moved directly into employment, representing a sharp decline (of 6.9 percentage points from the previous year), largely in response to the recession.

Scotland also has a highly flexible labour market, which is lightly regulated and now characterised by higher proportions of temporary and part-time jobs. Although this has disadvantages for jobseekers – in terms of limited security and phenomena like the 'zero hours contract' – it also has some advantages for young Scots compared to their continental peers. For example, part-time or temporary employment can provide a stepping-stone into something more permanent, allowing both the employee and the employer to test the water. So, although the quality of the work experience may at times be questionable, evidence does suggest that it is more likely to lead to further employment than being out of work.

In more highly regulated labour markets – for example, Belgium, France, Spain and Italy – there are fewer opportunities of this type (Barbieri, 2009). This is largely because their strong regulatory frameworks, designed to protect workers' rights, can actually create barriers for young people seeking labour market entry. Although this may be good for those already in employment, the features of these systems – high labour costs and strong employment protection – often make employers more reluctant to give new labour market entrants a chance. It can also exacerbate the barriers facing labour market entry for those young people outside the traditional recruitment channels, such as migrants.

Recent Organisation for Economic Co-operation and Development (OECD) research (Scarpetta et al, 2010) concludes that, based on data from nine countries, young people have a better chance of finding permanent work after a temporary job than from being unemployed. The report notes that:

> About 30-40% of school leavers in the OECD are thus estimated as being at risk of facing persistent difficulties in their access to stable employment. The OECD *Off to a Good Start: Jobs for Youth* (2010: 20) review clearly shows that the school-to-work transition is smoother in low-regulated labour markets where 'first jobs', even non standard ones, act rapidly as a stepping stone to a career. (Scarpetta et al, 2010, p 20)

In a European Union (EU) context, Scotland (together with the rest of the UK, Ireland and Portugal) is at one extreme of the spectrum in an economy with a high proportion of low-paid jobs and minimal job security. At the other end, the highly regulated models offer more job security and stable higher wages but with less scope for new jobs and consequent access issues for the young. In the middle are the highly praised Scandinavian countries, such as Denmark, with its flexicurity model offering low levels of job security compensated by high levels of labour market security (Sapir, 2003). Although the recent crisis has forced many EU member states to react, previous attempts to reform these structures to benefit young jobseekers have been defeated by trades unions, concerned about diluting hard-earned employment rights.[6]

Another structural issue that particularly affects young jobseekers relates to benefits entitlement. Since the 1980s young people in the UK under the age of 18 have been ineligible for unemployment benefit. As welfare is a reserved policy area this is currently a Westminster matter; however, the position here is largely mirrored in other developed industrial countries.[7] The withdrawal of benefits to under-18s in the UK was accompanied by the introduction of the Young Person's Guarantee (YPG) whereby unemployed young people were entitled to a place on a government training programme. This has now been replaced in Scotland by the 16+ Learning Choices programme, discussed below, in recognition of the failure of the YPG. One of the problems the guarantee created was that without any benefit entitlement under-18s had little incentive to register for support, making it harder to reach them once they left school. The Scottish government has recently taken steps to address this issue, which are also described later in this chapter.

Throughout this period, a familiar refrain has been from employers, voicing their concerns about the preparedness of young people for the labour market. Despite – or perhaps due to – continued changes within the curriculum, employers continue to portray school leavers as being poorly prepared for work. A recent study of Scottish employers noted that they identified school leavers' weaknesses including frequent absence, poor timekeeping and weak communication skills. The report concluded that there was a need to:

> ... work harder at the process of preparing school leavers for the workplace and provide an opportunity for the key stakeholders to look in detail at the options for achieving change. (Futureskills Scotland, 2006)

However, although government policy has encouraged schools to strengthen links with employers, it is often pupils who already have significant amounts of social capital who are first in the queue. For example, a Scottish government review of work experience in schools found that a high proportion of pupils had work placements found by their parents while those doing less well at school were likely to be excluded from any placement opportunity. It noted that 'the current model is not universal, with some of those who would benefit greatly from work experience being the least likely to get it' (Adams et al, 2008, p 33).

Policy response

In 2006 the Scottish government produced its own response to the issue through the publication of its NEET strategy, *More choices, more chances* (The Scottish Government, 2006). This underlined the scale of the problem, identifying Scotland as having the third highest NEET rate among OECD countries. It noted that despite rising attainment standards overall, there remained high levels of inequality within the education system. The strategy stressed the importance of early intervention to tackle the NEET challenge and encouraged the wide range of agencies with a stake in this agenda to collaborate more effectively.

More choices, more chances acknowledged the regional variations in NEET levels across the country, and although every local authority was allocated additional resources to implement the findings, seven 'hot spot' areas were prioritised.[8] The guidance letter from the Scottish Executive (as was) stated that these resources were to be used to:

- Strengthen collaborative planning and partnership working in order to reduce the risk of young people heading towards NEET (pre-16) and to assist those in the NEET group to migrate to a positive outcome;
- Establish a baseline from which to set targets to reduce the number of young people not in education, employment or training;
- Pilot new approaches and/or address gaps or weaknesses in the range of education, employability and specialist services ... and where funding is available to ensure longer-term sustainability.[9]

The SNP minority administration that took office in May 2007 continued the commitment to tackling the NEET issue set in train by its predecessor. However, during its period in office greater emphasis was placed on preventing the flow from school into negative destinations (that is, NEET). As part of its historic Concordat deal with local authorities, the SNP government established a performance framework against which Local Strategic Plans (Single Outcome Agreements) were gauged. One of these key indicators in the framework was the government's commitment to:

> Increase the proportion of school leavers (from Scottish publicly funded schools) in positive and sustained destinations (FE, HE, Employment or training). (The Scottish Government, 2007)

This focus on the younger end of the 16–19 group coincided with the reform of the senior curriculum in Scottish schools. In Scotland, these developments saw an alignment of anti-NEET activity with the direction of Scotland's education policy, particularly in relation to the modernising of the curriculum. For although Scotland has long prided itself on having a distinct and strong education system, there was increasing recognition that this does not benefit all young people. Indeed, in the initial launch of Curriculum for Excellence (CfE), the Scottish government alluded to the long underperforming tail in Scottish schools, and the fact that attainment levels among the bottom cohort had remained static for a decade. The response was an ambitious programme to modernise the curriculum whereby the 'senior phase' would allow for a more personalised offer for young people (The Scottish Government, 2009).

It is too early to state whether CfE will achieve its goals. In particular, it is too early to say whether it will help to engage those young people who have tended to be turned off by a secondary school offer which is largely perceived to be irrelevant for adult life. There is certainly an opportunity here to address one of the main structural weaknesses within the Scottish education system that contributes to the high levels of disengagement, which is the fragmentation between the vocational and the academic offer.

In recent years this has partly been addressed through the introduction of programmes like Skills for Work, and other school–college collaborative activities that have widened the curricular offer through introducing vocational programmes delivered in an environment beyond school. However, it is still the case that the 'academic' pupils tend not to engage in these subjects, giving them a second-class status within schools. It is also the case that the vocational pathway in Scottish schools remains undervalued and fragmented, unlike the most successful models across the continent. Here, I am thinking particularly of the dual system in place in Germany and Austria that ensures that a high quality vocational offer is embedded in the secondary school system from an early stage.

In Scotland, young people with a vocational ambition must navigate a different type of system beyond the compulsory education age. Although there are options and tasters related to vocational areas, these are presented as modular options rather than as part of a coherent learning pathway. An OECD review of the Scottish education system (OECD, 2007, p 133) identified this as an issue and concluded that:

> Were Scotland to follow the lead of some of its comparator nations, it would structure vocational options into programmes to span the compulsory and non-compulsory years. Its schools would offer structured pathways (which may link with college programmes) instead of unconnected courses or units which might be construed simply as exit visas.

Currently, the pathway is clear for those young people making a linear progression from school to higher education. It is far less so for young people whose aptitudes lie elsewhere or whose circumstances make this option difficult for them. Through CfE there is an opportunity to address this structural weakness, but this is an ambitious and major re-engineering exercise whose success is by no means guaranteed.[10] The commitment of the majority SNP government returned in May 2011 to reform post-16 education provides a further opportunity to address this longstanding fault line.[11]

The Scottish government's policy focus on positive school leaver destinations meant that during the initial years of the economic crisis, much of the policy leadership for addressing the problems faced by older teenagers was taken up by the Westminster government. During the latter stage of the Brown administration, the Labour government launched a series of interventions designed to stem the tide of rising youth unemployment – most notably the Future Jobs Fund and the YPG[12] (DWP, 2010).

Targeted at young people under the age of 25, these interventions were fully embraced in Scotland and through the Future Jobs Fund thousands of young people found temporary employment. Although there are often reservations about the benefit of wage subsidy programmes such as the Future Jobs Fund,[13] there is a strong evidence base to suggest that investing to keep young people in the labour market pays long-term dividends, particularly during downward economic cycles. In fact, the OECD, the IMF (International Monetary Fund) and the ILO (International Labour Organization) have stressed the value of such programmes and warned of the risk of creating a 'lost generation' by cutting them when the economy is still vulnerable (ILO/IMF, 2010).

The OECD (Scarpetta et al, 2010) cites the risk of repeating the experience in Japan of the 1990s where employers turned to 'fresh' graduates rather than those who had been trapped in unemployment once the economy picked up. However, in the UK these additional support measures aimed at young people – including the Future Jobs Fund – have been discontinued as part of the UK Coalition government's drive for short-term savings. However, as we note below, where the Scottish government has been able to retain measures to address youth unemployment, it has done so – such as retaining the Education Maintenance Allowances (EMAs) (discussed below), guaranteeing a learning opportunity for all Scottish 16- to 19-year-olds and supporting free higher education tuition fees. At the end of this chapter we explore these developments further and consider the extent to which it represents a growing divergence between UK and Scottish policy in relation to young people.

Operational response to the NEET issue

On the back of *More choices, more chances*, the Scottish government instigated a number of changes designed to tackle the NEET problem across the country. These can be grouped under a number of themes. One is *improved intelligence*, which has been assigned to Skills Development Scotland (SDS) to provide a lead. As part of this task, steps have been taken to provide better information from schools. This includes systems to better identify those at risk of becoming NEET, as well as more accurate data on post-school destinations. Related to this, baseline information at a local authority level allows for closer examination of performance against the government's commitment to support increasing proportions of leavers into positive destinations. Finally, the establishment of a national learning opportunities database was in response to the need for improved information on the learning supply side.

A second key theme relates to the restructuring of provision. At the national level, this has involved the government introducing a range of *new interventions* focused on the post-school transition point. One of the first key steps was the replacement of the discredited YPG with the 16+ Learning Choices model that seeks to provide every school leaver with an appropriate learning and skills opportunity.

The government took this further in an announcement made in September 2011 committing it to providing a learning or training place to every young person aged 16–19 under the banner of 'Opportunities for All'. In addition, the priority around targeting the most vulnerable was evident in the introduction of the Activity Agreements programme. This provides a personalised support programme to the most disengaged that is financially underpinned by the EMAs.[14]

At the local level, the ingredients for successfully tackling the NEET issue are well established, and there is ample evidence of *what works*. At the heart of this is coordinated agency activity underpinned by accurate intelligence on those young people most at risk. At its best, the partnership model is one where service providers recognise that the complex support needs of some young people mean that they require a customised support package mediated by a trusted intermediary. Voluntary and community-based organisations play an important role in this process, with the Prince's Trust, Fairbridge and Barnardo's active players across the country. Service delivery through keyworkers, often working on an outreach basis, has proven to be particularly effective at engaging disaffected young people.

Conclusion: a lost generation?

During the 2000s an evidence base was produced which underlined the long-term risks of youth unemployment – both for the individuals affected and for wider society. This identified the links between being NEET and other social problems addressed in this publication – for example, health and justice. This was very much a UK-wide phenomenon, initially prioritised by the first Blair administration. North of the border, there was a concerted policy drive to tackle the issue, led by successive Holyrood administrations. Therefore, until May 2010, the approach at both Scottish and UK levels was largely consistent.

The available data shows that the NEET figures in Scotland fell markedly in the years after 2003, when it was first consistently recorded, until 2007. In this four-year period the total number for Scotland fell from 27,550 to 20,840. However, during the initial recessionary years 2007–09 the figures rose back to 26,290. Then, against the UK pattern, the Scottish figures fell slightly in 2010, although at 25,170 they remained higher than at any time since 2006. From the viewpoint of 2011, it is too early to tell if the latest figures are a blip and whether numbers will again increase once the full impact of spending cuts in Scotland are felt.

However, what is becoming clear is a diverging policy approach to tackling youth unemployment and inactivity between Scotland and Westminster. At a time where the UK Coalition government has cut investment supporting youth employability – most notably through the axing of the Future Jobs Fund, scrapping of EMAs and the rise in tuition fees – the Scottish government's approach appears increasingly distinctive. In contrast it has retained EMAs, maintained a policy of no tuition fees, and the majority SNP administration has also pledged a learning opportunity for every 16- to 19-year-old through 'Opportunities for All'.

As we have seen in this chapter, a clear message from much of the evidence is the importance of supporting young people to stay in work and learning during a recession. A number of highly respected agencies – including the OECD, the ILO and the World Bank – draw this conclusion from their global experience. Yet this message is being differently interpreted north and south of the border, with marked distinctions in policy emerging.

There are limitations on the Scottish government's powers in this sphere, while employment and welfare remain reserved to London. However, it is evident that where it has scope, the SNP administration has shown much greater willingness to invest in tackling youth unemployment and inactivity than the UK Coalition government. Whether this distinctive approach will be enough to avoid the prospect of a 'lost generation', and whether it will yield very different results, remains to be seen.

Notes

[1] The phrase 'lost generation' has been much used during the current crisis. In Scotland, its first use was coined by Fiona Hyslop, then Cabinet Secretary, in January 2009, when during an economic debate in Parliament she said: "This for many Scots is the most difficult economic climate for over a generation". She warned that the "vulnerability" of young people in the employment market must be addressed "if we are to avoid creating a lost generation of young people like that witnessed in the 1980s" (reported in *The Herald*, 22 January 2009).

[2] The term 'NEET' is somewhat controversial. In Scotland, Fiona Hyslop discouraged its use while Cabinet Secretary, on the grounds that it is pejorative and negatively focused. However, it remains in widespread use in Scotland and throughout the rest of the UK and describes the situation of these young people. Consequently, it is used in this chapter as a shorthand term.

[3] The Scottish government's young offender learning and skills workstream found that the proportion of pupils with offending records leaving education into a positive destination was 41 per cent against an average of 87 per cent in 2007/08.

[4] Considerable research has been conducted into the media's negative portrayal of young people. This includes the Women in Journalism study 'Hoodies or alter boys?' which showed that over half the stories about young men in the media focused on crime.

[5] The Social Exclusion Unit report, *Reducing reoffending by ex-prisoners* (2002), noted that 63 per cent of young offenders were unemployed at the time of arrest.

[6] The most notable casualty was the scrapping of the proposed Villepin Youth contract reforms in France following the youth unrest in urban suburbs in 2006.

[7] Notable exceptions are Sweden, Finland, Ireland and Germany, where young people are entitled to full unemployment benefits.

[8] Glasgow, North Ayrshire, Dundee, East Ayrshire, West Dunbartonshire, Clackmannanshire and Inverclyde.

[9] Scottish Executive guidance letter to local authority chief executives and Community Planning Partnership chairs dated 15 August 2006.

[10] Witnessed in the difficulties experienced in the initial implementation of CfE in Scottish schools during 2010/11.

[11] In September 2011 Cabinet Secretary Mike Russell announced proposed post-16 education reforms designed to provide 'affordable, sustainable and high quality learning opportunities that are better aligned to Scotland's economic needs' (www.scotland.gov.uk/News/Releases/2011/09/14142913).

[12] Scotland had 10,675 temporary jobs approved for filling under the Future Jobs Fund programme by the end of March 2011. By July 2010, 5,870 young people had found an employment opportunity through the programme.

[13] Largely due to instances of deadweight, where subsidies discourage employers for investing in staff.

[14] EMAs are payments of up to £30 per week made to disadvantaged young people over 16 staying in learning and meeting agreed performance criteria.

Further resources

Allan, M. and Ainley, P. (2010) *Lost generation? New strategies for youth and education*, London: Continuum.

Hammer, T. (ed) (2003) *Youth unemployment and social exclusion in Europe: A comparative study*, Bristol: The Policy Press.

Petersen, A. and Mortimer, J. (2006) *Youth unemployment and society*, Cambridge: Cambridge University Press.

A data source for school leaver destinations in Scotland, based on an annual survey of school leavers, this provides national and local area data for post-school destinations: www.careers-scotland.org.uk/AboutCS/Initiatives/SLDR.asp

Scottish Government: Scotland performs provides details of the Scottish government's targets and performance framework including regular progress reviews: www.scotland.gov.uk/About/scotPerforms/performance

Department for Work and Pensions (DWP) Young Person's Guarantee statistics, a UK government department with data on interventions targeting young people as well as details of UK welfare-to-work policy and interventions: http://research.dwp.gov.uk/asd/asd1/jsa/ypg/ypg_oct2010.pdf

Women in Journalism, 'Hoodies or altar boys?', January 2009, research examining media attitudes to young people: www.womeninjournalism.co.uk/node/325

References

Adams, E., Smart, D., McGregor, A. and MacDougall, L. (2008) *Work experience in Scotland. Project report*, Edinburgh: Scottish Government (www.scotland.gov. uk/Publications/2008/11/27092915/13).

Arulampalam, W. (2001) 'Is unemployment really scarring? Effects of unemployment experiences on wages', *Economic Journal*, vol 111, November, pp 585-606.

Barbieri, P. (2009) 'Flexible employment and inequality in Europe', *European Sociological Review*, vol 25, issue 6, pp 621-8.

Bell, D.N.F. and Blanchflower, D. (2009) *What should be done about rising unemployment in the UK?*, Social Science Research Network (http://ssrn.com/abstract=1351203).

Bell, D. and Blanchflower, D. (2010) *Young people and recession: A lost generation?* (www.dartmouth.edu.blnchflr/papers/economic%20policy%20Article%20 v3_24.pdf).

Bradley, S. and Nguyen, A.N. (2004) 'The school-to-work transition', in G. Johnes and J. Johnes (eds) *International handbook on the economics of education*, Cheltenham: Edward Elgar.

Brookes, M., Goodall, E. and Heady, L. (2007) *Misspent youth: The costs of truancy and exclusion*, London: New Philanthropy Capital (www.philanthropycapital.org).

Brynner, J., Elias, P., McKnight, A., Pan, H. and Pierre, G. (2002) *Young people's changing routes to independence*, York: Joseph Rowntree Foundation (www.jrf. org.uk).

Canning, R. (1999) 'Post-16 education in Scotland: credentialism and inequality', *Journal of Vocational Education & Training*, vol 51, no 2, pp 185-98.

Coles, B., Godfrey, C., Keung, A., Parrott, S. and Bradshaw, J. (2010) *Estimating the life-time cost of NEET: 16-18 year olds not in education, employment or training*, York: University of York, York (www.york.ac.uk/spsw/research/neet).

DWP (Department for Work and Pensions) (October 2010) *Young Person's Guarantee official statistics*, October (http://research.dwp.gov.uk/asd/asd1/jsa/ypg/ypg_oct2010.pdf).

Futureskills Scotland (2006) *Scottish school leavers and their understanding of the world of work* (www.scotland.gov.uk/Resource/Doc/919/0065462.pdf).

Gregg, P.A. and Tominey, E. (2005) 'The wage scar from male youth unemployment', *Labour Economics*, vol 12, pp 487-509.

Howieson, C. (2004) *Destinations of early school leavers*, Edinburgh: University of Edinburgh (www.ces.ed.ac.uk/PDF%20Files/Brief028.pdf).

ILO (International Labour Organization/IMF (International Monetary Fund) (2010) 'The challenges of growth, employment and social cohesion', Oslo Conference Paper (www.osloconference2010.org/discussionpaper.pdf).

Ipsos MORI (2004) *Media images of young people* (www.ipsos-mori.com/researchpublications/researcharchive/poll.aspx?oItemId=761).

OECD (Organisation for Economic Co-operation and Development) (2007) *Quality and equity of schooling in Scotland* (www.oecd.org/document/18/0,3746,en_2649_39263231_39744402_1_1_1_1,00.html).

OECD (2010) *Off to a good start? Jobs for youth* (www.oecd.org/document/31/0,3746,en_2649_33927_46328479_1_1_1_1,00.html).

Sapir, A. (2003) *An agenda for a growing Europe*, Brussels: European Commission (www.euractiv.com/ndbtext/innovation/sapirreport.pdf).

Scarpetta, S., Sonnet, A. and Manfredi, T. (2010) *Rising youth unemployment during the crisis: How to prevent negative long-term consequences on a generation?*, Paris: Organisation for Economic Co-operation and Development (www.oecd.org/officialdocuments/displaydocumentpdf?cote=DELSA/ELSA/WD/SEM(2010)6&doclanguage=en).

Scottish Government, The (2006) *More choices, more chances*, Edinburgh: The Scottish Government (www.scotland.gov.uk/Publications/2006/06/13100205/0).

Scottish Government, The (2007) *Scotland performs*, Edinburgh: The Scottish Government (www.scotland.gov.uk/About/scotPerforms).

Scottish Government, The (2009) *Curriculum for Excellence – Building the curriculum 4: Skills for learning, skills for life and skills for work*, Edinburgh: The Scottish Government (www.ltscotland.org.uk/buildingyourcurriculum/policycontext/btc/btc4.asp).

Scottish Government, The (2010) *Young offender learning and skills workstream report*, Edinburgh: Scottish Government (www.scotland.gov.uk/Publications/2009/12/18103851/0).

Scottish Government, The (2011) *MCMC Group, NEET – SLDR and DWP benefits* (www.scotland.gov.uk/Topics/Statistics/Browse/Labour-Market/MCMC-E2).

Smyth, E. and McCoy, S. (2011) 'The dynamics of credentialism: Ireland from bust to boom (and back again)', *Research in Social Stratification and Mobility,* vol 29, issue 1, pp 91-106.

Social Exclusion Unit (1999) *Bridging the gap*, London: The Stationery Office.

Social Exclusion Unit (2002) *Reducing reoffending by ex-prisoners*, London: The Stationery Office (www.gos.gov.uk/497296/docs/219643/431872/468960/SEU_Report.pdf).

ELEVEN

Criminal justice, social inequalities and social justice

Hazel Croall

Introduction

Crime and criminal justice are intricately linked to the issues of welfare and social justice that form the focus of this collection. The clientele of police stations, courts and prisons are largely drawn from the most deprived groups and crime has a disproportionate impact on the poor. With its renowned Children's Hearings system and greater emphasis on rehabilitative social work with offenders, it has been argued that Scotland, before devolution, took a more welfarist and less punitive approach than many other jurisdictions, but that paradoxically, since devolution, there has been a process of 'detartanisation' (McAra, 2008; Croall et al, 2010; Munro et al, 2010), followed, arguably, by greater divergence and 'retartanisation' (McNeill, 2011) with the election of a Scottish National Party (SNP) minority Scottish government in 2007, a process which may well continue with the election of a majority SNP government in 2011.

This chapter begins by exploring the different ways in which crime, victimisation and criminal justice are linked to social inequalities in Scotland, before looking at the global and national context of criminal justice policy and the extent to which these have affected policies in Scotland. This broad analysis is followed by a brief account of key areas of criminal justice policy, looking at: youth justice, renowned internationally for its welfarist approach; imprisonment and community sentencing, topics featuring strongly in current debates; and, in contrast, the very different arrangements for corporate and environmental crime. Finally, it discusses issues of divergence and convergence, criminal and social justice before briefly considering some alternative approaches.

Crimes and social inequalities

It is first necessary to consider the controversial term 'crime' which, despite its widespread use, has defied legal, sociological or popular definition (Muncie et al, 2010; Croall, 2011). While often linked to criminal law, activities legally defined as crime change over time, and what people perceive to be 'criminal' is dependent on a cultural context. The negative stereotyping surrounding 'neds' in Scotland in the mid-2000s (a derogatory term applied to hooligans, louts or petty criminals), for example, amounted to the virtual criminalisation of some aspects of young people's behaviour and indeed style of dress. The label 'crime' or 'criminal' can also be used politically, as seen in the efforts of politicians to attribute the so-called 'riots' in several major English cities in August 2011 to 'criminality', thereby refuting any suggestions that social inequalities or government policies were to blame. What is perceived as crime affects whether acts are reported to the police by victims and witnesses and whether the police choose to take action and 'count' them as crime. Police activity can therefore 'create' crime – while it is often assumed that 'more bobbies on the beat' will reduce crime, it can also have the effect of inflating numbers of arrests and reported crimes, particularly in those areas where they choose to be 'on the beat'. Activities such as anti-social behaviour, groups such as young people, and areas can therefore be subjected to greater criminalisation. So contested is the concept of crime that some have argued for the use of the term 'social harm' which draws attention to the very different ways in which different 'harms' are subjected to law and censure (Tombs and Hillyard, 2004).

Official statistics about crime are therefore notoriously unreliable (Maguire, 2007; Croall, 2011) although they are often, misleadingly, used as an indicator of the success or otherwise of policies. The publication, in September 2010, of figures indicating that crime, including murders, knife crime and serious assaults, had fallen across Scotland in 2010 (Donnelly, 2010; The Scottish Government, 2010), and subsequent figures showing declining rates in 2011, have been claimed as successes for government policies and police initiatives (Leask and Devlin, 2011).

It is important to place these figures, and politicians' tendency to 'talk up' crime (McAra, 2008) in the context of consistently falling rates of crime, including youth crime (Burman, 2010), across the UK from around the mid-1990s, following steep rises from the late 1950s (Maguire, 2007; Reiner, 2007). Increases have variously been related to the enhanced opportunities provided by consumer goods and cars, to growing numbers of police, an increasing willingness to report crime and, from the mid-1980s onwards, to the massive social changes brought about by deindustrialisation and rising levels of unemployment, casual employment and income inequality (Reiner, 2007; Hale, 2009), said to be associated not only with crime but with a range of social issues (Wilkinson and Pickett, 2009). Recent decreases, particularly in property crime, can in large part be explained by technological factors such as increased security, particularly in relation to cars (Croall, 2011).

Scotland has seen consistently lower rates of victimisation than England and Wales and 2008/09 figures indicate rates of 23.4 per cent in England and Wales, 20.4 per cent in Scotland and 13.4 per cent in Northern Ireland (Muir, 2010). While in all jurisdictions violent crime forms a small proportion compared to property crime, these 2008/09 figures indicate that it constitutes 30 per cent of crime in Scotland, compared to 20 per cent in England and Wales. Crime has also not fallen as quickly in Scotland as in England. As in all jurisdictions, recorded crime rates are higher in cities such as Glasgow, which has been associated with a high murder rate (although this has recently fallen), Edinburgh and Dundee, with lowest rates in primarily rural areas such as Dumfries and Galloway, and the Northern region including the Highlands and Islands (The Scottish Government, 2008a; Mooney et al, 2010).

Crime is often popularly, however mythically (Hancock and Mooney, 2011), associated with social deprivation, with the 'dangerous classes' inhabiting 'dangerous' areas such as Scotland's 'schemes' – and the East End of Glasgow in particular has been negatively associated with the so-called underclass, 'Shettleston Man' or 'Broken Britain' (Law et al, 2010; Mooney et al, 2010; Croall, 2011). These areas are most often the focus of police and other initiatives against youth crime and underlie the current association of crime with the 'three "d's" of "drink, drugs and deprivation"' (The Scottish Government, 2007; McNeill, 2011).

Exploring what are complex relationships is far from easy. The socioeconomic status of convicted offenders is not recorded and they are far from representative. Nonetheless, a number of Scottish studies echo those from elsewhere and suggest that while involvement in crime is common for youth across the social spectrum, more serious and persistent offenders, including knife users and those involved in gang violence, are more likely come from the most deprived backgrounds (Bannister et al, 2010; McAra and McVie, 2010a; McVie, 2010). The class-based nature of the criminal justice process is starkly illustrated in research carried out for the Scottish Prison Service which related prisoners' postcodes to the socioeconomic classifications of their areas, and indicated that:

- 28 per cent of prisoners, compared with 10 per cent of the general population, came from the 'poorest council estates';
- half of the prisoner population came from 155 of 1,222 local government wards – all characterised by social deprivation;
- the male imprisonment rate from the 27 most deprived wards amounted to 953 per 100,000 of the population compared to the national average of 237;
- one in nine young men from the most deprived communities will have spent time in prison by the age of 23 (Houchin, 2005).

Inequalities are also seen in relation to victimisation. While rich and poor alike are victimised (the rich, for example, possess more goods and more conspicuous items such as desirable cars to tempt thieves), surveys suggest that the most deprived experience more kinds of crime more often, are more seriously affected by victimisation and are less able to protect themselves (Croall, 2007a). While these largely quantitative studies inadequately capture the 'lived reality' of crime, it is clear that life in some areas can involve daily experiences of verbal, racial or sexual harassment, threats of and actual violence along with vandalism, theft and burglary. The Scottish Index of Multiple Deprivation (SIMD) indicates that around one in ten people in the 15 per cent most deprived areas reported such crimes compared to one in 25 in the rest of Scotland (The Scottish Government,

2009). People from the most deprived areas are also more likely to report feeling unsafe and to see crime as a growing problem in their area (MacLeod et al, 2009).

Socioeconomic inequalities are strongly related to inequalities of age, gender and 'race' and ethnicity which cannot be fully explored here, and some of which are discussed in other chapters in this volume. Young people, who are more often on the street, thereby attracting more attention, are subject to more stringent policing and surveillance (McAra and McVie, 2005, 2007, 2010a). Young men are more likely to be convicted of crime than young women, and gender is a key factor in relation to domestic and other forms of violence. Many women in prison are victims of abuse and poverty (McMillan, 2010). Members of racial and ethnic groups, along with religious groups and people with disabilities, are also particularly vulnerable to harassment and so-called 'hate crime'. Although Scotland has a smaller and differently constituted minority ethnic population to that in England (fewer Afro-Caribbeans with Asians as the largest group), and did not see the urban unrest widely associated with racial groups in England such as the 'riots' of the 1980s popularly associated with Afro-Caribbeans and those of the 1990s and 2000s in Northern English towns associated with Asian youth (Webster, 2007), minority ethnic young people complain of racial harassment and 'over-policing' (Goodall et al, 2003; Croall and Frondigoun, 2010). The absence of 'riots' in Scotland in 2011 is briefly explored below.

The many attempts to account for these relationships cannot be discussed in depth here (Grover, 2008; Mooney et al, 2010; Croall, 2011). Many involve forms of 'poor blaming', from early sociological and criminological perspectives looking at 'sub'cultures or social 'dis'organisation, through notions of the criminal 'underclass' with its alleged 'dependency culture', to the later discourse of social exclusion – in itself often implying some fault in the poor or workless. There is, however, no simple or straightforward relationship between worklessness and crime, as crime rates can rise in times of affluence when there are more criminal opportunities *and* recession. Many studies suggest that crime is not necessarily related to absolute but to relative deprivation, and to widening economic inequalities (Young, 1999, 2007; Hale, 2009). Moreover, rather than unemployment per se, the growth of casual, poorly paid labour and deskilling are also important (Hale, 2009).

This must, however, be set against the vast amount of crime committed by more wealthy individuals, by corporations and state agencies. Often known as the crimes of the powerful, these are not generally regarded as crime and subject to far lower levels of criminalisation despite their considerable physical, economic and emotional impact. They include serious frauds, 'safety crime' (Tombs and Whyte, 2007), crimes against consumers and environmental or eco crime (Walters, 2010a, 2010b, 2010c; Croall, 2011). Fraud, for example, has been said to cost each Scottish citizen around £330 each year, and many of the 32 fatal and 2,721 major injuries to workers reported in Scotland in 2007/08 can be attributed to breaches or neglect of safety regulations (Tombs, 2010; Croall, 2011).

Of particular concern are cases in which mass deaths are subsequently attributed to failures on the part of management or regulators. Scottish cases include:

- The explosions on the Piper Alpha North Sea oil production platform in 1988 that killed 167 workers. While investigations identified shortcomings in preparations for a major emergency and in the Department of Energy's enforcement, the company, Occidental Petroleum Ltd, was not subsequently prosecuted for any offence (Ross and Croall, 2010).
- In December 1999, a family were killed in an explosion in Larkhall, attributed to leakage from severely corroded pipes that had been known about since 1986. Transco PLC were subsequently convicted for failing to replace the pipes and fined £15 million (Ross and Croall, 2010).
- In May 2004, an explosion caused by gas escaping from corroded pipes destroyed a factory in Maryhill, Glasgow owned by ICL Plastics, killing 9 workers and injuring 33. A subsequent report found that the company had not cooperated with the Health and Safety Executive (HSE) who in turn had failed to carry out inspections (Ross and Croall, 2010).

Environmental crime involves a range of offences including pollution, and a recent audit of 405 of Scotland's 'largest and most complex' industries revealed that almost 10 per cent failed annual Scottish Environment Protection Agency (SEPA) pollution inspections (Walters, 2010a). Of particular concern has been pollution associated with the defence and nuclear industries, which also illustrates state involvement. For example:

- The Dounreay nuclear power facilities have been responsible for recklessly releasing thousands of radioactive particles, and the UK government has attempted to cover up its negligence (Walters, 2010a). It was convicted and fined £140,000 in 2007 (Edwards, 2009).
- The Hunterston B plant in North Ayrshire has one of the worst records for safety incidents, having recorded 24 fires and leaks since 2001 (Edwards, 2009).
- Faslane, the nuclear submarine base, has been associated with a series of serious safety breaches, and the Ministry of Defence has admitted poor maintenance, training and staffing. SEPA has stated that it would close the base down if it had the legal powers (Edwards, 2009).

It is also important to recognise that the impact of corporate crime falls heavily on the most deprived (Croall, 2007b, 2011). It is very often workers, often in the least well paid and most casualised industries, whose safety is most endangered, and poorer consumers who have little choice but to buy cheap, but unsafe or substandard goods who are physically or economically harmed. Those living in the most deprived areas also suffer from the poorest air quality (Walters, 2010a).

Criminalisation, criminal and social justice

Criminal justice reflects and reinforces the operation of these inequalities through the process of criminalisation, which includes the designation of activities as 'crime', along with the operation of policing, the courts and sentencing. The introduction of Anti-Social Behaviour Orders (ASBOs), for example, effectively criminalised a whole range of 'incivilities', not hitherto regarded as crime, which were predominantly associated with areas of social housing (Burney, 2009). It will be seen below that a more punitive rhetoric towards youth crime from the 1990s was accompanied by increasing rates of imprisonment – despite the decreasing crime rates noted above. As outlined, policing is also important as the police must, in response to public, political and media pressure, prioritise certain crimes and areas for greater attention – choices which tend to involve street crime in specific areas.

A different discourse surrounds corporate, environmental and state 'offences', which are more often described as 'breaches' or 'exceedences' (Croall, 2004; Walters, 2010a) and subject not to policing and punishment, but to regulation and sanctions. A myriad of inspectorates, such as the HSE and SEPA, are responsible for law enforcement and tend to adopt a compliance model, in which the aim of agencies is perceived to be to protect the public by securing compliance (as opposed to bringing the guilty to justice) and that non-compliant (or offending) businesses will respond to persuasion and negotiation (Croall, 2004). This produces lower rates of prosecutions and is justified as reflecting the perceived need to balance the interests of industrial development and profits against those of protecting the public or the environment (Croall, 2004; Walters, 2010a, 2010b, 2010c). Thus the law is said to reflect the exercise of business influence. In a telling analysis, pre-dating the Piper Alpha disaster, Carson (1981) describes a 'political economy of speed' which involved pressures to extract North Sea oil as quickly as possible to maximise revenues and before regulatory regimes were fully developed.

While this chapter cannot deal with the many dimensions of inequality in the criminal justice process, there are clear indications that lower-class suspects and defendants are disadvantaged in relation to legal representation, making credible representations in court and receiving more interventionist sentences. In some respects the more affluent can 'buy' themselves out of heavier sentences, illustrated in aspects of monetary penalties. The Scottish 'Fiscal Fine' and more recently, the Fiscal Work Order, have been used as alternatives to prosecution, although the latter, directed at those who cannot pay fines, is more interventionist. As a sentence, fines can be related to offenders' means but also to the seriousness of the offence. This can result in the poorest being 'over-fined' and the more affluent 'under-fined' (Munro and McNeill, 2010). In an attempt to reduce the number of people imprisoned for defaulting on fines, a Supervised Attendance Order, again more interventionist, was introduced. While it had some success it produced an:

... emerging parallel system of low-end justice for people in poverty
.... and a bifurcation ... between ... those accused who can afford to
pay up and thereby maintain their autonomy and distance from the
justice system and those in poverty who cannot. (Munro and McNeill,
2010, p 221)

Criminal justice in Scotland: devolution and 'detartanisation'

Scotland was responsible for criminal law and justice long before devolution, and
had a distinctive legal culture (Young, 1997; Croall, 2005, 2006; McAra, 1999, 2008;
Croall et al, 2010). Scottish criminal justice must also, however, be placed within
the global context of 'penal transformations' in the latter part of the 20th century
(Garland, 1996). Rising rates of crime and the consequent costs of criminal justice,
combined with neoliberal notions of placing responsibility for crime on offenders
and their families, led, as in other policy areas, to the growth of actuarialism and
risk management, accompanied by 'popular punitivism' (Bottoms, 1994).

In the UK this was illustrated in the rhetoric and policies of Conservative
governments to whom welfarist policies were too 'soft', in the famous claim
that 'prison works' and in the recasting of community sentences as 'punishment'
in the community. The New Labour governments of the late 1990s and 2000s,
following the slogan 'Tough on crime, tough on the causes of crime', emphasised
risk management, evidence-based policy, the setting of targets and adopted a
moralising tone towards youth crime seen in the introduction of ASBOs and
associated Parenting and Curfew Orders. This 'punitive managerialism' (Cavadino
and Dignan, 2006) was also evident in comparatively high rates of imprisonment.

Before devolution, Scotland was generally perceived to have avoided populist
punitivism (Hutton, 1999), with more welfare-based arrangements persisting
in relation to the Children's Hearings system, criminal justice social work and
progressive prison policies (Young, 1997; McAra, 1999). While claims of a more
welfarist approach can be contested, as will be seen below, they have been associated
with a greater commitment to welfare in Scotland's civil society and political
culture (Garland, 1996; McAra, 1999). A distinctive criminal justice culture and
policy network, involving the Crown Office, Directors of Social Work and the
judiciary, reflected an 'other than England' emphasis and had enabled a resistance
to populist pressures from highly unpopular Conservative ministers (Cavadino
and Dignan, 2006).

While devolution could have been expected to see a continuation and indeed
a deepening of these differences, it is widely acknowledged that instead there
was a greater convergence and a process of 'detartanisation' accompanied by
greater punitiveness. McAra (2008) identifies an expansion of the criminal justice
architecture that involved increasing centralisation and ministerial control through,
for example, national strategies in relation to drugs, victims, youth crime and
courts. Penal welfarism gave way to public protection and risk management and
there was a fusion of criminal justice, social inclusion and social crime prevention

strategies with the introduction of ASBOs and similar community safety policies to those in England and Wales. While resisting these policies, the welfarist criminal justice establishment had lost its grip, as fighting crime became a means of securing political legitimacy and criminal justice became part of the political process. These processes, followed by a changed emphasis by the SNP-led government, can be illustrated in a brief exploration of some key areas of criminal justice.

Youth justice

Young offenders are very often seen as being in need of help rather than punishment, and all youth justice systems must find an appropriate balance between justice and welfare. Scotland has often been hailed as having one of the most enlightened, welfarist systems, deriving from the Kilbrandon Report of 1964 and its associated 'Kilbrandon philosophy' that prioritised the needs of the child and saw offending as a symptom of underlying problems. The Children's Hearings system, set up in 1968, is not, unlike other jurisdictions including England and Wales, a juvenile court, and deals with children who have offended alongside others requiring care and protection (McAra and McVie, 2010a, 2010b). It is less interventionist and involves fewer residential disposals (Cavadino and Dignan, 2006). Paradoxically however, Scotland has been widely criticised for having, at eight years, one of the lowest ages of criminal responsibility in Europe, for dealing with 16- to 18-year-olds in the adult criminal justice system and for relatively high rates of custodial sentencing for young people (McAra and McVie, 2010a; Muncie, 2011).

The Children's Hearings system was also criticised for being too 'soft', and youth crime was politicised from around the mid-1990s (Batchelor and Burman, 2010; McAra and McVie, 2010a). National standards and key performance indicators were introduced and the emphasis shifted from needs to risk assessment (McNeill, 2010). Persistent young offenders, a target of concern in England and Wales, were seen as a problem for the Children's Hearings system and 'fast-track' courts and youth courts for those over 16 were piloted. A model was slowly developing, argue McAra and McVie (2010b, p 182), which replaced the 'child' by 'an offender', who, with his/her parents, was pitched against the 'innocent victim' nested in a 'suffering community'. Successive reviews found the system to be under-resourced and it was widely felt that the Children's Hearings system was not 'flawed in design but in resourcing and execution' (McNeill, 2010, p 58).

Punitivism was particularly evident in the introduction of ASBOs, Dispersal Orders and Parenting Orders in 2004 in the face of concerted opposition from professional groups and experts. It was accompanied by particularly strong rhetoric from the then Labour Executive against youth crime and so-called 'neds' (Croall, 2006). Despite exhortations from ministers to use these orders, some local authorities used them only sparingly.

It is generally agreed that the SNP government of 2007–11 adopted a less punitive tone, was more prepared to listen (Mellon, 2009) and downplayed ASBOs and concerns about persistent young offenders (McNeill, 2010). Their 2008 document, *Preventing offending by young people: A framework for action* (The Scottish Government, 2008b), contains what McAra and McVie (2010a, 2010b) describe as an 'uneasy' mixture of welfarist, actuarialist and retributive influences. It begins with a positive statement about the contribution of young people to society (McNeill, 2010, p 51), stresses child well-being and links youth crime to education and health but at the same time favours early and intensive intervention for those designated as 'risky'. While the recent Criminal Justice and Licensing (Scotland) Act 2010 contains provisions that a child under 12 will not be prosecuted in the criminal courts, this falls short of reducing the age of criminal responsibility and leaves open the possibility that a child can have a criminal record (Norrie, 2010).

Offenders in prison and in the community

Young (1997, p 116) argued that Scotland has a reputation for 'penal harshness and for penal innovation', the latter referring to the celebrated work of the Barlinnie Special Unit for long-term prisoners. Despite decreasing crime rates and a range of alternative options, imprisonment rates have risen steadily. From having a lower rate up to the 1990s, in 2008 Scotland imprisoned 150 per 100,000 of its population compared to 152 for England and Wales. Furthermore, while sentencers perceive a rise in serious crime, this is not borne out by statistics (Tombs and Piacentini, 2010). There has also been an increase in remands in custody and in short sentences (Tombs, 2005). Penal harshness is also indicated in the continuation of the notorious habit of slopping out, well after it had been substantially reduced in England and Wales until it was made subject to human rights legislation. Despite successive attempts to reduce the use of prison for women, following a spate of suicides in Cornton Vale women's prison and arguments that many women in prison have committed only minor offences and are particularly likely to have suffered from abusive backgrounds and poverty, numbers have increased (Tombs, 2004; McMillan, 2010).

Contrary to claims that it 'works', imprisonment has been widely criticised. To Armstrong and McNeill (2009, p 2), 'prison remains a peculiar institution in which to imagine that rehabilitation can occur', and short sentences are generally felt to be expensive and to achieve little. The Scottish government explicitly sought to look at countries with lower imprisonment rates and proposed that there should be a presumption against sentences of less than six months. Opposition was so fierce, however, including arguments from the Labour opposition that dangerous criminals would be left on the street, that they had to 'climb down' (Morrison, 2009) to a presumption against sentences of less than three months, a policy included in recent legislation. Interestingly, Labour's stance on this issue has been said to conflict with the new Labour leader's reported position that reducing imprisonment does not amount to being soft on crime, and Conservative opposition is contradicted by suggestions by the English Justice Secretary for a sharp reduction in prison sentences of under 12 months (Johnson, 2010).

Scotland's arrangements for criminal justice social work have consistently been characterised as more welfarist. Scottish policies, unlike England and Wales, stressed the desirability of making more use of community sentences, emphasised social inclusion and, while adopting a 'what works?' approach, continued to emphasise offenders' needs as opposed to a more correctionalist approach which focuses on offenders as 'risks'. It fiercely resisted the creation, favoured by the Labour administration, of a single corrections agency and being cast as 'offender management', which, by rendering offenders as objects to be managed rather than humans with whom practitioners should engage, was seen as dissonant with Scottish traditions (Munro and McNeill, 2010).

While not abandoning rehabilitation, the SNP government has emphasised reparation, seen in the notion of community 'payback' which includes restorative justice, financial penalties, unpaid work, some restriction of liberty and paying back by working at change and engaging in activities to address offending behaviour. This can be viewed as an effort to 'sell' community alternatives to justify reducing imprisonment (Munro and McNeill, 2010). It differs, however, from the more punitive approach to 'payback' taken under the previous Labour government in England and Wales, which included suggestions that offenders wear bibs (Armstrong and McNeill, 2009).

Corporate and environmental crime

In many jurisdictions, following serious cases of mass deaths such as those outlined earlier, there have been calls for tougher laws and sentences to deal with corporate offenders. In England and Wales, the sinking of the Herald of Free Enterprise in Zeebrugge in 1987 with the loss of around 188 lives, along with a spate of rail crashes, led to a slow movement towards law reform.

A major difficulty in respect of corporate crime is how to make a company, a legal entity, responsible under *criminal* law that relies on the concept of *mens rea*, the guilty mind. A diffusion of responsibility within corporations enables corporate executives to blame employees, and employees to claim that they were 'only following orders' (Croall, 2004). Many jurisdictions have, following English law, developed a 'doctrine of identification', in which a person held to be the 'hands' or 'mind' of the company must be identified as responsible for offences (Ross and Croall, 2010). This inhibited successful prosecutions particularly as in large multinational corporations no one person could reasonably be expected to be aware of all breaches of regulations. Some jurisdictions attempted to moderate this doctrine by, for example, extending, as in Canada, responsibility to 'senior' managers; introducing notions of corporate as opposed to individual fault by attempting to aggregate responsibility; and, as in Australia, using the notion of the 'corporate culture' whereby a company could be convicted if it had allowed a culture to develop in which people could reasonably believe that behaviour, such as, for example, not using safety equipment, would be widely tolerated.

In Scotland an absence of prosecutions had left the law untested despite pressure for change in the wake of the Piper Alpha disaster in 1988. The Crown Office did attempt to indict Transco for culpable homicide, innovatively using arguments about aggregated responsibility. This was initially allowed but overturned on appeal, and the company was subsequently tried under health and safety legislation, which carries a lower penalty. This led to an Expert Group being set up to look at the law in the context of proposed new legislation in England and Wales. The group looked at other jurisdictions along with England and Wales, and their recommendations included creating an offence of corporate killing, with corporate liability based on organisational failure to ensure health and safety or on the existence of a corporate culture (Scottish Executive, 2005). It also proposed offences for individuals held responsible for death or serious injury.

Sentences for corporate offenders have also been criticised as too lenient. Even the 'record' fine given to Transco merely constituted 5 per cent of their after-tax profits and 1 per cent of their annual turnover. ICL were fined a total of £200,000, criticised in the press as amounting to a mere £44,000 for each life lost (*Edinburgh Evening News*, 28 August 2007). Sentences are limited by the so-called 'deterrence trap' – too high a fine can threaten a company's survival and thereby employment (Croall, 2005a; Ross and Croall, 2010). The Expert Group recommended that fines should be increased by relating them to a company's turnover or profit or through Equity Fines that penalise shareholders. It also suggested introducing corporate inquiry reports to accurately ascertain a company's means along with alternative sanctions such as corporate probation and community service, often advocated as particularly appropriate for companies (which could, for example, be asked to 'clean up' after pollution), and as underlining (by harmonising sentences for corporate and other offenders) the 'criminal' nature of offences (Croall, 2005a).

In the event, the Labour government decided that Scotland was not 'competent' to legislate in this area, which is close to Health and Safety and Company Law, both reserved matters, although this decision could be disputed (Ross and Croall, 2010). It was agreed that Scotland be included in the subsequent Corporate Manslaughter and Corporate Homicide Act of 2008, a much watered-down piece of legislation which adopts a senior management test but makes no provision for individual responsibility. The Act also envisages heavier sentences subject to guidelines. In Scotland a Private Member's Bill proposed by Dr Bill Wilson did attempt to introduce Equity Fines targeted at company shares; however, this also fell, in late 2010, on the grounds of competence, although corporate inquiry reports were included in the recent Criminal Justice and Licensing (Scotland) Act 2010.

These discussions were limited to cases involving death and serious injury and other corporate harms are, as seen above, less likely to lead to prosecution, particularly in Scotland where there was a lack of expertise within the Crown Office (Ross and Croall, 2010). This was acknowledged and specialist prosecution departments have been established for health and safety and environmental offences, indicating in respect of environmental crime that it is prepared to deal with it as crime (Walters, 2010a). But this must be seen in the context of regulatory law as a whole, which, with its bias against prosecution, and, moreover, severely reduced resources for inspections and investigations, has already been said to amount to regulatory degradation (Tombs and Whyte, 2009).

Conclusion

The above discussions clearly illustrate the role of socioeconomic inequalities in relation to crime and the close links between criminal and social justice. Some crimes are related to absolute poverty, others to relative deprivation and the 'humiliation' associated with being poor and marginalised (Young, 1999, 2007). As well as crimes of 'need', inequality also produces the crimes of 'greed' of wealthier individuals and corporations (Braithwaite, 1995), as Downes (2010, p 394) comments: 'feral bankers proved a far greater threat to moral decency and social cohesion than feral children'.

Criminal justice exacerbates social injustice, particularly where it involves 'intervention and intrusion in people's lives simply on the grounds that they are poor' (Munro et al, 2010, p 265). Scotland, argue Tombs and Piacentini (2010, p 249), 'imprisons the sick, the poor and the marginalized even though the overwhelming number of those in prison are not there for serious offences but for low level offences'. Punitive policies and early intervention with young offenders may push them further along the line to more persistent and serious offending (McAra and McVie, 2010a, 2010b). These kinds of policies are also exclusionary. Also important for social justice is the very different way in which corporate and environmental harms, which disproportionately affect the most deprived, are dealt with.

While applying to most jurisdictions, these considerations are particularly salient in Scotland, where 'a deep and persistent social polarisation between rich and poor' (Mooney et al, 2009, p 75) exceeds that in England (Mooney and Wright, 2009a). Indeed, the persistence of this inequality in itself suggests some scepticism about claims of the more welfarist approach of Scottish civic society and policy elites (Munro et al, 2010), claims also challenged by Muncie's (2011, p 49) observation that Scottish welfarism was 'essentially reserved for less serious "offenders" and/ or those below the age of 16'. Penal harshness has already been outlined and the much-hailed rehabilitative Barlinnie Special Unit is notable, argue Munro et al (2010), for being a never-repeated exception.

If welfarism is a 'myth', then 'detartanisation' can also be questioned, although most accept that there was considerable convergence post-devolution. The role of devolution is nonetheless complex and disentangling global, national, subnational and local influences is far from easy (Muncie, 2011). All four UK jurisdictions have, argues Muncie, been more punitive than many European countries in relation to, for example, ages of criminal responsibility, high rates of incarcerating young people and a climate of demonising youth. There have nonetheless been divergent trends. Wales has seen some 'dragonisation' of youth justice with a greater emphasis on the child, and Northern Ireland, with its distinctive history, has seen more emphasis on reparation. To Muncie (2011), local agencies and actors will always determine the ways in which national and subnational policies are activated on the ground.

McAra's arguments also, argue Munro et al (2010), imply that punitive discourses were alien to Scotland whereas what is exceptional was the continued dominance of values, including penal moderation, associated with liberal elitism. To them, the democratic structures following devolution provided space for the articulation of *existing* punitive values. The detartanisation argument is also limited in that it makes little reference to the context of widening structural inequalities (Munro et al, 2010) and refers to a rather restricted range of policies – it does not, for example, cover corporate and environmental crime.

The election of the first SNP government in 2007 brought about a new situation with, for the first time, different governing parties potentially providing space for further policy divergence (Mooney and Wright, 2009b; Munro et al, 2010). As Mooney and Wright (2009a, p 53) argue, 'nationalism as an organising principle leaves much room for manoeuvre particularly in relation to social policies', an observation also appropriate to criminal justice policy. This is seen, perhaps, in the 'uneasy' mixture of policies outlined above, with the less punitive tone towards aspects of youth justice, the aim of reducing numbers in prison and its emphasis on payback, which McNeill (2011) characterises as reflecting a longer tradition of collectivist corporatism in Scotland.

Conflicting approaches to criminal justice policy were evident in the Scottish parliamentary elections in 2011, in which Labour, largely supported by the Conservatives, adopted a punitivist approach, attacked the SNP as 'soft on crime', suggested strengthening ASBOs, promised to overturn the presumption against short prison sentences and promoted its policy of mandatory prison sentences for carrying knives (BBC, 2011a). This latter proposal in particular attracted intense public debate, involving claims and counter-claims about the costs of knife crime, including revelations that Labour had claimed that knife crime cost the NHS £500 million a year when this was actually the estimated cost to the NHS of all violence in Scotland (Barnes, 2011). The prison service disputed Labour's claims about resources and the police were also critical (*Holyrood Magazine*, 2011). The SNP, on the other hand, claimed credit for the apparent reduction in crime, which Labour disputed, and for their policy, supported by the Conservatives, of placing 1,000 more police officers on the beat. Their populist approach was also seen in their support for reparation, community payback schemes and the use of the assets seized from the proceeds of serious crime to support victims, all of which were used to support a populist claim that criminals should pay for their crimes (*Scottish Sun*, 2011). Policing also featured in the election, with all parties committed to retaining numbers of front-line officers, but disagreeing over proposals to create a national police force.

It is debatable how significant crime was in this particular election, with other issues, particularly health, education and employment, taking precedence. In a BBC poll, out of all criminal justice issues, only the policy of retaining numbers of police on the street featured in the top five voters' priorities (BBC, 2011b).

Mooney (2011) argues that the SNP outflanked Labour with their focus on student fees, opposition to the privatisation of the NHS and other 'classic' 'old Labour' policies. Indeed it could be argued that for this election at least, attempts to play the popular punitivism card and talk up crime, particularly knife and violent crime, as Labour did, failed.

Writing in January 2012 it is too early to predict the future shape of Scottish criminal justice policy under the second SNP administration, affected as it will inevitably be by severe budget cuts, and taking place in the broader context of debates about Scottish independence and Scottish society. The first months since the election have seen three extremely controversial issues involving criminal justice come to prominence – namely, sectarianism and 'hate crime', the national police force, and the role of the Supreme Court.

Before the election, in March 2011, the longstanding issue of sectarianism associated with Glasgow's football clubs was dramatically highlighted with suspected bombs being sent to Neil Lennon, the Celtic manager, and other high-profile Celtic supporters along with a particularly unruly Celtic–Rangers game. May 2011 saw further attempted attacks on Neil Lennon, and, in his first post-election speech, the First Minister pledged that the new government would take firm action on 'bigotry and booze', describing sectarianism as a 'parasite which must be eradicated' (BBC, 2011c). Fierce opposition followed an attempt to pass emergency legislation in the summer of 2011, but in December 2011, the government used its majority to pass the Offensive Behaviour at Football and Threatening Communications Bill, including provisions to increase the maximum prison sentences for some sectarian offences to five years, to act against sectarian chanting and to tackle the use of social networking sites and other electronic communications to organise violent clashes. Vocal opposition from a wide range of groups including not only opposition parties but also churches, Celtic and Rangers football clubs, the media and other high-profile commentators has attacked what they see as the Bill's rushed and ill-considered nature, raising important questions about exactly which behaviour will be encompassed, what is to count as 'offensive and threatening', and how it is to be enforced. Issues of human rights and freedom of speech have also been raised and the need for legislation contested (Macwhirter 2011). A range of measures emerging out of a Joint Action Group have also been introduced, including a prosecution team to support the police in relation to Football Banning Orders (O'Neill, 2011), a national football policing unit and the rescheduling of Celtic–Rangers games (BBC, 2011d).

The first session of the new Parliament includes legislation to create a Police Service for Scotland. Proposals for a National Police Force were subject to lengthy if inconclusive consultations before the election. It is argued that cost savings, said to amount to £390 million over five years and £1.9 billion over 15 years, are a major driver, with the Justice Secretary talking of making a 'virtue of necessity' . Whether or not these savings will indeed occur is, however, contested, and they will inevitably involve severe cuts in numbers of officers and civilian staff. Critics point to the difficulties of balancing resource considerations against pledges to retain numbers of front-line officers and also raise issues of local accountability and the 'quality' of policing, along with the potential dominance of the central belt (Hutcheon and Gordon, 2011; Reid, 2011; Rose 2012).

The significance of Scottish independence and the perhaps more explicit constitutional ambitions of the SNP government are indicated in the heated, and what was widely regarded as intemperate, reaction of the Scottish government to a UK Supreme Court decision upholding the Fraser appeal against conviction for murder following failure of the prosecution to disclose key information (Carrell, 2011; Robertson, 2011; Swarbrick, 2011). This had been preceded in 2009 by another important Supreme Court decision in the Scottish criminal case of Cadder that related to legal representation at police station interviews. Both cases hinged on claims of the violation of human rights by the Lord Advocate (in charge of prosecutions in Scotland), adjudication on which had been reserved to the UK Privy Council (functions taken over by the new UK Supreme Court) by the Scotland Act 1998. It had not been intended that the role of the High Court of the Justiciary as the final court of appeal in Scottish criminal cases should be challenged, and with it the historically distinct Scottish criminal jurisdiction and hierarchy of legal institutions, but that was the effect. In January 2012 the Lord President, head of the Scottish judiciary, submitted representations to the UK Parliament, recommending that the Scotland Bill be amended to restrict the Supreme Court jurisdiction to cases certified by the Scottish High Court as being of general public importance. This position is broadly similar to the recommendations of the 'McCluskey' review group set up by the Scottish Government (2011).

Issues involving criminal justice are likely therefore to be prominent in the next Parliament and will involve not only a continuation of existing themes in relation to youth justice, imprisonment and community payback, but highly contested issues which are likely to include discussions of the very nature and independence of Scottish criminal justice and which are likely to attract criticisms of the government for placing populist political sentiments above wider issues of human rights and liberalism, and resource constraints above considerations of accountability and the quality of services, let alone concerns over the interventionist nature of 'hate crime' legislation. Resource constraints are also significant in relation to the role and use of imprisonment.

Public spending cuts have a further significance in that, should they exacerbate inequalities, they might well increase some forms of crime. Downes (2010, p 394), for example, asks:

> What are the prospects for a crime rate rise to match that of the 1980s in the post-election context of public sector cuts and growing unemployment that seem the predictable response to the scale of the deficits incurred?

These issues have already surfaced in reactions to the 'riots' in English cities in August 2011, which many have popularly attributed to socioeconomic inequalities exacerbated in some instances by racial divisions. The absence of these kinds of disturbances in Scotland has occasioned considerable discussion, with the First Minister's allusions to the 'safer' and 'different' nature of Scotland, and claims, supported by apparently promising results from Glasgow's Community Initiative to Reduce Violence and the Violence Reduction Unit (Naysmith, 2011), leading to suggestions that England can learn from Scotland's example. The issue is, however, far more complex. As seen above, it is highly unlikely that the absence of 'riots' can be attributed to any differences in social inequality, although differences in the distribution of racial and ethnic groups may play a part. Also important are differences in so-called 'gang culture', with Scotland's gangs being more territorial and local, concentrated in peripheral estates, and with a greater focus on violence as opposed to the acquisitiveness which characterised many of the English disturbances (Taylor, 2011). A further factor may simply be Scottish weather as it was raining on the nights in question! Many have criticised the First Minister's response as overly complacent, and, as many of the cuts have still to bite, an increase in general levels of property crime and some form of public reaction on the part of excluded young people in Scotland cannot be ruled out (Roy, 2011).

Increases in corporate and environmental crimes are also likely as resources for enforcers lessen and companies seek to cut corners on safety or environmental protection (Tombs and Whyte, 2009; Croall, 2010). While ironically some cutbacks, such as those to the prison population, now proposed across the UK, might seem progressive, it is unlikely that resources will be provided to support criminal justice social work and the voluntary sector. Higher levels of crime or social disorder also risk increasing levels of punitiveness from the media, politicians and sentencers – the Labour Party, for example, continues to support mandatory life sentences for knife carriers despite opposition from many experts, including the police (Morrison, 2009).

Against this, the above considerations suggest the importance of policies seeking to reduce inequalities of income and wealth (Mooney et al, 2009). Recent research on involvement in gangs and knife carrying advocates policies involving socioeconomic improvement and increased opportunities for young people (Bannister et al, 2010; McVie, 2010). The risks of early intervention, outlined above, also support policies of minimum intervention (McAra and McVie, 2010a).

The different criminal status of corporate and environmental harms constitutes a further dimension of social injustice. Heavier sentences and specialist prosecution departments do serve to underline their 'criminal' status although recent evidence suggests a decreasing percentage of inspections and prosecutions (Williams, 2012). A more innovative approach could include these offences in the discourse of and institutional arrangements for community safety, particularly as these harms do constitute a threat to 'safer and stronger' communities (Croall, 2009). Introducing options such as Community Service Orders or indeed 'payback' for corporate offenders is also possible, and a fairer policy in relation to monetary penalties, more clearly related to offenders' ability to pay, could redress inequalities between all groups of offenders.

Acknowledgements

The author gratefully acknowledges Mary Munro's helpful comments and contribution.

Further resources

Croall, H., Mooney, G. and Munro, M. (2010) (eds) *Criminal justice in Scotland*, Cullompton: Willan Publishing.

McAra, L. (2008) 'Crime, criminology and criminal justice in Scotland', *European Journal of Criminology*, vol 5, no 4, pp 481-504.

For an excellent source that provides links to all the major sources of information and opinion on Scottish criminal justice, along with archives of key topics, see: www.cjscotland.org.uk

References

Armstrong, S. and McNeill, F. (2009) 'Choice versus crisis: how Scotland could transform thinking about prisons and punishment', *Criminal Justice Matters*, vol 75, pp 1, 2-4.

Bannister, J., Batchelor, S., Burman, M., Kintrea, K. and McVie, S. (2010) *Troublesome youth groups, gangs and knife carrying in Scotland*, Scottish Centre for Crime and Justice Research (www.scotland.gov.uk/Resource/Doc/324191/0104329.pdf).

Barnes, E. (2011) 'Labour's claim knife crime costs the NHS £500m a year is slammed as "a deception"', *Scotsman*, 20 April (www.scotsman.com/news/labour_s_claim_knife_crime_costs_the_nhs_163_500m_a_year_is_slammed_as_a_deception_1_1595743).

Batchelor, S. and Burman, M. (2010) 'The Children's Hearing system' in J. Johnstone and M. Burman (eds) *Youth justice*, Edinburgh: Dunedin, pp 14-26.

BBC (2011a) 'Issues guide: Crime and justice' (www.bbc.co.uk/news/uk-scotland-scotland-politics-12817703).

BBC (2011b) 'Scottish election: BBC poll shows Scots' top priorities', 11 April (www.bbc.co.uk/news/uk-scotland-scotland-politics-13029253).

BBC (2011c) 'Scottish Cabinet backs sectarian proposals', 25 May (www.bbc.co.uk/news/uk-scotland-13520683).

BBC (2011d) 'New Scottish police unit to tackle sectarianism' (www.bbc.co.uk/news/uk-scotland-glasgow-west-14105881).

Bottoms, A. (1994) 'The philosophy and politics of punishment and sentencing', in C. Clarkson and R. Morgan (eds) *The politics of sentencing reform*, Oxford: Oxford University Press, pp 17-49.

Braithwaite, J. (1995) 'Inequality and Republican criminology', in J. Hagan and R. Peterson (eds) *Crime and inequality*, Stanford, CA: Stanford University Press, pp 277-305.

Burman, M. (2010) 'What's the problem? The nature and extent of youth crime in Scotland', in J. Johnstone and M. Burman (eds) *Youth justice*, Edinburgh: Dunedin, pp 27-42.

Burney, E. (2009) *Making people behave*, Cullompton: Willan Publishing.

Carrell, S. (2011) 'Alex Salmond provokes fury with attack on UK Supreme Court', *The Guardian*, 1 June (www.guardian.co.uk/uk/2011/jun/01/alex-salmond-scotland-supreme-court).

Carson, W.G. (1981) *The other price of Britain's oil*, London: Martin Robertson.

Cavadino, M. and Dignan, J. (2006) *Penal systems: A comparative approach*, London: Sage Publications.

Croall, H. (2004) 'Combating financial crime: regulatory versus crime control approaches', *Journal of Financial Crime*, vol 11, no 1, p 45.

Croall, H. (2005a) 'Penalties for corporate homicide', Annex to Scottish Executive Expert Group on Corporate Homicide (www.scotland.gov.uk/Publications/2005/11/14133559/36003).

Croall, H. (2005b) 'Criminal justice in the devolved Scotland', in G. Mooney and G. Scott (eds) *Exploring social policy in the 'new' Scotland*, Bristol: The Policy Press, pp 177-98.

Croall, H. (2006) 'Criminal justice in post-devolutionary Scotland', *Critical Social Policy*, vol 26, no 3, pp 587-607.

Croall, H. (2007a) 'Social class, social exclusion, victims and crime', in P. Davies, P. Francis and C. Greer (eds) *Victims, crime and society*, London: Sage Publications, pp 50-77.

Croall, H. (2007b) 'Victims of white collar and corporate crime', in P. Davies, P. Francis and C. Greer (eds) *Victims, crime and society*, London: Sage Publications, pp 78-108.

Croall, H. (2009) 'Community safety and economic crime', *Criminology and Criminal Justice*, vol 9, no 2, pp 165-85.

Croall, H. (2010) 'Middle range business crime', in F. Brookman, M. Maguire, H. Pierpoint and T. Bennett (eds) *Handbook on crime*, Cullompton: Willan Publishing, pp 678-97.

Croall, H. (2011) *Crime and society in Britain* (2nd edn), London: Pearson.

Croall, H. and Frondigoun, L. (2010) 'Race, ethnicity, crime and justice in Scotland', in H. Croall, G. Mooney and M. Munro (eds) *Criminal justice in Scotland*, Cullompton: Willan Publishing, pp 111-31.

Croall, H., Mooney, G. and Munro, M. (2010) 'Criminal justice in contemporary Scotland: themes, issues and questions', in H. Croall, G. Mooney and M. Munro (eds) *Criminal justice in Scotland*, Cullompton: Willan Publishing, pp 3-20.

Donnelly, D. (2010) 'MacAskill: Scotland is winning the war on crime', *The Herald*, 8 September (www.heraldscotland.com/news/crime-courts/macaskill-scotland-is-winning-war-on-crime-1.1053590).

Downes, D. (2010) 'Counterblast: what went right? New Labour and crime control', *The Howard Journal*, vol 49, no 4, pp 394-7.

Edwards, R. (2009) 'Revealed: radioactive waste leak into the Clyde', *Sunday Herald*, 20 September (www.robedwards.com/2009/09/revealed-radioactive-waste-leak-from-hunterston.html).

Garland, D. (1996) 'The limits of the Sovereign State: strategies of crime control in contemporary society', *British Journal of Criminology*, vol 36, pp 445-71.

Goodall, K. with Choudri, R., Barbour, R. and Hilton, S. (2003) *The policing of racist incidents in Strathclyde*, Glasgow: University of Glasgow.

Grover, C. (2008) *Crime and inequality*, Cullompton: Willan Publishing.

Hale, C. (2009) 'Economic marginalization, social exclusion and crime', in C. Hale, K. Hayward, A. Wahidin and E. Wincup (eds) *Criminology* (2nd edn), Oxford: Oxford University Press, pp 365-84.

Hancock, L. and Mooney, G. (2011) '"Saints and scroungers": constructing the poverty and crime myth', *Criminal Justice Matters*, no 83, pp 26-7.

Holyrood Magazine (2011) 'Justice: clash over knife-crime policy', 20 April.

Houchin, R. (2005) *Social exclusion and imprisonment in Scotland*, Glasgow: Glasgow Caledonian University.

Hutcheon, P. and Gordon, T. (2011) 'SNP to legislate for single Scottish police force', *Sunday Herald*, 14 August, p 1 (www.heraldscotland.com/news/politics/snp-to-legislate-for-single-scottish-police-force-1.1117472).

Hutton, N. (1999) 'Sentencing in Scotland', in P. Duff and N. Hutton (eds) *Criminal justice in Scotland*, Aldershot: Ashgate/Dartmouth, pp 166-81.

Johnson, S (2010) 'Ed Miliband contradicts Iain Gray on sentencing', *The Telegraph*, 29 September.

Law, A., Mooney, G. and Helms, G. (2010) 'Urban "disorders", "problem places" and criminal justice in Scotland', in H. Croall, G. Mooney and M. Munro (eds) *Criminal justice in Scotland*, Cullompton: Willan Publishing, pp 43-66.

Leask, D. and Devlin, L. (2011) 'Revealed: Scots crime falls to lowest level since 1970s', *The Herald*, 1 August.

MacLeod, P., Page, L., Kinver, A., Iliasov, A., and Littlewood, M. and Williams, R. (2009) *2008/9 Scottish Crime and Justice Survey: First findings*, Edinburgh: Scottish Government Social Research (www.scotland.gov.uk/Resource/Doc/296333/0092084.pdf).

Macwhirter, I. (2011) 'This dumb, unjust law is Salmond's first own goal', *The Herald*, 15 December (www.heraldscotland.com/comment/columnists/this-dumb-unjust-law-is-salmonds-first-own-goal.16167952).

Maguire, M. (2007) 'Crime data and statistics', in M. Maguire, R. Morgan and R. Reiner (eds) *The Oxford handbook of criminology* (4th edn), Oxford: Clarendon Press.

McAra, L. (1999) 'The politics of penality: an overview of the development of penal policy in Scotland', in P. Duff and N. Hutton (eds) *Criminal justice in Scotland*, Aldershot: Ashgate/Dartmouth, pp 355-80.

McAra, L. (2008) 'Crime, criminology and criminal justice in Scotland', *European Journal of Criminology*, vol 5, no 4, pp 481-504.

McAra, L. and McVie, S. (2005) 'The usual suspects? Street-life, young people and the police', *Criminal Justice*, vol 5, no 1, pp 5-36.

McAra, L. and McVie, S. (2007) 'Youth justice? The impact of system contact on patterns of desistance from offending', *European Journal of Criminology*, vol 4, no 3, pp 315-45.

McAra, L. and McVie, S. (2010a) 'Youth crime and justice in Scotland', in H. Croall, G. Mooney and M. Munro (eds) *Criminal justice in Scotland*, Cullompton: Willan Publishing, pp 67-89.

McAra, L. and McVie, S. (2010b) 'Youth crime and justice: key messages from the Edinburgh Study of Youth Transitions and Crime', *Criminology and Criminal Justice*, vol 10, no 2, pp 179-209.

McMillan, L. (2010) 'Gender, crime and criminal justice in Scotland', in H. Croall, G. Mooney and M. Munro (eds) *Criminal justice in Scotland*, Cullompton: Willan Publishing, pp 90-110.

McNeill, F. (2010) 'Youth justice: policy, research and evidence', in J. Johnstone and M. Burman (eds) *Youth justice*, Edinburgh: Dunedin, pp 43-59.

McNeill, F. (2011) 'Determined to punish? Scotland's choice', in G. Hassan and R. Ilet (eds) *Radical Scotland: Arguments for self-determination*, Edinburgh: Luath Press.

McVie, S. (2010) *Gang membership and knife carrying: Findings from the Edinburgh Study of Youth Transitions and Crime*, Scottish Centre for Crime and Justice Research, Scottish Government Social Research (www.scotland.gov.uk/Publications/2010/09/09115209/9).

Mellon, M. (2009) 'On getting a good hearing: reform and justice for children' (www.cjscotland.org.uk/index.php/cjscotland/dynamic_page/?id=76).

Mooney, G. (2011) 'Scotland after May 2011: towards a "new" Scotland?', *Policy World*, summer, pp 10, 15.

Mooney, G. and Wright, S. (2009a) 'Wealthier *and* fairer? Reflecting on SNP proposals for tackling poverty, inequality and deprivation in Scotland', *Scottish Affairs*, vol 67, pp 49-56.

Mooney, G. and Wright, S. (2009b) 'Introduction: social policy in the devolved Scotland: towards a Scottish welfare state?', *Social Policy and Society*, vol 8, no 3, pp 361-5.

Mooney, G., Croall, H. and Munro, M. (2010) 'Social inequalities, criminal justice and discourses of social control in contemporary Scotland', in H. Croall, G. Mooney and M. Munro (eds) *Criminal justice in Scotland*, Cullompton: Willan Publishing, pp 21-42.

Mooney, G., Morelli, C. and Seaman, P. (2009) 'The question of economic growth and inequality in contemporary Scotland', *Scottish Affairs*, vol 67, pp 72-89.

Morrison, K. (2009) 'Handy guide to criminal justice in the Scottish Parliament September 2008-July 2009' (www.cjscotland.org.uk/pdfs/ScotParlannualreview0809.pdf).

Muir, R. (2010) 'Crime and justice after devolution', in G. Lodge and K. Schmuecker (eds) *Devolution in practice: Public policy differences in the UK*, London: Institute for Public Policy Research, pp 166-88.

Muncie, J. (2011) 'Illusions of difference: comparative youth justice in the devolved United Kingdom', *British Journal of Criminology*, vol 51, no 1, pp 40-57.

Muncie, J., Talbot, D. and Walters, R. (2010) 'Interrogating crime', in J. Muncie, D. Talbot and R. Walters (eds) *Crime: Local and global*, Cullompton: Willan Publishing, pp 1-36.

Munro, M. and McNeill, F. (2010) 'Fines, community sanctions and measures in Scotland', in H. Croall, G. Mooney and M. Munro (eds) *Criminal justice in Scotland*, Cullompton: Willan Publishing, pp 216-37.

Munro, M., Mooney, G. and Croall, H. (2010) 'Criminal justice in Scotland: overview and prospects', in H. Croall, G. Mooney and M. Munro (eds) *Criminal justice in Scotland*, Cullompton: Willan Publishing, pp 261-78.

Naysmith, S. (2011) 'Scottish gang scheme cuts offending in half', *The Herald*, 13 August.

Norrie, K. (2010) 'Criminalising children', *Journal of the Law Society of Scotland*, vol 55, no 7, pp 22-3.

O'Neill, C. (2011) 'Prosecution team to deal with football violence', *The Scotsman*, 6 August (www.scotsman.com/news/prosecution_team_to_deal_with_football_violence_1_1778163).

Reid, R. (2011) 'Seeking a solution', *Holyrood Magazine*, 27 June (www.holyrood.com/articles/2011/06/27/seeking-a-solution)

Reiner, R. (2007) *Law and order: An honest citizen's guide to crime and control*, Cambridge: Polity Press.

Robertson, J. (2011) 'Why the Supreme Court of UK has power to overturn Scots convictions', *The Scotsman*, 26 May (http://thescotsman.scotsman.com/legalissues/Why-the-Supreme-Court-of.6774511.jp).

Rose, G. (2012) 'Revealed, name for country's single force: the Police Service of Scotland', *The Scotsman*, 17 January.

Ross, J. and Croall, H. (2010) 'Corporate crime in Scotland', in H. Croall, G. Mooney and M. Munro (eds) *Criminal justice in Scotland*, Cullompton: Willan Publishing, pp 132-51.

Roy, K. (2011) 'In riot-free Scotland we had best not be complacent', *Scottish Review* (www.scottishreview.net/KRoy155.shtml?utm_source=Sign-Up.to&utm_medium=email&utm_campaign=245115-Can+riot-free+Scotland+afford+to+be+complacent%3F).

Scottish Executive (2005) Expert Group report on corporate homicide (www.scotland.gov.uk/Resource/Doc/1099/0019260.pdf).

Scottish Government, The (2007) *Scottish Crime Survey 2006* (www.scotland.gov.uk/News/Releases/2007/09/26155318).

Scottish Government, The (2008a) *Recorded crime in Scotland 2007/08*, Statistical Bulletin Crime and Justice Series, Edinburgh: The Scottish Government (www.scotland.gov.uk/Resource/Doc/239682/0066121.pdf).

Scottish Government, The (2008b) *Preventing offending by young people: A framework for action* (www.scotland.gov.uk/Resource/Doc/228013/0061713.pdf).

Scottish Government, The (2009) Analysis of SIMD against other indicators (www.scotland.gov.uk/Publications/2009/10/28104046/9).

Scottish Government, The (2010) 'Crime falls to 32 year low' (www.scotland.gov.uk/News/Releases/2010/09/07111730).

Scottish Government, The (2011) *Independent Review Group examining the relationship of the High Court of Justiciary and the United Kingdom Supreme Court* (www.scotland.gov.uk/About/supreme-court-review).

Scottish Sun (2011) 'Crime will pay ... for the victims' (www.thescottishsun.co.uk/scotsol/homepage/news/3501166/Crime-will-pay-for-the-victims.html).

Swarbrick, S. (2011) 'Salmond in the dock for Supreme Court "insults": leading lawyer attacks Salmond', *The Herald*, 11 June (www.heraldscotland.com/news/crime-courts/salmond-in-the-dock-for-supreme-court-insults-leading-lawyer-attacks-salmond-1.1111312).

Taylor, M. (2011) 'Why didn't the riots reach Scotland?', *The Guardian*, 16 August (www.guardian.co.uk/commentisfree/2011/aug/16/why-didn-t-riots-reach-scotland/print).

Tombs, J. (2004) 'From "a safer to a better way": transformations in penal policy for women', in G. McIvor (ed) *Women who offend*, London: Jessica Kingsley Publishers. .

Tombs, J. (2005) *Reducing the prison population: Penal policy and social choices*, Edinburgh: Scottish Consortium on Crime and Criminal Justice.

Tombs, S. (2010) 'Corporate violence and harm', in F. Brookman, M. Maguire, H. Pierpoint and T. Bennett (eds) *Handbook of crime*, Cullompton: Willan Publishing, pp 884-903.

Tombs, S. and Hillyard, P. (2004) 'Towards a political economy of harm: states, corporations and the production of inequality', in P. Hillyard, C. Pantazis, S. Tombs and D. Gordon (eds) *Beyond criminology: Taking harm seriously*, London: Pluto Press, pp 30-54.

Tombs, J. and Piacentini, L. (2010) 'Prisons and imprisonment in Scotland', in H. Croall, G. Mooney and M. Munro (eds) *Criminal justice in Scotland*, Cullompton: Willan Publishing, pp 238-60.

Tombs, S. and Whyte, D. (2007) *Safety crime*, Cullompton: Willan Publishing.

Tombs, S. and Whyte, D. (2009) 'A deadly consensus: worker safety and regulatory degradation under New Labour', *British Journal of Criminology*, vol 50, no 1, pp 46-65.

Walters, R. (2010a) 'Environmental crime in Scotland', in H. Croall, G. Mooney and M. Munro (eds) *Criminal justice in Scotland*, Cullompton: Willan Publishing, pp 152-74.

Walters, R. (2010b) 'Eco crime', in J. Muncie, D. Talbot and R. Walters (eds) *Crime: Local and global*, Cullompton: Willan Publishing, pp 173-208.

Walters, R. (2010c) 'Eco crime and air pollution', in F. Brookman, M. Maguire, H. Pierpoint and T. Bennett (eds) *Handbook on crime*, Cullompton: Willan Publishing, pp 867-83.

Webster, C. (2007) *Understanding race and crime*, Maidenhead: McGraw Hill and Open University Press.

Wilkinson, R.G. and Pickett, K. (2009) *The spirit level: Why more equal societies almost always do better*, London: Allen Lane.

Williams, M. (2012) 'Calls for action on accidents at work', *The Herald*, 9 January (www.heraldscotland.com/news/home-news/calls-for-action-on-accidents-at-work.16245417).

Young, P. (1997) *Crime and criminal justice in Scotland*, Edinburgh: The Stationery Office.

Young, J. (1999) *The exclusive society: Social exclusion, crime and difference in late modernity*, London: Sage Publications.

Young, J. (2007) *The vertigo of late modernity*, London: Sage Publications.

TWELVE

Working Scotland

Christine Bertram and Sharon Wright

Introduction

Work is intriguing in its capacity to mean everything and yet nothing. Nothing in as much as it is an unremarkable part of everyday life for the majority of people and everything for its centrality to our existence in capitalist societies. It is the very mundanity of work that belies its significance.[1] Work has the capacity to offer a source of identity and an arena to construct and enact social relations and roles. More than that, the extent to which work is exchanged for money (if at all and whether this is adequate, fair or extravagant) reflects important messages about status in relation to what and whose activities are valued by wider society. For many people, paid work is a necessity. For these reasons, work holds powerful meanings (Svendsen, 2008). Interpreting whether paid employment signifies alienation, oppression or empowerment depends on crucial questions about how it is structured and the conditions within which choices are made and the ways in which working interacts with aspects of personal and collective well-being (see Edgell, 2006; Strangleman and Warren, 2008).

It is perhaps because paid work is so central to social life in contemporary Scotland that it is so controversial to be without it. The public imagination is captivated by condemnatory reports of the so-called 'benefit dependency' of those who are currently out of work. Influential public figures like Iain Duncan Smith (UK Secretary of State for Work and Pensions) and Prime Minister David Cameron have sought popular political support by exploiting the stereotypical image of the workshy 'Shettleston Man' as a metaphor for 'Broken Scotland' (Smith, 2008; Mooney and Wright, 2011), implying at once that people in Scotland are insufficiently motivated for paid employment *and* that this is the source of deep and enduring social problems such as poverty and health inequalities.

However, Scotland's relationship with paid work is more complex than such stereotypes might suggest. Scotland's heritage is of hard work – both in agricultural toil and forged in the industrial powerhouse of the early 20th century. Rather than there being any deficit in the proportion of people working, Scotland has consistently maintained some of the highest employment rates in the world (The Scottish Government, 2010a). This is despite a major shift in the profile of the labour market, involving the dismantling of the manufacturing industry, which was the mainstay for generations of working-class men, and a rapid expansion of a feminised service sector, where low-paid and part-time work dominates.

Paid work in Scotland is also interesting from a policy perspective, because it presents an issue of friction in the devolution settlement. While the health of the Scottish economy is dependent on what happens in the labour market (as well as wider processes of globalisation), control over the majority of employment-related policy is held at Westminster, including: employment law, equal opportunities, social security and immigration. The key exception to this is the education and skills policy (including careers advice), which falls within the remit of the Scottish government. This means that the Scottish government is restricted in its capacity to set the terms of engagement for intervention that might address employment-related inequalities and injustices, such as inadequate wages, gendered occupational segregation or discrimination. Nevertheless, the government also plays a key role as a large-scale employer and procurer, with the ability to set and ensure good employment standards and practices of pay, for example, the Living Wage, and conditions for direct employees and contracted agencies.

In this chapter, we consider paid employment as a key site of inequality and injustice in Scotland. Rather than viewing paid employment as neutral or self-evidently beneficial for well-being, as successive UK Ministers for Work and Pensions have done (see Wright, 2009, p 203), we argue that people in different situations are positioned differently in relation to the demands and rewards of paid work, which may have a detrimental impact on their welfare. For example, since income is largely dependent on current or past employment for most people, constraints on the types of jobs (with their accompanying levels of security, pay and conditions) available to different social groups, such as socioeconomic groups, men and women or people from minority ethnic groups, are significant for lifelong inequalities in well-being, health and wealth. Here, we first outline the current state of the Scottish labour market, then highlight the distinctive combination of urban and rural areas, and illustrate the education and skill level of workers in Scotland before presenting gender as a case study of labour market inequality. We then consider the issue of being 'out of work' in Scotland: the construction of 'worklessness' as a social problem in relation to the benefit receipt of ill and disabled people; the development of welfare-to-work policies; and tensions between the goals of the Scottish government and strategies pursued by Westminster.

Paid work in Scotland

Scotland has maintained consistently high levels of employment above 70 per cent for the last decade (see Figure 12.1; The Scottish Government, 2010a). During 2006–09, Scotland held the top rate of employment in the UK, peaking in June 2007 at 76 per cent, exceeding the UK's highest ever[2] levels. In 2007, 29 local authority areas in Scotland had employment rates above 70 per cent, with nine local authority areas above 80 per cent (the Shetland Islands recorded 88.1 per cent), and only three dipping slightly below 70 per cent: Clackmannanshire at

69.4 per cent, Inverclyde at 68.4 per cent and Glasgow City with 66.9 per cent (The Scottish Government, 2010c). By 2009, the overall employment rate had reduced slightly to 73.9 per cent, with five local authorities having rates between 63.3 per cent (Glasgow) and 68.9 per cent (West Dunbartonshire). These high employment rates were accompanied by low unemployment, which remained stable at around 5 per cent between 2000 and 2010.

However, this robust picture of a nation hard at work was not the impression projected by Westminster politicians, who chose to justify harsh welfare reforms by focusing attention on the very small minority of people who were out of work in terms of 'widespread' so-called 'welfare dependency' (Fairclough, 2000; Mooney and Wright, 2011). The stigmatisation of being out of work, even with legitimate reason (for example, genuine disability, ill health or caring obligations), was also applied to whole neighbourhoods, such as the Glasgow East constituency (Mooney, 2009; see below). By deflecting attention away from historically and internationally high employment levels, exaggerating the extent of economic inactivity, inferring personal culpability without evidence and consciously stigmatising people who are out of work, politicians and policy makers have engaged in oppressive practices through the language of misrecognition (see also Fraser, 2005; Lister, 2008). This type of misrecognition denies the experiences, voices and identities of those who are subject to a 'devalued status' (Hobson, 2003, p 4). This public misrepresentation of people and place may therefore be interpreted as an example of politically endorsed widespread injustice.

The 2008 recession did have an impact on the employment rate, but this represents only a slight decline in the first instance (although there are projections to suggest that there will be substantial job losses, particularly in the public sector, following the UK Coalition government budget cuts; see Beveridge et al, 2010). In the quarter April to June 2010, the employment rate of 70.2 per cent was the second highest employment rate[3] among the four countries of the UK (ONS, 2010). The Scottish employment rate was on a similar level to England (70.9 per cent), and far surpassed employment levels in Wales and Northern Ireland (both just above 66 per cent). Even after the recession (2008–10), unemployment remained relatively low, below the EU average.

Scotland's success in maintaining very high employment levels in relation to other parts of the UK and by historical standards is further reinforced with international comparison. Figure 12.2 demonstrates that even after the 2008 recession, Scotland's employment rates remained above 70 per cent and outperformed most other rich nations.

Figure 12.1: Employment rates (ages 16–64) in the four countries of the UK, 1998–2010

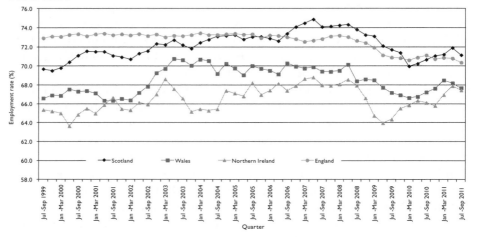

Source: The Scottish Government (2010a), derived from OECD Annual Population Survey

Figure 12.2: Employment rate (ages 15–64), international comparison, 2008 and 2009

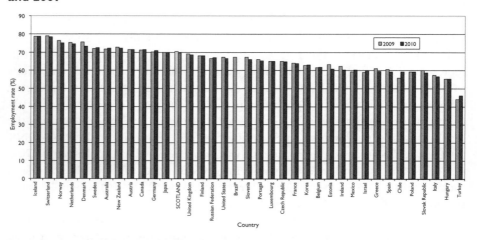

Source: The Scottish Government (2010a), derived from OECD Annual Population Survey

Transforming work

The strength of Scotland's overall employment rate is only one part of the story. Over the past century, Scotland's labour market has been changed beyond recognition – both in the type of work and the type of worker. Historically, Scotland's economy flourished through the combination of an agricultural base, pioneering scientific advances, along with entrepreneurial spirit and the persistent hard graft and determination of men, women and children. Migrant workers in the 19th century, mainly from Ireland, played an important role in this success. Engineering, coal and quarrying, iron, steel, the railways, textiles, chemicals, oil and whisky all prospered in their imperial heyday (Checkland and Checkland, 1989). By the 1960s, however, the boom had turned to bust. The thriving heavy industries that dominated the early part of the 20th century, such as the shipbuilding that earned Clydeside its reputation as the workshop of the world, were caught in a long collapse (cf Slaven, 1975). Between 1960 and 1975, 10,000 men per year were put out of work in manufacturing (Knox, 1999, p 254). Losses were especially bad in male-dominated skilled occupations, with 80,000 jobs disappearing between 1961 and 1971, which was worse than any loss in the preceding 50 years (Knox, 1999, p 254). By the late 1970s, the industries that had previously been most important, coal and shipbuilding, were on their knees (Knox, 1999). Thatcher's Conservative governments oversaw their final dismantling in the late 1970s and 1980s, and by the end of the 1980s, deindustrialisation was well advanced.

The loss of industry contributed to mass unemployment in the 1980s and uncovered prevalent ill health and disability that had been hidden within employment (Beatty and Fothergill, 1996; Alcock et al, 2003). The numbers of people having to claim benefits rose in response (see below) and the composition of the workforce changed. Inside the labour market, opportunities in agriculture also shrank and new types of work began to develop and mature. The service sector expanded, but not to the extent of replacing the jobs lost to manufacturing decline (Knox, 1999, p 288). By 1988, unemployment was falling, but jobs did not exist for all of those who needed them. A recession hit the UK in the early 1990s, although it was not experienced in the same way in Scotland (Audas and Mackay, 1997). Unemployment began to rise again to about 10 per cent (The Scottish Government, 2003). Meanwhile, jobs in hotels, business, financial services and health and social care continued to expand throughout the 1990s and have been projected to continue to grow (Futureskills Scotland, 2007). Added to this were significant changes that had an impact on the conditions for engaging with employers, including the weakening of trades unions, deregulation and worsening social security provision (Gregg and Wadsworth, 1999). When unemployment began to drop again in the mid to late 1990s, large numbers of people still remained outside the labour market, receiving benefits because of their ill health or disability, rather than for unemployment (DWP, 2006). Low-paid, low-quality and precarious employment proliferated and many workers were left in insecure jobs, but had less power than they would have had previously to protect against employers' demands (Gregg and Manning, 1997). On the other hand, changing social security policies meant greater pressure to remain in employment.

If the idea of a 'job for life' ever held true, albeit for a minority of male workers, it had certainly lost its legitimacy by the late 20th century, and, taken with the devastation of Scottish manufacturing, meant a definite shift in demand for skills away from those needed in predominantly manual jobs in the skilled trades, such as process-oriented and elementary occupations (Futureskills Scotland, 2007). This created challenges for many working-class men (Webster, 2000) who were not positioned strongly to compete for new higher-skilled, professional occupations, or those in sales, customer and personal services occupations requiring either high levels of education or a 'soft skills' set (Futureskills Scotland, 2007). In 1982, the majority of workers were men, who worked full time. However, since then, the size of the labour force has expanded steadily and particularly the share of women has grown (Futureskills Scotland, 2007). While 90 per cent of working-age men were in employment in the 1960s, this figure fell to less than 80 per cent by 2005. Conversely, less than 50 per cent of working-age women were employed in the 1960s, while in 2005 this had grown to over 70 per cent (Macpherson, 2008). In 2007, the labour market participation of men and women was nearly equal, and this trend is projected to continue (Futureskills Scotland, 2007). The shift from full-time, lifelong jobs towards low-paid, part-time and temporary work was also gendered from the point of view that new opportunities arose for women. However, while the 'feminisation' of paid work allowed for increasing numbers of women to balance earning with unpaid care activities, 'flexibility' is not necessarily on employees' terms, and problems with in-work poverty, inadequate childcare and conflicting demands on limited time have remained (Crompton, 1999; Burchardt, 2008; Millar, 2008; The Scottish Government, 2010d). This highlights issues of equality and social justice, especially for primary caregivers. For instance, Taylor-Gooby (2005) examined public attitudes towards social justice and found that the public placed much more emphasis on gender equality in the workplace than at home, meaning that it was socially acceptable that women forgo earnings (and thus potentially higher pensions) while looking after their young children. He concluded that policies were not adequate to support a balance of work and family life.

Urban and rural dimensions

Another distinguishing feature of Scotland's labour market is presented by patterns of settlement around a diverse landscape. There is a contrast between the urban concentrations (mainly in the central belt, where Edinburgh and Glasgow account for more than a fifth of the whole population of Scotland) and large areas of sparsely populated remote highlands and islands (where the population density is lower than 10 persons per square kilometre). When it comes to paid employment, the impacts of problems like low pay, poor working conditions and insecure employment face all workers in Scotland; however, there is another set of issues facing urban and rural labour markets that are noticeably different. Workers in rural areas travel further to work than workers in urban areas (Futureskills Scotland, 2006, p 22). In contrast, people in lower-paid jobs tend to live closer to their workplace than people in managerial and professional occupations. Futureskills Scotland (2006, p 45) predicted that the rural labour market in Scotland will remain broadly stable and that there will not be substantial changes in the industrial and occupational structures in the rural areas. However, the Scottish population is set to mainly grow in urban areas, especially in large towns like Inverness, Stirling and Perth (Futureskills Scotland, 2006), and with it, demand for both jobs and workers.

We can see this most clearly in the demand for migrant workers. In the wake of increasing demographic imbalances, with a top-heavy demographic profile, declining fertility rates and high levels of out-migration (see also Chapter Six, this volume), Scotland generally has a very different need for migrant workers than other parts of the UK (de Lima and Wright, 2009), although within Scotland different localities vary in this regard. This can be traced back to high levels of emigration from Scotland in the post-Second World War era, which included groups of potentially high-earning, productive and talented workers (Knox, 1999). Out-flows of working-age adults continue to affect rural areas in particular (Jamieson and Groves, 2008). Scotland generally, and rural communities in particular, have relied heavily on migrant workers (certainly as far back as the 19th century when Irish workers played an important role in filling labour shortages), most recently from Central and Eastern Europe, to fill employment gaps caused by youth out-migration and low levels of unemployment (Jamieson and Groves, 2008; see also Chapter Six, this volume). Work opportunities in Scotland's rural areas are typically located in the low-pay/low-skill agriculture and services sectors (de Lima, 2008).

In disadvantaged urban areas, such as much of Glasgow, the problem is not so much the rise of low-paid jobs and demand for migrant labour as the decline of job opportunities, the social exclusion of those without paid employment and a response that does not address the specific needs of localities. The loss of whole industries and the associated high levels of unemployment did little to improve the health or prospects of people living in the unhealthy environments where poverty is concentrated. Lindsay (2010) found that long-term unemployed people had gradually drifted into social exclusion and isolation because they participated less in social activities, had less social interaction and, as a consequence, had less opportunity to use social networks for jobseeking. UK and Scottish government policies have attempted to focus economic recovery policies not only on the regeneration of the physical environment but also on the regeneration of the labour force through increasing 'employability'. However, this remaking of the labour force has involved creating flexibility mainly on terms that are beneficial to employers rather than employees. Helms and Cumbers (2006) argue that while employment policy is made at UK level, implementation needs to be adapted to the local level and its specific historic labour market context to produce effective outcomes, which might then be seen as a form of distinctive Scottish labour market policy.

Education and skills

Labour market inequalities, then, are to be found in urban and rural areas. They are, however, also connected to levels of education and skills. Education and skills policy is one of the few employment-related policy areas directed by the Scottish government and has been identified as a key area for stronger local intervention (Froy and Giguère, 2010). Overall, the Scottish workforce is well educated. In a comparison with some OECD (Organisation for Economic Co-operation and Development) countries and the regions of the UK, Scotland has the lowest rate of people with no or low qualifications; it ranks top for people of working age with qualifications above NVQ3 or NVQ4; second highest for 25- to 64-year-olds participating in education and training; and ranks in the top five for 15-year-olds achieving the highest proficiency in reading, maths and science (Futureskills Scotland, 2005). The 2008 Employer Skills Survey reinforced this result. However, attainment gaps persist between different income groups, with poverty acting as a barrier to children and young people achieving their educational potential (Telfer, 2011), an issue explored in Chapter Ten (this volume).

Education and skills policy in Scotland is very closely linked to economic policy, with Scottish government policy calling for the skills required to accelerate economic recovery and maintain sustainable growth in its updated skills policy (The Scottish Government, 2010b). The strategy focuses on providing opportunities for skills development and for these skills to be effectively used in the workplace. It aims to support people and businesses and calls for close partnership working of public, private and third sector organisations to support the strategy. It further sets high-level targets via the National Training Programmes for 2010/11 to achieve '15,000 Modern Apprenticeship starts, 14,500 training places to support the unemployed and 5,000 new flexible training opportunities to meet the needs of businesses' (The Scottish Government 2010b, p 7), thus indirectly linking support for unemployed people with education and skills and economic development. However, challenges still exist in relation to education and skills, particularly where there are mismatches between supply and demand.

Hard-to-fill jobs and skills gaps

Despite having a relatively well-educated workforce, there are still mismatches between the education and skills of workers/jobseekers and employer demand. One outcome of this situation is the persistence of 'hard-to-fill' vacancies. At the time of the 2008 Employer and Skills Survey, there were nearly 70,000 vacancies (equivalent to 3.1 per cent of all employees), about half of which were considered 'hard to fill'. Employers' stated reasons for why positions were hard to fill included a lack of applications, lack of the necessary attitude/motivation/personality in applicants, and a lack of skills/qualifications and experience. However, more than 50 per cent of hard-to-fill jobs were due to reasons other than skills shortage. Employers were aware that they often had difficulty filling open positions due to a general shortage of applicants, low wages or unattractive terms and conditions (Futureskills Scotland, 2009). This illustrates a key tension of employment relations, where employers' interests in minimising costs and maximising profits (once confined to the private sector, but spreading increasingly to other sectors) can motivate strategies to depress wages and limit the generosity of employment conditions. At a basic level, with in-work poverty an enduring issue, low wages are not simply an issue of jobseeker preference, but a matter of inadequate income to meet basic necessities.

A small number of employers reported skills gaps, meaning that existing employees are not fully proficient in their job – usually due to the introduction of new technology or working practices (Futureskills Scotland, 2009). The segregation between the industries where the majority of skills gaps were perceived was notable. They usually occurred in occupations that required lower skills and qualifications and were most common in the hotel and restaurant industry. The occupations where the highest rate of skills gaps was identified by employers included elementary occupations, sales and customer service and personal service occupations (the latter two being female-dominated occupations). Training was most frequently offered in occupations that required higher skill levels. Managers, professionals or associate professionals were most likely to have received training, while workers in elementary occupations, sales and customer service were least likely (Futureskills Scotland, 2009). The result is that in male-dominated occupations, training was more common and frequent, whereas female-dominated occupations struggled with training and qualifications. This means that women frequently occupy jobs that have a poor quality of work due to low pay and unattractive conditions, and that offer little training or potential for advancement. Keep (2010) argues that it is not the skills supply that presents a major barrier to a globally competitive economy but rather that it is businesses that need to use the available skills more effectively, although the difficult task for policy makers is to match skills demand by industry and the skills supply through individuals and educational institutions.

Labour market inequalities: a gender case study

Thus far we have outlined key trends of paid work in Scotland (in rates of employment and unemployment), explored dramatic changes in the nature of jobs, highlighted urban/rural distinctions and overviewed issues of education and skills. However, in order to understand what employment means to people in Scotland, we also have to recognise that social groups are situated differently in relation to the demands and rewards of paid employment and obligations, such as caregiving, outside of the labour market, and this is a key source of injustice. While work can be a valuable source of meaningful fulfilment, it may instead be a source of suffering and exploitation. Scotland's labour market remains deeply divided, like others around the world, meaning that opportunities are not equally available to all and, despite a generation of equal opportunities legislation, discrimination remains a live issue. Here, we explore the example of gendered labour market inequalities as an illustrative case study of the extent and nature of workplace injustice.

The segregation into male- and female-dominated occupations is quite distinct in Scotland, compared with other parts of Great Britain. In 2008, 77 per cent of employees in health and social care and 75 per cent of employees in education were women. In contrast, 75 per cent of employees in manufacturing, 76 per cent of employees in transport, storage and communication and 93 per cent of workers in construction were men (Macpherson, 2008). This is further highlighted by the fact that 60 per cent of female employees work part time compared to only 9 per cent of men (EOC, 2006b). This split is further highlighted when looking at particular sectors. Personal service, administration and sales occupations are predominantly female, whereas senior management, process and plant operations and the skilled trades are male-dominated (see Table 12.1). When compared to the average in Great Britain for 2006, there was a slightly higher percentage of women in full-time employment in Scotland. Additionally, there are slightly more women in professional and managerial occupations in Scotland compared to the rest of Great Britain, while the level of employment in the female-dominated occupations is nearly the same. This slight shift may be a consequence of the increasing share of female workers in the Scottish labour market. Nevertheless, the gender segregation according to industry sectors and occupations is quite pronounced. One of the explanations for the dominance of women in the care and education professions is the perceived low status of the work due to poor pay and work conditions as well as a lack of opportunities for progression. However, there appears to be a stereotyping effect due to the view that working with children is more socially acceptable for women than men (Macpherson, 2008).

Table 12.1: Employment and employment by occupation in Scotland and Great Britain

	Scotland		Great Britain	
	Women	**Men**	**Women**	**Men**
Employment (%)	68	78	67	79
Full-time	60	91	58	91
Part-time	40	9	42	9
Employment by occupation (%)				
Personal service	83	17	84	16
Administrative and secretarial	82	18	81	19
Sales and customer service	68	32	69	31
Associate professions and technical	50	50	50	50
Professional	48	52	42	58
Elementary	42	58	45	55
Managers and senior officials	36	64	34	66
Process, plant and machine operatives	12	88	13	87
Skilled trades	8	92	8	92

Source: EOC (2006a, 2006b)

The hourly pay gap between men and women in Scotland is significant, with women earning 11 per cent less than men in full-time employment, and 33 per cent less in part-time employment. However, when compared to the average of all of Great Britain, the pay gap in Scotland is significantly less, largely because on average men and women in Scotland are paid less than the average salary across Great Britain. On average, women across Great Britain earn 17 per cent less in full-time employment and almost 40 per cent less than men in part-time employment. The gender pay gap becomes even more apparent, when broken down by industry sector (see Table 12.2). There are no specific Scottish figures but the British data show the largest gap exists in the financial services sector, with an overall rate of 41 per cent. Surprisingly, however, the health and social work sector, which consists of mostly female-dominated occupations, comes a close second with a gender pay gap of 38 per cent. The smallest gender pay gap is in the transportation and communications sector with only 9 per cent. Not unexpectedly, the pay gap in the public sector is marginally smaller than in the private sector.

Table 12.2: Pay and income and full-time earnings per sector in Scotland and Great Britain

	Scotland			Great Britain		
	Women	**Men**	**Pay gap (%)**	**Women**	**Men**	**Pay gap (%)**
Pay and income (£/hr)						
Full-time	11.37	12.91	11.9	11.67	14.08	17.1
Part-time	8.57	9.22	33.6	8.68	9.81	38.4
Full-time earnings by sector (£/hr)						
Banking, insurance, pension provision				13.98	23.89	41.4
Health and social work				11.54	17.03	32.2
Real estate, renting				12.7	16.66	23.8
Wholesale, retail				9.02	11.54	21.8
Public administration and defence				11.62	14.44	19.5
Manufacturing				10.38	12.89	19.5
Hotel and restaurant				7.12	8.55	16.7
Construction				10.83	12.35	12.3
Education				13.87	15.68	11.5
Transport and communication				11.02	12.09	8.9
Public sector				13.18	15.20	13.3
Private sector				10.65	13.75	22.5

Source: EOC (2006a, 2006b)

Childcare

Earlier we argued that policy responses can reduce skills gaps and inequality of access to different types of jobs. When it comes to gender inequality for working parents a further and highly important area is childcare. Women's employment patterns are also affected by the availability of affordable high-quality childcare. One Scottish policy was introduced in 1998, when the Scottish Office produced the Green Paper that became the Scottish government's childcare strategy, with clear links to employment and employability (Scottish Office, 2007). One of its aims was to enable parents to work or engage in education. The strategy aimed to make high-quality affordable childcare available in every area. In order to match supply and demand, 32 childcare partnerships were set up to monitor provision and quality and make suggestions to improve the provision in the local authority area. They consisted of a mix of local authority leaders, public, private and third sector organisations providing childcare, the NHS, education providers, employment services providers and parents. Locally, the Childcare Information Service was established to provide orientation and work towards meeting national standards. The Scottish government's interventions to increase the availability of childcare went hand-in-hand with the UK policy on tax credits – with the Working Tax Credit offering top-ups to inadequate wages and a childcare element to help with costs, along with the Child Tax Credit offering payments for each child. The Scottish government initiative was the Working for Families Fund, which provided additional services for those both in and moving towards work, that is, those claiming or likely to shortly claim for childcare costs. In some instances the Working for Families Fund topped up the childcare allowance in the Child Tax Credit (McQuaid et al, 2009, 2010). However, UK Coalition spending cuts threaten arrangements and support for in-work incomes and childcare.

Being 'out of work'

The first part of this chapter has provided an overview of employment levels in Scotland, the transformation of the profile of the labour market, an introduction to key features (such as the need for migrant workers in dispersed rural labour markets) and an illustration of gendered labour market inequalities. In this section, we consider another key issue for contemporary debate – being out of paid work. This issue has attracted a great deal of interest from politicians, policy makers, the press and the wider entertainment media. As we have argued above, the controversy surrounding being out of work highlights the centrality of paid employment to social life in Scotland. It is distinctly ironic, however, that policies and discourses directed at those without work became so vociferous at a time when employment levels were at an all-time high (see above) and unemployment had been consistently low for a decade (Nickell, 1999). In this sense, the presentation of 'the problem' to the public, especially by Westminster politicians (both in the UK Labour governments between 1997 and 2010, as well as the 2010 Conservative–

Liberal Democrat Coalition) has been somewhat disingenuous. The contents of successive reform packages (1997–2010) have been disguised when presented to the public, through media reports during election campaigns that exemplified for instance the population of the Glasgow East constituency as representative of all perceived problems with benefits and their recipients. The particular local problems were over-generalised towards success and failure of welfare policies, thus misrepresenting the people and places of Scotland while using the discourse to support stricter conditions for benefit receipt (Mooney, 2009; Mooney and Wright, 2011). Some analysts go further, to suggest that the misrecognition of powerless groups actually constitutes a powerful form of oppressive injustice (Lister 2004, 2008; Fraser, 2005; Wright, 2011). At UK level (where social security policies are made), there has been a distinct shift in discourses about claiming benefits (Fairclough, 2000), in which those without paid employment have been stigmatised and subjected to a 'devalued status' (Hobson, 2003, p 4) as 'dependent' (Freud, 2007). A good example of how reform discourse has been manipulated is *No one written off* (DWP, 2008), within which paid employment for lone parents and disabled people was presented positively as offering the key to an empowered life, better health and an escape from poverty. The implication was that paid employment was a *right* for disadvantaged groups and that reforms offered support to realise these rights. However, in reality, the policy changes (see below) mainly increased pressure on benefit recipients to look for work, without effective mechanisms to increase access to vacancies, increase the supply of employment or ensure that jobs paid above-poverty wages. Rather than ensuring that benefit recipients were no longer 'written off', the policy changes introduced greater compulsion and work-related conditionality for disadvantaged groups, which restricted access to financial support in times of need and reinforced the message that ill health or disability and caring responsibilities (a form of unpaid work) were no longer legitimate grounds for absence from the labour market. In terms of discourse, for more than a decade welfare-to-work policies have reproduced dichotomies between the preferred state of 'independence', associated only with paid work, and the stigmatised state of 'dependence' on welfare (Lewis, 1998). This underplays the potential for paid employment to be experienced as a source of alienation, oppression or exploitation. It also overlooks the impact of paid employment on time available for alternative activities, which might offer greater scope for promoting well-being (Burchardt, 2008).

Since the late 1990s, the UK government has sought to reduce social security expenditure by requiring benefit recipients to take specific actions to look for paid work. The Scottish government has very little control over this area of policy making, which is reserved for Westminster. Welfare reforms began in relation to unemployed people with a tightening of eligibility conditions and the harshening of sanctions, when Jobseeker's Allowance was introduced by the outgoing Conservative government in 1997. On coming to power in 1997, the New Labour government prioritised reform of the benefits system, which they targeted first at lone parents, by withdrawing the Lone Parent Premium of Income Support and the One Parent Benefit, which increased financial hardship for lone parents making new claims. It was only after this first cost-cutting exercise that the Labour government turned their attention towards 'making work pay', by introducing the National Minimum Wage in 1999 and improving the system for topping up low wages by introducing tax credits for those with inadequate wages (Millar, 2002). The commitment to eradicate child poverty by 2020 was also introduced around this time, as were a range of New Deal employment programmes to provide advice to help groups look for work (this was mandatory for long-term unemployed 18- to 24-year-olds and those aged 25 plus, but voluntary for lone parents and disabled people).

In the early 21st century, the New Labour government introduced a new phase of radical welfare reforms that followed the aim to raise the employment rate to 80 per cent, by moving people 'off benefits and into work' (DWP, 2006). This was not a solution to unemployment, which was at a historic low, but a measure to encourage and compel those who had previously been excused from the labour market, for reasons of caring responsibilities, ill health or disability, to look for work. Labour market inactivity was reconstructed as 'worklessness', with the implication that almost everyone should now be looking for work. Further improvements to the Working Tax Credit, Child Tax Credit and steps to increase the availability of affordable high-quality childcare helped lone parents in particular, but analysis shows that overall welfare-to-work policies have failed to meet their objectives in Scotland (Adams and Thomas, 2007).

The enduring picture is one in which the majority of people in Scotland are in paid employment. At the end of 2008, there were 1.7 million working-age households, consisting of 3.2 million people, in Scotland, of which 294,000 households (or 553,600 people) were 'workless' (Johnson, 2009). The highest rate of 'workless' households, where no one had a job, could be found in Glasgow City (28.9 per cent of working-age households in Glasgow), which was the second highest in all of the UK, after Inner City London. However, overall, Scotland had the highest rate of working households among the four countries in the UK and the second lowest rate of workless households. 'Worklessness' seemed to be particularly focused in the central belt and the Borders region of Scotland, with rural areas and the Isles much less affected. Anyadike-Danes (2010) found that there was a clear North–South distribution in the amount of people claiming Incapacity Benefit, which was closely linked to the industrial heritage of northern areas because Incapacity Benefit claimants in the North were more likely to suffer from musculo-skeletal diseases than their southern counterparts. Prior to 2008, Glasgow was the city with the highest count of Incapacity Benefit claimants in the UK, with almost one fifth of the working-age population claiming Incapacity Benefit (Webster et al, 2010). However, the claimant count has fallen sharply since 2003, and although still twice as high as elsewhere in the UK, it is suggested that improvement has occurred because of a general strengthening of the local labour market, rather than as a result of employment programmes such as the Working Neighbourhoods Pilot or Action Zones.

In September 2010, 6.9 per cent of men in Scotland were claiming Jobseeker's Allowance but only 2.9 per cent of women were claiming (ONS, 2010b). Of all benefit claimants, 16.3 per cent were claiming for longer than 12 months. A total of 765,000 people in Scotland were economically inactive between January and December 2009, with 28.9 per cent of them saying they had long-term health problems. Twenty-five per cent of those who were economically inactive said they wanted a job. In 2009, unemployment was slightly lower in Scotland than the UK average (7.0 per cent compared to 7.6 per cent). The areas with the highest unemployment rate were North Ayrshire and Glasgow City, with unemployment levels in excess of 10 per cent, while the lowest unemployment rates could be found on the Shetland and Orkney Isles (around 2.5 per cent) and on the mainland in Aberdeenshire (2.9 per cent), Aberdeen City (4.1 per cent) and Perth & Kinross (4.2 per cent) (ONS, 2010b). Unemployment has been very low in Scotland for the last decade, which has contributed to exceptionally low levels of long-term unemployment. Rises in unemployment following the 2008 recession may be reflected in high long-term unemployment in years to come. However, the Scottish context for the introduction of coercive welfare-to-work policies was one in which record proportions of people already had jobs and unemployment was at its lowest sustained level since the immediate post-war era (Nickell, 1999).

Conclusion

This chapter has provided an overview of key issues relating to work in Scotland, highlighting issues of inequality and injustice. First, we demonstrated the very high levels of employment that preceded the 2008 recession, which were combined with low unemployment but high levels of benefit receipt for illness and disability. Second, we outlined the restructuring of the Scottish labour market that transformed an industrial powerhouse into a service economy in the space of a century, demonstrating the differential impacts of this for particular localities and for men and women. Attention was then paid to the differing issues affecting urban and rural areas, which have required migrant labour to sustain local communities. The state of the workforce in terms of education and skills was then summarised, before focusing on a case study of enduring injustice in relation to gendered labour market segregation. The final section highlighted the issue of being out of work, which has been controversial in political and media debates, with negative constructions and misrepresentations of benefit recipients becoming an almost daily aspect of life. Overall, the Scottish labour market can be seen as active, vibrant and productive, but within the labour market powerful divisions remain, structuring the opportunities for lifelong earning potential available to different social groups and reinforcing long-term disadvantages. Ongoing tensions exist between the Scottish government and the UK government, particularly in relation to policy areas where Scotland's needs are not met by policies controlled at Westminster – in particular, immigration and social security. A viable solution to address these tensions could consist of a two-pronged approach involving decentralisation of Westminster decision-making power to the local level linked in with increased economic development opportunities by the Scottish government (The Scottish Government, 2011): first, through a decentralisation of policy-making power from Westminster to the local level, labour market programmes could be targeted to specific local historic backgrounds and labour market needs, as suggested by Helms and Cumbers (2006), to address specific problems; and second, through increased support for Local Regeneration Agencies by the Scottish government to drive a strengthening of the labour market, which has been shown to be more effective than the blanket approach of, for instance, Action Zones. However, the current misfit, between issues of employment-related social justice and Holyrood's capacity to take effective action to address them, leaves gaps that are unlikely to disappear.

Notes

[1] We are grateful to Ian McIntosh for this point and for his questioning of taken-for-granted assumptions relating to the lived reality of paid work.

[2] Since comparable records began in 1971 (National Statistics, 2008).

[3] 'Employment rate' means the proportion of the working-age population (women aged 16–59, men aged 16–64) population in paid employment (of at least one hour per week).

Further resources

A key starting point for understanding work and welfare in Scotland is: Helms, G. (2006) 'Work to welfare: welfare to work?', in G. Mooney, T. Sweeney and A. Law (eds) *Social care: Health and welfare in contemporary Scotland*, Paisley: Kynoch & Blaney, pp 123-43.

The UK-wide system of social security and tax credits is overviewed in: Millar, J. (ed) (2009) *Understanding social security: Issues for policy and practice*, Bristol: The Policy Press.

For more detail on the history of work in Scotland see: Mulhern, M.A., Beech, J. and Thompson, E. (eds) (2011) *The working life of the Scots, Vol 7, Scottish life and society: A compendium of Scottish ethnology*, Edinburgh: John Donald.

The Scottish Government website provides details of education and skills policy, as well as immigration and area-based anti-poverty initiatives that promote access or support people in gaining or retaining employment: www.scotland.gov.uk

For further statistics and analysis of labour market issues, see: www.scotland.gov.uk/Topics/Statistics/Browse/Labour-Market

For details on UK-wide social security and 'welfare' policies and initiatives, see the Department for Work and Pensions: www.dwp.gov.uk/

The Poverty Site includes an extensive section on 'Working age', with useful data and analysis of different aspects of working and claiming benefits: www.poverty. org.uk/s57/index.shtml

References

Adams, J. and Thomas, R. (2007) 'Active labour market policy in Scotland: does it make a difference?', *International Journal of Manpower*, vol 28, no 1, pp 30-41.

Alcock, P., Beatty, C., Fothergill, S., Macmillan, R. and Yeandle, S. (2003) *Work to welfare: How men become detached from the labour market*, Cambridge: Cambridge University Press.

Anyadike-Danes, M. (2010) 'What is the problem, exactly? The distribution of Incapacity Benefit claimants' conditions across British regions', *Policy Studies*, vol 31, no 2, pp 187-202.

Audas, R. and Mackay, R. (1997) 'A tale of two recessions', *Regional Studies*, vol 31, no 9, pp 867-74.

Beatty, C. and Fothergill, S. (1996) 'Labour market adjustment in areas of chronic industrial decline: the case of UK coalfields', *Regional Studies*, vol 34, no 7, pp 627-40.

Beveridge, C.W., McIntosh, N. and Wilson, R. (2010) *Independent budget review: The report of Scotland's Independent Budget Review Panel*, Edinburgh: APS Group Scotland.

Burchardt, T. (2008) *Time and income poverty*, CASEreport 57, London: London School of Economics and Political Science.

Checkland, O. and Checkland, S. (1989) *Industry and ethos: Scotland 1832-1914*, Edinburgh: Edinburgh University Press.

Crompton, R. (ed) (1999) *Restructuring gender relations and employment: The decline of the male breadwinner model*, Oxford: Oxford University Press.

de Lima, P. (2008) 'Poverty and social exclusion in rural areas', Final Report, Annex I, Country Studies, Scotland, in P. Bertolini, M. Marco Montanari and V. Peragine, *Poverty and social exclusion in rural areas*, Brussels: European Commission.

de Lima, P. and Wright, S. (2009) 'Welcoming migrants? Migrant labour in rural Scotland', *Social Policy and Society*, vol 8, no 3, pp 391-404.

DWP (Department for Work and Pensions) (2006) *A new deal for welfare: Empowering people to work*, London: The Stationery Office.

DWP (2008) *No one written off: Reforming welfare to reward responsibility*, London: The Stationery Office.

Edgell, S. (2006) *The sociology of work: Continuity and change in paid and unpaid work*, London: Sage Publications.

EOC (Equal Opportunities Commission) (2006a) *Facts about women and men in Great Britain 2006*, Manchester: EOC.

EOC (2006b) *Facts about women and men in Scotland 2006*, Manchester: EOC.

Fairclough, N. (2000) *New Labour, new language?*, London: Routledge.

Fraser, N. (2005) 'Reframing justice in a globalizing world', *New Left Review*, no 36, pp 69-88.

Freud, D. (2007) *Reducing dependency, increasing opportunity: Options for the future of welfare to work: An independent report to the Department for Work and Pensions*, London: Corporate Document Services.

Froy, F. and Giguère, S., (2010) *Putting in place jobs that last: A guide to rebuilding quality employment at local level*, Paris: Organisation for Economic Co-operation and Development.

Futureskills Scotland (2005) *International comparisons of Scotland's labour market and skills performance – Summary report*, Glasgow: Futureskills Scotland Scottish Enterprise.

Futureskills Scotland (2006) *The Scottish labour market 2006*, Glasgow: Futureskills Scotland Scottish Enterprise.

Futureskills Scotland (2007) *Labour market projections 2007 to 2017*, Glasgow: Futureskills Scotland Scottish Enterprise.

Futureskills Scotland (2009) *Skills in Scotland 2008*, Edinburgh: The Scottish Government.

Gregg, P. and Manning, A. (1997) 'Labour market regulation and unemployment', in D. Snower and G. de la Dehesa (eds) *Unemployment policy: Government options for the labour market*, Cambridge: Cambridge University Press, pp 395–420.

Gregg, P. and Wadsworth, J. (eds) (1999) *The state of working Britain*, Manchester: Manchester University Press.

Helms, G. and Cumbers, A. (2006) 'Regulating the new urban poor: local labour market control in an old industrial city', *Space & Polity*, vol 10, no 1, pp 67-86.

Hobson, B. (2003) 'Introduction', in B. Hobson (ed) *Recognition struggles and social movements*, Cambridge: Cambridge University Press, pp 1-17.

Jamieson, L. and Groves, L. (2008) *A review of the research literature to explore the key drivers of youth out-migration from rural Scotland*, Edinburgh: The Scottish Government.

Johnson, J. (2009) 'Households and the labour market for local areas', *Economic & Labour Market Review*, vol 3, no 11, London: Office for National Statistics, pp 24-31.

Keep, E. (2010) *The challenges and dilemmas of public skills policy and investment*, Histon: East of England Developing Agency.

Knox, W. (1999) *Industrial nation: Work, culture and society in Scotland, 1800-present*, Edinburgh: Edinburgh University Press.

Lewis, J. (1998) '"Work", "welfare" and lone mothers', *Political Quarterly*, vol 69, no 1, pp 4-13.

Lindsay, C. (2010) 'In a lonely place? Social networks, job seeking and the experience of long-term unemployment', *Social Policy and Society*, vol 9, no 1, pp 25-37.

Lister, R. (2004) *Poverty*, Cambridge: Polity Press.

Lister, R. (2008) 'Recognition and voice: the challenge for social justice', in T. Craig, T. Burchardt and S. Macpherson (eds) *Tackling occupational segregation in Scotland: A report of activities from the Scottish Government Cross-Directorate Occupational Segregation Working Group*, Edinburgh: Scottish Government, pp 105–22.

Macpherson, S. (2008) *Tackling occupational segregation in Scotland: a report of activities from the Scottish Government Cross-directorate Occupational Segregation Group*, Edinburgh: Scottish Government.

McQuaid, R., Bond, S. and Fuertes, V. (2009) *Evaluation of the Working for Families Fund (2004-2008)*, Edinburgh: The Scottish Government.

McQuaid, R., Bond, S. and Fuertes, V. (2010) *How can parents escape from recurrent poverty?*, York: Joseph Rowntree Foundation.

Millar, J. (2002) 'Adjusting welfare policies to stimulate job entry: the example of the United Kingdom', in H. Sarfati and G. Bonoli (eds) *Labour market and social protection reforms in international perspective: Parallel or converging tracks?*, Aldershot: Ashgate/ISSA (International Social Security Association), pp 266–84.

Millar J. (2008) 'Making work pay, making tax credits work: an assessment with specific reference to lone parent employment', *International Social Security Review*, vol 61, no 2, pp 21–38.

Mooney, G. (2009) 'The "Broken Society" election: class hatred and the politics of poverty and place in Glasgow East', *Social Policy and Society*, vol 8, no 4, pp 437–50.

Mooney, G. and Wright, S. (2011) 'Presenting poverty', in J.H. McKendrick, G. Mooney, J. Dickie and P. Kelly (eds) *Poverty in Scotland 2011: Towards a more equal Scotland*, London: Child Poverty Action Group, pp 133–45.

Nickell, S. (1999) 'Unemployment in Britain', in P. Gregg and J. Wadsworth (eds) *The state of working Britain*, Manchester: Manchester University Press.

ONS (Office for National Statistics) (2010a) *High level summary of statistics trend*, Last update: Thursday, 19 August 2010 (www.scotland.gov.uk/Topics/Statistics/Browse/Labour-Market).

ONS (2010b) *Labour market statistics regional monthly data* (www.statistics.gov.uk/STATBASE/Product.asp?vlnk=15084).

Scottish Government, The (2003) *Scottish economic statistics, 2003* (www.scotland.gov.uk/Publications/2003/04/17042/21542).

Scottish Government, The (2010a) *Employment and economic activity – Employment rate* (www.scotland.gov.uk/Topics/Statistics/Browse/Labour-Market/TrendEconomicActivity).

Scottish Government, The (2010b) *Skills for Scotland: Accelerating the recovery and increasing sustainable economic growth*, Edinburgh: The Scottish Government.

Scottish Government, The (2010c) *Local area labour markets in Scotland: Statistics from the Annual Population Survey 2009* (www.scotland.gov.uk/Publications/2010/07/29103916/5).

Scottish Government, The (2010d) *Poverty and income inequality in Scotland: 2008/09* (www.scotland.gov.uk/Publications/2010/05/povertystats0809/Q/ Page/2).

Scottish Government, The (2011) *The Government economic strategy*, Edinburgh: The Scottish Government (www.scotland.gov.uk/ Publications/2011/09/13091128/0).

Scottish Office (1998) *Meeting the Childcare Challenge: A Childcare Strategy for Scotland*, Edinburgh: Scottish Office.

Slaven, A. (1975) *The development of the West of Scotland, 1750–1960*, London: Routledge & Kegan Paul.

Smith, I.D. (2008) 'Living and dying, on welfare in Glasgow East', *The Daily Telegraph*, 13 July.

Strangleman, T. and Warren, T. (2008) *Work and society: Sociological approaches, themes and methods*, London: Routledge.

Svendsen, L. (2008) *Work*, Stocksfield: Acumen.

Taylor-Gooby, P. (2005) *Attitudes to social justice*, London: Institute for Public Policy Research.

Telfer, C. (2011) 'Education', in J.H. McKendrick, G. Mooney, J. Dickie and P. Kelly (eds) *Poverty in Scotland 2011: Towards a more equal Scotland*, London: Child Poverty Action Group, pp 173-8.

Webster, D. (2000) 'The geographical concentration of labour market disadvantage', *Oxford Review of Economic Policy*, vol 16, no 1, pp 114-28.

Webster, D., Arnott, J., Brown, J., Turok, I., Mitchell, R. and MacDonald, E.B. (2010) 'Falling Incapacity Benefit claims in a former industrial city: policy impacts or labour market improvement?', *Policy Studies*, vol 31, vol 2, pp 163-85.

Wright, S. (2009) 'Welfare to work', in J. Millar (ed) *Understanding social security*, Bristol: The Policy Press, pp 193-212.

Wright, S. (2011) 'Relinquishing rights? The impact of activation on citizenship for lone parents in the UK', in S. Betzelt and S. Bothfeld (eds) *Activation and labour market reforms in Europe: Challenges to social citizenship*, Basingstoke: Palgrave, pp 59-78.

THIRTEEN

Social housing and homelessness policies: reconciling social justice and social mix

Kim McKee and Danny Phillips

Introduction

While housing policies already had a distinctive Scottish flavour even before devolution, the creation of the Scottish Parliament in 1999 has allowed further policy divergence (see, for example, Maclennan and O'Sullivan, 2008). As Kintrea (2006) highlights, the first term of the Scottish Parliament resulted in a number of high-level policy goals centred on social justice, social cohesion, economic competitiveness and empowerment. Both the policy documents and memoranda in circulation at this time highlighted that housing reform was 'to contribute to policy objectives that are broader and more fundamental than new arrangements for the delivery of housing services' (Kintrea, 2006, p 190). This chapter focuses on the first two of these articulated goals, social justice and social cohesion, and in doing so illuminates the progress and contradictions that have characterised social housing and homelessness reforms in a devolved Scotland. While social justice is concerned with equal opportunities and rights of access to social rented housing, social cohesion relates to social mix and is intimately connected to wider public policy debates around social capital, social networks and the most appropriate solution to tackling concentrations of poverty.

In order to explore these key themes in more depth, this chapter begins with an overview of housing policy in devolved Scotland. This is followed by a detailed focus on the homelessness legislation in Scotland following devolution in 1999, which has been recognised internationally for its progressive principles and strong commitment to social justice by extending the rights of homeless households to access social housing. This is followed in turn by a discussion of social housing and social mix, connecting the homelessness agenda to wider debates about concentrations of poverty and the appropriate role of social housing in a devolved Scotland. The final substantive section further develops this argument with reference to the policy shift from social to affordable housing, which was first initiated under the Labour–Liberal Democrat Coalition and has continued under the Scottish National Party (SNP) government. This policy agenda is concerned with promoting low-cost homeownership as a vehicle to secure greater social mix at the neighbourhood level. However, it has the further effect of 'normalising' homeownership and marginalising social housing (McIntyre and McKee, 2009).

This chapter concludes by underlining the mismatch between homelessness reforms underpinned by the policy objective of social justice, and government initiatives concerned with promoting social cohesion through tenure mix. While the political commitment to ending homelessness is a laudable one, it has nonetheless exacerbated concentrations of poverty and disadvantage within the social rented sector, reinforcing the image of social housing as a residual tenure of last resort. However, as this chapter argues, the future of social housing in Scotland could be transformed if the Parliament were to use its devolved powers to pursue a distinctly Scottish approach to social housing reform, one that is tenure-neutral in nature, and that recognises the positive social contribution the sector can make. At present, however, social housing policy in Scotland is largely focused on meeting the requirements of the politically iconic homelessness legislation and its ambitious 2012 target to end homelessness.

Social housing in Scotland: policy context since 1999

Scotland has the highest proportion of social housing in the UK. It houses one in four of the Scottish population, and accounts for nearly 40 per cent of the tenure structure in some urban local authority areas such as Glasgow and Dundee. There have, however, been significant changes within the social rented sector in recent decades, not least the growth of the housing association movement, because of UK and devolved government support for housing stock transfer,[1] coupled with more favourable funding regimes for registered social landlords (RSLs)[2] (Pawson and Mullins, 2010). In 1981, while 52 per cent of Scottish dwellings were in the local authority sector and 2 per cent in the housing association sector, by 2006 this had changed to 15 and 10 per cent respectively (Wilcox, 2007, p 101). This emphasises not only the changing tenure balance within the social rented sector, but also the growth in homeownership during this period.

The Right to Buy policy introduced by Margaret Thatcher's Conservative government in 1980 played an important role in growing homeownership by enabling sitting tenants to buy their council house at discounted rates (Newhaven Research, 2005; King, 2010). Given Scotland's historic tenure structure, current levels of homeownership (65 per cent) would have been difficult to achieve without the prior existence of a large public sector that could be privatised (McKee, 2010a). Despite the massive impact this policy has across all housing tenures, reforms to the Right to Buy have been contradictory in the period since the establishment of devolution. While the Housing (Scotland) Act 2001 extended the 'right' to *all social housing tenants*, at the same time it made the discounts less generous for new tenants to the sector. Moreover, the SNP government's Housing (Scotland) Act 2010 scrapped the 'right' for both new social housing and new tenants. This measure is arguably not only decades too late given the Right to Buy has already significantly reduced the overall volume of social housing for rent, but also contradicts other government policy objectives around tenure mix and social cohesion, by reducing the opportunity for low-cost homeownership (McKee, 2010a).

There are now 26 local authority landlords and over 200 RSLs in Scotland (SHR, 2010, p 2). In contrast to the rest of the UK, small, community-based landlords dominate the RSL sector in Scotland. Over 80 per cent manage a housing stock of less than 2,000 homes, and unlike in other parts of the UK, tenants and other local residents dominate their governing bodies (SHR, 2010; see also McKee, 2010c). These community-controlled housing associations are geographically concentrated in the west of Scotland and have become lead agencies in area-based regeneration initiatives, supported by the Wider Role Fund (Scott, 1997). Their strong connection to, and understanding of, local interests enables them to act as 'anchor' organisations in their communities, adding value to existing statutory and voluntary services (McKee, 2011).

The growth in whole stock transfer since devolution has, however, also created a small number of very large social landlords in Glasgow, Dumfries and Galloway, Inverclyde and the Scottish Borders. Between them, these big four housing associations own a third of the RSL housing stock (SHR, 2010, p 2). Denounced by critics (including tenants' groups and trades unions) as the latest phase of housing privatisation (Daly et al, 2005; Ginsburg, 2005), stock transfer was an important policy priority of the first Scottish administration. Despite being rebadged and sold to tenants as 'community ownership' (Daly et al, 2005), it has, however, lost momentum in recent years, not least because of the problems in delivering this agenda in Glasgow (McKee, 2009a, 2009b).

A further distinctive feature of social housing in Scotland is the existence of a single Scottish secure tenancy. This was a product of the Housing (Scotland) Act 2001, and ended differential rights between housing association and council tenants by creating a single tenancy across the social rented sector (Scott, 2004). In policy terms, this was integral to the success of rolling out stock transfer on a much larger scale, as it made stock transfer more palatable to tenants. It ends the previous distinction between assured and secure tenants by giving all social housing tenants (regardless of whether their landlord is a local authority or an RSL) the same rights in terms of succession, assignation and security of tenure (Scott, 2004). Unlike in the rest of the UK there is also a single regulatory framework in Scotland. Created by the Housing (Scotland) Act 2010 the new Scottish Housing Regulator (formerly Communities Scotland) now has responsibility for monitoring and assessing the quality of housing services provided by both local authorities and RSLs. The previous 2001 Act introduced a common set of performance standards for social landlords, a more user-centred inspection process, and also enhanced the Regulator's powers of intervention. Comparisons across different types of social landlord highlight that in general local authority landlords are poorer performers (SHR, 2009). However, this finding needs to be contextualised given the different funding regimes and cultures of performance that exist across the sector.

Following the change of administration in 2007 and the election of the SNP government, initiatives to support new building in the social rented sector have been pursued, such as the National Housing Trust and the Council Housing Building Fund (The Scottish Government, 2009, 2010, 2011). The SNP have also rejected the dramatic social housing reforms currently being pursued in England, which will end tenancies for life and move towards market rents (CLG, 2010). Nonetheless, questions have been raised about the 'black hole' in the SNP's plans for building new social housing, given that the Comprehensive Spending Review cut over 30 per cent from the affordable housing budget (SFHA, 2011; Shelter, 2011).

Homelessness policy represents a final distinctive aspect of housing reform in the period since 1999. The Parliament has introduced a plethora of reforms designed to strengthen homeless households' rights to access social housing. This legislation is unique and progressive, not only in UK terms but also internationally, and is explored in more detail in the next section.

A progressive homelessness agenda?

Prior to devolution, all homelessness policy in the UK was within the legal framework of the Housing (Homeless Persons) Act 1977 (which was consolidated into two separate Scottish and English Acts in the mid-1980s). The 1977 Act required local authorities to provide accommodation for people seeking rehousing due to homelessness. However, their homelessness must also have been 'unintentional', they had to meet the criteria of 'priority need' (that is, their household includes a child, pregnant woman or other vulnerable person), and they also had to have a 'local connection' with the area (Fitzpatrick, 2004; Anderson, 2007, 2009). Homeless people not deemed in 'priority need' were offered only advice and assistance, while those in 'priority need' but deemed intentionally homeless were only entitled to temporary accommodation for a time-limited period (Fitzpatrick, 2004).

Despite its clear limitations, the 1977 Act was a significant piece of legislation that, for the first time, granted homeless households rights to long-term accommodation, as well as 'reasonable preference' in the allocation of council housing. Nonetheless, it has also been fundamental in changing the socioeconomic characteristics of new social housing tenants, further contributing to the residualisation of the sector (King, 2010). Residualisation refers to the way in which social housing has become a residual tenure, housing the poorest, most vulnerable sections of society (Forrest and Murie, 1988). In addition, the 1977 Act was criticised for creating a 'perverse incentive to "manufacture" homelessness', an argument that resulted in a reduction of local authorities' homelessness obligations in England under John Major's Conservative government of the 1990s (Fitzpatrick, 2004, p 185).

Since devolution, homelessness policy was high on the new Scottish Parliament's agenda. In 1999, a Homelessness Task Force was established and chaired by the Minister with responsibility for Social Justice (which included housing). Membership of the Task Force was inclusive, and included representatives from across the public and voluntary sectors as well as civil servants. The Task Force's most significant proposals were legislative changes to improve the rights of homeless people. The most radical recommendation was that 'priority need' in the Housing (Homeless Persons) Act 1977 should be removed within a decade (by 2012), with a proposal to gradually widen the definition until the distinction between those in priority need and those who were not was eventually rendered redundant. The gradual shift over time was also to enable local authorities, which have statutory responsibility for meeting homelessness obligations, to mobilise the necessary resources and partnership arrangements to implement this legislation (Homelessness Task Force, 2002).

The reliance of local authorities on other housing partners is a direct result of the growth in whole stock transfer – another policy priority of the first administration of the Scottish Parliament. Because of the stock transfer of public sector housing to RSLs, some cities, such as Glasgow, now have no council housing, and are thus reliant on housing providers in both the voluntary and private sectors to discharge their homeless responsibilities. The Housing (Scotland) Act 2001 introduced a duty on RSLs to comply with requests from local authorities to accommodate unintentionally homeless households in priority need, and also to give homeless households 'reasonable preference' in their allocation policies (Fitzpatrick, 2004). This has exacerbated tensions between RSLs, located in the voluntary sector, and central government, with landlords frustrated at government dictating to them how they should manage their housing (McKee, 2008).

The key recommendations of the Task Force were embodied in the Homelessness etc (Scotland) Act 2003, with some of their initial findings also incorporated in the Housing (Scotland) Act 2001. Overall, this landmark and progressive legislation is internationally recognised as being at the forefront of tackling homelessness by extending the rights offered to homeless households (Shelter, 2007; Anderson, 2009). While the centrepiece of the 2003 Act was its ambitious 2012 target, it also made provisions to soften the 'intentionality' and 'local connection' tests, and required landlords and lenders to notify the local authority of any pending eviction or repossession. As Fitzpatrick (2004, p 192) emphasises:

> ... the 'vision' ... enacted in the 2003 Act is that by 2012, everyone who is homeless in Scotland will be entitled to permanent re-housing, except for a small number of intentionally homeless people for whom this right will be suspended temporarily.

While much policy analysis concentrates on the 2003 Act, it is important not to overlook the earlier provisions of the Housing (Scotland) Act 2001 which also strengthened the rights of individual homeless households in a number of important ways. For example, the 2001 Act required local authorities to provide interim accommodation pending inquiries to *all homeless applicants*; to provide *permanent accommodation* to unintentionally homeless people in priority need; and a right to temporary accommodation for non-priority homeless applicants. These measures effectively brought 'the rights of those non-priority applicants in line with those of intentionally homeless households in priority need', and from a resource perspective place an 'onerous new demand on local authorities ... to provide interim and temporary accommodation to non-priority groups' (Fitzpatrick, 2004, p 189).

These tensions highlight the paradoxical nature of the homelessness legislation in Scotland. While the extension of homeless people's rights on the one hand is to be welcomed, this landmark legislation nonetheless puts pressure on the social housing system. Despite the demands it makes on social housing allocations, the 2003 Act has not been matched by any significant increase in housing supply, other than restrictions to the Right to Buy, coupled with support for some small-scale new building, as mentioned earlier. This has resulted in an increased emphasis on the private rented sector in order to meet statutory obligations with regards to homelessness.

Failure to attend to the issue of housing supply is critical. Analysis of the SCORE (Scottish Continuous Recording System) lettings data highlights that the proportion of households accessing social housing through the statutory homelessness route has more than doubled since the legislation was introduced post-devolution (SCORE, 2003, 2010). Any increase in the number of homeless households that local authorities have a responsibility to rehouse ultimately limits the availability of social housing lettings for other potential tenants not coming through the homelessness route.

As is explored in more detail in the next section, this has the effect of restricting access to social housing to the most vulnerable groups in society, exacerbating existing concentrations of poverty within the sector. It also compounds the sector's role as welfare housing, precluding any kind of radical alternative. Despite the potential social (in)justice implications of these policy tensions, there was little opposition to the homelessness legislation in the first term of the Scottish Parliament, and the SNP government has largely continued with the homeless agenda set out by the previous Labour–Liberal Democrat Coalition. The establishment of what Fitzpatrick (2004, p 192) terms an 'inalienable right to (some type of) accommodation and support' is a radical departure not only from the previous Scottish position, but from what is happening in other parts of the UK.

Progress towards meeting the 2012 target has nonetheless been mixed (Anderson 2007, 2009; Nolan and Maclean, 2008; Wilcox et al, 2010). Under an interim target set by the Scottish government, local authorities should have halved the percentage of households assessed as not being in priority need by 2009. While the majority of local authorities are now meeting this, research by Pawson et al (2007) suggests that homelessness prevention should be given greater importance as Scotland moves towards the 2012 target (as has been the case elsewhere in the UK). This is because extending 'rights to housing' does not address the social and economic causes of homelessness (Anderson, 2009). Focusing the homelessness agenda on housing-led solutions may also downplay the equally important issue of support. Without sufficient support and service structures to maintain the tenancy, formerly homeless households may simply drift back to the streets (see, for example, Atherton and McNaughton Nicholls, 2008).

Social housing and social mix

Increasing homeless households' rights to access social housing – while a laudable aim – nonetheless reinforces the expectation that social housing exists only to cater for those in the most severe housing need. A key criticism of social housing reforms under devolution is that they have failed to envision any radical future for the sector as a mainstream tenure of choice, and have instead largely accepted its role as welfare housing for the most vulnerable sections of society. Social housing has always been the 'wobbly pillar' of the welfare state as it has never provided the same universal provision as other public services, such as comprehensive education or the National Health Service (NHS) (Malpass, 2010). Nonetheless, at its peak in the early 1980s it housed half the Scottish population and historically there has never been the same stigma attached to renting from a social landlord in Scotland as compared to other parts of the UK. This was because it was traditionally a larger tenure that housed a more general cross-section of the population. It was quite 'normal' for working families in the 1970s and 1980s to live in social housing (or council housing as it was more commonly known then).

Analysis of current housing policies, however, highlights an unwillingness to return to this wider role, with allocation policies remaining very much focused on supporting those in extreme housing need, such as the homeless. Despite the SNP's professed commitment to tenure neutrality, in policy terms they continue to think of social housing as simply welfare housing and a tenure of last resort, as opposed to a more mainstream tenure that individual households may positively choose to opt into. In *Firm foundations* the Scottish government actually describes social landlords as 'the providers of homes for the most vulnerable in society' (The Scottish Government, 2007, p 25), and conceives the sector as a residual tenure that supports people at particular times in their lives, offering a 'safety net at a time of personal crisis' or 'first home before entering owner-occupation' (The Scottish Government, 2007, p 34). However, as long as the sector remains solely the preserve of the poorest, most vulnerable sections of society, then aspirations around social cohesion and social mix are going to be difficult to achieve.

Allocating social housing on the basis of most extreme need ultimately leads to greater concentrations of poverty and disadvantage. Analysis of the SCORE (2010) interim lettings data for 2010/11 highlights that a third of households in the social rented sector are unemployed, 16 per cent retired, and 9 per cent long-term sick or disabled. Given these high levels of economic inactivity, it is perhaps not surprising that the average weekly household income for social renters in Scotland is only £207, and over two thirds are reliant on some form of housing benefit. Combined figures relating to unemployment and household income reflect the type of households that tend to be concentrated within the sector: older households (17 per cent), single parent households (19 per cent) and single adult households (37 per cent). Moreover, 28 per cent of those households allocated a social rented property during the reporting period came through the homelessness route. This figure underlines how the homelessness route is now the only mechanism to access social housing in many areas, resulting in households strategically presenting themselves as 'homeless' to jump the waiting list queue.

Such concentrations of poverty and disadvantage have a knock-on effect on housing management, for if social housing is only a welfare safety-net for people with no other choices, then it becomes a much more difficult sector to manage. The homelessness legislation is a good example of this. Prior to the 2001 Act RSLs were able to reject households on the grounds of their past behaviour in order to protect the social order of their local communities (Kintrea, 2006). Now they can do this much less easily, as removing the rules on 'intentionality' means that those households who have lost their home through anti-social behaviour now have rights to rehousing through the homelessness route. This not only contradicts ministers' tough rhetoric on anti-social behaviour, but makes housing management at the community level much more challenging (Flint, 2004; Kintrea, 2006). This is a frustration expressed not only by landlords, but increasingly by social housing tenants themselves, who feel powerless in the process of social housing allocations, and also angry at its outcomes, as the system is perceived to act against 'hard working families' who wish to remain in their local area close to their existing kin networks (McKee, 2008, 2009b; Nolan and Maclean, 2008; Anderson, 2009). This sentiment reflects the heterogeneity of social housing estates, and the way in which tenants themselves make moral judgements about other tenants, in the same way that welfare professionals have historically always made distinctions between the 'deserving' and 'undeserving' poor (Ravetz, 2001; Johnstone and Mooney, 2007).

As Kintrea (2006, p 198) observes, it seems that 'social justice for some is being bought at the expense of access to housing for slightly less badly off groups'. While the Housing (Scotland) Act 2001, and other subsequent reforms, have focused on improving the quality of social housing, and making the sector even more accessible to homeless people, the limits of the devolution settlement perhaps precludes a more radical vision. Many of the key mechanisms that structure the housing system and the attractiveness of particular tenures lie outside the scope of the Scottish Parliament, such as the housing benefit and tax system (Gibb, 2004; Kintrea, 2006; McKee, 2010a).

Given these tensions within the devolution settlement, the Scottish government, like the Scottish Executive before them, have pursued a policy of tenure mix in order to tackle concentrations of poverty. The policy objective here is both to attract more affluent households and to retain 'successful' local households, within areas traditionally dominated by social housing, and in doing so increase social mix and the role model effect at the neighbourhood level. Creating a better balance of tenure, house types and incomes is deemed pivotal not only in tackling concentrations of deprivation, but also in realising government aspirations for more cohesive, sustainable communities (Scottish Executive, 2005; The Scottish Government, 2007, 2010, 2011). This is important in the Scottish housing policy context given the spatial concentrations of poverty within social housing estates. Nonetheless, not only does this policy objective assume that public housing estates have failed, but it also ignores that the evidence base for mixed communities remains highly contested (see, for example, Graham et al, 2009; Lupton and Fuller, 2009; van Ham and Manley, 2010). To develop this argument further, the next section explores the way this tenure mix agenda has been delivered in Scotland through low-cost homeownership initiatives. It is argued this represents a shift in government priorities from social to affordable housing, and further supports the 'normalisation' of homeownership.

From social to affordable housing

A central aspect of Scottish housing policy in recent years has been tenure mix through low-cost homeownership, which the Scottish government (2007) has branded as LIFT (low-cost initiatives for first-time buyers). Increasing homeownership among low and middle-income groups has emerged here as an important strand of housing-led regeneration (McIntyre and McKee, 2009; McKee, 2010b). Policy vehicles to encourage this include, for example, GRO grants to support owner-occupation in areas with little private housing; the inclusion of affordable housing in new private housing developments using planning gains; and the promotion of shared ownership, and more recently shared equity, intermediate housing products (see, for example, Bramley et al, 2007; Munro, 2007; Wallace, 2008; McKee, 2010a, 2010b). Uniting this plethora of different schemes and policy initiatives is a political ambition to help people realise their aspirations for homeownership, with a particular emphasis on first-time buyers, especially those currently living in the rental sector or with relatives. As such, these schemes build on previously successful low-cost homeownership initiatives such as the Right to Buy (see, for example, Newhaven Research, 2005).

Although not new, these initiatives are a small but increasingly important segment of the housing market as affordability problems are exacerbated by the economic downturn. A key impact of the recession has been that mortgage finance is now more heavily constrained, with larger, more onerous deposit requirements proving to be a particular barrier for young households trying to access the housing ladder for the first time. As figures from the Council for Mortgage Lenders (for 2009) highlight, the average deposit requirement for first-time buyers in the UK is now 25 per cent, with the average age of a first-time buyer without parental support now 37 years (cited in The Scottish Government, 2010, p 10). At the same time, the new era of fiscal austerity and public sector budget cuts announced by the UK Coalition government at Westminster has put social housing budgets under threat. Housing is not a protected area of public spending in the same way as education and health, as reflected in the recent Scottish Comprehensive Spending Review. Consequently, the idea of social housing is now being reimagined as affordable housing. This represents an important and significant departure from the traditional model of social *rented* housing, towards housing for *sale* through low-cost homeownership initiatives. While this policy shift is couched in the language of meeting individual aspiration, it is important to note the public cost of low-cost homeownership is significantly less than for traditional social rented housing, and represents a considerable saving to the public purse. Such schemes also shift responsibility for housing provision downwards from the state to the individual consumer, representing a further example of rolling back the state.

Continuing to promote homeownership to low-income groups at a time when the economy is struggling is, however, neither risk-free nor unproblematic (Newhaven Research and the University of Glasgow, 2008; McIntyre and McKee, 2009). Some of the most popular low-cost homeownership initiatives, such as shared equity,[3] are more bureaucratically administered and restrictive than traditional social housing tenancies; at the same time, low-income purchasers are paying more for their borrowing due to limited availability of mortgage products (McKee, 2010b). Evidence also suggests purchasers are becoming trapped in an intermediate tenure that they cannot move out of (Wallace, 2008; McKee, 2010b). Despite being sold the dream of homeownership, becoming a 'full' homeowner in the conventional sense is financially not within their reach. These research findings, combined with current restrictions on public sector spending, raise the question of whether it is appropriate for government to concentrate scarce resources on housing for sale at a time when social housing waiting lists continue to grow.

Instead of pursuing tenure mix at the expense of marginalising the social rented sector perhaps the Scottish government could use the downturn as a positive opportunity to rethink its attitude to tenure and adopt truly tenure-neutral policies, which would enable the social rented sector to play a greater 'social' role during these difficult economic times. Promoting affordable housing at a time when what the country arguably needs is more social housing not only further marginalises and stigmatises the sector, but also ultimately compounds its role as a welfare safety-net for the most vulnerable. Moreover, social housing policies that favour those in extreme need are in direct opposition to aspirations for social mix. As Arthurson (2008, p 15) argues, 'the resultant stigma attached to a residualised social housing tenure makes social interaction across different housing tenures even less likely'.

Historically, social (and more specifically council housing) in Scotland has housed a much broader section of the population than this. It has the potential to do so once again through policy initiatives such as mid-market rent, or more radically by rethinking how we allocate social rented housing and prioritise different groups in housing need. In contrast to most other European countries and English-speaking nations there is currently no income test requirement to access social housing in the UK. In principle, then, the allocations policy could be adapted to diversify the social characteristics of new tenants entering the sector, not least because genuine social mix at this micro (street) level is more likely to deliver the positive social interactions and role model effects described by the literature than at the meso (neighbourhood) level (Arthurson, 2008). Nonetheless, it could be argued that tenure mix, even where it is successful, only ever addresses the symptoms rather than the causes of structural inequalities. Housing policy on its own cannot resolve the problems (often referred to as neighbourhood effects) that are caused by concentrated poverty.

Conclusion

Two key policy objectives of housing reforms since devolution have been social justice and social cohesion. While the former has been achieved by extending the rights of homeless households to access social housing through the provisions of the Housing (Scotland) Act 2001 and the Homelessness etc (Scotland) Act 2003, the latter is brought into focus through the shift from social to affordable housing via low-cost homeownership initiatives, currently branded as LIFT. At one level both these policy objectives have delivered positive housing outcomes: the homelessness legislation is progressive and internationally renowned, while low-cost homeownership schemes offer one route to tackle the problem of housing affordability, and also encourage greater tenure mix at the neighbourhood level in regeneration areas.

On the other hand, both these policies are in constant tension and not necessarily mutually compatible. While the homelessness legislation in Scotland certainly delivers social justice for a very vulnerable group in society, as Kintrea (2006) has observed, it does so at the expense of other slightly less well-off groups who would also like to access social housing. As a nation, if we are interested in social justice, should we not be pursuing social justice for all, instead of social justice for some? The more social housing that is allocated to statutory homeless households then the less there is available to let to the wider population who would also like a social housing tenancy, unless we build more social housing, that is. The current situation not only exacerbates concentrations of poverty and disadvantage in the social rented sector, undermining aspirations for social mix, but also compounds the sector's role as a marginal tenure, as opposed to a proactive and positive choice. Social housing's residual status has been further underlined by the rhetoric of affordable housing, which is currently being emphasised at the expense of traditional social rented housing.

The implicit and explicit policy discourse underpinning both the homelessness legislation and low-cost homeownership initiatives is that homeownership is the natural, tenure of choice: those who can afford to buy should be encouraged to do so, with social rented housing being reduced to a welfare safety-net for those who cannot. The question remains, however — is this what we want the future of social housing to be? Given Scotland prides itself on a commitment to social justice, should the Scottish Parliament not have bigger ambitions for the social rented sector? It once housed over half of Scottish households, and given the increasingly difficult mortgage market, not to mention the precarious labour market situation many Scottish families are in, is now not the time to be embracing and promoting the positive social contribution the social rented sector can make? While this would mark a significant departure from housing policy developments elsewhere in the UK, is that not the whole point of devolution, to pursue distinctly Scottish policy agendas?

Although the current devolution settlement imposes a number of restrictions on the Parliament, there is scope for MSPs (Members of the Scottish Parliament) to act and think differently on these important social justice and social policy questions. This in turn opens up the possibility for the introduction of more tenure-neutral policies, which would support a greater role for social housing, such as funding for significant new social housing developments, and a rethink of the current social housing allocations policy to encourage greater social mix within the tenure. At present, however, social housing policy in Scotland remains largely focused on homelessness and meeting the 2012 target. While there is much to admire about this legislation, not least its political commitment to improving the rights of a very vulnerable group within society, there seems to be little critical discussion of the impact it undoubtedly has on the social rented sector more broadly. The future of social housing in Scotland can be transformed, but only if there is the political will and a commitment of public resources to allow this transformation to happen.

Notes

[1] Housing stock transfer refers to the sale of housing from public sector landlords (local authority or Scottish Homes) to not-for-profit landlords located in the voluntary sector (housing associations or cooperatives).

[2] 'Registered social landlord' is an umbrella term for not-for-profit landlords who provide affordable housing for rent to households in 'need'. This includes housing associations and cooperatives. In contrast to local authority housing providers, RSLs are located in the third sector as opposed to the public sector.

[3] Shared equity effectively acts like an interest-free loan. Purchasers buy a smaller stake in the property (normally between 60 and 80 per cent), with this smaller mortgage equating to a smaller deposit requirement and a lower monthly mortgage payment. After two years purchasers have the option to increase their stake up to 100 per cent; however, they are the legal owner and responsible for all repair and maintenance. When the property is sold both the purchaser and the developer (normally an RSL) split any equity gains.

Further resources

Kintrea, K. (2006) 'Having it all? Housing reform under devolution', *Housing Studies*, vol 21, no 2, pp 187–207.

McKee, K. (2010) 'The end of the Right to Buy and the future of social housing in Scotland', *Local Economy*, vol 25, no 4, pp 319–27.

Sim, D. (ed) (2004) *Housing and public policy in post-devolution Scotland*, Coventry and York: Chartered Institute of Housing and Joseph Rowntree Foundation.

The Scottish Government housing website: www.scotland.gov.uk/Topics/Built-Environment/Housing

Scottish Continuous Recording System (SCORE): www.scoreonline.org.uk/index.cfm

Shelter: http://scotland.shelter.org.uk/

References

Anderson, I. (2007) 'Sustainable solutions to homelessness: the Scottish case', *European Journal of Homelessness*, vol 1, pp 163–83.

Anderson, I. (2009) 'Homelessness policy in Scotland: a complete safety net by 2012?', in S. Fitzpatrick, D. Quilgars and N. Pleace (eds) *Homelessness in the UK: Problems and solutions*, Coventry: Chartered Institute of Housing, pp 107–24.

Arthurson, K. (2008) 'Theorising social mix: spatial scale and resident interaction', Paper presented at the Australasian Housing Researcher's Conference (http://mams.rmit.edu.au/kj0qpcv9t0vy.pdf).

Atherton, I. and McNaughton Nicholls, C. (2008) '"Housing First" as a means of addressing multiple needs and homelessness', *European Journal of Homelessness*, vol 2, pp 289–303.

Bramley, G., Morgan, J. and Littlewood, M. (2007) *Initial evaluation of the Open Market Homestake Pilot*, Research Report 87, Edinburgh: Communities Scotland.

CLG (Communities and Local Government) (2010) *Local decisions: A fairer future for social housing*, London: CLG.

Daly, G., Mooney, G., Poole, L. and Davis, H. (2005) 'Housing stock transfer in Birmingham and Glasgow: the contrasting experiences of two UK cities', *European Journal of Housing Policy*, vol 5, no 3, pp 327–41.

Fitzpatrick, S. (2004) 'Homelessness policy in Scotland', in D. Sim (ed) *Housing and public policy in post-devolution Scotland*, Coventry and York: Chartered Institute of Housing and Joseph Rowntree Foundation, pp 183–98.

Flint, J. (2004) 'The responsible tenant: housing governance and the politics of behaviour', *Housing Studies*, vol 19, no 6, pp 893–910.

Forrest, R. and Murie, A. (1988) *Selling the welfare state: The privatisation of public housing*, London: Routledge.

Gibb, K. (2004) 'At the margins of devolution? Fiscal autonomy, housing policy and housing benefit', *Scottish Affairs*, vol 48, pp 111-32.

Ginsburg, N. (2005) 'The privatization of council housing', *Critical Social Policy*, vol 25, no 1, pp 115-35.

Graham, E., Manley, D., Hiscock, R., Boyle, P. and Doherty, J. (2009) 'Mixing housing tenures: is it good for social well-being?', *Urban Studies*, vol 46, no 1, pp 139-65.

Homelessness Task Force (2002) *Helping homeless people: An action plan for prevention and effective response*, Homelessness Task Force Final Report, Edinburgh: Scottish Executive.

Johnstone, C. and Mooney, G. (2007) '"Problem" people, "problem" spaces? New Labour and council estates', in R. Atkinson and G. Helms (eds) *Securing an urban renaissance: Crime, community, and British urban policy*, Bristol: The Policy Press, pp 125-39.

King, P. (2010) *Housing policy transformed: The Right to Buy and the desire to own*, Bristol: The Policy Press.

Kintrea, K. (2006) 'Having it all? Housing reform under devolution', *Housing Studies*, vol 21, no 2, pp 187-207.

Lupton, R. and Fuller, C. (2009) 'Mixed communities: a new approach to spatially concentrated poverty in England', *International Journal of Urban and Regional Research*, vol 33, no 4, pp 1014-28.

Maclennan, D. and O'Sullivan, T. (2008) *Housing policies for Scotland: Challenges and changes*, York: Joseph Rowntree Foundation.

Malpass, P. (2010) 'Housing and the new welfare state', *Housing Studies*, vol 23, no 1, pp 1-19.

McIntyre, Z. and McKee, K. (2009) 'Creating sustainable communities through tenure-mix: the responsibilisation of marginal homeowners in Scotland', *Geojournal* (www.springerlink.com/content/90xg83643pq14g79/fulltext.pdf).

McKee, K. (2008) 'Transforming Scotland's public sector housing through community ownership: the re-territorialisation of housing governance?', *Space and Polity*, vol 12, no 2, pp 183-96.

McKee, K. (2009a) 'Learning lessons from stock transfer: the challenges in delivering second stage transfer in Glasgow', *People, Place and Policy Online*, vol 3, no 1, pp 16-27.

McKee, K. (2009b) 'Empowering Glasgow's tenants through community ownership?', *Local Economy*, vol 24, no 4, pp 299-309.

McKee, K. (2010a) 'The end of the Right to Buy and the future of social housing in Scotland', *Local Economy*, vol 25, no 4, pp 319-27.

McKee, K. (2010b) 'Promoting homeownership at the margins: the experience of low-cost homeownership purchasers in regeneration areas', *People, Place and Policy Online*, vol 4, no 2, pp 38-49.

McKee, K. (2010c) 'The future of community housing: some thoughts and reflections', *People, Place and Policy Online.*, vol 4, no 3, pp 103–10.

McKee, K. (2011) *Glasgow and West of Scotland Forum of Housing Associations' response to the Scottish Government's regeneration discussion document: Building a sustainable future* (www.gwsf.org.uk/uploads/GWSFregenmay2011webversion.pdf).

Munro, M. (2007) 'Evaluating policy towards increasing owner occupation', *Housing Studies*, vol 22, no 2, pp 243–60.

Newhaven Research (2005) *Right to Buy in Scotland: Impacts of the current policy framework and options for reform*, Edinburgh: Chartered Institute of Housing Scotland.

Newhaven Research and University of Glasgow (2008) *The credit crunch and the Scottish housing system*, Edinburgh: Chartered Institute of Housing Scotland.

Nolan, M. and Maclean, I. (2008) *Towards 2012: Homelessness Support Project*, Report to Convention of Scottish Local Authorities (COSLA), Association of Local Authority Chief Housing Officers (ALACHO) and the Scottish Government, April, Edinburgh: The Scottish Government.

Pawson, H. and Mullins, D. (2010) *After council housing: Britain's new social landlords*, Basingstoke: Palgrave Macmillan.

Pawson, H., Davidson, E. and Netto, G. (2007) *Evaluation of homelessness prevention activities in Scotland*, Edinburgh: Scottish Executive.

Ravetz, A. (2001) *Council housing and culture: The history of a social experiment*, London: Routledge.

SCORE (Scottish Continuous Recording System) (2003) *Scottish Continuous Recording System: 2003-2004 annual digest*, St Andrews: SCORE, Centre for Housing Research.

SCORE (2010) *Midyear report 2010/11*, St Andrews: SCORE, Centre for Housing Research.

Scott, S. (1997) *1988 and all that: The changing role of housing associations in Scotland*, Occasional Paper 31, Glasgow: Centre for Housing Research, University of Glasgow.

Scott, S. (2004) 'Managing housing in the social rented sector', in D. Sim (ed) *Housing and public policy in post-devolution Scotland*, Coventry and York: Chartered Institute of Housing and Joseph Rowntree Foundation, pp 33–51.

Scottish Executive (2005) *Homes for Scotland's people: A Scottish housing policy statement*, Edinburgh: Scottish Executive.

Scottish Government, The (2007) *Firm foundations: The future of housing in Scotland*, Edinburgh: The Scottish Government.

Scottish Government, The (2009) *Increasing affordable housing supply from limited public resources: The proposed National Housing Trust Initiative*, Edinburgh: The Scottish Government.

Scottish Government, The (2010) *Housing: Fresh thinking, new ideas*, Edinburgh: The Scottish Government.

Scottish Government, The (2011) *Homes fit for the 21st century: The Scottish Government's strategy and action plan for housing in the next decade 2011-2020*, Edinburgh: The Scottish Government.

SFHA (Scottish Federation of Housing Associations) (2011) 'Affordable housing cut by over 30% – SFHA reaction', *News* (www.sfha.co.uk/sfha/latest-news/affordable-housing-cut-by-over-30-sfha-reaction/menu-id-8.html).

Shelter (2007) *Homelessness prevention report*, Edinburgh: Shelter Scotland.

Shelter (2011) 'Black hole at heart of SNP government's social homes funding', Press Release, June (http://scotland.shelter.org.uk/media/press_releases/press_release_folder/2011/black_hole_at_heart_of_snp_governments_social_homes_funding).

SHR (Scottish Housing Regulator) (2009) *Social landlords in Scotland: Shaping up for improvement*, Glasgow: SHR.

SHR (2010) *Registered social landlords in Scotland: Summary facts and figures 2008/09*, Glasgow: SHR.

van Ham, M. and Manley, D. (2010) 'The effect of housing tenure-mix on labour market outcomes: a longitudinal investigation of neighbourhood effects', *Journal of Economic Geography*, vol 10, pp 257-82.

Wallace, A. (2008) *Achieving mobility in the intermediate housing market: Moving up and moving on?*, York and Coventry: Joseph Rowntree Foundation and Chartered Institute of Housing.

Wilcox, S. (2007) *UK Housing Review 2007/08*, Coventry and York: Chartered Institute of Housing/Building Societies Association.

Wilcox, S., Fitzpatrick, S., Stephens, M., Pleace, N., Wallace, A. and Rhodes, D. (2010) *The impact of devolution: Housing and homelessness*, York: Joseph Rowntree Foundation.

FOURTEEN

Environmental justice: a question of social justice?

Eurig Scandrett

Introduction: locating Scottish environmental policy

Environmental policy is only one contributor to socio-environmental change. Other factors include ecological changes, ideological shifts and other policies in the context of global and local economic trends. This is not to underplay the significance of policy in relation to the environment, but to locate it in relation to these other factors. Where policy aims for social justice in relation to the distribution of environmental factors we can refer to 'environmental justice' policy. The high point of such environmental justice policy in Scotland was the Labour–Liberal Democrat Coalition government under First Minister Jack McConnell, from the end of 2001 to May 2007, which succeeded in attenuating aspects of environmental policy onto a narrative of social democracy. However, it can be argued that the policy ultimately failed to influence the causes of environmental injustice in market-led economic policy (Scandrett, 2010).

Scott and Mooney (2009) argue that the minority Scottish National Party (SNP) government of 2007–11 successfully managed to position itself to the left of Labour on poverty policy, while continuing to hold the tension between social democracy and neoliberalism in practice: indeed, this Janus positioning may have contributed to its subsequent success in the May 2011 elections. It is argued here that the first SNP government similarly adopted a public position as 'more environmental' than Labour, while in practice its environmental policies have lacked cohesion, and are divorced from social policies. Having positioned itself as pro-business but with a clear social agenda and with less need to win support from other parties in Parliament, it remains to be seen whether the majority SNP government is able to bring more coherence to its socio-environmental policies. During the term of the first SNP government of 2007–11, however, some evidence could be seen of the increasing influence of an alternative ideology of ecological modernisation (EM), which seeks to integrate environmental policy into a capitalist economy.

This chapter argues that social justice in environmental policy must be understood in its local, global and intergenerational dimensions. Applying this analysis to developments in land use planning, climate change and waste management by successive Scottish governments helps to reveal competing class interests through combining elements of social democracy, neoliberalism and the emerging ideology of EM.

EM theory (Hajer, 1995) can be understood as a compromise between the logic of capital accumulation and the interests of the environment, in much the same way as social democracy was a settlement between capital accumulation and the interests of the working class – except that it is highly problematic to refer to 'the environment' having 'interests'. EM is therefore an attempted settlement between capitalism and the interests of the social class that originally developed a discourse of environmental protection – the professional class.[1] Dryzek et al (2003) argue that EM is the mechanism by which a 'green state' is emerging in several Western countries, as environmentalists are incorporated into the state apparatus much as the working class were in social democracy and the bourgeoisie in liberal representative democracy. However, 'environmentalists' are not a class in the same way as the bourgeoisie or the working class. It is argued here that technical-bureaucratic environmentalists ('envirocrats') of the professional class are increasingly aligned with bourgeois interests in what might be seen as a changing hegemonic class alliance (Gramsci, 1971).

Justice and the environment in Scotland

Social justice, in relation to the environment, has three dimensions: local, global and intergenerational. Local environmental damage disproportionately affects social groups who experience social and economic oppression, in particular people living with poverty, working-class, racialised and indigenous communities (Bullard, 1990, 2005; Agyeman et al, 2003). The term 'environmental justice' originates in the US movement against environmental racism, where environmentally polluting activities are disproportionately located beside African-American, Latino and Native American communities. In Scotland, environmental injustices are correlated primarily with class. Dunion (2003) and Agents for Environmental Justice and Scandrett (2003) document examples of working-class communities which have resisted polluting developments including the Greengairs landfill site, Douglas opencast coal mine (both in North Lanarkshire) and Baldovie incinerator in Dundee. Several studies have identified correlations between environmental pollution and indices of deprivation in Scotland (Fairburn et al, 2005) and elsewhere in the UK (Walker et al, 2003).

Second, the global distribution of resource consumption is highly unequal. Rich countries, including Scotland, consume higher levels of fossil fuels, water, metals and minerals, and thus place a greater burden on the global environment than the poorer countries of the South. Moreover, in addition to this North–South inequality in resource consumption, there is an unequal control over resources between classes within countries and regions throughout the world.

Finally, global resources are being depleted, and the ecological and geological cycles on which societies depend are threatened with irreversible damage. This constitutes an injustice to future generations who will be left with the legacy of environmental destruction. Intergenerational justice must therefore be a key component of environmental policy (Barry, 1978; Smith, 1998) as recognised in the definition of 'sustainable development' of the World Commission on Environment and Development (1987, para 27): development that 'meets the needs of the present without compromising the ability of future generations to meet their own needs'. Resource exhaustion and the destruction of ecosystem functions will have a detrimental impact on future generations of all classes, but especially oppressed subaltern classes, including peasant and tribal communities.

Social justice as applied to environmental policy in Scotland must therefore take into consideration aspects of local environmental justice, equalising international consumption distribution and intergenerational justice. These three dimensions of environmental injustice, while conceptually distinct, interact with and reinforce each other. For Scotland to contribute to global and intergenerational justice requires a considerable reduction in the total consumption of natural resources, but to achieve local environmental justice it is important to recognise both the current unequal levels of resource consumption, and the unequal power over resource consumption. Poor people in Scotland consume lower levels of resources than the rich, and also have less control over the resources that they use, for example, in the form of energy.

A further application of social justice to the environment, whether categories of social justice can legitimately be applied to the human treatment of the non-human environment, is beyond the scope of this chapter. However, we ignore the interrelationships between human societies and the diversity of biological species, genetic resources and ecosystems at our peril. The global destruction of biodiversity, which has accelerated in the past 200 years, has led to an ecosystem far more vulnerable to disruption and catastrophe, which inevitably has a disproportionate impact on the poorest sections of society. Environmental injustice therefore constitutes a social relation that nevertheless occurs within a complex ecological context.

Here, the local, global and intergenerational dimensions of environmental justice are explored in relation to Scottish policies on development planning, climate change and waste management. In each case, recent policy developments are scrutinised against what a socially just policy would entail and then explored in relation to their ideological content. This analysis draws on political ecology (Hayward, 1994; Guha and Martinez-Alier, 1998; Blaikie, 1999), an approach that takes seriously the structural politics of social inequality and exploitation as well as the complexity of the relationship between human societies and the biological and geophysical environment.

Political ecology of Scotland

One method of assessing the extent to which any country lives within its ecological limits is to compare the 'net primary production' of the land with the population which it supports. At subsistence level, Scotland's carrying capacity has been estimated at nearly five-and-a-half million people (Moffatt, 1996), although this takes no account of modern lifestyles, for which the 'ecological footprint' provides a useful corrective. Moffatt calculated that in 1995, Scotland's population and lifestyle required a land area 20 per cent greater than could be provided by sustainable exploitation of the productive capacity of Scotland's land. Scotland's population therefore can only be sustained by a net import of resources and/or exploiting non-renewable resources.

Under a capitalist mode of production, however, natural production capacity can be substituted by capital. In other words, exploiting an exhaustible natural resource in order to generate capital will leave future generations better off by inheriting that capital than they would be with a legacy of unexploited natural resource – although within any generation, the distribution of the capital would be unequal. Over the period 1988–92, Moffatt calculated that environmental depreciation was more than compensated for by capital growth (Moffatt, 1996, p 82).

In a stronger attempt to assess global and intergenerational justice, Friends of the Earth Scotland (FoES) calculated Scotland's resource consumption in comparison with a measure of socially equitable sustainable consumption called 'environmental space'. This metric calculates the resources that can be used and pollutants emitted 'without damaging the capacity of the planet to support ourselves and other species' (FoES, 1996, p 7). Most significantly, this measure includes the Equity Principle, 'a fair division of access to global resources' (FoES, 1996, p 8), which recognises the disproportionate per capita resource use in countries in the global North. On that basis, the consumption of most non-renewable resources in Scotland would need to reduce by between 58 per cent for iron and 84 per cent for copper.

These measurements focus on global and intergenerational justice. Measures of local environmental justice have been relatively recent. The most significant research to date has been conducted by Fairburn et al (2005) who identified positive correlations between poverty and industrial pollution, derelict land and the quality of air and river water, and negative correlations with access to green space.

Such statistical correlations provide evidence that Scotland encounters the same phenomenon as elsewhere in the world: the poorest and socially exploited experience the worst environmental conditions. However, statistical correlations measure one moment in a dynamic process, and the absence of such a correlation does not 'prove' that there is no environmental injustice occurring. Economic activity under capitalism tends to shift costs onto the environment, and 'environmental justice' emerged as a mobilising frame in a social movement of communities fighting against resultant local pollution. The tensions between environmental justice as statistical correlation, as social process and as social policy remain important for analysing its role in social welfare in Scotland (Scandrett, 2007).

Environmental policy

Environmental policy is fully devolved to Scotland's Parliament. However, in order to understand how Scottish environmental policy is produced, how social and economic policy have an impact on the environment and vice versa, requires an analytical approach which does justice to the complexity of the interaction between social and environmental processes at a local and global level. The Scottish environment is shaped by geophysical, climatological and ecological processes well beyond the controls of any political institution in Scotland. Opportunities in and constraints to environmental policy making in Scotland are established at UK, EU and international level, as well as through the influence of other powerful actors, not least the transnational flows of capital.

Even since the formation of Scotland's Parliament, fully devolved environmental policy making has always confronted its wider context. Energy policy is reserved to Westminster while the location and impact of power stations is devolved. The same pollutant affecting the same person is the responsibility of either the (devolved) Scottish Environment Protection Agency (SEPA) or the (reserved) Health and Safety Executive (HSE) depending on whether that person is at home or at work. Most Scottish and UK environmental policy is driven and structured by European directives and international protocols. It is therefore impossible to explore environmental policy in Scotland without considering its global context.

Economies convert natural resources – soil, oil, timber, minerals and so on – into useful products and energy, which are distributed and consumed leaving behind unusable materials which are managed as waste. Each of the stages of extraction, manufacturing, distribution, consumption and waste disposal has its own economy – and in a market system its own potential for profit – its own social distribution and its own environmental impact. When we are looking at Scotland's environmental policy in the context of social justice, it is therefore important to assess who is benefiting from and who is being affected by the interactions between society and environment, which may be influenced by political practice in Scotland. By political practice we must include economic decision making, social movement action and any other social processes in which power is distributed and contested, as well as the making and implementation of policy.

We now turn to specific developments in policy that have occurred in recent times in order to assess its ideological direction of travel. Three areas of policy are examined: development planning policy, climate change policy and waste policy. The first highlights the tension between social democracy and neoliberalism; the second demonstrates growing influence of EMA as a depoliticised and technical approach to environmental policy, alongside resistance from some environmentalists and working-class communities; and the third illustrates a further marketisation of environmental policy that constitutes a threat to local environmental justice.

Development planning policy

Development planning is the administrative system that allocates land to different forms of development and puts constraints on the types of development that can occur. It is therefore a legal structure with opportunities for addressing local environmental justice issues. A socially just development planning system would seek to optimise local control of development, or at least the criteria by which development is judged, within the constraints of wider social benefit, such as the protection of ecosystem functions, safety issues, preventing exploitation, fair distributions of costs and benefits and so on. The details of how these are interpreted is a matter for democratic debate, but the basic functions of a development planning system that contributes to justice would fulfil these functions.

In fact, development planning in Scotland has many of these features. Development plans are open to public scrutiny guided by social need and government principles. Once approved, individual developments are expected to adhere to nationally agreed principles that are designed to reflect the social good. Intergenerational and global justice are not considered as criteria for planning but there is no inherent reason within the system that prevents this. Where the system breaks down is the privileging of the cost–benefit analysis of the developer, which is excluded from the planning process. Developers make economic decisions of what to develop but the logic of their cost–benefit analysis is not subject to democratic scrutiny. Planning controls *where* development occurs, not *what* or *whether* it occurs. Alternative models of development planning exist, such as multi-criteria analysis, centralised planning or stakeholder agreements. The strengths and weaknesses of these alternatives are not the subject of this chapter (see O'Connor, 2000a), but rather illustrate that cost–benefit calculations need not precede democratic scrutiny or the constraints of socially beneficial criteria.

The incorporation of social and environmental criteria into cost–benefit analysis through the direct costing of ecological and socially beneficial goods and services, or else indirectly through 'contingent valuation' (such as measures of 'willingness to pay'), is a controversial issue in economics. Some authors argue that allocating a price to such 'external' costs is a way of internalising the social and environmental benefits to cost–benefit analysis (see, for example, Pearce et al, 1989). This is a favoured strategy within EM theory and is influential in policy making at a European as well as a UK and Scottish level (see, for example, HM Treasury, 2003). Others (for example, Martinez-Alier, 2002) are highly critical of this approach, however, arguing that it is impossible to reflect the value of socio-environmental benefits such as people's health or the global climate in terms of price, and where this is attempted it will inevitably disadvantage those with least financial leverage. The wealthy can use economic advantage to protect their environment whereas the poorest are forced to choose between livelihood and a clean environment. Some economists have attempted to combine these approaches and discern conditions under which environmental cost-benefit analysis is appropriate and where it is not (O'Connor, 2000b).

The Scottish Planning Act 2006 was delivered by the Labour–Liberal Democrat Coalition of 2003–07 under First Minister Jack McConnell, in other words by the administration that had done most to integrate environmental justice and social justice, albeit without affecting a neoliberal economic policy privileging market forces (Scandrett, 2010). Planning reform had been driven by two opposing forces: that from business interests who complained that the planning system was a bureaucratic impediment to economic growth; and from many local communities and environmental campaigners who argued that the system was inaccessible, rigged in the developers' favour and too often unable to prevent unwanted developments. The Act therefore attempted to address both of these contradictory pressures and develop a 'much more inclusive and efficient planning system to improve community involvement, support the economy, and help it to grow in a sustainable way' (The Scottish Government, 2007). Although the Bill was initiated by the McConnell Executive it was implemented almost entirely under the minority SNP administration between 2007 and 2011.

The Act seeks to resolve the contradiction between economic growth and social accountability, not by opening the developer's economic decision to democratic scrutiny but by separating out different categories of development. For most development decisions, developers are encouraged to front-load public consultation. A few major 'national developments' published in the *National Planning Framework 2* (The Scottish Government, 2008) are regarded as of significant national importance and subject to considerably reduced public consultation. These national developments are the most controversial, including strategic airport enhancements, the Cockenzie gas-fired and Hunterston coal-fired power stations, and have provoked direct action, local opposition and judicial review respectively. Meanwhile, concerns from community groups about the conduct of developers and local authorities in permitting developments against the wishes of the public continue (see Planning Democracy, 2010).

In summary then, development planning reform has occurred within the framework of the tension between (weak) social democracy and (strong) neoliberalism. It has certainly not resolved the conflict between these and is having the effect of shifting the site of conflict elsewhere, into conflicts between local authorities and national government, into the courts, and into direct action.

Climate change policy

Climate change is a global environmental issue par excellence. Anthropogenic global warming is causing climate change through the enhanced greenhouse effect, in which a range of 'greenhouse gases' are accumulating in the atmosphere as a result of major developments in production throughout the world. While many policies affect the activities that contribute to climate change, including agriculture and food systems, construction, planning and waste management, most attention has focused on fossil fuels – oil, coal, gas – the burning of which emits carbon dioxide. Fossil fuels retain the sun's energy and atmospheric carbon that were fixed during the five million years of the Carboniferous period. A significant amount of this carbon has been re-emitted into the atmosphere over a period of only 200 years, causing major disruption to global chemical, climatic and ecological systems. The science of such a complexity of systems involves some uncertainty, although it is clear that the current rate of emissions is leading to increased frequency of major floods, droughts, storms, sea level rise, coastal erosion and outbreaks of disease, disproportionately affecting the poorest people in the most vulnerable environments.

Obtaining international agreement on coordinated action to reduce carbon dioxide emissions has proved notoriously difficult, largely as a result of the intransigence of the US that (with the exception of Kuwait) emits the highest level of carbon dioxide per capita. Since the Framework Convention on Climate Change was established in 1992, an international process of policy development expects developed countries to reduce carbon dioxide emissions (for an introduction to climate change policy, see FitzRoy and Papyrakis, 2010).

The extent of carbon dioxide reductions required involves consideration of social justice. Clearly an irreversibly disrupted climate is an unjust legacy to bequeath to future generations and greenhouse gases need to be maintained within limits that minimise ecological damage. Friends of the Earth's use of environmental space measurements suggests that carbon dioxide emissions of 1.7 tonnes per capita per year fulfils the criteria of global and intergenerational justice – if implemented globally, all citizens throughout the world would have an equal right to use fossil fuels, and the total emissions would not exceed the absorption capacity of the global carbon cycle (FoES, 1996; McLaren et al, 2009). This translates to a reduction for Scotland of 80 per cent.

One problem with the environmental space index is that it takes no account of the unequal history of carbon dioxide emissions: the ecological debt (Simms, 2005). Khor (2009) has estimated that 600 billion tonnes of carbon is the total carbon budget over the fossil fuel era between 1800 and 2050, of which 40 per cent has already been 'consumed' by the 20 per cent of the world's population in the rich countries. For developing countries even to maintain their current per capita emission levels, they 'would need to reduce their emissions by 213% by 2050' (Khor, 2009, p 29)!

In any meaningful sense, for Scotland to make its contribution to global and intergenerational justice would require a rapid reduction in our dependence on fossil fuels to as close to zero as possible. However, in order to achieve local environmental and social justice, this would have to be done in a managed, redistributional way. Within Scotland, the rich consume fossil fuels at a greater rate: they travel further, especially by private car and aeroplane, and make greater use of imported goods and energy-intensive products; while the poor have less control over where they live, how they travel and the amount of fuel they need to keep themselves warm and clean (Dunion, 2003). Achieving social justice would require a major investment in public transport, insulation of the housing stock and other structural energy-saving initiatives, a transfer to Scotland's abundant sources of renewable energy generation and planned transition arrangements for workers in the fossil fuel industry to diversify into alternative employment (TUC, 2008).

Despite the then First Minister McConnell recognising climate change as an environmental injustice (Scottish Executive, 2002), little was done during his government to move towards a socially just climate policy. The early years following the SNP's election in May 2007, moreover, provided a typically incoherent approach to climate policy. Transport policy seemed to be motivated by a mixture of populism, business friendliness and distance from the previous administration. Within the first year of their government, the SNP backed private transport against public by abolishing bridge tolls, opposing road pricing, scrapping the Bus Travel Development Fund and attempting to cancel Edinburgh's tram scheme. On the other hand, they also abolished the Air Travel Development Fund, while simultaneously backing strategic development of three Scottish airports. In exchange for the support of the Green MSPs (Members of Scottish Parliament), the SNP government established the Climate Challenge Fund, in which £27.4 million supported 250 community-based carbon reduction projects. On the other hand, by late 2010, the government's energy efficiency action plan had been delayed six times and its home insulation scheme had reached a tiny fraction of those targeted (Edwards, 2010).

However, the Climate Change Act 2009 (achieved following the largest lobby of Parliament since its inception) contains among the most ambitious piece of legislation of any government. It constitutes a framework to cut all greenhouse gas emissions by at least 80 per cent by 2050, with an interim target of 42 per cent by 2020 and mandatory annual national targets to be met by all public sector bodies. 'Scotland aims to become a leading nation in developing a sustainable way of life, reducing the impact its people have on the local and global environment' (The Scottish Government, 2009, p 1).

The mechanisms of achieving these cuts were not specified in the Act, although the delivery plan suggests that carbon pricing, technological development and consumer behaviour change, with an emphasis on economic cost-effectiveness, will be the drivers rather than regulation (although see Edwards, 2010). With the exception of recognising the importance of fuel poverty there is little recognition of the differential impact of the greenhouse gas reduction measures on people who are experiencing poverty (see Chapter Five, this volume), or the use of mechanisms that might promote local environmental justice. There is a risk that this will lead to the use of easier, cheaper and socially inequitable approaches such as carbon price-driven market demand. The increasing influence of EM is seen in this policy, in which markets are the primary tool of policy, manipulated or simulated by the state.

It is possible that these are the early stages of the incremental influence of 'envirocrats' among public servants and policy advisers close to government.

Political shifts that increase the influence of the professional class are taking the form of technical resolutions to environmental problems, rather than political arguments about the relationship between society and ecology. This is an area of environmental policy where we are likely to see ideological struggle in the near future.

Away from the government-sponsored policy agenda, there are developments in Scotland that are affecting climate change. The evolution of direct action environmentalism has been a significant development across the UK since the 1980s, partially in response to the increasing professionalisation and bureaucratisation of environmental non-governmental organisations (NGOs) (Seel et al, 2000), and climate change has been a particular focus for sections of this movement, including the annual Camp for Climate Action, which occupies land near to a significant source of carbon dioxide emissions as a basis for targeted direct action. In Scotland there has been some recognition among direct action environmentalists of the relationship between climate-damaging activities and social injustice. Annetts et al (2009) have documented the struggle against the M77 motorway extension during the mid-1990s that revolved around the 'Pollok Free State' alliance between direct action anarchists and local working-class communities in Glasgow. Coal Action Scotland (ca 2009), with origins in Earth First! and Camp for Climate Action, has targeted opencast coal sites and made a deliberate attempt to build alliances with local working-class community action against opencast. 'Plane Stupid' anti-airport expansion activists have held 'convergence' events with fuel poverty campaigners in Clydebank, under the flight path of Glasgow airport. As part of the Camp for Climate Action at the Royal Bank of Scotland headquarters in Edinburgh in August 2010, connections were made between direct action environmentalists in Workers' Climate Action and local trades union representatives in the Edinburgh area (Scandrett et al, 2012).

Thus, on policy related to climate change there is evidence that the SNP government adopted approaches which improve intergenerational and international justice, even though weak on local environmental justice. The extent to which progress has occurred seems to have been the result of popular pressure from a range of civil society groups, but especially the environmental NGOs and envirocrats within the policy community. There is capacity for protest to make further concessions on local justice and some evidence that alliances are starting to form between climate activists and working-class communities and trades unions.

Waste policy

Achieving intergenerational justice for waste requires that future generations are not left with materials that cannot be adequately absorbed, without damage, by ecological cycles. Since the 1992 Basel Convention on the Control of Transboundary Movements of Hazardous Wastes, global waste injustice has been reduced and the disposal of waste is normally in the same country as the materials consumed. There are exceptions to this, however, since export for recycling is permitted in the Convention, and UK computer waste has been traced to India and China where reusable materials can be stripped out profitably by low-cost, unorganised labour under poorly implemented controls (Kalra, 2004). There is also an illegal international trade in waste. However, the vast majority of waste is required to be managed as close as possible to where it was consumed, and local environmental injustice is a significant issue.

The relationship between waste facility location and poverty is unclear. Fairburn et al (2005) found a slight peak in waste facility incidence adjacent to both the bottom and top quintile of the deprivation index (see also Scandrett et al, 2000; Walker et al, 2003). However, statistical correlations measure only a snapshot in a complex process of economic and social change and conflicts over waste facilities have been an important feature of environmental justice struggles in Scotland. Jack McConnell made his 2002 announcement on environmental justice following a visit to Greengairs landfill site, which had been the focus of a sustained conflict over dumping toxic waste (Scottish Executive, 2002; Dunion, 2003).

In 2010, the Scottish government produced Scotland's Zero Waste Plan (SZWP) which aimed to cut waste through a familiar hierarchy of reducing initial resource content, reusing products, recycling of material components and reclaiming residual energy content. This plan is probably the most consistent example of the use of EM thinking so far, employing state-manipulated, market-led, 'closed loop' management of resources (that is, treating waste in one part of the production process as a resource for another part). The policy approach is based on maximising the economic value of waste materials in order to stimulate business activities in reuse, recycling and recovery of energy. The primary targets were geared towards the SNP's flagship 'sustainable economic growth', through state manipulation of markets on the basis of information feedback. This combination of technical and entrepreneurial activity is indicative of EM and serves the interests primarily of business and the professional class. However, there is a small recognition of the need to reflect the interests of workers through, for example, the need to 'Improve skill levels and health and safety' (The Scottish Government, 2010, p 9) in a sector notorious for poor employment terms and hazardous working conditions.

The balance between class interests is struck by details of how data are collected, the level of voluntarism versus regulation in achieving goals and the extent of public subsidy of private capital accumulation through infrastructural investment, education, business support and so on. In much of this, the SZWP is uncommitted, delaying decisions, for example, on its interpretation of waste prevention, whether adopting a social (per capita) or economistic (per unit GNP) measure (The Scottish Government, 2010, p 2). In general the tendency is towards market solutions, for example, 'Driv[ing] innovation by defining the outcomes of a zero waste Scotland, without being prescriptive about the means' (The Scottish Government, 2010, p 9), positioning the policy at the 'weak' end of EM approaches, compatible with neoliberalism.

Significantly, the SZWP makes no reference to inequality of any kind, even though resource use and waste production is class-related. Wealthier sectors of the population, with high consumption levels, use higher amounts of resources per capita and therefore produce more waste – the 'effluence of affluence'. Moreover, poorer communities have less control over their resource consumption and waste production, low incomes being translated into less choice, and in the absence of material wealth, income tends to be needed for material consumption. The relationship between class and patterns of waste production and exposure are complex and require further research, although the SZWP shows no interest in this, preferring to focus on studies which facilitate business development around maximising the economic value of waste.

Most important is the development of policy towards waste incineration. The location of new 'energy from waste' incineration plants continues to be the source of social conflict, exacerbated because of the tendency for incinerators to be located in poor communities. On mainland Scotland, the only large-scale municipal incinerator in operation, located between the working-class communities of Whitfield and Douglas in Dundee, has been a focus for social protest since its construction (Scandrett, 2002). There have been several attempts to establish new incinerators in different parts of Scotland, mostly close to working-class communities and always accompanied by fierce protests. Many of these local campaigns have joined together into a national campaign, Green Alternatives to Incineration in Scotland (www.gainscotland.org.uk).

The SZWP has taken a position cautiously in favour of further energy from waste incinerators, with a strong commercial justification. 'For energy from waste to be truly sustainable it should only be used for resource streams which cannot practicably offer greater environmental *and economic benefits* through reuse or recycling' (The Scottish Government, 2010, p 9; emphasis added). However, it does not identify the risk of such facilities disproportionately affecting poor communities and in fact, through recommending the location of waste facilities on existing industrial or contaminated land, could serve to reproduce this environmental injustice (The Scottish Government, 2010, Annex 2, p 4). There is evidence of negative health impacts on communities living near to incinerators (FoE, 2002), and the location of waste incinerators therefore seems likely to become an important area of social conflict in the future.

Conclusion

The high point of environmental justice policy in Scotland between 2002 and 2007 was achieved through the attenuation of environmental concerns onto a social democratic discourse, albeit ultimately rendered impotent through the preferential influence of neoliberal economics. The SNP government that followed simultaneously positioned itself as both more social democratic and more environmental than Labour, while in practice adopted inconsistent positions and policies on social justice and the environment, with no integration between these two. The outcome is that the 2007–11 SNP government developed some environmentally beneficial but class-blind policies that look set to continue after winning a second term with an absolute majority. Within these policies, increasing influence of EM can be discerned, not as a result of political leadership but through the influence of 'envirocrats' within and close to government, as well as environmental NGOs, who have largely also downplayed environmental justice. Despite some positive impacts, there is a risk in this development that environmentally beneficial policies are presented as technical solutions to scientific problems, when in fact they involve political choices that benefit some sections of society and cost others.

This is far from being a settled trajectory, however, and battles over specific policies that affect sectoral interests continue. The election in 2010 of a Conservative–Liberal Democrat Coalition government in Westminster, claiming to be the UK's 'greenest government ever', started pursuing savage cuts in the public sector and essentially privatising social policy to the 'Big Society' of profit and non-profit-distributing enterprises and voluntary groups. Zac Goldsmith, inheritor of the Goldsmith millionaire dynasty, former *Ecologist* editor and self-proclaimed 'Burkean environmentalist', was elected as a Tory MP and became Prime Minister David Cameron's adviser on environmental issues. At the same time, the 2010 General Election saw the first member of the Westminster Parliament from the Green Party, the respected left winger Caroline Lucas.

A growing influential direct action environmental movement across the UK has, particularly in Scotland, started to make connections between the abstract objectives of environmental protection and the specific struggles of communities directly affected by pollution (for example, Coal Action Scotland, ca 2009). The trades union movement, despite a continuing legacy of putting short-term job protection above wider social and environmental concerns, is initiating important steps towards environmental policy in workers' interests.

Environmental policy is likely to be a site for increasing skirmishes in the war of position, albeit often disguised as technical problem solving. Moreover, in a capitalist economy such as Scotland's, economic growth, economic efficiency and capital accumulation necessarily involve shifting costs outwith the economic calculus onto the cheapest possible sink, whether that be the natural environment, poorer countries, workers' health, disempowered communities or future generations (Martinez-Alier, 2002). Environmental injustice is caused by this logic of capital growth and it is unlikely that social justice can be achieved under capitalism (Jackson, 2009). Increasing environmental justice in all its dimensions is an important component of the transition to a post-capitalist society. In this context, it is necessary to analyse the alliances of classes that are forming to defend collective interests. In practice this involves stronger connections between working-class movements, including trades unions and community action groups, and environmentalists, across the spectrum from grassroots environmental justice campaigners, direct action environmentalists, NGOs and even the envirocrats.

Note

[1] The term 'professional class' is used to describe the salaried professional and technical workers distinguished by a high level of access to education and whose position in the labour market is determined by their use of specialist knowledge. In the literature these are variously referred to as professional-managerial, 'new middle class', knowledge class and so on (or at least sections of these classes). The term is used here heuristically and its use does not imply a position within the debates in Marxist and Weberian sociology on whether these workers should be regarded as a discrete class, intermediate between classes or in a contradictory class location (see Burris, 2005, for an overview, and also Wright, 2009). Yearley (1994) points out that Western environmentalism, which advocates lower economic growth, is largely supported from this class despite its dependence on public investment of significant economic surplus.

Further resources

Agyeman, J., Bullard, R.D. and Evans, B. (2003) *Just sustainabilities: Development in an unequal world*, London: Earthscan.

Dunion, K. (2003) *Troublemakers: The struggle for environmental justice in Scotland*, Edinburgh: Edinburgh University Press.

Harvey, D. (1996) *Justice, nature and the geography of difference*, Oxford: Blackwell.

McLaren, D., Bullock, S. and Yousuf, N. (2009) *Tomorrow's world: Britain's share in a sustainable future*, London: Earthscan.

Martinez-Alier, J. (2002) *Environmentalism of the poor: A study of ecological conflicts and valuation*, Cheltenham: Edward Elgar.

SNIFFER (2004): www.sniffer.org.uk/Webcontrol/Secure/ClientSpecific/ResourceManagement/UploadedFiles/UE4(03)01.pdf

Friends of the Earth Scotland: www.foe-scotland.org.uk

Green Alternatives to Incineration in Scotland: www.gainscotland.org.uk

Planning Democracy: www.planningdemocracy.org.uk

Rob Edwards: www.robedwards.com/climate_change/

References

Agents for Environmental Justice and Scandrett, E. (2003) *Voices from the grassroots*, Redressing the Balance Handbook No 4, Edinburgh: Friends of the Earth Scotland.

Agyeman, J., Bullard, R.D. and Evans, B. (2003) *Just sustainabilities: Development in an unequal world*, London: Earthscan.

Annetts, J., Law, A., McNeish, W. and Mooney, G. (2009) *Understanding social welfare movements*, Bristol: The Policy Press.

Barry, B. (1978) 'Justice between generations', in P. Hoder and J. Raz (eds) *Law, morality and society*, Oxford: Clarendon Press, pp 268-84.

Blaikie, P.M. (1999) 'A review of political ecology', *Zeitschrift für Wirtschaftsgeographie*, vol 43, pp 131-47.

Bullard, R.D. (1990) *Dumping in Dixie: Race, class, and environmental quality*, Boulder, CO: Westview.

Bullard, R.D. (2005) *The quest for environmental justice: Human rights and the politics of pollution*, San Francisco, CA: Sierra Club.

Burris, V. (2005) 'The future of class analysis: reflections on "class structure and political ideology" and "class structure and political ideology"', in R.F. Levine (ed) *Enriching the sociological imagination: How radical sociology changed the discipline*, Boulder, CO: Paradigm Publishers, pp 133-63.

Coal Action Scotland (ca 2009) *Mainshill: Stories from the woods*, Anti Copyright.

Dryzek, J.S., Downes, D., Hunold, C., Schlosberg, D. and Hernes, H.-K. (2003) *Green states and social movements: Environmentalism in the US, UK, Germany and Norway*, Oxford: Oxford University Press.

Dunion, K. (2003) *Troublemakers: The struggle for environmental justice in Scotland*, Edinburgh: Edinburgh University Press.

Edwards, R. (2010) 'Winning the war on cars: how ministers plan to cut climate pollution', *Sunday Herald*, 5 September; 'Home insulation scheme failing to reach many homes', *Sunday Herald*, 27 June; 'Anger over repeated delays to energy-saving plan', *Sunday Herald*, 13 June (www.robedwards.com/climate_change/).

Fairburn, J., Walker, G., Smith, G. and Mitchell, G. (2005) *Investigating environmental justice in Scotland: Links between measures of environmental quality and social deprivation*, Project UE4(03)01, Edinburgh: SNIFFER.

FitzRoy, F.R. and Papyrakis, E. (2010) *An introduction to climate change economics and policy*, London: Earthscan.

FoE (Friends of the Earth) (2002) *Incineration and health issues*, Briefing, London: FoE (www.foe.co.uk/resource/briefings/incineration_health_issues.pdf).

FoES (Friends of the Earth Scotland) (1996) *Towards a sustainable Scotland*, Edinburgh: FoES.

Gramsci, A. (1971) *Selections from the Prison notebooks* (translated by Quentin Hoare and Geoffrey Nowell Smith), London: Lawrence & Wishart.

Guha, R. and Martinez Alier, J. (1998) 'From political economy to political ecology', in R. Guha and J. Martinez Alier, *Varieties of environmentalism: Essays North and South*, London: Earthscan, pp 22-45.

Hajer, M.A. (1995) *The politics of environmental discourse: Ecological modernisation and the policy process*, Oxford: Oxford University Press.

Hayward, T. (1994) 'The meaning of political ecology', *Radical Philosophy*, vol 66, spring, pp 11-20.

HM Treasury (2003) *The green book: Appraisal and evaluation in central government* (with 2011 update), London: The Stationery Office (www.hm-treasury.gov.uk/d/green_book_complete.pdf).

Jackson, T. (2009) *Prosperity without growth: The transition to a sustainable economy*, London: Sustainable Development Commission.

Kalra, V. (2004) *E-waste in India – System failure imminent*, New Delhi: Toxics Link.

Khor, M. (2009) 'Copenhagen battle for climate action with equity', *Economic & Political Weekly*, 28 November, vol xliv, no 48.

Martinez-Alier, J. (2002) *Environmentalism of the poor: A study of ecological conflicts and valuation*, Cheltenham: Edward Elgar.

McLaren, D., Bullock, S. and Yousuf, N. (2009) *Tomorrow's world: Britain's share in a sustainable future*, London: Earthscan.

Moffatt, I. (1996) *Sustainable development: Principles, analysis and policies*, London: Parthenon.

O'Connor, M. (2000a) 'Pathways for environmental evaluation: a walk in the (Hanging) Gardens of Babylon', *Special Issue: Social Processes of Environmental Valuation, Ecological Economics*, vol 34, pp 175-93.

O'Connor, M. (2000b) *Natural capital environmental valuation in Europe*, Policy Research Brief Number 3, Cambridge: Cambridge Research for the Environment.

Pearce, D.W. Markandya, A. and Barbier, E.B. (1989) *Blueprint for a green economy*, London: Earthscan.

Planning Democracy (2010) www.planningdemocracy.org.uk

Scandrett, E. (2002) 'Environmental justice', in L. Adams, M. Amos and J. Munro (eds) *Promoting health: Politics and practice*, London: Sage Publications, pp 58-62.

Scandrett, E. (2007) 'Environmental justice in Scotland: policy, pedagogy and praxis', *Environmental Research Letters*, vol 2, no 4 (www.stacks.iop.org/ERL/2/045002).

Scandrett, E. (2010) 'Environmental justice in Scotland: incorporation and conflict', in N. Davidson, P. McCafferty and D. Miller (ed) *Neoliberal Scotland: Class and society in a stateless nation*, Newcastle: Cambridge Scholars Publishing, pp 183-201.

Scandrett, E., Crowther, J. and McGregor, C. (2012, forthcoming) 'Poverty, protest and popular education in discourses of climate change', in A. Carvalho and T.R. Peterson (eds) *Climate change communication and the transformation of politics*, London: Cambria.

Scandrett, E., Dunion K. and McBride, G. (2000) 'The campaign for environmental justice in Scotland', *Local Environment*, vol 5, no 4, pp 467-74.

Scott, G. and Mooney, G. (2009) 'Poverty and social justice in the devolved Scotland: neoliberalism meets social democracy?', *Social Policy and Society*, vol 3, no 4, pp 379-89.

Scottish Executive (2002) Environmental justice speech in South Africa (www. scotland.gov.uk/News/Releases/2002/09/2156).

Scottish Government, The (2007) *A brief guide to the 2006 Scottish Act* (www. scotland.gov.uk/Publications/2007/03/07131521/1).

Scottish Government, The (2008) *National Planning Framework for Scotland 2*, Edinburgh: The Scottish Government (www.scotland.gov.uk/ Publications/2008/12/12093953/0).

Scottish Government, The (2009) *Climate change delivery plan: Meeting Scotland's statutory climate change targets*, Edinburgh: The Scottish Government (www. scotland.gov.uk/Publications/2009/06/18103720/11).

Scottish Government, The (2010) *Scotland's Zero Waste Plan*, Edinburgh: The Scottish Government (www.scotland.gov.uk/Publications/2010/06/08092645/11).

Seel, B., Paterson, M. and Doherty, B. (2000) *Direct action in British environmentalism*, Oxford: Routledge.

Simms, A. (2005) *Ecological debt: The health of the planet and the wealth of nations*, London: Pluto Press.

Smith, M.J. (1998) *Ecologism: Towards ecological citizenship*, Milton Keynes: Open University Press.

TUC (Trades Union Congress) (2008) *A green and fair future: For a just transition to a low carbon economy*, Touchtone Briefing No 3 (www.tuc.org.uk/touchstone/ justtransition/greenfuture.pdf).

Walker, G., Fairburn, J., Smith, G. and Mitchell, G. (2003) *Environmental quality and social deprivation*, R&D Technical Report E2-067/1/TR, Environment Agency (www.geography.lancs.ac.uk/envjustice/downloads/technicalreport.pdf).

WCED (World Commission on Environment and Development) (chair: G.H. Brundtland) (1987) *Our common future*, Oxford: Oxford University Press (www. un-documents.net/ocf-ov.htm#I.3).

Wright, E.O. (2009) 'Understanding class: towards an integrated analytical approach', *New Left Review*, vol 60, November-December, pp 101-16.

Yearley, S. (1994) 'Social movements and environmental change', in T. Benton and M. Redclift (eds) *Social theory and the global environment*, London: Routledge, pp 150-68.

FIFTEEN

Conclusion: towards a new phase of devolution?

Gill Scott and Gerry Mooney

Social justice: still a matter for concern?

Our earlier text, *Exploring social policy in the 'new' Scotland*, concluded that:

> ... one of the most interesting challenges facing social policy makers in Scotland was to see how far it is possible to *at least* moderate the sharp social divisions and inequalities that characterise the UK as a whole. (Mooney and Scott, 2005, p 270; emphasis in original)

It is a challenge that the First Minister, Alex Salmond, also recognised in his 'Taking Scotland forward' speech, made to Parliament in the first few weeks after the historic Scottish National Party (SNP) election victory of May 2011, when he said,

> ... the struggle for fairness, equality, tolerance, rights of free speech and thought – these are struggles which are never won – they require constant vigilance and courage. (Salmond, 2011a)

Reviewing policy developments through the lens of social justice is an important task in Scotland, as elsewhere. Much has been made of the support for and capacity of a devolved government openly claiming to redress inequalities. In Chapter One we argued that such an analysis remains important as devolution coninues to evolve. Three reasons underlay this argument: first, the evidence that inequalities, albeit more heterogeneous than in the past, still persist and affect the quality of life of many Scottish citizens; second, because politicians still claim they are responding to a distinctive belief held by the people of Scotland in fairness and social justice; and third, because there is increasing evidence that the Scottish electorate think that strengthening the powers of a devolved parliament could allow better solutions to Scottish problems – in January 2012, 58% of Scottish voters were recorded as favouring the 'devolution max' option, that is, more powers for the Scottish Parliament, short of full independence(Settle and Devlin, 2012).

The contributors to this book have addressed the issue of social justice in a number of ways. They have identified the nature of inequalities, to a greater or lesser extent, and have also highlighted the extent to which social justice is or is not informing policy development. It is an important issue to explore when a distinctively Scottish political agenda has become increasingly identifiable, but also when both Scottish and UK welfare decisions and policy are, at the same time, having major negative effects on the social welfare of Scottish citizens. Authors, here, have identified successes and failures in the policies since 2005 but have also provided some ideas of alternative ways to achieve a more just society in the future. There is plenty here as people in Scotland are offered a referendum for independence – a referendum that the Scottish Government in 2012 saw as necessary to 'build a better society' (Scottish Government, 2012). They also show that the political will to make decisions in Scotland to reduce social inequality cannot be assured alongside moves to raise the powers of a devolved Scottish government or towards independence.

Social justice, social welfare and nation building

The future of social welfare is one of the most important issues of our times, be it in Scotland, the UK or other areas of the world, where welfare has been a key element of social life. Social policy is in a state of flux, affected by economic, political and social change that is threatening moves towards greater equality (Cantillon, 2010). It is not a new phenomenon: a number of analysts characterised the welfare state as being under siege even before the economic crisis of the new century, analysts, moreover, who see welfare as being recast in new directions, where social justice is seen as less 'affordable' (Esping-Andersen, 1996; Ferguson et al, 2002; Pearce and Paxton, 2005).

Scotland is no different in this respect from other countries and, as the chapters of this book illustrate, no site of policy is exempt from the winds of economic and social change, and political debate. Budget deficits, privatisation, the marketisation of economic and social activities, increasing national and international competition, increasing inequalities, ageing of the population, changes in family structure, accelerated technological change – they are all factors producing similar problems across Europe, but solutions often differ and choices matter. Indeed comparative research highlights strong differences in the welfare models that nations adopt when responding to economic, social and population change. Factors affecting the adoption of what Esping-Andersen (1990) calls a social democratic model rather than a corporatist regime, or of a liberal rather than a care-based model have been much debated, as too have the reasons for the different paths of social welfare being developed in new European Union (EU) member states (Moreno and Palier, 2004). However, can lessons about possible policy direction be learned from such an analysis? While we know that welfare in the UK is not the same as welfare in, for example, Sweden or the US, can those models be used to inform policy in Scotland and, indeed, can changes in the governance of Scotland within the UK offer other countries lessons about developing a new model of welfare, distinguishable from that of the rest of the UK? Is it really worth looking at the processes of policy formulation in Scotland and the real and potential impact of Scottish-based policy?

The answer from the authors here is that analysis of Scottish policy development is invaluable within and beyond the borders of Scotland. Their discussions show how important it is to recognise the extent to which global forces determine the fate of national and subnational welfare states, as well as how the welfare reforms of the UK have an impact on poverty and inequality in Scotland. At the same time they show that it is useful to ask if there are other ways of 'doing policy' and whether substate nationalism can affect policy. The interaction between social policy change and demands today for more devolved powers for Scotland, as well as growing support for Scottish independence has, until relatively recently, been largely ignored by academic research, but this book has shown that there are lessons in Scotland that could help promote new approaches to equality in other contexts. We know lessons can be learned from other small countries like Sweden, for example, where jobs have been created more successfully than in other countries, thereby keeping unemployment in check and inequality less extreme (Begg et al, 2007). Regions like Catalonia in Spain also appear to have policy lessons for others – the region seems to be better placed than others to retain and develop the economic and social provision that might place it in a stronger position to find a route out of the recession (Teague, 2006). In the same way examining social policy in Scotland can also contribute much to policy learning, not least because the experience in Scotland highlights how substate nationalism and policy development can go hand in hand.

This is not unique to Scotland. Using the experience of nationalism and social policy decentralisation in Canada and Belgium as examples, Beland and Lecours (2007, 2008, 2010) argue that substate nationalism represents a powerful force for the decentralisation of social policy (Beland and Lecours, 2007, p 405). They provide two reasons for why this is the case. First, social programmes are more likely than other types of programmes to touch people in everyday life. As a consequence governments running these programmes can establish direct and tangible links with a population – a potent nation-building tool. Second, discussion around specific social policy alternatives can easily be conducted as a debate over core values, principles and identities. In this respect the language of social policy is similar to discourse of nationalism insofar as one group can argue to have more of a certain quality (for example, egalitarianism or entrepreneurship) than the other. Their argument offers a potential explanation for the Scottish 'policy and nation' formula that we have identified in the different policy areas covered in the book. Throughout the devolution process the interplay of social policy and social justice has been a major defining feature of devolved government in Scotland. But examining the First Minister's speech of May 2011, 'Taking Scotland forward', again, such an argument is being taken further – it suggests that policy change for a better society is only possible with independence:

> My aim is now, has been in the past, and always will be: to deliver
> a better society for the people of Scotland. It happens that we need
> full powers to do this but the people come before the powers, the
> community before the constitution, the children before the state.
> (Salmond, 2011a)

There is little doubt that continuing claims will be made to the essentially 'Scottish' character of policies, with economic and social policy making tied to the pursuit of a particular vision for Scotland in the 21st century. In this respect social policy has a crucial role to play in nation building, and while this is not unique to Scotland, nonetheless it appears to have a particular potency in the Scottish context (see McEwen, 2002, 2006; Mooney and Williams, 2006; Williams and Mooney, 2008; Hassan, 2009; Mooney and Scott, 2011; Law and Mooney, 2012b).

Changing UK context: welfare cuts and the Scotland Bill

As we look to the next five years we have to recognise that it is a very different policy context and a new phase of devolution that faces the SNP as well as Scottish society in general. It is a context where public attitudes towards more distinctly Scottish directions in policy will lead to greater expectations and a greater divergence between UK and Scottish policy. It is also one where attempts to address the tensions between the UK and Scottish governments have been proposed, most notably in the Scotland Bill that was approved by the Westminster government in 2011. Such tensions are bound to increase as we head towards a referendum on independence now scheduled to take place in 2014.

To be implemented the Bill would have to be passed by the Scottish Parliament. That looks unlikely. As highlighted in Chapters One and Two, the SNP are opposed to the Bill in its present form, arguing that it does not go far enough or give sufficient increase in powers to raise revenue. They call for far more power to be devolved than the Bill allows. What the process shows is that while there is no agreement on whether 'devolution max' or full-blown independence will be the final position, there is currently political will in both Scotland and England towards greater powers for the Scottish Parliament – and hence greater potential for policy divergence in the next decade.

European and UK-wide economic change and UK-wide changes in welfare spending have had an unequal and uneven impact on people in all four nations of the UK. Recent decisions made at UK level about the benefits system will, for example, have serious implications for child poverty in Scotland. In Scotland cuts in the budget from London, an 11 per cent reduction for 2011–12 on the 2010–11 level (The Scottish Government, 2011b), mean the expansion of public services of earlier phases of devolution will be curtailed. Public announcements will be of reductions in services rather than expansions of popular policies of the last 10 years, such as free travel for over-60s, free prescriptions, abolition of tuition fees and free personal care.

Reflecting the reductions in public sector employment at a UK level, Scotland's public sector workforce is in the front line of service cuts. There are over 500,000 public sector workers in Scotland (and another 104,000 in reserved, Westminster-controlled) public sector departments such as the civil service, just over a quarter of the entire workforce – a higher proportion than in England. In some areas, including Glasgow where 34 per cent of the workforce is in the public sector and in Eilean Siar (Western Isles) where this figure reaches 43 per cent (Dorling and Thomas, 2011), the proportion of public sector workers is considerably higher, and there are many areas where the local authority, education sector or the NHS is the largest single employer. What makes the situation in Scotland even more complex is that the majority of the public services targeted for spending and job cuts are in devolved areas, that is, they lie under the direct control of the Scottish government, and it is the Scottish government that will have to implement cuts and make the decisions where cuts will fall (and it was the Scottish government which in late 2010 imposed a pay freeze for public sector workers and which was extended by a further year in the September 2011 budget announcement; see The Scottish Government, 2011b). The Scottish budget comes entirely from the UK Parliament. Chancellor George Osborne announced in 2010 that the annual £30 billion Scottish budget will be cut by around £1 billion per year in real terms for four years. By 2015 the expectation is that, even with the Scotland Bill, the Scottish budget will be back at the level of 2005, and it has been estimated that over 100,000 public sector jobs will be lost by this time.

European context

The UK political context is not the only one to affect policy and the interaction of social policy and nation building in Scotland. A number of our authors make reference to the impact of European funding and the use of European models by policy makers in developing Scottish policy, or at least in making decisions about the models of service delivery and pattern of beneficiaries. This is not an insignificant reference. The EU may not have been particularly successful in creating a common framework for European social policy (Moreno and Palier, 2004), but with over half of the Scottish government's workload originating in the European policy arena, and given the Scottish government's responsibility for implementing EU Directives in devolved areas, Scotland's devolved institutions have had to adapt to the growing Europeanisation of the UK policy process. Scott Greer suggests that:

> ... the upshot is that the EU is not a happy place for regional governments to develop distinctive social models. (Greer, 2009, p 179)

Since many of the devolved policy areas are also areas of European funding programmes and initiatives, policy approaches originating in Europe have often been adopted, particularly in the areas of education, training, youth, social inclusion and employment programmes (Birrell, 2009). The amount of funding is not insignificant. When the European Regional Development Fund (ERDF) was first created in 1975, Scotland was the third largest recipient of funds in the European Community (EC) and it was a significant beneficiary of the Structural Funds throughout the 1980s and 1990s (Bachtler et al, 2007). While such funding is now much reduced, the impact of EU funding on domestic policy can be a significant one (Verschraegen et al, 2011).

Before the Euro crisis of 2011, SNP politicians had seldom made much of this impact of EU funding but they have played with the idea of joining the EU as an independent state:

> The SNP believes that Independence in Europe is the logical next step for Scotland to take on its road to becoming a normal, democratic, European nation, just like Denmark, Ireland or Luxembourg. (SNP, 2011)

They have also drawn on small European democracies to highlight the possibilities of small nations' independence. SNP leader Alex Salmond regularly argues, for example, that the success of countries like Norway shows an independent Scotland would flourish. His claims in 2006 (Salmond, 2006) that:

> Scotland can change to a better future and be part of northern Europe's arc of prosperity ...

came to haunt him as Ireland and Iceland – part of his North European 'arc of prosperity' – saw the collapse of their banking systems. Nevertheless, interest in the Nordic nations has increased and political parties in Scotland are starting to examine examples of multi-level governance and social policy development that have worked well in Scandinavia (Nordic Horizons, 2012).

Despite the difficulties with the comparisons drawn with Iceland and Ireland, the point that is increasingly being made by politicians from different parties is that enhanced devolution, or even independence, could be a framework within which alternative policy responses to those that currently exist could be developed. There are obviously strong economic and political forces that might limit the extent of change, but as all the contributors to this book suggest, there are possibilities for change in the way in which welfare is delivered if social justice is to be pursued. In 1996 Esping-Andersen argued that:

> The political problem today is how to forge coalitions for an alternative, post-industrial model of social citizenship and egalitarianism. (Esping-Andersen, 1996, p 267)

Imagining a different future

Esping-Andersen's conclusion is one that raises important questions for countries such as Scotland, leaving aside the contention around what is meant by a post-industrial model! But exactly what sort of future would we suggest, which coalitions would work and how important is it to Scotland's future to consider policy options? It certainly seems that devolution, with all its new voices, is now embraced by the vast majority of Scottish voters. Coalition government has also been tried and tested and, while independence was not in early 2012 the favoured position of most Scots, support for independence has increased since 2011, although it is not as yet clear how solid this level of support is. It does seem as if greater powers are preferred to maintain and develop distinctive aspects of Scotland's public sector and social policy.

It has, however, been a changing process and it is noticeable that each of the four elections has reflected a changing pattern of interaction between social policy and national identity. For Hassan the 2011 elections mattered because:

> The incremental caution, conservatism and stasis of much of Scottish institutional life is slowly coming to an end; given that Scotland is not about to embrace a marketised, privatised society the question is still open what will come next. The Scottish Parliament is where a large part of this will be played out, whereas the Westminster orientated commentary draws succour from the fact that what really matters is the UK elections and that those are the big boys' league that Scottish Labour will continue to win. This ignores that the contest for Scotland's future will be decided in Scottish elections, and not at Westminster. (Hassan, 2011)

If Hassan is right, then the move towards a civic nationalism in Scotland is an important one, and policy options become increasingly important for the Scottish people. In the May 2011 Scottish elections all the major parties offered a model of future policy that differed somewhat from the rest of the UK. There was a shared commitment to a Council Tax freeze, a commitment to a greener future, free university tuition fees for students in higher education (rejected by the Conservatives), and efficiency gains in public sector spending. The nature of social welfare in the future was understood to be important by all, responding to a perception that Scotland is a country where potent collective traditions and commitments to egalitarianism exist and social policy matters. At the same time, economic growth and prosperity were seen as essential if moves towards equality were to be pursued. Before the financial crash the SNP had presented a vision of Scotland as a modern, competitive country able to stand for itself in the context of a globalised world economy. The vision was of an independent country prospering on the back of sustainable economic growth built around knowledge and other leading sectors, supported by a low tax regime and an efficient government and public sector, and reflected the perspective that globalisation is an opportunity more than a risk or threat to Scotland's future development. There was a tension here, between the Celtic neoliberals who wanted to emulate the bank-led market economies of Iceland and Ireland and those who preferred the Nordic model of high tax and high spend countries like Denmark and Finland. Certainly the Celtic neoliberals were, and are, largely in tune with the neoliberal world view of New Labour and of the Conservative–Liberal Democrat UK Coalition government, and the global failure of this neoliberal vision in the context of far-reaching economic and financial crisis has yet to see the SNP and New Labour fully abandon neoliberal premises and models. The 'modernised nationalism' of the SNP, explored by Arnott and Ozga in their chapter in this book and elsewhere (Arnott and Ozga, 2010a, 2010b), or what Law and Mooney term 'competitive nationalism' (Law and Mooney, 2010, 2012a), remains in step with a neoliberal approach and vision (see also Davidson et al, 2010).

Building the new Scotland of the 21st century, however, involves a reconceptualisation and a reimagining of Scotland, a changing nation, as well as a changing nationalism. The fact that there is a specific social policy-making agenda, around social integration, inclusion and a policy rhetoric around fairness and solidarity does not detract from or contradict neoliberal assumptions as these are wedded to the national project of growth and prosperity. The naturalisation of 'Scotland' and the renationalisation of economic and social policy as in the Scottish 'national interest' are key components of this project. During the May 2011 Scottish election campaign and in its immediate aftermath, the SNP made considerable play of its vision of a 'better Scotland', proclaiming their outstanding election success as 'a victory for a society and a nation' (Salmond, 2011b). In the period of the fourth Scottish Parliament, with the SNP forming a majority government, there has been more of a similar language and emphasis, as they move towards the 2014 referendum on independence for Scotland. The interplay between nation building and social policy making in Scotland is therefore about to enter a new and more significant phase. It is, however, likely to be slower and more incremental than some might have expected. In the First Minister's legislative statement to Parliament on 7 September 2011 (Salmond, 2011a), much of the speech was devoted to criticising the Coalition's economic policies and, while outlining 16 pieces of legislation to be presented to Parliament, including the establishment of a single national police force for Scotland and guaranteed training places or jobs for 16- to 19-year-olds, the speech stopped far short of presenting ideas for a radically different or independent Scotland.

Despite this recognition of slow but steady change, the significance for the nature of welfare in the country should not be underestimated and may, as in Canada and Belgium, be a positive one for welfare outcomes (Beland and Lecours, 2010). In Canada the nationalist mobilisation of Québec has contributed to differences in welfare entitlements across the country, with welfare state expansion being favoured in Québec because of progressive ideas. Can that happen in Scotland?

In 2005 we suggested that innovative and radical ideas for policy change were needed. We argued, among other things, that the multiple inequalities that characterised Scotland needed to be addressed and social inclusion needed to be reinterpreted as more than paid employment, high-quality and non-market-based public services were key to Scotland's future and had a key role to play in tackling inequalities. In 2005 we claimed that policy innovation in Scotland was possible and necessary if social injustice was to be addressed. Since that time market liberalisation has increased and economic and social cohesion has been under more threat – innovation is needed even more. Chapters One and Two have highlighted the very wide powers that Scotland has as a devolved nation to introduce such innovation – some of the widest powers of any devolved state. Alex Law argues in Chapter Two that the space exists for greater social and territorial justice within Scotland and other authors have outlined the extent of possibilities for addressing social inequality and injustice in Scotland.

Changes that come within the remit of the devolved settlement are shown and discussed across the chapters. The three policy options discussed in Chapter Three give some idea of how the 'policy space' of devolution could be exploited to reduce income and wealth inequalities. Maintaining and developing universal service provision such as free prescriptions and university tuition are suggested because there are real economic and social benefits from generating equality. Addressing income inequality through minimum wage strategies such as the Living Wage is advanced because it has a progressive impact on the lowest paid and is something on which the public sector could lead. And finally, Morelli and Seaman propose the replacement of Council Tax by a local income tax because low-income households could be made exempt. As they note none of these suggestions is particularly far reaching, but few have been adopted despite the rhetoric of social justice and the room for manoeuvre in a devolved Scotland. The explanation given is that the political will of those in power since 1997 to fully address inequalities does not exist – continuing inequality is not the result of a flawed devolved settlement.

Similar arguments are made in Chapters Four, Five and Six. Sinclair and McKendrick in Chapter Four point to the uniquely benign circumstances of continuous economic growth and relative political harmony, which marked the first three Scottish governments between 1999 and 2011 and opened up possibilities for the reduction of poverty. Their conclusion, however, is that the opportunities were never fully exploited. Scott, in Chapter Five, identifies how regeneration policy has been put onto the policy agenda but without the resources to make much change and with a continuation of place rather than people as its focus – reflecting a lack of will to fully develop key equalities measures. If the First Minister's claim that 'Modern Scotland is also built on equality' (Salmond, 2011b) is to have resonance, then serious efforts to incorporate equalities thinking into social policy development is needed.

De Lima in Chapter Six similarly highlights how new spaces for debate on issues of identity and belonging were opened up by devolution, particularly through the equal opportunities powers granted under the Scotland Act 1998. However, she also shows that this has not led to any real difference in the lives of minority ethnic groups in Scotland as the main emphasis has been on addressing labour market skills gaps and shortages in order to contribute to Scotland's economic growth. The politics of recognition for women and minority ethnic groups has been achieved to some extent since 1999, but bolder steps are demanded in Chapters Four to Six to pursue the politics of redistribution. Will it happen? Sinclair and McKendrick in Chapter Four argue that there is a real possibility that it could, as the poorer economic environment since 2008 may force policy makers and citizens to make choices that would lead to greater divergence than ever before between Scotland and other parts of the UK, especially England. De Lima further argues that we must be careful in such a situation not to be driven by purely instrumental policies. Her argument is in relation to policies on migration – if they are based on a labour market that cannot provide quality employment and are developed in isolation from social justice concerns then the discrimination experienced by some minority ethnic groups and individuals will not disappear. A similar point is made by Adams in Chapter Ten where, despite every indication that policy makers of almost all the political parties are committed to supporting young people, the focus has been on driving down the NEET (not in education, employment or training) figures, and less attention has been accorded to the problems of poverty and intergenerational disadvantage that would prevent the loss of a generation in the current economic environment. Throughout Chapters Four, Five and Six the impact on social inequalities of unequal access to quality employment is raised as an increasingly important factor that policy must address. Chapter Twelve explores this more deeply, highlighting the way in which the restructuring of the Scottish labour market has had an impact on men and women, particular localities and on different minority ethnic groups. Powerful labour market divisions are shown to persist and policy solutions are seen to be affected by ongoing tensions between the Scottish and UK governments. For Bertram and Wright solutions need to be made more local. Their argument is that local labour market programmes are needed to target specific local historical backgrounds and labour market needs and more support is needed for Local Regeneration Agencies – a situation hampered by the devolution settlement that limits Holyrood's capacity to take effective action.

Chapters Seven, Eight and Nine give us some more detailed idea of how services are being developed in a devolved Scotland, the extent to which they address social injustices and the extent to which they draw from and contribute to international lessons about policy. Poole in Chapter Seven argues that positive steps have been made under devolution to tackle those factors in the physical and social environment which reduce positive health outcomes – improving housing, regenerating urban environments, building resilience and capacity in communities. Major improvements in working together across departmental and professional boundaries in the field of health and social care have been seen but for Poole there has, once again, been a lack of political will to grapple fully with the progressive policies of redistribution needed in relation to income, wealth, opportunity and cultural access that lie at the heart of health inequalities. Dumbleton and McPhail's discussion of social services (Chapter Eight) offers a more positive evaluation of change in social services since devolution. They argue that Scotland can be rightly proud of innovations such as increased service user involvement in the care service and in children's services, the approach of *Getting it right for every child*. Introduced in 2008, *Getting it right for every child*, with its integrated and holistic approach to supporting the well-being of children and underpinned by social perspectives of equality and human rights, is internationally recognised as a model of policy, but it is argued here that such positive developments in this field are threatened by a combination of non-ring-fenced local authority budgets and the impact of the global financial crisis together with the responses to the crisis by the UK and Scottish governments, as well as a lack of concern for broader social justice issues that leads to a 'blaming the victim' mentality among policy makers. Dumbleton and McPhail's reference to the international standing of Scotland's children's services reminds us that the 'welfare nationalism' of Scotland may use other models for policy development than reference its own or UK past and present experiences.

Arnott and Ozga's discussion of education policy (Chapter Nine) suggests that while the alignment of economic and social justice agendas has been attempted in Scotland's educational policy in much the same way as in England, there are important differences and they derive certainly from an SNP desire to align Scotland's educational system more closely with the smaller democracies of Europe. Europe was an important reference point for SNP educational policy – the social justice agendas in education that remain intact and supported by the public in smaller democracies such as Sweden and Denmark have helped to shape a Scottish agenda which is markedly different from the increasing involvement of private interests in education, the raising of tuition fees and the abolition of Educational Maintenance Awards seen in England. For Arnott and Ozga, education has come to be seen as having an important role in the shaping and support of national identity in Scotland and the pursuit of social justice through education along the lines of Denmark and Sweden represent an important part of the rhetoric, if not reality, of educational provision.

The analysis of criminal justice policy in Chapter Eleven suggests that, just as with education policy, the room for manoeuvre in policy created by devolution and national identity is worth examining. Croall outlines the less punitive and authoritarian tone towards youth justice in Scotland in comparison with England and Wales, the aim of reducing numbers in prison and emphasis on payback that could be seen to reflect a distinctive approach to criminal justice. However, she also argues that public spending cuts, particularly those exacerbating inequalities, might well exacerbate some forms of crime. Increases in corporate crime and environmental crimes are more likely as resources to enforce existing laws are reduced. Plans to reduce the size of the prison population are not likely to be matched with the necessary support for criminal justice social work or the voluntary sector. Scotland may have a distinctive criminal justice system but that does not mean it is not facing considerable difficulties in developing policies that meet the needs of a changing society.

Two of the remaining three chapters, Chapter Twelve on housing and Chapter Thirteen on environmental justice, remind us of the significance of the models that Arnott and Ozga suggest have been rejected as part of a distinctively Scottish vision or reimagining of the future – marketisation. During the last 20 years, as the economy came increasingly to be built around ever more deregulated markets, something approaching a housing crisis has emerged, environmental threats have increased, and political choices have been made to reduce their impact in Scotland. Scandrett in Chapter Fourteen argues that since 2002 environmental concerns and social democratic discourse have coincided at times but in inconsistent ways, and were less integrated with social justice concerns as the economic crisis began to bite. He sees the high point as between 2002 and 2007 when there was an attempt to integrate environmental concerns and social justice measures. Since then environmentally beneficial but class-blind policies have been more common – technical solutions to scientific problems without a clear recognition of the struggles of communities affected by pollution. In a capitalist economy such as Scotland's, the logic of economic growth creates greater environmental injustice, and for Scandrett the answer lies not only in top-down policy but in the development of stronger connections between working-class movements, community action groups and environmentalists ranging from grassroots environmental justice campaigners to 'envirocrats'.

Chapter Thirteen on housing highlights an area where Scotland has always had considerable independence of policy direction, but notes some of the unintended consequences when a social justice initiative occurs without recognition of the full complexities of access to resources. Two key policy objectives in housing reform are identified: the rights of homeless households to access social housing through the provisions of Housing Acts in Scotland and the extension of low-cost homeownership initiatives. The homelessness legislation is progressive and internationally renowned and low-cost homeownership schemes offer a route to tackle the problem of housing affordability and housing tenure mix. For McKee and Phillips these two policies are unfortunately in constant tension and not necessarily compatible: the homelessness legislation delivers social justice for a very vulnerable group but does so at the expense of other slightly less well-off groups who would also like access to social housing. Their conclusion is that although the current devolution settlement imposes a number of restrictions, there is scope for the introduction of more tenure-neutral policies that would support a greater role for social housing as a whole. The conclusion of Chapter Thirteen is that funding for new social housing and policies to encourage greater social mix within current social housing are needed. The social rented sector once housed over half of Scottish households – the increasingly difficult mortgage market and the precarious labour market situation of many households across Scotland means that, as in the past, the private sector cannot deliver to the housing needs of a large proportion of the population. Developing the necessary policy depends, however, on political will and the commitment of public resources.

While the contributors' discussions of policy solutions in this book are wide-ranging, what is clear is that there are no single or even simple technical solutions – they are affected by economic change, political and social contestation and political will – but, as even the Christie Commission, established by the Scottish government to review the future of Scotland's public services, concludes:

> ... irrespective of the current economic challenges, a radical change in the design and delivery of public services is necessary to tackle the deep-rooted social problems that persist in communities across the country. (The Scottish Government, 2011a, p 4)

Looking ahead

'We are now the national party of Scotland – acting in the interests of all of Scotland', commented First Minister Salmond in the aftermath of the SNP's monumental victory in the May 2011 Scottish elections. As noted above, we are likely to hear much more of this play to nation and the Scottish national interests in the years to come. However, two issues need to be considered if a 'nation that is fair and just' (Salmond, 2011b) is to be achieved alongside the strengthened powers of devolution or independence for Scotland. These are, first, the changed economic context and second, an unspoken but real tension between the pursuit of territorial and social justice.

The wider economic context that surrounds Scottish devolution and policy making as we complete this book in tearly 2012 is somewhat different from the context of the late 1990s. An Audit Scotland report in 2011 concluded 'Scotland's finances are facing a "worst case scenario" in the coming years and public bodies may struggle to manage their budgets" (Audit Scotland, 2011). The future for Scotland's public sector and the possibility of a 'policy-led' move towards nationalism now looks highly vulnerable, despite the wholehearted desire to be distinctly 'Scottish'. Budget cuts to the level of £1.3 billion were announced in the first budget statement following the election in May 2011 (The Scottish Government, 2011b). The amount is obviously directly related to the reduction in the Block Grant from Westminster and reflects cuts in public finance across the UK as a whole. Their impact is likely to be long-lasting, certainly on public services as a whole but also on economic growth even if, as John Swinney, the Cabinet Secretary for Finance and Sustainable Growth, claimed it is:

> ... an approach to public spending that presents alternatives to the course set by the UK Government that best meets the needs of the people of Scotland. (The Scottish Government, 2011b)

So, despite the fact that the SNP will govern Scotland until 2016 with a commitment to the 'Scottish national interest', this does not mean it will be easy to fund its preferred policies. Nor does it mean that its neoliberal-based economic growth agenda will be diluted. Indeed, the opposite is likely to be the case. Competitive tax regimes for business, a business-friendly environment and economic growth will dominate any commitment to a socially just social policy making, with social policy measures mobilised as part of the goal of a competitive successful Scotland, that is, in relation to the reimagined Scotland of the future.

However, we are entering a period not seen before, and one which few could have imagined emerging. There is scope and potential for divergent policy making, and for some radical policies to emerge. Social justice and social policy will continue to be key features of the Scottish political and policyscapes in the immediate future, just as they have been since the start of the long process of devolution, a process that has now entered a new and perhaps even more dynamic phase. Despite this, we cannot ignore the fact that tension exists between two forms of justice: territorial and social. Devolution for Scotland has been driven by a strong sense that 'Scotland' had fared particularly badly under successive Conservative UK governments. Demands for devolution were essentially demands for territorial justice for the Scottish nation. The introduction of devolution addressed the crisis of legitimation that the UK state faced in Scotland in the 1990s. However, through the renationalisation of politics in Scotland, and through the vehicle of social policy making in particular, claims for further territorial justice in the shape of 'more devolution', 'devolution max', if not full independence, are increasingly merged with demands for fairness, for social justice. Politics in Scotland in recent times has moved significantly from a concern with class to nation. Social justice demands come to be interpreted, understood and represented in a narrative which speaks of Scotland becoming a 'better nation', 'a nation that is fair and just' through policies that will 'make the nation proud' (Salmond, 2011a). While a policy rhetoric that foregrounds fairness and justice is to be welcomed, unless it is combined with a programme of redistributive justice, this means that the vexed question of social justice is likely to be a more difficult one to address than the largely constitutionally understood issue of territorial justice.

References

Arnott, M. and Ozga, J. (2010a) 'Education and nationalism: the discourse of education policy in Scotland', *Discourse: Studies in the Cultural Politics of Education*, vol 31, no 3, pp 335-50.

Arnott, M. and Ozga, J. (2010b) 'Nationalism, governance and policy making in Scotland: the Scottish National Party in power', *Public Money and Management*, vol 30, no 2, pp 91-6.

Audit Scotland (2011) *Scotland's public finances: Addressing the challenges*, Edinburgh: Audit Scotland.

Bachtler, J., Vironen, H. and Mitchie, R. (2007) *Scotland Europa: EU funding programmes 2007-2013: A comparative analysis of EU funding and policy support structures*, Glasgow: European Policy Research Centre.

Begg, I., Jurai Draxer, J. and Mortensen, J. (2007) *Is social Europe fit for globalisation? A study on the impact of globalisation in the European Union*, Brussels: Centre for European Policy Studies.

Beland, D. and Lecours, A. (2007) 'Federalism, nationalism and social policy decentralisation in Canada and Belgium', *Regional and Federal Studies*, vol 17, no 4, pp 405-19.

Beland, D. and Lecours, A. (2008) *Nationalism and social policy: The politics of territorial solidarity*, Oxford: Oxford University Press.

Beland, D. and Lecours, A. (2010) 'Does nationalism trigger welfare-state disintegration? Social policy and territorial mobilisation in Belgium and Canada', *Environment and Planning C: Government and Policy*, vol 28, pp 420-34.

Birrell, D. (2009) *The impact of devolution on social policy*, Bristol: The Policy Press.

Cantillon, B. (2010) *Crisis and the welfare state: The need for a new distributional agenda*, Oxford: Foundation for Law, Justice and Society, University of Oxford.

Commission on Scottish Devolution (2009) *Serving Scotland better: Scotland and the United Kingdom in the 21st century*, Final Report (Calman Commission), presented to the presiding officer of the Scottish Parliament.

Davidson, N., McCafferty, P. and Millen, D. (eds) (2010) *Neoliberal Scotland: Class and society in a stateless nation*, Newcastle: Cambridge Scholars Publishing.

Dorling, D. and Thomas, B. (2011) 'Mapping inequalities in Britain', *Sociology Review*, vol 21, no 1, pp 15-19.

Esping-Andersen, G. (1990) *The three worlds of welfare capitalism*, Princeton, NJ: Princeton University Press.

Esping-Andersen, G. (ed) (1996) *Welfare states in transition: National adaptations in global economies*, London: Sage Publications.

Ferguson, I., Lavalette, M. and Mooney, G. (2002) *Rethinking welfare: A critical perspective*, London: Sage Publications.

Greer, S. (ed) (2009) *Devolution and social citizenship in the UK*, Bristol: The Policy Press.

Hassan, G. (ed) (2009) *The modern SNP: From protest to power*, Edinburgh: Edinburgh University Press.

Hassan, G. (2011) *What is happening to Scottish politics, its future and why it matters* (www.gerryhassan.com/?p=1641).

Law, A. and Mooney, G. (2010) 'Financialisation and proletarianisation: changing landscapes of neoliberal Scotland', in N. Davidson, P. McCafferty and D. Miller (eds) *Neoliberal Scotland: Class and society in a stateless nation*, Newcastle: Cambridge Scholars Publishing, pp 137-59.

Law, A. and Mooney, G. (2012a) 'Competitive nationalism: state, class and the forms of capital in devolved Scotland', *Environment and Planning C: Government and Policy*, vol 30, no 1, pp 62-77.

Law, A. and Mooney, G. (2012b) 'Devolution in a "stateless nation": nation-building and social policy in Scotland', *Social Policy and Administration*, vol 46, no 2, pp 161-77.

MacLeod, A. and Davidson, L. (2011) 'Poll boost for SNP as backing for split grows', *The Times*, 7 September.

McEwen, N. (2002) 'State welfare nationalism: the territorial impact of welfare state development in Scotland', *Regional and Federal Studies*, vol 12, no 1, pp 66-90.

McEwen, N. (2006) *Nationalism and the state: Welfare and identity in Scotland and Quebec*, Brussels: Peter Lang.

Mooney, G. and Scott, G. (eds) (2005) *Exploring social policy in the 'new' Scotland*, Bristol: The Policy Press.

Mooney, G. and Scott, G. (2011) 'Social justice, social welfare and devolution: nationalism and social policy making in Scotland', *Poverty and Public Policy*, vol 3, no 4, art 5.

Mooney, G. and Williams, C. (2006) 'Forging new "ways of life"? Social policy and national building in devolved Scotland and Wales', *Critical Social Policy*, vol 26, no 3, pp 608-29.

Moreno, L. and Palier, B. (2004) 'The Europeanization of welfare: paradigm shifts and social policy reforms', Conference paper, ESPANET.

Nordic Horizons (2012) *McKommunes: People-sized local government*, Conference report (www.nordichorizons.org).

Pearce, N. and Paxton, W. (2005) *Social justice: Building a fairer Britain*, London: Politico's.

Salmond, A. (2006) 'Scotland can join Europe's arc of prosperity', Scottish National Party Press Release (www.snp.org/node/10359).

Salmond, A. (2011a) 'The First Minister's Statement to Parliament: the Government's Programme for Scotland, 2011-2012', 7 September (www.scotland.gov.uk/About/programme-for-government/2011-2012).

Salmond, A. (2011b) 'First Minister's Statement: Taking Scotland forward', 26 May (www.scotland.gov.uk/News/Speeches/FM-Statement-26-05-11).

Scottish Government, The (2011a) *Report on the future delivery of public services by the Commission*, chair: Dr Campbell Christie, 29 June (www.scotland.gov.uk/Publications/2011/06/27154527/0).

Scottish Government, The (2011b) *Scotland's spending plans and draft budget 2011-12*, Edinburgh: The Scottish Government (www.scotland.gov.uk/Resource/Doc/331661/0107923.pdf).

Scottish Government, The (2012) *Your Scotland, your referendum: Consultation*, Edinburgh: The Scottish Government.

Settle, M. and Devlin, K. (2012) 'New poll builds pressure for devo-max question', *The Herald*, 17 January.

SNP (Scottish National Party) (2011) *Independence in Europe* (www.snp.org/node/254).

Teague, P. (2006) 'Deliberative governance and EU social policy', in C. Pierson and F.G. Castles (eds) *The welfare state reader*, London: Polity Press, pp 269-88.

Verschraegen, G., Vahnhercke, B. and Verpoorten, R. (2011) 'The European Social Fund and domestic activation policies: Europeanisation mechanisms', *Journal of Economic and Social Policy*, vol 21, no 1, pp 55-72.

Williams, C. and Mooney, G. (2008) 'Decentering social policy? Devolution and the discipline of social policy, a commentary', *Journal of Social Policy*, vol 37, no 3, pp 1-18.

Index

Page references for notes are followed by n